A HISTORY OF ROME

A History of Rome

FROM 753 B.C. TO A.D. 410

CYRIL E. ROBINSON

Methuen Educational Ltd

LONDON · TORONTO · SYDNEY · WELLINGTON

This book was originally published in August, 1935
It has been reprinted nine times
Reprinted 1963 and 1966
Reprinted 1971 by Methuen Educational Ltd
11 New Fetter Lane London E.C.4
Reprinted 1974

Printed in Great Britain by
Butler & Tanner Ltd, Frome and London

SBN 423 87420 9

PREFACE

IT is unfortunate that so often in the past the study of Roman History has been divided into two halves. To restore some sense of its unity and continuity is the purpose of this book. In the redistribution of emphasis which is imposed by such a task there is gain as well as loss. The story of the Republic's rise is less vital and less interesting than that of its later phases, and few readers will regret its curtailment. On the other hand it is a pity that the study of the Empire is so frequently cut short at the period of the Antonines. The Decline and Fall is a fascinating spectacle, and though full detail of its narrative is not perhaps desirable, some account of its course and causes can scarcely fail to be instructive.

I have once more to acknowledge my debt to Mr. G. T. Griffith, Fellow of Gonville and Caius College, Cambridge, who has kindly read my manuscript. I am also indebted to members of the Warburg Institute who have assisted me in procuring several of my illustrations.

C. E. R.

CONTENTS

PART I. THE ROMAN REPUBLIC

PART II. THE ROMAN EMPIRE

ILLUSTRATIONS

    **Photo: *Anderson, Rome.*   †*Photo: Boissonnas, Geneva.*
    ‡*Photo: Alinari, Florence.*

MAPS

PART I

THE ROMAN REPUBLIC

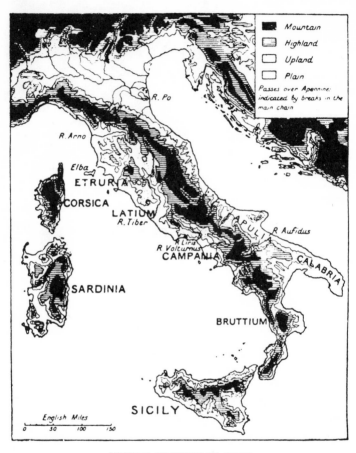

Mountain
Highland
Upland
Plain

Passes over Apennine:
indicated by breaks in the
main chain

R. Po

R. Arno

Elba

ETRURIA

CORSICA

LATIUM

R. Tiber

R. Liris

R. Volturnus

CAMPANIA

APULIA

R Aufidus

CALABRIA

SARDINIA

BRUTTIUM

SICILY

English Miles

0   50   100   150

PHYSICAL FEATURES OF ITALY

CHAPTER I

LAND AND PEOPLE

ITALY is without question the loveliest country of Europe. The air is softer than in Greece, the mountains less stark, the valleys more fertile, the vegetation more luxuriant. But here perhaps certain distinctions should be made. In the first place, it must be remembered that three-quarters of the whole peninsula consists of hill-country or mountain. For the vast chain of the Apennines not merely runs continuously throughout its entire length, but also spans more than half its breadth from sea to sea. Now (setting aside the wide expanse of the Po Valley, which in ancient times was not considered a part of Italy at all), the eastern or Adriatic shore is for the most part without charm, fertility, or importance. In its northern sector the coastal strip between the mountains and the sea is a mere ribbon so narrow at some points as barely to admit the passage of a road; then, after the somewhat richer valley of the Aufidus, the landscape broadens out into a wide moorland plateau, yet this so droughty, windswept, and inhospitable as to play but little part in history proper. It was indeed of no small importance to the early fortunes of the Italian folk that their more profitable lands faced not towards Greece and the old culture of the Orient, but towards the more backward countries of Africa and Spain. For on the western side of the great watershed which catches abundant moisture from the south-west winds, there are fertile valleys lying high among the mountains and numerous rivers such as the Volturnus, the Tiber, and the Arno, whose waters travel down to feed the rich alluvium of the coastal plains. These plains, though larger than on the Adriatic shores, are of no very great extent. Campania, in the south, was equivalent in area to a large-sized English county. Latium, in the centre, was upwards of a hundred miles in length, but a good walker could cross it at any point within a single day. To the north of this lay Etruria, which, owing to volcanic upheavals, was a confused medley of pleasant valleys, wild mountain, water-logged marsh, and hill-girt lakes—a district which geographically no less than historically lay somewhat separate and aloof from the rest of Italy.

In immemorial days volcanoes were both numerous and active along this western coast; and its plains were for this reason left almost untenanted by the primitive inhabitants of the peninsula. Of these, a short, long-headed race of rudimentary culture, very little is known. In historic times their descendants were still to be found in the Ligurian mountains above Genoa and in moorlands of Apulia and Calabria in the south-east. Elsewhere, however, at a very early date they were either absorbed or evicted by invaders coming from beyond the Alps—the true Italian race. The original home of this extremely virile people appears to have been in the Danube basin or even farther north. They were, in fact, a branch of that great Indo-European stock, tribes of which in the process of migration found their way into many lands. For from the language that they spoke was derived not merely the Italian tongue, but Greek, German, Anglo-Saxon, and Sanskrit, in which was written the sacred poetry of ancient Hindustan.[1]

About 2000 B.C. a group of these wandering folk penetrated the Alps and settled down among the northern lakes of Italy, where for safety's sake they built their houses on wooden piles placed well out in the water. Other tribes must presently have followed; and from about 1500 onwards the process of southward infiltration must have begun. By 1000 B.C. or thereabouts the various tribes had settled down into the areas which they henceforward were to occupy; and differences of dialect long persisted, marking some primitive distinction between the tribes which settled in Umbria, the tribes which settled in the plain of Latium and the tribes which settled in the upland valleys of the central Apennines. More important however, was the influence of geographical environment on the political institutions of these various groups. The settlers

---

[1] The kinship of the different languages may be illustrated by such a word as the Sanskrit *Pita*, Greek πατήρ, Latin *pater*, German *Vater*, and English *father*.

who made their home among the upland valleys—the Aequi,
Marsi, Hernici, Samnites, and the rest—were so well protected

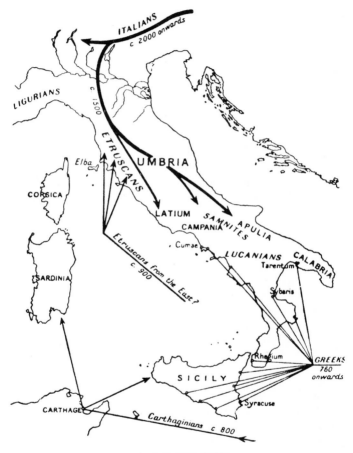

ITALY, EARLY MIGRATIONS

against attack by the surrounding mountain-ridges that there
was little inducement for their scattered villages to combine
for concerted measures of defence; and, though each tribe

would recognize the leadership of its own chief, they remained content with that, and never developed the habit of closer political union.

In the level plain of Latium, on the other hand, the situation was different. Here, in the absence of any natural barrier of defence, there was every inducement for the inhabitants of the widely scattered villages to coalesce in groups, each group having its separate stronghold whither to rally in case of war. Since trade, too, developed more naturally among the dwellers on a plain, such groups would find it convenient to have some common market wherein to exchange their goods. Last but not least, the ties of a common religion encouraged them to meet together for the celebration of its rites and festivals. Thus was evolved a new form of community[1] known to history as the city state, in which the inhabitants of a comparatively small district, though not of necessity quitting their scattered homes, had come to group themselves around a central town that served them not merely as stronghold, market-place, and common sanctuary, but also (what was still more important) as a political capital.

In order to understand the political institutions of such city states, we must look back to the primitive customs of the Italian folk when they came first to settle. They were then, like those kindred tribes who settled down in Greece, at what is called the *patriarchal* stage. In other words, the family was the unit on which their organization was based, and in each family the authority of the father was supreme. So too in their communities or clans, composed as each was of a group of families, the chieftain, like the father, then held supreme authority. In war-time he was leader of the host, in peace-time priest and judge. When he needed advice, he called into consultation the heads of the various families: but in matters of high importance—a declaration of war, the making of laws, or the selection of a new chief—the final decision lay with the whole assembled folk. In early times political institutions changed slowly, if at all; and when in due course the city state came into being, it was of these three

[1] Somewhat earlier, of course, city states of a similar type had been evolved in Greece.

elements—-a chief or king, an advisory council of elders or *patres*, and an assembly or *comitium* of the citizens—that its constitution was composed.

During the second half of the seventh century B.C. it appears that some forty of such city states sprang up in Latium; and the sense of tribal unity between these 'Latins', as they called themselves, had further led to the formation of a League between them. Its chief purpose was religious; and the centre at which the members met for the celebration of their common festivals was Mount Albanus near the middle of the plain. How far the League may have also served the purpose of concerted self-defence, we have no means of knowing; but sooner or later under the pressure of foreign foes there was bound to arise the opportunity for one of the forty cities, more powerful than the rest, to take the lead. But, before the time arrived for such a leadership, a new stimulus to Latin culture was first to infuse the needful strength into the city which achieved it. The stimulus came from the country lying between the Arno and the Tiber—Etruria.

CHAPTER II

THE ETRUSCANS AND ROME

I. THE GROWTH OF ETRUSCAN POWER

BEFORE we can follow farther the fortunes of the cities of the Latin. Plain, we must first turn to consider the history of two neighbouring districts in which very different civilizations had meanwhile been taking root. The first is Etruria; and here at once we are confronted with a strange enigma. Herodotus, the Greek historian, declared that this tract of country in North-west Italy was colonized by seafarers from Lydia in Asia Minor. The ancients endorsed the view that the Etruscans came from the East; and the character of certain of their religious rites—in particular, divination from the entrails of slain beasts—suggests an affinity with Mesopotamian cults. On the other hand, modern archaeologists have discerned a still more striking similarity

between the art of Etruria and the art of ancient Crete; and
it seems not improbable that Etruscan culture was developed
not by Asiatic invaders from beyond the sea, but by the
aboriginal inhabitants of Italy itself—of kindred blood to the
inhabitants of Crete—whom an admixture of the vigorous

LATIUM, DURING THE MONARCHY AND EARLY REPUBLIC

Indo-European invaders somehow impelled to fresh activity
and enterprise.

Be that as it may, it is certain at least that from about the
ninth century B.C. a flourishing civilization arose in the country
lying between the Arno and the Tiber. Certain it is, too, that
the authors of this civilization were of a very different type
from the Italians proper. Of their early history no records
are available; for, though we possess many thousands of their

inscriptions, the meaning of these has never been deciphered. From archaeological finds, however, especially from paintings and other objects found in the rock-hewn tombs in which their dead were buried, we have abundant evidence of their customs and appearance. They were thick-set of limb, supercilious of feature, and in character, so far as can be judged, dour, sensuous, and cruel. They loved the spectacle of brutal sports; and their religion—very different from the cheerful and imaginative creed of the Indo-Europeans—was a sinister worship of demon deities. Their wealth, which was considerable, was partly based on the skill of their metal-workers, then unrivalled in the world, who drew on the copper of their own mines around Volterra and from the adjacent island of Elba. They were great merchants, too, and traffic with Levantine ports brought them jewels and other luxuries from Egypt, Phoenicia, and elsewhere.

But there was another quarter in which they also traded and from contact with which they drew an inspiration even more vital to their culture. From the eighth century onwards both Sicily and the southern coasts of Italy had been gradually re-peopled by colonists from Greece. At Tarentum, Rhegium, and even as far north as Cumae and Naples in Campania there were now flourishing Greek towns. There are few good harbours in Italy; but what there are lie mostly in the south, and it was not unnatural that, as members of a great seafaring race, the new settlers should have made good use of them. A prosperous trade sprang up both with East and West and thus contact had soon been made with Etruria.

The debt of the Etruscans to the Greeks was great. From them they learnt the art of writing, using a somewhat altered form of the Hellenic alphabet. They adopted the Greek type of military equipment. Their temples, though made not of stone, but of timber-work encased with brightly coloured tiles, bore a close resemblance to the Greek architectural style, and the influence of Greek art can especially be traced in some of their terra-cotta statues and even more in their painted pottery. In one respect, however, the Etruscans may be said to have learnt nothing from the Greeks. Their political institutions showed none of the Hellenic love for freedom and self-government. Their princes were sheer autocrats, living, like medieval barons, in hill-top castles fortified with massive masonry. Like medieval barons, too, they lorded it proudly over the local peasantry, who laboured for them as serfs. Nor was there any tendency towards league or political union between their various towns. Each Etruscan prince was an independent tyrant of his petty kingdom; and it was not unnatural that, as time wore on, other adventurous spirits, lacking a kingdom of their own, sought to win one by foreign conquest. The first of these crossed the Apennines and founded cities in the valley of the Po. Then others took ship to Campania, where they did the same. The marshy lands of Latium did not for a while attract them; but towards the end of the seventh century, when the Latins, as we have seen, were engaged in coalescing into small city states, these too began to feel the pressure from the north. First Veii, then Fidenae, and finally Praeneste fell into Etruscan hands, and it seemed as though the whole of Latium was destined to succumb—a necessary prelude, it would seem, to the further expansion of the Etruscans' power over Campania and the south. One city, however, still stood across their path. It held a key position, at the Tiber crossing nearest to the sea, and so commanded the land-route along the Latin coast—the nearest route to Campania. The name of this city was Rome.

II. ROME AND THE ETRUSCANS

The early history of Rome, previous to the period of Etruscan expansion, is unhappily obscure. No record, except for legendary tales, appears to have survived; but later on, in the third and second centuries B.C., these tales were woven into historical sequence, and a highly fanciful chronology was evolved. The story of Rome's origin (fixed for no sound reason at 753 B.C.) was treated as a sequel to the tales of Greek mythology, according to which, the hero Aeneas having sailed from Troy to the shores of Latium, his son Ascanius or Iulus there founded Alba Longa. There is no need to rehearse the still more famous story how two of Iulus' descendants, Romulus and Remus, miraculously escaped the vengeance of a wicked uncle and proceeded to found a city of their own on the site of the Seven Hills, or how, during the celebration of a common religious festival with the neighbouring tribe of Sabines, its new inhabitants succeeded with unpardonable violence in procuring indispensable wives. Excavation at least confirms the fact that the earliest settlers, who burnt their dead, amalgamated later with intruding squatters who preferred to bury theirs, and who in all probability hailed from the Sabine hinterland.

More solid ground is reached when we arrive at the epoch of Rome's early kings. In later times much study was devoted to the city's origins by such antiquarians as the Elder Cato and Varro, and their work culminated in the great History compiled by Livy in Augustus' reign. According to Livy's narrative the first king whom we can regard as in any true sense historical was a Sabine, Numa Pompilius. He was said to have been the organizer of the State religion—its annual cycle of festivals, and the institution of its priestly 'guilds'. There is nothing improbable in the story; and it is a significant fact that in the Calendar drawn up by Julius Caesar larger lettering was employed to distinguish certain feasts, concerned for the most part with agricultural operations, which clearly must have been of high antiquity. The next king, Tullus Hostilius, a Latin, was credited with the destruction of Alba Longa, and in corroboration of this we have evidence that not long afterwards Aricia became the religious centre of the Latin League. Under Ancus Martius, the third king, there occurred two innovations: the building of a bridge across the Tiber and the construction of a harbour at Ostia on the river's mouth, both pointing to a growth of trade and suggesting at least some contact with the merchants of Etruria. What seems certain is that the Etruscans' effort towards southerly expansion, to which we referred above, was at this time in full blast; and the strange thing is that they apparently got hold of Rome without a struggle.

For the next king to ascend the throne was of Etruscan blood. Tarquin, the name by which he was known, is simply the Etruscan title for a king. But tradition told that he entered the city unromantically in an ox-cart, and there is no evidence whatever of military conquest. The natural inference is that, having settled at Rome as a trader, he succeeded by sheer strength of character in securing his election to the throne. Certainly the forceful rule of the Tarquin and his two successors well accords with the belief that a new type of monarch was now directing the city's policy. The Elder Tarquin's power, just as it was peaceably won, seems not to have been based in any way on force. So far from hearing of a foreign garrison, we have evidence that one quarter of Rome—as its name the 'Vicus Tuscus' shows—was given up to peaceful Etruscan traders. Certainly the city's wealth grew rapidly. It may be that maritime traffic was developed; but the chief source of profit would seem to have been the toll dues levied upon passing merchandise, since, as we said above, Rome stood on the best overland route between Etruria and the south. The wealth thus gotten was put to sound use. Etruscans, if they knew anything, understood how to make a city both strong and imposing; and under the Elder Tarquin's successor, Servius Tullius, Rome was in many ways transformed.

This Servius, whether himself of Etruscan birth, or (on more reliable evidence) a Latin, had at least the wisdom to continue his predecessor's policy. He was a man of large ideas and dominating personality, and amongst other things he is credited with having built the first real fortifications of the city. The 'Servian Wall', as it was called, whether of stone construction or merely a mound surmounted by a timber palisade, was planned on a wide circuit. It included not merely the Capitol (or Citadel), the Palatine, and the other low hills which surround the central valley of the Forum, but also the outlying spur called the Aventine. On this latter hill, moreover, Servius built a temple to Diana, a notable adornment of the hitherto boorish city. Skilled craftsmen, we may be sure, were imported from outside for such an undertaking, but the purely mechanical work was done by the forced labour of the somewhat unwilling inhabitants. For Servius' power, even if first conferred upon him by the Assembly of the citizens, was based upon the support of the upper class of landowners. The fact is that in Rome, as in other city states of the period, the prestige and power of the aristocracy was great. The Advisory Council or Senate, which consisted of leading nobles, played an important part in the direction of policy; and even in the Assembly, or *comitia*, as we shall see, Servius himself gave to this upper class a preponderating influence.

For, above all else, the reign of this far-sighted monarch was remarkable for a complete reorganization of Rome's institutions. First and foremost the purpose of his reforms was to make her a military State. For service in the army, and for the collection of the war-tax he divided the citizens into a series of classes corresponding to their wealth.[1] First came the richest class, who, possessing the wherewithal to furnish a horse, were scheduled to serve as *equites* or knights. The moderately rich, who could afford heavy armour, served in the front ranks of the foot. The remaining classes of poorer citizens, who could afford no more than light equipment, marched in reserve. The military unit at this date was known as a 'century' (though this term can scarcely have signified exactly a hundred men), and the number of centuries furnished by the different classes varied. The class of Knights provided 18 centuries, the Heavy Foot 80; while the remaining classes, put together, provided 93 in all. That the total of centuries provided by the poor was smaller than the total provided by the rich was highly significant. For according to Servius' reforms the same basis of organization which was employed in summoning the host was also employed in counting the votes of the Assembly.

In the Roman Assembly, it must be understood, decisions were not taken on the usual principle of 'one man, one vote'. Instead of this the voters were divided into groups, and decisions were taken on a majority of group-votes—each group-vote being of course determined by a majority among its members. Hitherto for this purpose the citizen-body had been divided into groups of families, known as 'curiae' or clans —a manifest survival of the patriarchal age. But Servius had

---

[1] The account of this assessment, as given by later historians, presents many difficulties—not least that the 'as', or coin by which values were said to be reckoned, did not at this early date exist as a coined currency. So some authorities think that the Servian constitution was in reality the product of a later age—perhaps the period of the Samnite Wars.

other ideas. In place of the Assembly-by-clans[1] he substituted an Assembly-by-centuries. In other words, the two richest classes, which furnished 98 centuries to the army, were divided into 98 voting-groups, and on the same principle the poorer classes, though naturally more numerous, into no more than 93. By such an arrangement, therefore (and not without some justice), the men who bore the brunt of the fighting were given also the chief voice in political decisions. In the new Assembly-by-centuries, moreover, the preponderance of the aristocratic vote was further reinforced by the strict military discipline under which its business was conducted. It met on the Campus Martius, a drill-ground outside the city. During its sessions a red flag was hoisted on the Capitol. A bugler sounded the summons and the voters themselves were mar-shalled as though for parade. Thus, for better or for worse, the stamp of militarism was set upon Rome's political institu-tions. As a result, her citizen-body, unlike the citizen-bodies of contemporary Greek States, developed a habit of orderly conduct and strict obedience to authority which was at once its pride and its strength, and Rome became, in short— what she was ever after to remain- -a pre-eminently soldier State.

Though the traditional account of Servius' constitution presents some difficulties (so much so that certain historians have even doubted whether it dated from so early a time) there can be no question that Rome was already becoming a power in the land. In many other cities of Latium, not merely Veii and Fidenae in the north, but also Tusculum and Praeneste in the east, and Velitrae, Lanuvium, and Ardea to the south, Etruscan princes had secured control. The Latin League was in danger of disruption, and it seems to have been the ambition of Rome's monarchs to rally its remaining members under their leadership. Servius Tullius is known to have made a treaty with them; and it may be inferred that in building his temple on the Aventine he intended to make it the religious centre of the League. His successor, Tarquin the Proud, was even more ambitious. Probably with the same end in view, he too built

[1] The Assembly-by-clans, or *comitia curiata*, was not altogether abolished, but was permitted to survive for purely ceremonial purposes.

a temple—this time a temple of Jupiter on the Citadel or Capitol, an imposing structure with gabled portico, overlayed after the Etruscan fashion with brightly coloured tiles. That the Latins would appreciate his designs was scarcely to be expected; and by a series of campaigns he sought to impose by force a union unattainable by good will. His success appears to have been considerable. For under the terms of a treaty, which according to the Greek historian Polybius was negotiated between Rome and Carthage soon after the Tarquin's fall, Ardea, Antium, Laurentum, Tarracina, and other Latin cities were recognized as 'subject to Rome.

Her domination was unpopular; and the character of the second Tarquin did nothing to mitigate the Latins' dislike of it. As may be inferred from his title 'The Proud', he was a domineering tyrant. At Rome he maintained his power by means of an armed bodyguard; and so much was he detested that an act of brutal insolence done by his son Sextus to a lady named Lucretia was sufficient to unthrone him. Following the lead of two nobles, Brutus and Valerius, the citizens rallied and drove the whole hated family out. When with the aid of Veii and other Etruscan towns Tarquin returned to the attack he was repulsed. Not to be thwarted, he sought other and more powerful allies. In aid of his cause Lars Porsenna, the powerful prince of Etruscan Clusium, gathered a great host which captured the Janiculum Hill on the farther side of the Tiber, and but for Horatius Cocles' heroic defence of the bridge-head would have taken Rome itself. Nor was this the end of Lars Porsenna's efforts. For to judge by the evidence of a late Roman writer according to which he forbade its inhabitants the use of iron weapons, it would seem that at one time Lars Porsenna must actually have gained control over the countryside and perhaps even over the city. It was not till the famous battle fought in 496 at Lake Regillus, hard by Tusculum, that Rome was finally freed from the Etruscan menace.

Once liberty was gained and the commonwealth established the memory of the monarchy became an object of bitter detestation among the Roman people. Nevertheless, it can scarcely be denied that they owed very much to the strong rule of the Etruscan kings. What they had gained on the political and military side there is no need to recapitulate; but another debt well worth noting was the introduction of a new architectural style. The architecture of the Romans was their one outstanding achievement in the field of art, and, though much of it was modelled on the 'beam and gable' construction of the Greeks, it contained one feature which undoubtedly was learnt from the Etruscan craftsmen—the arch. For drains, roofed over with a circular vault of stone, have been discovered in the Forum, some of which certainly date from the Etruscan occupation. But beyond all else, we may conclude by saying, the national character of the Romans—their forceful, stern, imperious spirit—must surely have been derived, in part at least, from their brief but fruitful contact with this alien race. For intermarriage cannot have failed to leave its mark behind, and much Etruscan blood must actually have flowed in the veins of many a noble family at Rome.

CHAPTER III

THE REPUBLIC AND ITS ORDEAL

AT the time of the Tarquins' expulsion, the vast majority of Rome's citizens, and certainly all her leading citizens, were still farmers. Most agricultural communities are by nature conservative; and at Rome, if anywhere, reverence for tradition—the *mos majorum*, or ancestral custom, as they called it—was immensely strong. When a new set of circumstances arose her people showed a shrewd practical instinct for adapting their old methods to meet it. So century after century they built up their intricate constitution, adding a new official here or making an adjustment there, till it resembled the fabric of some great Gothic cathedral, a motley patchwork of superimposed parts, yet still a uniform whole. In short, violent breaks with the past were avoided at all costs; and so it was at the establishment of the Republic. Though the monarchy was abolished, nothing else was changed; and in its place were substituted a pair of magistrates called consuls, annually elected, but otherwise possessing to all intents the same power as the kings.[1] These consuls commanded the host in battle. Even in peace-time they held complete authority for life or death over the citizens, whom they could flog or execute at will. The functions of administering justice and controlling the State finance were equally under their control. But, such responsibilities proving too onerous without assistance, they were given a couple of subordinates, called 'quaestors' or 'inquisitors', whose duty it was to arrest criminals and superintend the revenue.

The creation of two consuls rather than one did something, too, to ease the burden of the office, but its real purpose was to minimize the risk lest some ambitious individual might re-establish the monarchy. For each consul had an absolute power of veto over his colleague's acts—an expedient which, one might think, would soon have led to a deadlock. In times of special crisis, it is true, when unity of command seemed essential to the Republic's preservation, a single dictator was appointed, normally for a period of six months. But, as a rule, the dual magistracy was maintained without a hitch; for the Romans had a shrewd knack of working what was apparently unworkable, and an admirable tradition of sanity and self-restraint made them ready to subordinate their private ambitions to the common weal.

Nor must it be forgotten that, if the consuls were the chief executive of the State, the direction of policy lay in other hands. The Senate, though still an advisory council, contained within itself all the accumulated wisdom and experience of the leading citizens. It was well-nigh impossible for officials who changed with every year to run counter to the authority of so weighty a body. Even the Centuriate Assembly itself, though technically possessing the final say in all matters of importance, was inevitably subject to direction from above. On occasions, it is true, the citizens asserted themselves to good purpose; and in the first year of the Republic they extorted a concession whereby appeal was permitted to the Assembly's verdict against the consul's power of arbitrary

[1] The religious functions of the king, however, were transferred to a high-priest, or *pontifex maximus*, chosen from among the leading citizens.

execution.[1] Generally speaking, however, the Romans felt an extraordinary respect for their social superiors. The 'nobles'—men, that is, of 'known' and ancient pedigree—were regarded with something like awe; and the Senate, selected by the consuls from among such nobles, experienced little difficulty in getting their own way.

The exclusive attitude of these aristocrats, however, led almost from the first to very great dissatisfaction among a certain class of the population. Not that these aristocrats were what we ourselves should regard as very refined or cultured folk. Rome, let us repeat, was an agricultural community. Even the proudest of her citizens were farmers—rough, hard-bitten, practical folk—and often active farmers at that. Every one knows the story 'how, when a dictator was required, men were sent to find an ex-consul Cincinnatus and found him toiling in his shirt-sleeves at the tail of a plough. Nevertheless, in an agricultural community there inevitably arise certain social distinctions. Any one familiar with the rural life of English villages knows how the old-established inhabitants look down upon new-comers and what strict distinctions are drawn between the 'classes'. So it was also at Rome. Certain families had appropriated to themselves, as a hereditary right, the privileges of holding public offices. They also claimed a knowledge of the unwritten law, not understood by the vulgar herd. They held the mysterious secrets of the ritual of State religion. They had even gone so far as to pretend to an almost magical superiority of blood; and these 'patrician' families, as they were called, refused to intermarry with the lesser order of 'plebeians'.

How precisely the plebeian class was composed is matter for conjecture. Some of them no doubt were alien craftsmen or traders who, with the growing prosperity of Rome under the Tarquins, had been induced to take up their residence in the city. The vast majority, however, must have been landless citizens. For though in the far-back days of the original settlement every member of the community would have been allotted

---

[1] This was called the 'Valerian Law of Appeal'. Actually it only applied within the radius of the city itself. Beyond that citizens were considered to be on active service.

THE FORUM, TEMPLE OF SATURN

ETRUSCAN BRONZE LION

each his holding, the increase of population had produced severe competition; and the less successful farmers, falling into debt, would eventually lose their holdings and take the position of mere labourers on the lands of the more successful. It was even common enough for a debtor to pledge his own person in payment, and on default to become the slave of his creditor. Against such a state of things the plebeians could look for no adequate redress. For they were wholly at the mercy of patrician magistrates, who not unnaturally favoured the land-owners of their own class. So, if anything was to be done to right the wrong, the plebeians felt that they must do it them-selves. One weapon indeed they had—they were *indispensable* as soldiers. The times were critical. In 496 the renewed threat of Etruscan domination had been narrowly averted at the battle of Lake Regillus. In 494 marauders from the Volscian moun-tains had threatened southern Latium and Rome had been forced to send her army thither. Many plebeian soldiers had marched in the ranks, and on their return home it dawned on them that the best way to air their grievances was simply to 'go on strike'. So, instead of re-entering Rome, they marched off in a body to the Sacred Mount, some three miles from the city and asserted their intention of founding there a new city of their own. Negotiations followed, and at last a concession was offered which brought them back to Rome. A new type of magistrate was to be created under the title of 'tribunes', whose special function it was, in the case of arrest for debt, to inter-vene between the patrician magistrate and his plebeian victim. To secure him against physical violence the tribune was given a guarantee that his person should be inviolate or 'sacrosanct', and any assailant therefore subject to a religious curse. These new officials were of course plebeians (at the outset two in number, but raised subsequently to ten), and they were to be elected annually by a meeting of plebeians only.

Thus for the time being the danger of civil discord was averted. But externally Rome now drew in her horns. Her pretensions to the hegemony of the Latin League were aban-doned, and in 493, on the initiative, it is said, of Spurius Cassius, she made a fresh treaty accepting a position of equality among her sister States of the plain, and even agreeing

to share with them the commandership in war. This compromise was timely, for war was imminent both upon the
north front and the south. The Etruscan menace, it is true,
was no longer what it had been. Almost simultaneously with
Rome's expulsion of the Tarquin, the other cities of Latium had
recovered their independence, and even in Campania the
Etruscan occupation was ended by a great victory won by the
Greeks in the vicinity of Cumae, where Hieron, the tyrant of
Syracuse, lent them valuable aid (474). But if the worst of
the struggle against the Etruscans was now over, the Republic
had yet to reckon with the neighbouring town of Veii, which
they still retained; and there was much desultory fighting
between the two bitter rivals, in which Rome suffered at least
one calamitous reverse. Meanwhile, on the southern front she
was engaged in constant warfare, as much in the Latins' cause
as in her own. There the Aequi and the Volsci, two predatory
tribes from the surrounding mountains, were overrunning the
plain. At one time the Volsci, it is said, pressed forward to the
very gates of Rome, led, so the story goes, by the exiled
Roman general Coriolanus, who was only dissuaded from sack-
ing the city by the prayers of his own mother. Under Cincinnatus, the hero of the ploughing episode above related, another
serious incursion of the Aequi was defeated, and by about 460
a respite was secured.

But unhappily peace abroad spelt further discord at home,
and the plebeians, who had closed their ranks in the face of the
enemy, now renewed their agitation. This time their demand
was that the unwritten law, which the patrician magistrates
interpreted and administered at will, should at length be
codified. In 454 a commission was dispatched to Athens to
study that city's laws; and in 451, in place of the regular
consuls, a Board of ten officials, called 'decemviri', was
appointed to formulate a code. In 450, the work being still
unfinished, a fresh Board of ten was elected, but at the end of
the year a startling development occurred. The Board of ten
refused to lay down their office. This met with strong opposition, for the prospect of a permanent tyranny of ten was little
to the taste of the constitutionally-minded Romans. A disgraceful episode brought the crisis to a head. Appius Claudius,

the leading member of the Board, had fallen in love with a
girl named Verginia, and, with unscrupulous effrontery, he
employed his magisterial powers to declare her a slave and so
get her into his clutches. Her father, horror-struck, seized up
a knife from an adjacent butcher's stall and plunged it into his
own daughter's heart. A tremendous commotion followed.
The soldiers, then under arms, went 'on strike' once more.
Claudius was executed, the Board of ten deposed, and in the
following year, 449, two consuls, Valerius and Horatius, were
duly elected once more.

Among their first measures was the promulgation of the
famous Valerio-Horatian laws—the very charter of plebeian
liberties. Thereby twelve tables of statutes, previously drawn
up by the two successive Boards, became the recognized code
of the State. It was great gain for the citizens at last to know
precisely where they stood under the law; but there is little
reason to suppose that the formulae of the Tables materially
differed from the traditional usage of unwritten custom. Thus,
the harsh practice of enslavement for debt was still retained;
and for private injuries redress, instead of being enforced by
fine or other official punishment, was left in the hands of the
complainant. 'If a man break another's limb and satisfy not,
on him may he retaliate.' In one respect, however, the code
revealed that instinct for just dealing which ever afterwards
was typical of the national character; for it was enacted that
a commercial bargain, even if made merely by word of mouth,
should be considered binding on the contracting parties. One
serious grievance remained, the ban on intermarriage between
patrician and plebeian families; but by a law passed in 445 this
too was removed once and for all. Under the Valerio-Horatian
legislation an important political advance was made. For
official sanction was now given to the holding of a plebeian
assembly, organized not by 'centuries', the military unit,
but according to geographical districts known as 'tribes'[1]
or wards. It is probable that henceforward the quaestors
as well as the tribunes were elected by this plebeian body;

[1] These 'tribe'-districts appear to have been the basis on which the
war-tax was collected—and the word trib-unes' is of course derived
from the same root.

and at any rate, its discussions could not fail to have some weight.

Such an opportunity to air their grievances was doubtless a great assistance to the plebeians' cause; and, though they were still debarred from the consulship—a serious curtailment of their political liberties—a compromise was presently effected which for the time being sufficed to pacify them. In 444 the consuls were temporarily replaced by six military tribunes drawn from the plebeian as well as from the patrician class. During the remainder of the century Rome was more often than not engaged in war; and the compromise of 444 was so necessary to the maintenance of her internal unity that the experiment was often repeated. For fifty out of the next eighty years military tribunes continued to be elected.

The campaigns of this period completed the work begun during the first half of the century. In 431 a great victory won near Mount Algidus began the process of driving back the hill-tribes, who still harried southern Latium, into their mountain fastnesses; and a dozen years or so later the plain was thoroughly cleared of these Volscian and Aequan intruders. Then in 406 began a ten years' struggle with the neighbouring town of Veii, and at length in 396 this great Etruscan citadel was captured by the Roman general Camillus. The story goes (though quite uncorroborated by recent examination of the site) that the besiegers drove a tunnel underground, and, appearing suddenly from the very bowels of the earth, surprised the garrison in the midst of a sacrifice. Be that as it may, the town was sacked, its inhabitants enslaved, and its territory annexed. Thus by the beginning of the fourth century B.C. not merely had Rome more than doubled her territory, but by her leadership of the Latin League against their southern enemies she had re-established her position as the foremost city of the plain. Her future fortunes seemed assured, when suddenly, like a bolt from the blue, there fell upon her the worst calamity in all her history.

Among the forests and swamps of Central Europe great hordes of Celts or Gauls were at this time wandering in search of lands or plunder—an adventurous race, gigantic in stature, hard drinkers, lovers of the chase, unstable and impetuous by temperament. In war they were formidable fighters, rushing naked into battle and wielding their iron claymores with an *élan* before which even the disciplined soldiery of southern Europe was apt at first sight to quail. Towards the end of the fifth century a tribe of them, the Insubres, had entered the Po Valley from across the Alps and expelled the Etruscan settlers. Other bands followed. Some settled down to agriculture and became in time good farmers. In 391, however, another tribe, the Senones, under their chieftain Brennus, crossed the Apennines and appeared before the Etruscan town of Clusium. A desperate appeal for help went south to Rome, and her envoys, appearing at an unlucky moment, joined in the battle on the Etruscan side. Reparation was demanded for this violation of neutrality—and refused. It was no more than four days' march from Clusium to Rome; and presently came the appalling news that the Gauls were on the move. Eleven miles from the city, where the little River Allia flows into the Tiber, the Roman army met the barbarian hordes, and broke. On the morrow the city was entered. The streets were empty. But in the Forum, seated each on his ivory chair and staff in hand, the Gauls found the elders of the State silent and motionless as statues. An inquisitive fellow stroked the beard of one, and the old man, striking back, was promptly killed. The others shared his fate. Meanwhile, the bulk of the inhabitants had taken refuge in the neighbouring town of Caere. Only on the Citadel did a patriot band hold out. For seven months the Gauls made repeated onslaughts on the stronghold, then, wearying of the struggle, accepted gold to betake themselves off. But Rome was left in ashes, and all she had gained by a century of effort had vanished in a moment. The blow to her prestige was terrible, and all her old enemies seized the chance to profit by her downfall. The southern Etruscans, whom she had recently mastered, threw off her yoke. The Aequi and the Volsci renewed their depredations; and even the Latin allies were openly disaffected. Rome weathered the storm; but how serious had been the crisis was shown by the desperate proposal, defeated only by the efforts of the great Camillus, that the city should be abandoned and its inhabitants bodily transferred to the more defensible fortress of Veii.

Socially and politically such a catastrophe was a great leveller. Rich and poor alike had lost their homes. Ancient buildings, the very stronghold of aristocratic tradition, had been utterly destroyed. Above all, every class had shared in the ordeal; and it is little wonder that the plebeians felt a new determination to assert their full rights of citizenship. Throughout a long series of wearisome campaigns they had fought for the State; and what had they got for it all? War bore hardly on the common soldier's livelihood. Campaigns, it is true, were brief; but they usually took place at a season of the year when harvests had to be gathered; and having left his farm in less capable hands, the farmer-soldier would often return to find himself ruined, so that he must abandon his holding and become a hireling labourer. Thus, while the estates of patrician landowners grew, there was a corresponding increase in the numbers of the landless poor. The crying need of the plebeians at this date was for more land.

Now, as it happened, there were large parts of Roman territory—originally perhaps the royal domain of the former kings—which were now the property of the State and known as Public Land or *Ager Publicus*. Further additions had been made to it when, as after the conquest of Veii, new territory had been annexed. But what seemed grossly unfair to the plebeians was that the bulk of Veientine territory, instead of being divided up and leased out to small-holders, was rented by large proprietors as pasturage. The result was that after the Gallic Sack agitation broke out afresh. In their assembly the plebeians now enjoyed opportunity for consultation, and in their tribunes they had spokesmen. In 376 two tribunes, C. Licinius Stolo and L. Sextius Lateranus, came forward with concrete proposals for reform. The history of the next ten years is one long tale of violence and intrigue. So bitter was the conflict that at one time sheer anarchy prevailed. At last, in 367, the great Camillus was made dictator, and thanks to his good offices a settlement was reached and the Licinian proposals were allowed to become law.

The reforms therein contained covered a wide field. First, the tenure of Public Land was to be strictly limited. No man might for the future rent more than 300 acres, or graze more than 100 cattle or 500 sheep upon the common waste. Secondly, the lot of debtors was alleviated by permission to deduct from their total debt the amount of interest already paid. This set a sound precedent for bankruptcy proceedings, on which further improvements were presently made; and the practice of enslavement for debt came virtually to an end. Last, but not least, it was enacted that of the two yearly consuls one should always from henceforth be a plebeian. It may be that in this matter the patricians' opposition was somewhat weakened by the fact that the consulship, though still supreme, was no longer the sole important office of State; for with the growth of Rome's territory and population public business had outgrown the capacity of a single pair of magistrates. Already in 443 many of the consuls' duties had been transferred to a couple of censors, elected once in every five years. These censors arranged the leases of public lands and contracts for building and road-making. They controlled the civic register for tax-collection and war-service, and, perhaps most important of all, they superintended the personnel of the Senate, with power to eject members for political or even moral misbehaviour. Now, simultaneously with the Licinian reforms, came the creation of further officials—a praetor, who took over from the consul the administration of justice; and two aediles, who superintended municipal affairs—the food-supply in times of famine, the upkeep of temples, and the organization of public games.

It was naturally not long before the plebeians gained admission to these newly created posts,[1] and during the ensuing years the political influence of the plebeian masses was to show a marked advance. Their numbers were steadily increasing, till by the middle of the fourth century the total of Rome's citizens numbered 200,000 males. About the same time the introduction of an official currency proved a great stimulus to trade. The harbour at Ostia, which had fallen into disuse, was rehabilitated, and a growing commercial element in the city developed a new spirit of adventurous enterprise. Even among the agriculturalists—the vast majority of the community—

[1] A plebeian first became censor in 356, praetor in 337, and, to cap it all, high-priest in 300.

there was no lack of enthusiasm for a policy of expansion, bred of an insatiable demand for land. To all these men—farmers and traders alike—the pride of their new-won liberties must have acted as an incentive to common effort. The happy termination of the century-long conflict between the rival orders had infused a new patriotism into the body politic; and it was in the strength of a united nation that Rome set out upon her stupendous task of rebuilding her shattered fortunes, and, more than this, of asserting her supremacy over the whole of Italy.

CHAPTER IV

THE CONQUEST OF ITALY

I. ROME'S RECOVERY

NATIONAL character alone is seldom sufficient to account for a people's success in conquering its neighbours. Geographical· factors also tell, and in this respect Rome was fortunate. Along the western coast of Italy ran what may be termed a natural corridor, consisting of the plain of Campania, the plain of Latium, and, in continuation northward, the valley of the Tiber, which led up into the heart of Umbria and Etruria. From her situation midway upon this corridor Rome was able to send her armies north or south at discretion, and (what was still more important) to penetrate the valleys of the central Apennines, which debouched upon the plains. When faced by a combination of many foes she was thus able to divide their forces and overcome the resistance, first of one group, then of another.

The conquest of Italy, however, was not the work of a moment, and Rome had first to consolidate her position against old enemies. The last had not been heard, for instance, of the Gallic marauders. In 360, and again ten years later, fresh bands of them crossed the Apennines and surged up to the very gates of the city before they were beaten back. It was not till 332 that a treaty of peace was arranged with them, and even that was not long to last. There was trouble too with the Etruscans; and as the fruit of her victory Rome

Setia
Fregellae
Privernum
Interamna
Bovianum
Mediolanum
INSUBRES
Cremona
Lautulae
Formiae
Placentia
Anxur
(Tarracina)
Minturnae
BOII
R. Volturnus
Beneventum
Via Aemilia 187
Capua
Caudium
Saticula
R. Rubicon
Ariminum
AGER GALLICUS
Liternum
Nola
Pisa
Cumae
Naples
ETRURIA
Volaterra
Sena Gallica
Baiae
Puteoli
Vesuvius
Arretium
U
Pompeii
L. Trasimene
Sentinum
M
B
Clusium
PICENUM
R
CAMPANIA
A
Castrum Novum
Telamon
Narnia
Hadria
Ciminian
SABINES
Forest
Carsioli
Alba Fucens
Caere
Aequi
Marsi
Paeligni
Tusculum
Ardea
Sora
Bovianum
Hernici
Satricum
Fregellae
Antium
Volsci
Luceria
Anxur
R. Lifis
Ausculum
Capua
Via Appia
Cumae
Caudium
(Later)
Veseris
Venusia
Naples
Mt. Vesuvius

- Roman Citizen Colonies
- Latin Colonies
312 signifies date of Road
.... approximate frontier of Roman
Territory in 241 B.C.

Paestum
Tarentum
LUCANIA
Heraclea
English Miles
0   50   100
Thurii

R. C

ROME'S CONQUEST OF ITALY

annexed a considerable strip of territory immediately north of the Tiber. But despite these interruptions her main pre-occupation was still to reassert her hegemony over Latium itself. So greatly had her strength now grown that her sister cities of the League could scarcely resist, though they much resented, her claim to leadership; and here too her territorial ambitions led to the annexation of the Pomptine Marshlands at the south end of the plain, directly abutting on the Volscian hills.

Thus in two directions had begun the process of expansion which was to end in bringing the entire peninsula under the rule of the Republic.

Many factors contributed to her success; but more important than her geographical position, more important than even her military prowess, were the political methods whereby she con-trived to conciliate as well as to conquer. Throughout their history the Roman people displayed a surprising readiness to recognize the rights of other folk, and even to extend to them the privileges of citizenship which they themselves enjoyed. These privileges were twofold. The citizen, in the first place, possessed certain *personal* rights; his commercial contracts, his tenure of property, the validity of his marriage and of his bequests by will, and, above all, the security of his person against the arbitrary violence of magistrates or others, all these were assured of sanction and protection in the Roman courts of law. Secondly, in *public* affairs, he was entitled to vote in the Assembly and to hold political office. Now, already in her relations with her sister States of the Latin League, Rome had accorded to their members the same private rights as her own citizens possessed; that is to say, if a citizen of any Latin city entered into any contract with a Roman, such a contract was regarded as legally valid. Such rights were accordingly known as 'Latin' rights; and the advantages thereby bestowed were much appreciated by Rome's neighbours. But her policy did not stop short there. In 381, after overcoming the adjacent town of Tusculum, she generously admitted it to terms of further privilege. Hereby the citizens of Tusculum became in a full sense citizens of Rome, even capable, that is to say, of holding public office.

Their rights of managing their own local affairs were not indeed impaired by such incorporation in the Roman State, but they were compelled to pay the war-tax like other Roman citizens, and in token of this imposition a town thus treated was known as a *muni-cipium* or 'burden-holder'. As Rome's conquests spread, it became her custom to confer this status on cities already accustomed to the practice of self-government; sometimes it carried full franchise, but more often the 'Latin' or half-franchise, though this with the understanding that, their loyalty once proven, promotion to the higher privilege would automatically follow.

Where, however, the inhabitants of conquered territory were either little to be trusted or too uncivilized for urban development, Rome employed another device. Lacking as she did a standing army, she could not post a permanent garrison in such a district, but she sent instead a party of landless citizens (of which she had enough and to spare), annexing sufficient territory to provide them all with farms and establishing a fortified town at its centre. Such a community of planters was known as a *colonia* or colony. Sometimes the planters were Romans with full rights, sometimes Romans and Latins mixed, with 'Latin' or half-franchise. In either case they served not merely as a military outpost at some strategic point in a district of doubtful loyalty, but often too as pioneers of civilization, spreading the social and political ideas of Rome among the backward parts of Italy.

Hitherto, apart from two or three colonies which had been planted in Latium itself, there had been no strategic motive for a further development of this policy. But now with the reassertion of her hegemony of the plain and the extension of her own frontier to the foot of the Volscian hills, the time was near at hand when the Republic would carry her arms into more distant regions, there to employ in one degree or another the same political methods which she had already employed nearer home. Nor was the acquisition of fresh territory, in the first instance at any rate, the motive which led her on to her career of conquest. For, strange as it may seem in so militarist a State, it was not in accordance with the Republic's principles to make war unprovoked, but always either in self-defence against an enemy's attack or in response to an appeal for assistance from some friendly State. It was the latter reason which was presently to bring her into conflict with the most formidable of all Italian hill-tribes—the Samnites.

II. THE SAMNITE WARS

The plain of Campania, the most fertile perhaps of the whole peninsula, was originally inhabited by a folk called the Ausones. Over these the Greek colonies at Cumae and Naples (as well as the temporary Etruscan occupation noted above) had exercised some cultural influence, but this did not avail to protect them against intruders from the hinterland. Soon after the expulsion of the Etruscan princes, about the middle of the fifth century B.C., some Samnites, descending from their upland dales, had overrun the plain, and, settling there, had developed Capua into a prosperous town, which became the centre of a league of many Campanian cities. When in 343 these Oscans, as they came to be called, were attacked in their turn by fresh marauding parties from their kinsmen of the dales, they appealed for help to Rome. Rome sent her army south[1] and beat back the invaders. But this was not the end of the episode. When peace was made in 341, she left a garrison in Capua and made it clear that she regarded Campania as under her protection.

This decision, as we shall see, had very important repercussions upon Rome's relations with the Latin League. Seeing her thus embarking on new ventures of which they themselves might be asked to bear the burden and she get all the profit, they resolved to make a stand. Their demands were drastic. They insisted not merely that they should be given full citizenship, like Tusculum, but that one of the Roman consuls and half the Roman Senate should be drawn from their ranks. If such terms had been accepted, it would have meant that the Roman Assembly too would have been swamped by Latin voters, and the Republic's independence of action overridden.

---

[1] The strange thing is, however, that during her struggle with the Gauls, Rome had made a treaty with the Samnites; and the inconsistency of her policy seems to throw some doubt on the whole story of this war.

No compromise seemed possible and her answer was war to the knife.

Her situation, already critical, was rendered even more so when the Campanians joined the Latins. But with the aid of the Samnite dalesmen (now her allies under the terms of the peace treaty of 341) she succeeded in driving her foes southward down the Campanian coast. Near Mount Vesuvius was fought a decisive battle. Great tales were told of Roman heroism, and it was said that Decius Mus, the consul, having vowed his life to the infernal deities, plunged with head veiled into the thickest of the fight, and by his noble self-sacrifice assured the triumph of his country's arms. The collapse of the Latins rang the death-knell of their League. But Rome's terms were generous. So far from depriving the defeated States of their old rights of the half-franchise, she even admitted some, as she had admitted Tusculum, to the full privileges of citizenship. But on one point she was firm. None were to be allowed to make alliances with any but herself. Isolated each from each, it would be next to impossible for them to raise rebellion; and thus early in her history the Republic recognized the importance of the principle—frequently to be followed in dealing with other enemies—'Divide and Rule'.

With the disappearance of the Latin League, Rome and the Samnites remained the two chief powers in Italy; and despite their recent alliance there was little prospect of lasting peace between them; for the virile mountaineers with a rapidly increasing population could not long be expected to resist the lure of the rich Campanian plains. They were a race of natural warriors, and their only weakness lay in their lack of political unity. Yet, widely scattered though they were among their secluded dales, they had a strong sense of tribal patriotism, and when seriously challenged and attacked in their own country they were capable of rallying fiercely to the common cause, and under the command of their chosen *generalissimo* they would fight with a grim tenacity which it was to take all Rome's strength to master.

With the extension of her power into Campania, Rome must clearly have foreseen the inevitability of a clash with these formidable mountaineers; and steps were taken betimes to

garrison the approaches into the southern plain. In 329 a
colony was planted at Anxur (or Tarracina) commanding the
coastal route thither and in 328 at Fregellae on the inland
route to the east of the Volscian hills. A year later came a
further opportunity to intervene in Campania. Faction had
broken out in Naples, and one party having hired some
Samnites to assist them, the other party appealed to Rome.
Rome sent an army[1] and drove the mercenaries out. But the
fat was now in the fire, for the Samnites of the dales, resenting
the defeat of their fellow-countrymen, made it a *casus belli*.
So began the struggle which was to last on and off for more
than a third of a century.

For some years the fighting was desultory and indecisive.
The Samnites for their part failed in their attempts to take
Fregellae; yet they could not be brought to open battle in the
plains. At last, in 321, came a rumour that their army had
marched eastwards against the inhabitants of Apulia, who had
recently become the allies of Rome. Here, thought the two
consuls, Veturius and Postumus, was a chance to follow them
and force a decision upon advantageous ground. So up they
climbed towards the passes, and in the neighbourhood of
Caudium they threaded through a narrow defile. Beyond this
they emerged into a broad, meadowed valley, reached the head
of it, and found this blocked by a strong Samnite force; then
turning on their tracks, retired towards the narrow defile and
found that blocked too. They were caught in a trap. Their
desperate attempts to break away were unavailing, and eventually they were starved into surrender. The terms imposed by
Pontius, the Samnite *generalissimo*, were harsh. All Rome's
acquisitions in the south were to be abandoned. Six hundred
Roman knights were to be left as hostages. The rest of the
army was to disarm, pass under the 'yoke'[2] as a token of
disgrace, and march home in their shirts. The shamefaced
army slunk into the city under cover of night and shut themselves up in their houses, and the Senate were left to make the

---

[1] As the campaign outlasted the year one of the consuls was left in
his command as 'pro-consul' or 'consuls' substitute'—an important
precedent for the future.

[2] A pair of spears stuck in the ground and supporting a third on top.

best of a bad business. The tale told by later historians that the two consuls were sent back in chains to the Samnites and the lost ground brilliantly recovered can merely have been an attempt to gloze over the catastrophe. Rome required a breathing-space in which to re-equip her army, and she used it to excellent purpose. For one most important lesson had been taken well to heart. In mountain warfare the phalanx or massed formation (first taught to Rome by the Etruscans and learnt by them from Greece) was at a hopeless disadvantage. It was certainly no match for the Samnites, who fought in small mobile detachments first discharging a volley of casting-spears or javelins, then following this up at a rush with their short stabbing swords. The only possible course for the Romans was to adopt similar tactics. Accordingly, the legions were equipped, after the Samnite pattern, with javelin (or *pilum*) and short-sword. Each legion was divided into 'maniples' (or 'handfuls') 120 men strong. In battle the maniples were ranged in three successive lines, leaving a fair gap between each maniple; and they attacked, like the Samnites, first with volley, then with rush, the front line, if unsuccessful, giving way and permitting the second to pass forward through its gaps. So flexible was this formation and so well adaptable to every circumstance of warfare that it became the permanent basis of Rome's military methods and the secret of her unparalleled record of success in many wars and many lands.

On the resumption of hostilities in 316 it was determined to attempt the encirclement of Samnium from the east as well as from the west. So while one army operated in the neighbourhood of Caudium another was sent to Apulia with the purpose of founding a colony at Luceria as a base for operations on this further flank. So risky a dissipation of the Roman forces gave the enemy their chance. In strong force they suddenly broke out across northern Campania, and, reaching the sea, took the coastal route for Latium, beat the army of reserve at Lautulae, and pushed on nearly to Rome. Happily the Latins stood firm in their allegiance; and in 314 the legions, recalled from Campania, overwhelmed the invaders near the scene of the recent defeat. Nevertheless, the blow to the Republic's prestige had serious consequences. In 310 the Etruscans declared war on her, followed by the Italian tribes of the central Apennines—the Marsi, Hernici, Aequi, and Paeligni. It was an uncomfortable moment; but thanks to the advantage of her strategical position Rome was able to divide the members of this powerful combination and strike down each in turn. In 304 the Samnites themselves agreed to terms and abandoned their claim to Campania.

The fact was that the Republic's genius for organization was telling. She had already begun the construction of a military high-road towards the south—known, after the censor Appius Claudius, as the Appian Way. She had planted colonies at Interamna and Saticula in upper and lower Campania; and she now drove a wedge between her northern and southern enemies by planting others at Carsioli and Alba Fucens in the central Apennines. Thus the Samnites were hemmed in by Roman outposts in every quarter save the south. Their position looked hopeless; but in 299 came a golden opportunity for a last desperate throw. Of recent years Central Europe had once more been in commotion. Fresh parties of Gauls had crossed the Alps, and their arrival had stimulated their kinsmen of the Lombard Plain to new activity. Leaguing themselves with several Etruscan cities, they hung menacingly in the north; and the Samnites, seizing their chance, renewed the war. But the Romans were ready, and this time they struck up into the heart of Samnium. Bovianum, the ancient contre of its tribal League, was captured, and fire and sword went through the scattered villages of the dales. But the Samnite army was not beaten yet, and in 296 it slipped away along the eastern coast and joined hands with a large force of Gauls in the neighbourhood of Sentinum. It was perhaps the strongest combination which Rome had ever yet been called upon to meet. But before the enemy could cross the Apennines the two consuls, Decius and Fabius, followed on their tracks and, coming up with them, won a complete victory.

The battle of Sentinum was a landmark in Rome's progress towards a complete mastery of the peninsula, for the Samnite resistance now collapsed. The planting of a colony at Venusia upon their southern flank completed their encirclement, and

in 290 peace was made. Seven years later a fresh inroad of
the Gauls was defeated near Lake Vadimo in Etruria, and this
was a signal for Rome to bring the Etruscan cities, which had
lent help to the barbarians, under her own control. On the
farther side of the Apennines a regular string of colonies
had meanwhile been planted along the Adriatic shore, and
a strip of territory, known as the *Ager Gallicus* and reaching as far northwards as the River Rubicon, was formally
annexed.

The political treatment of the various districts, which in the
course of these long campaigns had been brought under Roman
rule, differed widely. The cities of Campania had been given
the half-franchise, with prospect of ultimate promotion to full
rights. The Samnites and other tribes which were unripe for
incorporation in the Roman political system were given the
less honourable status of *socii* or allies, bound to furnish a
contingent of soldiers on demand, and, though left to manage
their own internal affairs, allowed no independence of external
policy. The Etruscans were given a similar status; but,
despite their ancient civilization and political development,
their outlandish speech and alien habits still excited Rome's
suspicion; and whereas treaties with other allies were concluded 'for ever', the Etruscans were only admitted to terms
for a specified period of years.

As a result of such arrangements the peoples of Italy became
the members of a wide confederacy, all linked to Rome by
treaty. At the centre lay the Roman territory proper—an
area now of several hundred square miles. Round this was a
still larger area—including Latium, parts of Campania, and
after 268 the Sabine hills—which, by grants of civic franchise
in one degree or the other, was virtually incorporated in the
Roman State. Outside this again lay the less privileged
members of the Confederacy—the Etruscans, the Samnites,
and the other tribes of the central Apennines, over which
Rome's numerous colonies, whether of full or of 'Latin' rights,
kept an ever-watchful eye. The only States which still
remained outside the scope of the Republic's influence were
the Greek cities of the south and their wild neighbours of
the mountainous hinterland; but before she could conquer

these, a stern test—perhaps the sternest that she had yet encountered—was now immediately awaiting her.

III. THE WAR WITH PYRRHUS

Hitherto the chief motive underlying Rome's policy of expansion had been, as we have said, the need of finding more land for her poorer citizens, and this need the plantation of so many colonies must have gone far to satisfy. Nevertheless, the growth of a democratic spirit, which the Licinian reforms had awoken in the populace, was now beginning to make itself felt in other ways. In 287 a law called the *Lex Hortensia* endowed the Plebeian Assembly-by-tribes with powers of legislation parallel and equal to the powers of the more aristocratic Centuriate Assembly;[1] and one effect of this reform was to breed—especially among the commercial element—a more adventurous attitude towards foreign policy. Nor was this attitude to be long before finding an outlet.

In southern Italy, as we have already seen, were many flourishing cities of Greek colonists. While they had grown wealthy on trade, their citizens had lost much of their virility, and, when pestered, as they often were, by their predatory neighbours of the Lucanian and Bruttian mountains, they used their wealth to hire outside assistance. At one time Sparta, and again more recently Agathocles, the tyrant of Syracuse, had sent troops to fight their battles. But Agathocles having died in 289, they were forced to turn elsewhere; and seven years later the town of Thurii, when attacked by the Lucanians, sent an appeal to Rome. Though the Senate hung back, the tribune leaders of the Plebeian Assembly insisted on sending a contingent south. The expedition was successful; but it caused considerable annoyance among the people of Tarentum, who, being accustomed to act as champions to these south Italian cities, resented such an intrusion on their own preserve. A

---

[1] The apparent anomaly of two sovereign bodies existing side by side was not so great as might appear. The voters of which they were composed were not in point of fact very different, since the plebeians now formed the great majority of the citizens. It became, moreover, a more or less regular practice to leave law-making to the Tribal Assembly and election of the senior magistrates to the Centuriate Assembly.

little later, when a small Roman squadron put into their harbour, they raked up an old treaty forbidding right of entry to these southern waters, and attacking it sank four vessels. Envoys sent to protest against this high-handed action were denied a hearing by the silly populace, who laughed at their bad Greek and pelted them with filth. 'It shall be wiped out in blood,' said a Roman; and war was declared on the ill-mannered town.

At this period—the aftermath of Alexander's wars—Greece was full of mercenary soldiers; and the Tarentines, distrusting their own feeble powers of resistance, sent post-haste to ask the aid of Pyrrhus, the ruling prince of Epirus and a relative of Alexander himself. He was an impulsive, adventurous, and distinctly unstable character, eager to emulate his great kins-man's career of conquest, and, as far as soldiering was concerned, an expert commander of troops. The force he brought with him to Italy consisted of professional fighters, trained in the tactics which had recently conquered the East—a phalanx of heavy armed foot, about 20,000 strong, marshalled in serried ranks to a great depth and with a front which bristled with the projecting heads of their long lances; a well-drilled cavalry; and (what to the Romans was a terrifying novelty, the more so since horses will never face them) a herd of twenty elephants. Near Heraclea in the summer of 280 the two armies met. In battle it was the business of the phalanx to hold the opposing infantry, leaving their cavalry to do the rest; and while the Roman legions were hurling themselves ineffectually against the hedge of lances, their horse fled at the elephants' approach, and they found themselves surrounded. The rout cost them 7,000 men, but it cost Pyrrhus himself 4,000—a loss he was less able to afford. Thinking that a dash on Rome would bring her allies to his side, he hurriedly marched north, and actually arrived within forty miles of the city before he realized his error and retired. His offers of peace were indignantly rejected by the war-party at Rome; and the winter was spent in drilling fresh troops, for the first time partly levied from the lowest class of citizens.

In the spring of 279 Pyrrhus, reinforced by some Samnites and Lucanians, advanced up the Adriatic coast; and near

Asculum, east of Venusia, he once more encountered the legions. This time, on rougher ground, they managed throughout an entire day to hold the enemy; but on the morrow their front was breached by the onset of the elephants and they retired with heavy loss. But the effort had cost their opponents as dearly as before—another 'Pyrrhic' victory; and it was presently followed by a retirement to Tarentum. Disheartened by the feebleness of his Greek allies, whom he found to be a pack of incorrigible loungers, Pyrrhus was half-minded to throw up the war; and aptly enough at this moment came an invitation from Sicily.

There the Carthaginians were renewing their oft-repeated endeavour to gain full control of the island. They had attacked Syracuse, and the citizens in desperation sent for Pyrrhus to save them (278). He went, and in a whirlwind campaign drove off the besiegers, swept clear most of the island, and after meditating an invasion of Carthage itself abandoned the idea—and returned to Italy. But his case now seemed well-nigh desperate. His Lucanian allies deserted him, his own forces had dwindled, and the Romans were stronger than ever. He tried by a night march to surprise one of their armies near Maleventum, went astray in the dark, and when he met them, suffered a severe defeat. Even some of his elephants were captured. He knew now that the game was up; and in the autumn of 275 he slipped away with troops numbering little more than a third of what he had brought over. Finally, in 272 the garrison he had left in Tarentum was withdrawn and the town surrendered. Rome's terms were generous. She posted a detachment of troops on the citadel, but otherwise she left Tarentum and the other Greek colonies free to govern themselves. Her only stipulation was that they should supply a quota of warships on demand.

This last provision was a symptom that the Republic was beginning to feel the need for a fleet. Some forty years earlier, it is true, two officials had been appointed to control her naval organization, but since the few ships she possessed were not fitted with decks for the operation of marines they can scarcely have been intended for anything more than the transport of troops or supplies. Her energies indeed had been fully employed upon land. Much of it had gone to the plantation of her numerous colonies, to which at the conclusion of the Pyrrhic War she had added one at Maleventum (now re-christened Beneventum[1]) and another at Posidonia (or Paestum) on the south-west coast. For the further consolidation of her power over Italy she was busy developing a system of strategic roads. The making of roads was indeed one of the few arts in which the Romans excelled. They were of solidly built structure, often raised like causeways above the surrounding level, normally paved and planned to run straight as an arrow from point to point. Already the Via Appia had been carried south into Campania and across the Samnite passes as far south as Venusia. The great north road, later known as the Via Flaminia, reached as far as Narnia; and eastwards a third struck up into the central Apennines. Such a system afforded passage not merely to Rome's legions, but also to her officials and merchants; and more than anything else it hastened the dissemination of her speech and habits throughout the scattered members of her confederation. Thanks to her political methods such influences spread rapidly. Large areas were well on the way to being thoroughly Romanized.

The truth is that the making of a nation had begun; and even the outside world was aware of it. The Republic's spectacular triumph over Pyrrhus had attracted the attention of Ptolemy Philadelphus, who now ruled the Egyptian portion of Alexander's empire. He sent a friendly embassy to Rome, and she for her part sent envoys back again. Thus the sons of men who thirty years before had been engaged in a life-and-death struggle with half-barbarous hill-tribes now found themselves treated on equal terms of courtesy by the proudest monarch of the day. The first stage in Rome's course was accomplished. She had become a World Power.

[1] That is, 'Wel-come' instead of 'Ill-come'.

CHAPTER V

CITY AND CULTURE

I. THE CITY

THANKS to modern excavation, supplemented by the record of historians, the topography of Rome is fairly well established. The Forum, which has now been laid completely bare, was of course at all times the centre of the city's life; but at this early epoch it was still a market-place lined with the stalls of greengrocers and butchers. Here, too, most public business was transacted. At the north-west corner was the Curia or Senate House, said to have been built by the king Tullus Hostilius. In front of it lay a square enclosure, the Comitium, in which the Tribal Assembly held its meetings till, outgrowing the space, it moved into the Forum proper. Between the Comitium and the Forum stood the speaker's platform, which after 338, when it was adorned with 'beaks' sawn off some captured galleys, received its famous nickname of the 'Rostra'. Rising above the west end of the Forum lay the Capitol, approached by an abruptly winding road; on the south the Palatine, where better-class Romans for the most part had their houses, and on the farther side of which was the Circus Maximus or Racecourse. The most populous part of the city, crowded with the unwholesome tenements of the poor, spread over the lower slopes and valleys of the Quirinal, Viminal, and Esquiline hills, which spread fanwise on the opposite or north side of the Forum. The opportunity, which the Gallic Sack afforded, of rebuilding the city on a well-ordered plan was unhappily missed; and a natural impatience led to haphazard methods which produced the hideous slums of later years. On the other hand, the temples had escaped the fury of the Gauls, who were extremely superstitious. Of these Tarquin's Temple of Jupiter still stood upon the Capitol, the rest mainly round the Forum. Here, for instance, was the Temple of Saturn, the earliest monument of the Republican times; the Temple of Castor, commemorating the victory of Regillus; and another to Con-cord, celebrating the union of the orders in 367. In front of

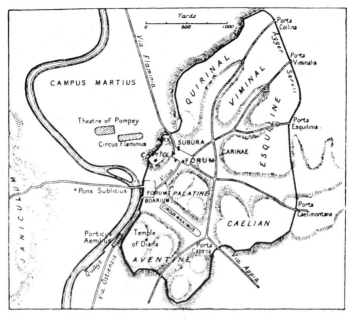

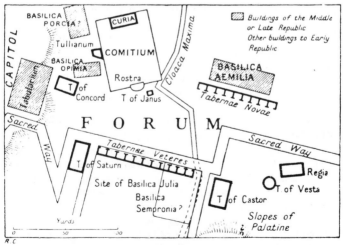

ROME AND THE FORUM

the Comitium stood the small square shrine of Janus, the doors
of which were only closed when the Republic was at peace; and
finally at the farther end of the Forum was the circular Temple
of Vesta, containing a sacred hearth which was symbolic of
the State as was the domestic hearth of the family, and
whereon the Vestal priestesses, vowed to perpetual virginity,
tended, on pain of execution for neglect, the flame of an
undying fire.

Such multiplicity of deities was the natural outcome of a
polytheistic creed; and the tendency to increase rather than
diminish their number was due partly to the character of the
Romans' own religion, partly to their racial aptitude for
borrowing other peoples' ideas. The primitive faith of the
Italian folk had been not unimaginative. They believed that
all the world about them was permeated by supernatural
powers—potent for good or ill. There were spirits in the woods
and rivers, a spirit of the sea and of the sky. There were even
spirits in the most concrete commonplace things. Janus was
the spirit of the door, Vesta of the hearth. There was even a
nasty little spirit known as 'Robigo' or Blight. Agricultural
prosperity was naturally considered to be dependent on such
spirits' favour; and most of the early festivals—the Satur-
nalia, for instance, held at sowing-time—were dedicated to
their propitiation. But by and by fresh attributes were
assigned to these rustic deities, and Mars, to take one example,
became the god of war. Even abstractions were personified
and the spirit of concord, as we have seen, received a temple;
so too did the spirit of purification, called Cloacina, the patron-
deity of drains.

Now the very elasticity of the Romans' religious conceptions
had a dangerous side; for it paved the way for the incorporation of foreign ideas. From the Etruscans they had early
learnt to endow their invisible spirits with a local habitation
and a human form. From neighbouring cities too they
adopted many new deities—Minerva, the patroness of arts,
from Etruscan Falerii; and Castor and Pollux from Tusculum.
It was a more serious matter when contact with the Greeks of
Campania led to an assimilation of Hellenic theology. For the
Romans had soon begun to identify their gods with the gods

of Greece—Jupiter with Zeus, Mars with Ares, Minerva with Pallas Athene, and so on. Eventually even Bacchus, a most un-Roman god, was accepted and identified with Liber. Thus the primitive animism of the old Italian faith was supplanted by anthropomorphic conceptions originating in Greece. It was not a wholesome change, for the tales of Greek mythology, however beautiful in fancy, were not calculated to exert a sound moral influence; and religion, once divorced from the live issues of daily conduct, declined at length into unedifying superstition. So the monotonous effort to propitiate the unseen powers, with its routine of sacrifice and festival, and its ridiculous attempts to prognosticate the future from the examination of entrails or the flight of birds, lost all power to elevate; and later, when the habit of thinking grew, the hollowness of its pretensions provoked the inevitable reaction towards scepticism and doubt.

There remained, however, one element in the Roman religion which, associated as it was with the central institution of their social system, retained a special sanctity and even a real significance—the religion of the home. For at Rome every household possessed its separate altar and its peculiar gods. These were the Lares and Penates, the one originally connected with the bounds and ways of the family estate, the other with the store-cupboard. Both had come to represent the spirit of the home, and so became the symbol of that deeply rooted instinct for family life which was the source of all that was noblest in the Roman character. The priest of the domestic cult was the paterfamilias. He served its altar and embodied in his own person the 'genius' of the home. Thus armed with a divine sanction he ruled like a despot over his petty kingdom. There was no limit set to his arbitrary power. He could even put his children to death, with nothing said. But the stern discipline of his rule was tempered by affectionate regard. Cato, the arch-Roman, considered a wife and a son to be 'the holiest of holy things'. Over his wife a man held almost complete authority; and legally she had no independent rights. Yet the Roman matron was no downtrodden creature. Her activities were not confined, as were her Hellenic cousin's, to the duties and seclusion of the home; and, as early legends show, she often played an important part in public life. There can in fact be little doubt that the influence of Roman wives and mothers had a steadying influence over the political as well as the private behaviour of their men-folk.

It was not the habit in the best days of the Republic to hire a nurse or tutor for the Roman boy. He grew up under his parents' eye, and accompanied his father on business or in sport. Absolute obedience was the first rule of his life and *pietas* or loyalty to home and parents was the quality most highly esteemed at Rome. Strong home affections beget a natural pride in the family's tradition; and the ideal of conduct which every Roman father strove to teach his son was well defined—manly endurance, dignity of bearing, an almost puritanical suppression of the feelings, and, above all, an unswerving devotion to the common weal. Such lessons were pointed by the legendary tales of Cincinnatus, Horatius Cocles, or other self-sacrificing heroes of the days gone by.

Such an education in the moral virtues is most effective and most permanent only in a community where men are little accustomed to think for themselves. The average Roman of this epoch was a somewhat stolid, unimaginative farmer, cultivating with the aid of his sons and perhaps a few free labourers an estate of modest acreage. If he could read and write, that was all the education that was expected of him; and being intellectually too lazy to criticize or rebel, he was content to follow blindly in the routine of life prescribed for him by the immemorial custom of his forebears. But the time was near at hand when a policy of territorial expansion would bring him into contact with other influences. Already with the Pyrrhic War and the conquest of South Italy was beginning the slow, but historically vital, process whereby the Romans were to be introduced to the ideas and culture of Greece. The next stage in that process was to come with their conquest of Sicily, and to this the inevitable conflict with the rival power of Carthage was now about to guide them.

CHAPTER VI

THE FIRST PUNIC WAR

THE Mediterranean world of the third century B.C. fell into two fairly well-defined halves. Throughout the eastern half a more or less homogeneous Hellenistic culture, originated by the city states of Greece, Sicily, and Asia Minor, had been widely disseminated as the result of Alexander's conquests. At his death, it is true, the vast empire which he had founded went to pieces, and from it his generals had carved out great dominions for themselves. The successors of his European viceroy ruled in Macedon, aspiring to the supremacy over the whole of Greece. The Seleucid Dynasty, from their capital at Antioch in Syria, ruled Mesopotamia and most of Asia Minor. The Ptolemies of Alexandria ruled Egypt. But despite the political disruption of his empire the cultural unity which Alexander had given it survived. A debased form of the Greek tongue was becoming the lingua franca of the Levant. Greek art and literature flourished at Alexandria and elsewhere; and even among the exclusive Rabbis of Jerusalem the influences of Greek thought began to permeate. Meanwhile in the western half of the Mediterannean Hellenism had as yet little hold. Of the two great powers which were now to contest its mastery, Rome, as we have seen, was still in a comparatively backward state. Carthage, on the other hand, belonged to an order of civilization which had little in common with either Greece or Rome.

The Carthaginian people were of Semitic stock, being descended from Phoenicians, who in the ninth century had founded the town of Kirjath or Carthage on the north African coast. In character they were a dour, cruel, and fanatical folk. Their religion was gross and horrible, and its chief deities were Astarte, the unedifying Moon Goddess, and Moloch the Fire Lord, into whose furnace, at times of dire extremity, they were even known to cast their children. Like the Phoenicians, they were primarily traders. Their ships voyaged to Britain for tin; their caravans drew gold, ivory, and precious stones from the dark interior of the Continent.

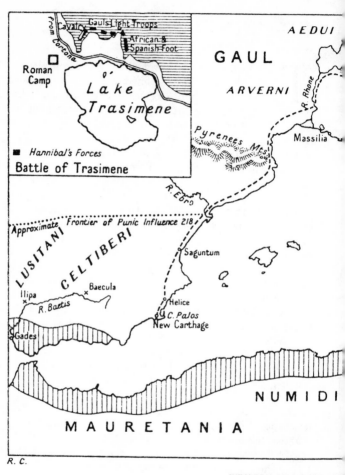

Battle of Trasimene

Roman Camp

Lake Trasimene

Cavalry (from Cortona)

Gauls Light Troops

African & Spanish Foot

■ Hannibal's Forces

GAUL

AEDUI

ARVERNI

R. Rhone

Massilia

Pyrenees Mts

R. Ebro

Approximate Frontier of Punic Influence 218

LUSITANI

CELTIBERI

Saguntum

Baecula

Ilipa

R. Baetis

Helice

C. Palos

New Carthage

Gades

NUMIDIA

MAURETANIA

R. C.

VENETI
Aquileia
Mediolanum
INSUBRES Placentia
Parma
Mutina
Lucca
Faesulae
Ariminum
R. Metaurus
Sena Gallica
R. Arno
Arretium
Cortona
L. Trasimene
ETRURIA
UMBRIA
Pharos
Issa
ILLYRIA
Scodra
Lissus
Subines
Rome
SAMNIUM
Aufidus
CAMPANIA
APULIA
Cannae
Canusium
Capua
Nola
Naples
Tarentum
LUCANIA
CORSICA
SARDINIA
Corcyra
EPIRUS
BRUTTIUM Croton
Messana
M. Ercte
Panormus
Mylae
Rhegium
Orepana
Aegates Is.
Motya
Himera
Lilybaeum
Agrigentum
Syracuse
C. Farina
Ecnomus
Utica
R. Bagradas
Carthage
Zama

---- Line of Hannibal's March
× Site of Battle
▥ Area of Punic Empire in 264 B.C.
English Miles
0   100   200   300

PERIOD OF THE PUNIC WARS

But from the sixth century onwards began a period of territorial expansion. In the Libyan hinterland they reduced the natives to serfdom. They extended their sway over the desert tribes of Numidia and over southern Spain; Sardinia, valuable for its metals, became theirs; and they annexed to themselves the trade-stations first planted by the Phoenicians on the western shores of Sicily—Panormus, Motya, and Lilybaeum. From these various sources they drew an immense revenue partly by custom dues and partly by tribute; and they used it to build up not merely a powerful navy, but also a large mercenary army, reinforced by regiments pressed from their subjects in Africa and Spain. Political power lay in the hands of a ruling caste of landlords and merchants. Except at times of extreme crisis the popular Assembly possessed no voice at all; and the State's policy was directed by a council of leading citizens, guided by a small inner committee of its own members. The two chief magistrates called 'Shophetim,[1] or 'suffetes', were elected annually; but their military commanders were allowed a much longer term—an arrangement which was to give them a manifest advantage over the changing consuls of Rome. Thanks to her commercial supremacy Carthage had become the richest city in the world. On the seas she had no rival. The western waters of the Mediterranean were to all intents and purposes a 'Carthaginian Lake', and her object was to close them, if possible, to all vessels save her own. The treaty made with, Rome in early days, for instance, forbade the sailing of any Roman vessel west of the Fair Promontory near Carthage; and it was clear enough that, if the Republic desired any considerable extension of her commercial enterprise, she would sooner or later have to reckon with these formidable rivals.

The inevitable bone of contention between the two great powers was the island of Sicily. For two centuries at least the Carthaginians had persisted in their attempt to extend their grasp beyond the harbours they already possessed upon the western coast. Invasion after invasion had been beaten back by the stalwart resistance of the Greek settlers, but after the withdrawal of Pyrrhus in 276 the Carthaginians had

[1] The same title was used for the 'judges' of the early Israelites.

reoccupied the greater part of the island. Two states retained their independence—the kingdom of Syracuse, now ruled by the young Prince Hiero, and the little town of Messana at the north-east corner of the island. This town was in the possession of a party of freelance mercenaries who called themselves 'Mamertines' or 'children of Mars'; and in 265, finding themselves hard pressed by Hiero's troops, they secured the protection of a Carthaginian garrison. Then, suddenly changing their minds, they appealed to Rome. The Senate shrank from the venture, but the popular party, perceiving that the Carthaginians, once ensconced in Messana, would command the all-important trade-route through the narrow straits, insisted on overruling the Senate's decision, and in 264 two legions were commissioned to march south.

It seems a strangely audacious adventure on which this insignificant force was embarking; but under cover of night they slipped across the straits, occupied Messana (which had already ejected the Carthaginian garrison), and, when faced by a combination of Hiero's troops and a fresh Carthaginian army under Hanno, succeeded in beating them back. Truth to tell, the enterprise was not so hazardous as might at first sight appear. The Carthaginians, unaccustomed as they were to meet with any opposition either by land or sea, did not keep their fleet or army on a standing basis. In peace-time the fleet was normally laid up in dock, and rowers would have to be collected and trained before it could be put into commission. Even the mobilization of adequate land-forces would take time, for mercenaries had to be hired from Greece, Spain, or other quarters. So the Romans could count on a breathing space, and very well they used it. In 263 they attacked Syracuse and forced Hiero to become their ally. In the following year they laid siege to Agrigentum, and, when Hanno brought an army to relieve it, defeated him heavily. In 260, however, the Carthaginian fleet was ready, and it proceeded to cruise round Sicily and terrorize the coast. If the Romans, thus marooned on the island, were to escape complete disaster, there was only one expedient—they too must organize a fleet.

Hitherto, as we have seen, the Republic possessed few warships of her own, and even those of her Greek allies were no match for the towering galleons of Carthage. But by good luck an enemy quinquereme had been stranded off Bruttium, and on the model of this the Italian shipwrights built a hundred new vessels of the larger type. Crews were trained to row on a scaffold of benches erected ashore. But the real hope of Rome lay in the superiority of her marines, provided that these, in accordance with the tactics of the day, could get aboard an enemy vessel. So by an ingenious device each ship was fitted with a hinged gangway, which could be lowered suddenly from a masthead and get a grip on the enemy's deck by an iron spike, nicknamed the *corvus* or crowsbill. The sequel to these preparations was a series of astonishing victories over the hitherto invincible navy of Carthage. In 260 the consul Duillius won a crushing victory off Mylae, not far from Messana. Two years later a success was gained off Sardinia, and Corsica was captured. Finally, near Cape Ecnomus on the southern shore of Sicily, Regulus and Manlius, the consuls for 256, defeated the enemy in a tremendous set battle in which over 300 vessels were engaged on each side.

The Carthaginian collapse was the more disastrous, since on this occasion the Romans were aiming at something more than the supremacy at sea. In Sicily itself the enemy strongholds at the west end of the island still defied their efforts; and the government had begun to feel that the shortest way to win Sicily was to strike direct at Carthage herself. Accordingly, after their victory at Ecnomus, the fleet and its accompanying transports proceeded to the African coast; and though for the rest of the year the Romans contented themselves with ravaging the country, the case of Carthage seemed desperate. During the ensuing winter, however, the arrival of a Greek mercenary contingent put a new complexion on affairs. Their commander Xanthippus, a professional trainer of troops, reorganized the garrison on Greek tactical methods; and even the unwarlike citizens turned out to drill. The result was that, when spring came, the Romans suffered overwhelming defeat. Regulus (whose colleague Manlius had been recalled) was captured; and every one knows the story how some six years later he was sent home on parole to convey overtures of peace, and how, having courageously refused to recommend the terms he had

AN ETRUSCAN APOLLO

been sent to sponsor, he went back to captivity in Carthage, where he died.

The tragic breakdown of this attempt to carry the war on to African soil marked the beginning of a decline in the Republic's fortunes. For the long-distance voyages which it necessarily involved proved too much for the skill of her pilots. Fleet after fleet was lost at sea through inefficient navigation. First a squadron of 350 ships, dispatched to the relief of Regulus, was caught in a storm off Sicily and all but eighty foundered. In 253 a second squadron, while returning from a raid on the Libyan coast, was also wrecked. Even their capacity to meet the Carthaginians in battle was seriously impaired; and in 249 what remained of Rome's naval forces were defeated in the harbour of Drepana[1] and a large convoy of her transports went down in a storm. The loss of her supremacy at sea reacted seriously on land-operations. In 254, it is true, the great Carthaginian fortress at Panormus had been captured, and the Roman army set to work to invest Lilybaeum. But they could make little headway. They found it impossible to prevent enemy blockade-runners from revictualling the town, and, worse still, with the destruction of their own fleet and transports it became increasingly difficult to keep their troops supplied, so that convoys had to be sent overland by way of the narrow straits.

Rome faced her troubles with dogged courage. When in 249 Regulus came over with proposed terms of peace they were indignantly rejected and the attack on Lilybaeum was pressed on. Two years later the siege was still in progress when there came out to Sicily a new Carthaginian general named Hamilcar Barca. In contrast to the half-hearted policy of the home government, this young man's ambition was wholly set on the defeat of Rome. Making his base on Mount Ercte in the rear of Panormus, he harried the besiegers of Lilybaeum by a series of raids. Their communications were in danger, and it became clear that if the fortress was ever to be taken Rome must regain the command of the sea.

[1] The famous story is told how the Roman commander P. Claudius was warned before the battle that the omens were against him, since the sacred chickens, carried aboard, would not eat. 'Then they shall drink,' he replied, and had them thrown into the sea.

A tremendous effort was put forth. Loans were raised, and the empty treasury was replenished; even women contributed their jewellery. And in 242 a fleet of 200 new vessels put out under Lutatius Catulus for Drepana. It was not till a year later that the Carthaginian navy, which the negligence of a listless government had allowed to fall to pieces, was ready to face the new challenge. It met Catulus outside Drepana near the Aegates Islands, and, manned as it was with raw crews, it was utterly annihilated. Carthage accepted defeat and Hamilcar was left to negotiate the terms—an indemnity of 3,200 talents or 500,000 pounds, a guarantee not to sail her warships into Italian waters, and above all the abandonment of all claim to Sicily.

Rome's annexation of the island naturally followed, and it proved to be one of the most important landmarks in her history. Hitherto in her dealings with the peoples she had conquered she had always treated them, as we have seen, more as confederate allies than as subjects; and even here those Sicilian cities which had assisted her to victory received similar indulgence. With Syracuse, for example, she concluded an alliance 'for ever'. Messana and other cities were given a status analogous to that of the south Italian Greeks. Of them she asked no tribute any more than she had asked it of her Italian allies. But with the rest of the islanders her policy was different. The expenses of the war had been heavy; the necessity of garrisoning the country would mean further outlay; and the temptation to recoup herself was strong. It was the Republic's habit, moreover, to accept the state of things she found already existing, and the Sicilian people were accustomed to pay tithes. Some had paid them to Carthage, some to Hiero; and the latter's method of assessment was so much more systematic that it was now actually adopted. The burden which it placed upon the natives was certainly not excessive. Pasture-land was liable to a money-tax (*scriptura*) paid on every head of grazing stock, and on crops a tithe or tenth was levied. The first charge on the latter was to provide for the needs of the garrison. What remained was transported to Rome, where, owing to the growing exhaustion of the Latin farms, additional supplies were very welcome. The collection of these tithes was farmed out to contractors—either Sicilians or resident Romans—who paid a lump sum down to the government and were then entitled to recoup themselves by charging the natives a fraction over the prescribed tenth. At first a quaestor was sent out to superintend these arrangements; but it was soon discovered that a more responsible official would be needed for the command of the garrison and the administration of justice. So from 227 onwards two additional praetors were elected at Rome, one for Sicily, the other for Corsica and Sardinia, an additional annexation made in 239. These praetors' powers, like the consuls' at home, were extremely autocratic—more military than civilian in character. Far removed as they were, too, from the constraints of public opinion at home and the watchful eyes of democratic tribunes, they wielded an authority even greater than the consuls, ruling like despots over their little kingdom. Though at the outset there is no reason to suspect any gross misgovernment, the inauguration of the provincial system had no very wholesome effect upon the Roman people. It marked the birth of a grasping spirit which was new in the national character, and which unhappily grew with years.

One other consequence of the annexation of Sicily remains to be noted. The representatives of Rome who found their way into the island—whether traders, tax-collectors, soldiers, or officials—there came into contact with a luxurious and decadent culture in which the bad traits of Hellenism prevailed over the good. The ostentatious display and frivolity of Hiero's court at Syracuse could not fail to exercise an attraction on the simple-minded Italians; and it is not long before we find plays being acted at Rome which, though rewritten in Latin, were closely modelled on the none too moral comedies of the Greek dramatists. Thus the staid, puritanical morality of the Republic was subjected for the first time to an influence which was eventually to undermine the very foundations of its strength.

CHAPTER VII

BETWEEN THE WARS

I. ROMAN EXPANSION

THE struggle with Carthage, though it had lasted a quarter of a century and had strained Rome's resources to the uttermost, left her stronger than ever. Despite the continuous demands upon their man-power, the members of her confederacy had (with the exception of one town, Falerii) stood by her loyally. Her troops had gained valuable experience. Her improvised fleet had won the command of the seas; and in the aftermath of the war the same spirit of enterprise which had carried the Republic into it drove her on to embrace fresh opportunities of overseas adventure. In 239, when the Carthaginian garrison in Sardinia mutinied against its home-government, Rome rushed in to lend it assistance, and succeeded in extorting from her now helpless rival not merely the cession of the island but another large indemnity.

Still more important were the events which led her to embark on a policy of expansion eastwards. With the adjacent peninsula of Greece she had hitherto had no official dealings; but a considerable trade ran across the Adriatic, and it was in protection of this trade that the next campaign was to be undertaken. Among the creeks and islands of the Illyrian coast, on the farther shore of the Adriatic, were ensconced a race of piratical freebooters, who under the energetic leadership of their ambitious queen named Teuta had become a regular scourge to cross-sea shipping. In 230 these rascals caught a party of Italian merchants and put some of them to death. Envoys sent to protest were attacked on their homeward voyage, and the Senate, losing patience, sent a fleet to end the nuisance. The fleet made for Corcyra, which was in Illyrian hands; Demetrius of Pharos, a dependent of Queen Teuta, conveniently turned traitor to his mistress. As a reward he was left in possession of the island under the protectorate of Rome; and further to safeguard the trade-route a strip of territory on the Epirot mainland opposite was formally annexed.

This apparently harmless step led indirectly to the most momentous consequences. For Rome, having once intervened in the affairs of the Greek peninsula, could not easily draw back. To the states of the Peloponnese indeed the suppression of piracy was a godsend, and they loaded the Republic with demonstrations of gratitude. But Antigonus Doson, the ruling King of Macedon, regarded her interference in a very different light. Like his predecessors, he considered the whole peninsula as his own special preserve, and as soon as ever Rome's back was turned he began to befriend the buccaneer Demetrius, who resumed his old game on the sea. In 221 Antigonus' successor, Philip V, continued this policy; and, as may well be imagined, he was none too pleased when Rome intervened once more to suppress Demetrius and even captured his island stronghold of Pharos. This blow to Macedonian pretensions was not readily forgotten; and, when the Republic became engaged in her life-and-death struggle with Carthage, King Philip, as we shall see, was ready to take sides with her enemy. Thus, by a series of incidents which had begun with the necessity of destroying some impudent pirates, Rome was to be led on, in the ultimate issue, to the conquest of Macedon and Greece.

If we look for the motive force which lay behind the Republic's foreign policy during these critical years we shall find it, as we found it during the recent Punic War, in the continued ascendancy of the popular party. The more cautious Senate was often pushed into action against its better judgment; and even within Italy itself there had been occasion for strong difference of opinion. In 232 the popular party, led by the tribune C. Flaminius, had insisted on parcelling out into allotments for small-holders the *Ager Gallicus* or border-country on the north-east frontier, which the Senate, presumably for purposes of revenue, had wished to retain as public land and lease out to rich tenants. A wiser plan, which may indeed have been in the Senate's mind, would have been to strengthen this dangerous frontier by the plantation of a colony. For the Gauls of the Po Valley, stimulated by a fresh influx of tribes from beyond the Alps, were once more upon the war-path. The Boii and Lingones, who lived south of the Po, leagued themselves with the Insubres of Mediolanum (or

Milan) and the Taurini, whose district lay round the modern Turin; and in 225 a formidable host again broke across the Apennines into Etruria. But the Romans were prepared and had made their dispositions. By skilful strategy troops from Sardinia were landed in the invaders' rear, and these, co-operating with two other armies, drove them westwards against the coast, till at Telamon they were brought to bay and practically wiped out. The opportunity to reduce the whole Gallic population of the northern plain was too good to be missed. First the territory of the Boii was overrun; then Mediolanum was taken; and finally, with the exception of the Ligurian mountains, the whole of this wide district fell under the power of Rome. Distrusting the fickle temper of the Gauls, she did not enrol them as members of her confederacy. But she took steps towards keeping control over the Po Valley by planting colonies at Placentia on the nearer bank and at Cremona on the farther. Meanwhile the strategic high road towards the north was carried as far as Ariminum on the Adriatic coast, and named after Flaminius (now censor) the Via Flaminia. The Republic, it is clear, had already begun to envisage an extension of her frontier to the line of the Alps— the natural boundary of Italy; but unhappily for her this prudent policy of self-defence was incomplete, and the Gallic tribes' allegiance insufficiently secured, when the twenty-three years' respite in her struggle with Carthage ended, and the army of Hannibal was able to break across the Alpine barrier unopposed. What were the events which led to the renewal of the conflict, and how Carthage herself had fared during the interval, it is now time to consider.

II. CARTHAGINIAN RECOVERY

Though historical evidence is lacking on the point, there can be little doubt that some time during the course of the First Punic War Carthage lost her hold on southern Spain. A shrinkage of revenue must have resulted; and this may very possibly account for the feebleness shown by the government during the later stages of the war, and still more for their failure to pay off their mercenary troops at its conclusion. The indignant soldiers came out in mutiny (which incidentally led, as we have seen, to the further loss of Sardinia); and for three years a horrible internecine conflict racked the unhappy country. It is known to history as the Truceless War. The mercenaries killed, mutilated, and tortured all who fell into their hands. The citizens threw their prisoners to be trampled on by elephants. The government's cause was finally saved, as it had nearly been saved in Sicily, by leadership of Hamilcar Barca; and when at last the mutiny was put down this man was given an army to undertake the reconquest of Spain.

Landing at Gades (or Cadiz) in 237, Hamilcar first overran the south-west corner of the peninsula, then pushed his success up the Mediterranean coast, until in 227 he lost his life by drowning in a river near Helice. His son-in-law Hasdrubal, who now assumed the command, proceeded to found New Carthage on the south-east coast to be the naval base, arsenal, and fortified capital of the new Spanish Empire. Thence he extended his control over the mountainous hinterland, exploited the silver-mines in which the neighbourhood was rich, and enlarged his own forces by recruiting the native tribesmen. But such rapid progress of the Punic leader was, in one quarter at least, regarded with grave concern. The ancient Greek colony of Massilia (or Marseilles) at the Rhône mouth had long been a rival to Carthaginian traders; and, though a line of demarcation between their respective spheres of influence had been drawn at Cape Palos, the encroachments of Hasdrubal had widely overstepped this stipulated boundary. The Massiliots, justifiably indignant, made an appeal to Rome, who had long been their ally; and Rome's remonstrances were so effective that Hasdrubal in 225 gave a specific undertaking that he would in future keep to the south side of the River Ebro.

Had Rome taken no further steps, all perhaps would have been well; but she presently proceeded to strike up an alliance with the independent Spanish city of Saguntum, which lay south of the Ebro and so well within the area now allotted to Carthage. Since Saguntum had not been mentioned in the foregoing settlement, it was a moot point whether Rome's action was legitimate or no. But in any case it led to the most disastrous consequences. In 221 Hasdrubal was murdered, and Hamilcar's young son Hannibal stepped into his command. Two years later he suddenly attacked Saguntum, and after a siege of eight months took it. There can be little doubt that this high-handed measure was intended as a point-blank challenge to Rome, and was in fact the culmination of a long and deep-laid policy. Hannibal's father, Hamilcar, from the moment he set foot in Spain, had had but one goal in view—the building up of resources of man-power and money wherewith to avenge the recent humiliation of his country's arms. The story is told how, before leaving Carthage, he had taken his young son to Moloch's Temple, and, bidding him lay his hand on the altar, had made him swear undying enmity to Rome. The fulfilment of that vow was from first to last the dominant motive of Hannibal's career. His preparations were now completed. He was ready to strike; but there was one obstacle in his path. The home-government had no enthusiasm for the resumption of the war; and if they were to be drawn into it, there must be a *casus belli* which they could not possibly evade. In Saguntum, Hannibal found his opportunity. He could argue on the one hand that he was within his rights in attacking it, since it lay within his sphere of influence. He must have known, upon the other hand, that the Romans would never overlook this treatment of their ally. Sure enough, though they made no effort to rescue the doomed town, they sent an embassy to Carthage. After some dis-cussion, Quintus Fabius, its leader, gathered his cloak into two folds. 'I carry here War and Peace,' he cried. 'Which shall I give you?' 'Which you will,' came the answer—and he shook out the fold of war.

CHAPTER VIII

THE SECOND PUNIC WAR

I. FIRST PHASE TO CANNAE

ON the face of it Hannibal's decision to invade Italy seems the most foolhardy of adventures. He was pitting his strength against a country which possessed an almost inexhaustible reserve of man-power. On the estimate of a census taken some years before, the Romans could draw on 700,000 foot (counting allies as well as citizens) and 70,000 horse. Their infantry, though composed of yeoman soldiers called up from the plough, were at this date the finest in the world. Equipped with helmet, cuirass, and greaves, and carrying a large shield, two javelins, and a sword, they were trained in the tactics learnt during the Samnite Wars; and fought with a dogged courage which, as had often been shown, was capable of winning battles in despite of the inexperience of their consular commanders. Against these admirable troops the striking-force at Hannibal's disposal appeared a mere handful. He could not even take his full complement along with him to Italy. Some he was forced to send across to mount guard over western Africa, some he left behind with his brother Hasdrubal in Spain. His army of invasion, therefore, was limited to 30,000 infantry and 9,000 horse. But their quality was good. The infantry was a veteran force conscripted from Africa and Spain and trained to a high efficiency under his own eye. His Numidian cavalry were incomparably superior to anything which the Republic could produce.

Yet, when all is said, it remains astonishing that with this tiny force Hannibal should have undertaken an overland march through nearly 1,000 miles of country and there embarked on a campaign in which, as he must have known, his communications would be severed and even a single defeat might well mean complete disaster. The truth is that in reality he had no other choice. His home-government, as we have said, showed no eagerness for the war. Their navy had never recovered its spirit or efficiency. It was incapable of conducting transports for an attack by sea; and to await a proper mobilization would in any case have been perilous. For Hannibal rightly divined that the Roman strategy would be an offensive against Africa or Spain, and it was essential that he himself should get his blow in first. Two calculations, moreover, served to justify his boldness. In the first place, having learnt through his agents how much the Gauls of the Lombard Plain resented their recent subjugation, he counted on their assistance. In the second place, he believed that

Rome, like Carthage, was equally unpopular with her other subjects; and though apparently not hoping to capture the city itself, he expected her Italian confederacy to fall to pieces at the first sign of her defeat. The fact was, however, that more than anything else Hannibal's enlistment of the Gauls—their age-long enemy—rallied the Italians' resistance against him; and in the earlier stages of the war at least there were to be no defections from Rome.

All the more remarkable, therefore, was the brilliance of the triumphs which Hannibal achieved, and the secret of them must be found in his own powers of leadership. He was now twenty-nine years of age, a wiry athlete trained to run and box and capable of enduring the privations of a bivouac or the strain of the longest march. Over the troops which he commanded he exercised a fascination little short of miraculous, so that throughout all the long years of the distant and wearisome campaign their loyalty never faltered. In the field he showed an ingenuity of ruse and manœuvre which completely outwitted his slow-thinking opponents. Roman accusations of his 'Punic' perfidy had little foundation in fact, but there was a deep strain of Semitic fanaticism in his character; for he was extremely superstitious and a believer in dreams. Yet he was well educated too, having all the culture of Carthage, and well versed in the history of Hellenic warfare. Diplomatic as well as strategical conceptions played a large part in his schemes; and, what is invariably the mark of great commanders, he displayed a keen imaginative insight into the psychology of his opponents.

Though the Romans never seem to have anticipated an invasion of their own territory, they had laid plans in a leisurely fashion for an invasion of the enemy's. Even before Hannibal crossed the Rhône and disappeared into the east Publius Scipio, one of the consuls, arrived with a fleet of transports at Marseilles, *en route* for an invasion of Spain. On learning the startling news, and after actually visiting the camp which Hannibal had just quitted, he left his brother Gnaeus Scipio to continue the Spanish offensive, and himself hurried back to Italy. Meanwhile a second expedition under the other consul, Sempronius, had set out for Africa. While still in Sicilian waters the news had reached them too. But, though summoned home, their return was slow; and thus North Italy was left to the inadequate protection of new and half-trained levies at the very moment when Hannibal arrived.

Hannibal, for his part, had made good marching. He left New Carthage in May and the Rhône in August. With the aid of guides lent by friendly Gauls he made the passage of the Alps. His exact route is the subject of much controversy; and even Polybius' careful account, written two generations later, is topographically obscure, though it seems to favour the Little St. Bernard Pass. During the ascent there was trouble with the terrified mountaineers. Boulders were hurled from the surrounding crags, and stragglers seldom returned. But the descent was far more terrible. Snow began to fall. The men sank in the drifts. The track was trampled to ice. The elephants, of which Hannibal had brought a couple of score, slithered in grotesque panic. At one point the march was held up by a landslip till the engineers made a new path. The loss of life was serious; and when in late autumn the plains were finally reached the survivors were sick and exhausted. It was lucky for Hannibal that he could supplement his depleted force with volunteer contingents of Gauls. Speed was still his chief object, and he pressed on towards the Po. Here Scipio was awaiting him with troops hastily raised for the purpose. North of the river a cavalry engagement on a tributary stream, the Ticinus, went heavily against the Romans, and they retired to the south bank of the Po, where Sempronius, freshly back from Sicily, soon joined them. Here Hannibal followed them; but he knew better than to assault their camp, which lay on high ground behind the River Trebia. One early December morning, when sleet was falling fast, his skirmishers, by feigned flight, enticed the Romans out across the river, already swollen breast-high by winter spates, and so on to the plain beyond, where he had them at his mercy. Their cavalry were routed, their wings enveloped, and finally on their rear came a surprise attack from a party hidden in the reed-beds of a watercourse. Though surrounded, the legions fought with splendid courage; but no more than 10,000 men succeeded in breaking through. The victory decided the fate of the northern plains; for now all the Gauls came out for Hannibal, and he spent the winter in reorganizing the forces and curbing the impatience of these somewhat embarrassing allies.

In the spring of 217 Hannibal was ready to move south. He had two choices before him. He might strike down the eastern coast, where Servilius, one of the consuls, was awaiting him at Ariminum; or he might cross the Apennines and descend by a more westerly route through Etruria, where lay Flaminius, the old popular champion, now Servilius' colleague in the consulship. Hannibal chose the latter route, and, crossing the Apennines, plunged through the flooded valley of the Arno, where incidentally he caught ophthalmia and lost an eye. Burning and plundering as he went, he passed southward through Etruria, hoping to draw Flaminius out from his entrenchments at Arretium; and, when Flaminius refused to budge, marched past him down the road which led towards Rome. South of Cortona this road, as it skirted the borders of Lake Trasimene, entered a narrow strip of plain enclosed by a crescent of surrounding hills, either spur of which came close down to the waterside. Here, knowing that Flaminius was now hard upon his heels, Hannibal resolved to lay his trap. Overnight he lined the surrounding hills with troops, the best on the two spurs commanding the narrow gaps through which the road passed southward. Next day the morning mist lay heavy over the borders of the lake when suddenly through the tense silence there fell on the expectant ears of the watchers on the hill-tops the sound of a column tramping along the road beneath. The Romans could neither see nor be seen; and not till the tail of their column had passed completely through the first gap did they become aware of the presence of the foe. Then on an instant the hills were alive with shouting. The gap was closed behind them; the gap ahead was closed; and, almost before they knew it, they were attacked on all sides at once.

'Then the rout began' (says Livy in a memorable passage); 'they fled in blind panic up the steep hill-sides or into the narrow defiles, a struggling mass of men and weapons. Large numbers, finding no other way of escape, waded out into the shallows and plunged shoulder deep in the water.

Some in their desperate terror attempted to swim for safety; but the distance rendered this hopeless, and they either lost their nerve and were drowned in the deep water, or, exhausted by their futile efforts, they struggled forlornly back into the shallows and were there cut down by the enemy cavalry, who plunged in after them. . . . The issue was already decided when the sun's growing heat dispersed the mist and full daylight broke; and then in brilliant sunshine mountain and plain revealed the awful scene of carnage and the utter catastrophe of the Republic's arms.'

Only a remnant succeeded in breaking through to safety, and even these were overtaken and captured the next day.

At Rome the news fell like a thunderclap; but the Senate kept their heads and appointed as dictator Quintus Fabius Maximus, a shrewd, imperturbable aristocrat. Under his direction the bridges were broken down, the fortifications repaired, and the enemy's arrival awaited. But Hannibal had brought no siege-train with him. His main hope was still to temporize and win over the Italians to his side. So, judging Samnium and the south to be the most likely area of disaffection, he recrossed the Apennines and passed south-eastwards into Apulia. Fabius, gathering new legions and picking up the army of Servilius, followed him, and, regaining touch, began his famous strategy of 'delay'. Try as he might, Hannibal could not bring his elusive enemy to battle, and yet wherever he went he found himself dogged. Once, having crossed into Campania, he found his retreat cut off by a Roman force which blocked the pass behind him. Only his ingenuity saved him. At nightfall he tied lighted faggots to the horns of a herd of oxen and drove them up the mountain-side into the darkness. The Romans naturally pursued this imaginary foe, and by morning the true enemy had slipped through the unguarded pass.

Towards the end of the year, however, there were ominous symptoms of impatience at Fabius' dilatory tactics. Even the soldiers at the front nicknamed him 'Hannibal's lackey'; and his unpopularity resulted in the ridiculous appointment of Minucius, his own master of horse, to a share in his dictatorship. Worse still, in electing the consuls for 216 the Assembly's choice fell on Terentius Varro, a vulgar, pushful braggart, reputed in later days to have been a mere butcher's son; and, though a patrician Aemilius Paullus was elected as his colleague, it was clear that the policy of caution was to give place to a vigorous offensive.

Accordingly the spring of 216 saw the dispatch of two consular armies, some 50,000 strong (counting citizens and confederates), by far the largest force Rome had yet put into the field. Paullus and Varro had definite instructions to engage in open battle; and by the normal arrangement they undertook the command upon alternate days. Hannibal, who had wintered in Apulia, could have asked nothing better. Living as they did upon the country-side, his troops were already on short commons and spoiling for a fight. The level country too gave excellent ground for the manœuvre of his cavalry. So he awaited the Romans near Cannae on the lower Aufidus; and, astutely calculating the day of the hot-headed Varro's command, he provoked an engagement by harrying the Romans' watering-parties. Then, taking up such a position that the prevalent sirocco drove blinding sand-clouds in his opponents' faces, he lured on their eager charge by yielding with his advanced centre, swept away their flanking cavalry with his own Spanish and Numidian horse, and, finally swinging forward his wings on their now unguarded flanks, held the legions completely enveloped in a ring of steel. What followed was simple butchery. Packed in dense formation (for, mistrusting his raw levies, Varro seems to have relied upon sheer weight of numbers), the Romans stood unable to use their weapons and waiting until it was their turn to die. Enormous numbers were killed or captured; and Varro almost alone among the officers escaped with a remnant to Canusium.

Rome was without an army; and though the Senate with magnificent *sang-froid* controlled the frenzied populace and manned the walls with slaves and boys, the city seemed doomed. 'In five days,' said a Punic officer, 'we shall sup on the Capitol.' But Hannibal did not march. Perhaps the prospect of a siege still daunted him. In any case, as we have said, the destruction of Rome was not so much his aim as the disruption of her confederacy. And now at last, after Cannae, its loyalty was shaken. In many Campanian towns the poorer classes resented the domination of the rich who governed in Rome's interest and, seizing their chance, went over to the side of Hannibal. Even Capua, the second city in Italy, joined him. The Lucanians, Bruttians, and even some Samnites followed suit. But there the rot stayed. Not one of Rome's colonies deserted her. Even in the disaffected area they stood like rocks amid a turbulent sea. What was more surprising, the Greeks of the south remained staunch. Thus in the third year of the war, and despite her many defeats, the Republic was still very far from beaten; and at this rate of progress it was clear that in the long run she could outlast Hannibal. She still possessed enormous reservoirs of manpower. Though the south had suffered severely from the enemy's depredations, the farms of central Italy were untouched. Finance had at one time caused acute anxiety to the government; for the war had paralysed trade and men took to hoarding; but by an ingenious manipulation of the currency the hoarders were induced to bring in their coins for reminting. The war-tax was doubled. Restrictions were placed on private extravagance; and even women's trinkets were melted down for the Treasury. So the financial crisis had at last been overcome.

Most important of all, the popular party having been completely discredited by the failure of their nominees, the Senate henceforward took complete control. It was realized that a frequent change of generals was futile, and experienced officers were wisely entrusted with prolonged commands. The cautious Fabius and his impulsive fellow-veteran Marcellus—the 'shield and spear of Rome' as they were called—became consuls again and again. The armies were divided into small detachments, which, while avoiding battle, dogged Hannibal at every step. It was an amazing spectacle—the whole of this great country concentrating its strength against a mere handful of worn-out veterans, yet so terrified by the memory of Trasimene and Cannae that they dared not risk a decision against the incomparable skill of its commander. He was like a lion baited by a pack of dogs. None the less, they were slowly getting the better of him. Even the adherence of Capua and other towns now caused him more embarrassment than benefit; for, while engaged in one district, he would learn that his protégés had been attacked in another. If he went to their aid the same trouble arose in his rear. In short, the whole character of the war changed, and sieges, not battles, became the order of the day. But for this branch of warfare Hannibal was ill provided, and though he made great efforts to capture both Naples and Tarentum, he could make no impression.

II. THE STRUGGLE WIDENS

This was for him the more disastrous, since his chief requirement was now to gain a good port in southern Italy. For he was in sore need of supplies and reinforcements. The Gauls were tiring of the profitless struggle and deserting him. No troops had as yet come through to him from Spain; and so far as the war in Italy was concerned his prospects looked black indeed. But one important result of his victory at Cannae had been to widen the area of conflict, and bring him fresh hope of assistance in other quarters. The news of his great triumph had stirred immense enthusiasm at Carthage. The listless government woke up. The fleet was put in commission, and made an attack, though an unsuccessful attack, on Sardinia (215). In 213 came an opportunity to intervene in Sicily. After Hiero's death two years before, Syracuse had fallen a prey to faction; and Carthaginian agents soon stirred the populace into rebellion against Rome. The natural strength of the city, situated as it was on a highly defensible peninsula, had been further increased by war-engines designed by the world-famous mathematician Archimedes. So, though the consul Marcellus promptly laid it under siege, he at first could make little headway. In 212, however, taking advantage of a festival when the sentinels were drunk, he got possession of the western heights, called Epipolae, which overlooked the town. The Carthaginian army, which had come to raise the siege, was wiped out by a terrible plague; and in the following year a Carthaginian fleet, dispatched for a last effort, turned tail without a blow. After that, treachery soon did its work and the city was entered. A ferocious sack ensued; and against Marcellus' orders Archimedes himself was among the victims.

By 210 the remaining rebel cities were reduced. Their territory was confiscated and either returned to its former owners at a rental or leased to Italian exploiters. The Syracusan domain was merged in the province.

Rome's supremacy at sea was responsible for much more than the reduction of Sicily. It was unquestionably decisive of the whole issue of the war; and but for the failure of his fleet Hannibal might well have procured invaluable assistance from another quarter besides Africa or Spain. For the news of his successes had much impressed King Philip of Macedon, who was only too eager for a chance to wipe off old scores against Rome; and after Cannae he entered into an alliance with Hannibal.[1] But the troops he promised to send never crossed the Adriatic. Whenever the Carthaginian fleet appeared in these waters it was scared off by the appearance of the strong Roman patrols. The Republic even turned the tables on Philip by stirring up trouble for him in the Peloponnese. So it was not from Macedon, as it turned out, that Hannibal could look for the much-needed reinforcements. Spain remained his only hope. But even from here, we must remember, the sea passage to Italy was barred by Rome's naval supremacy; and to understand the reason why no overland march had been attempted we must pause to consider the course of the campaign on this front.

The decision of Publius Scipio in 218 to leave a Roman army to operate in Spain had been endorsed by the government, and in the following spring he was sent out as pro-consul to join his brother Gnaeus. A ding-dong struggle had then begun for the line of the River Ebro. In that year a Carthaginian attack by both land and sea had been repulsed near the river-mouth, partly with the aid of Massiliot vessels; and in 216 the two brothers took the offensive. Step by step Hasdrubal was driven back, till in 214 he was recalled from Spain to deal with a revolt of a Numidian chief called Syphax. During his absence the Romans not merely captured Saguntum and all the intervening coast, but carried the war into the mountains of the hinterland, and enlisted many native tribesmen on their

---

[1] The understanding probably was that in return for his services Hannibal should later help Philip to complete the reduction of Greece.

side. The instability of such allies, however, was soon fatally
revealed. For on Hasdrubal's return in 212 they deserted their
new masters, and in two successive battles in the Baetis valley
the Romans were overwhelmed. Both the Scipios lost their
lives; and by this terrible disaster nearly all their gains south
of the Ebro were wiped out.

At Rome it seems that the more experienced leaders shrank
from the responsibility of the Spanish command; and the
Assembly's vote fell on a young man still in his twenties, the
dead pro-consul's son and namesake, Publius Cornelius Scipio.
The personality of this celebrated general was one of extraordinary charm; but his rare gifts of imagination and initiative
were apt to arouse the nervous fears of the more conservative
senators; for he was a pioneer of the growing interest in Greek
culture, and his liberal outlook made him impatient of the
conventional restraints of Roman political life. Nor did the
brutal traditions of Roman generalship appeal to his chivalrous
temperament. He could quell a mutiny without bloodshed
and capture a town without massacre. At the same time he
had an almost superstitious belief in his own star, and strange
tales were told of his mysterious visits paid at the dead of
night to the temples of the gods. It was not for nothing that
the Roman people shared his confidence.

Scipio's career in Spain began brilliantly. In 209, while the
enemy's armies were still scattered, he made a sudden dash and
took New Carthage by surprise. The enemy were compelled
to fall back on Gades as their future base; and in 208 Scipio
followed up his success by defeating Hasdrubal near Baecula.
But owing to the difficulty of the country he was unable to
keep touch with the retreating enemy; and somewhat later in
the year, while he was far away in southern Spain, there came
the appalling news that Hasdrubal had slipped across the
unguarded passes of the western Pyrenees and was on his way
to join his brother Hannibal.

In order to appreciate how things now stood in Italy we
must glance back at the events which had occurred there during
the interval. There, as the years went by, it became clear that
the war was simply one of exhaustion. Even Rome was
suffering severely. Corn was running out and supplies had to

be brought from Egypt. So great was the strain upon the country's manhood that a quarter perhaps of all the adult males were serving by land or sea; and at one time twelve Latin colonies refused to supply more troops. Worse still, Hannibal's efforts had at last been bearing fruit. In 213 he had won over the town of Tarentum (though the fort commanding the harbour still defied him); and the loyalty of the Etruscans was more than doubtful. The Senate determined on a tremendous effort. Their armies were sent to lay siege to Capua, and a double ring of palisaded entrenchments was drawn round the city, one against sorties from within and the other against relief from without. Hannibal knew that failure to save the threatened city would imperil his prospect of winning more allies, and in a desperate attempt to divert the besiegers he turned at length to march on Rome. He moved slowly up through Latium, plundering and burning as he went and driving terror-stricken refugees before him. Three miles from the capital he halted on the River Anio, hoping panic would do its work. But the Senate refused to recall more than a single army from Capua; and so great was men's confidence within the city that, when the ground on which the Carthaginians had encamped was put up for auction, it realized its normal price. Hannibal's bluff had failed. One day he rode right up to the Colline Gate and threw a spear into the city; then rode away and disappeared with his army into the Sabine hills. Next year (211) Capua had fallen and was made a terrible example. Many leading citizens took poison; others were scourged and beheaded. A number of the inhabitants were sold as slaves, and their territory confiscated. Two years later Tarentum suffered the same fate. But, try as they might, the Romans were as far as ever from defeating Hannibal. Their only hope lay in wearing him out; and it may well be imagined with what horror they learnt, in the autumn of 208, that Hasdrubal was marching on Italy.

The season was by then too far advanced for Hasdrubal to make the passage of the Alps, and the Romans had time to make their dispositions for the following spring. Of the two consuls for 207 Claudius Nero was sent south to keep watch on Hannibal. Livius Salinator, his colleague, went north to the neighbourhood of Ariminum, and on Hasdrubal's approach fell back across the River Metaurus to Sena Gallica. Meanwhile in Apulia Hannibal was marching this way and that, anxiously awaiting news from his brother. It was due to his restless movements that the dispatch-riders sent to arrange a rendez-vous in Umbria failed to find him and fell into the hands of Roman foragers. Nero took the situation at a glance. Acting on his own initiative, he left the bulk of his army to watch Hannibal, and himself with 7,000 men raced north. One morning a double call on the Roman bugles gave Hasdrubal the hint that the camp at Sena Gallica contained no longer one army but two. That night he fell back hurriedly; and, when he reached the Metaurus, now swollen in spate, he missed the ford in the darkness. Next day, as he moved up the southern bank, the Romans closed in on him. His Gallic contingents got out of hand and he was utterly defeated.

Not many days later, as Hannibal was still waiting in Apulia, more impatient than ever at the unaccountable delay, something, flung through the air, pitched and rolled within the ramparts of his camp. Somebody picked it up. It was the head of Hasdrubal. Then Hannibal knew that he had lost the war. Retiring into the toe of the peninsula, he con-tinued as best he could to maintain himself among the wooded mountains of Bruttium.

The real issue of the struggle now shifted to Spain and there centred round the activities of the young Scipio. In the same year as the Metaurus, he had redressed his so nearly fatal blunder by winning a great victory over the remaining enemy troops in the neighbourhood of Ilipa. As a result the whole of the southern coast now fell into his hands; and he followed this up by capturing the Carthaginian base at Gades on the Atlantic coast. His attractive personality gained him great popularity among the natives, who at one time actually offered him the crown; but Scipio was no longer interested in Spain. He saw that, if final victory was ever to be achieved, it must be achieved on African soil; and with this end in view he returned to Rome and secured his election to the consulship for 205. The Senate, haunted by the memory of Regulus' ill-starred expedition, was aghast at Scipio's project. Hannibal, they argued, was still on Italian soil. The Carthaginians were still making desperate efforts to relieve him; and though one of their fleets went down in a storm off Sardinia, Mago, his youngest brother, had somehow got across and was maintaining a precarious footing among Ligurian mountains in the north. It was therefore scarcely the moment in the Senate's view to undertake the hazard of an expedition into Africa. But Scipio would brook no refusal. He made it clear that, if thwarted, he would appeal to the Assembly over the Senate's head, and proceeded to call for volunteers, who flocked readily to the standard of the popular young leader. The Senate had no choice but to give him the command of Sicily, which he required as a base for the coming operations; and, as a further precaution of safety, peace was made with Philip of Macedon, who, if the Republic's naval forces were to be concentrated in southern waters, might well have proved an uncomfortable menace to her rear.

Scipio spent the year of 205 in completing his preparations in Sicily, and meanwhile his friend Laelius went ahead to make what arrangements he could for gaining assistance in Numidia. Scipio, while still in Spain, had already been in communication with the nomad tribesmen; and their two leading chiefs, Massinissa and Syphax, had shown some readiness to revolt against Carthage. At this point, however, they unfortunately fell out between themselves, both claiming the hand of Sophinisba, the beautiful daughter of the Carthaginian general, Hannibal Gisco; and Syphax, winning the lady, had transferred his allegiance to the Carthaginian side and driven his rival into the desert. The loss of these prospective allies, the value of whose cavalry was an important factor in his plans, was a serious blow to Scipio when in 204 he landed in Africa and attacked Utica. So hard pressed was he indeed by Syphax and Gisco that he had to abandon the siege. In the following year, however, he defeated them in two successive battles, and the prestige of his success swung round the wavering Numidians to his side.

The Carthaginian Government, now thoroughly alarmed, first sued for peace, then refused to face the terms offered. But while the parleys were in progress Hannibal escaped by sea from Italy, and bringing with him the shattered remnant of his force arrived at Carthage. During the winter he did what he could to put fresh heart into the dispirited troops. Next year (202) he moved south-west into the interior, where he won some successes against Massinissa's tribesmen; and finally near Zama, about five days' march from Carthage, he was brought to battle by the Roman host. On that last stricken field the odds were too great even for Hannibal's genius. The Numidian cavalry, once his most dreaded arm, were now ranged with the enemy. The charge of his elephants miscarried; for the Romans opened lanes in their battle-line and the bewildered beasts either charged harmlessly through or turned in blind terror to trample their own ranks. Finally the half-trained mercenaries of his front line broke before the charge of the legions, and at this his African and Carthaginian reserves fled from the field.

Carthage was down, and the terms were far more severe than those offered a twelvemonth earlier—an indemnity of 10,000 talents to be paid within fifty years; the destruction of her entire war-fleet with the exception of ten vessels; the abandonment of all foreign possessions; the grant of an independent status to Massinissa as King of Numidia; and, most galling of all, an undertaking to make neither war nor treaty with any one, unless with the express sanction of Rome. Thus, to all intents and purposes, she was reduced to the position of a vassal State.

During the tragic years of his country's humiliation Hannibal showed the true measure of his greatness, setting patiently to work to rebuild on better lines her shattered fortunes. The collection of money for the huge indemnity caused great distress; and in 196 the overtaxed populace, resenting the selfish mismanagement of the oligarchical regime, called on the great general to take control. Being elected suffete, he made that office once more a real power in the land. He introduced a system of direct democratic election to the chief Council of State; and so successful were his financial measures that at the end of five years it was possible to offer Rome complete and final payment. Yet, like a true patriot, he made no attempt to perpetuate his power and calmly laid down his office at the appointed term. His political enemies, however, took a mean revenge. By sending secret denunciations to Rome they worked on the Senate's nerves, and, though Scipio generously spoke out on behalf of his old enemy, the surrender of Hannibal was demanded (195). Rather than compromise his country he went into voluntary exile, where we shall hear of him again.

III. THE EFFECTS OF THE WAR

The Second Punic War, as it has been declared, was the most important war in history; and it is not too much to say that it decided the fortunes of Mediterranean civilization for six centuries to come; for by delivering into Rome's hand the undisputed control of the sea, it opened the way to a career of further conquest, and, what is perhaps even more significant, it so changed the trend of her political development that from this time onward we can begin to discern the domineering and despotic temper which was to colour the whole course of her Imperialism. She had entered the war as the head of a confederacy of allies; but in the course of the ordeal, when her back was against the wall, she had swept aside all niceties of political privilege and ruled them like a dictator. Her ruthless demands for men and money had placed an almost intolerable strain upon their loyalty; and when this failed them, as at Capua and Tarentum, she had struck back with a ferocity which must have cowed the rest. Even the twelve Latin colonies which had pleaded utter exhaustion were subsequently compelled to supply double contingents; and when the war was over Rome's attitude did not alter—she still continued to treat even her more privileged allies rather as subjects than as equals. In 188, it is true, she admitted Arpinum and two other towns to full citizenship; but there the extension of the franchise stopped short. Even members of 'Latin' communities who had migrated to the capital and thereby legitimately established their claim to civic rights, were frequently struck off the register, so jealous had the citizen-body become of its valuable privileges.

Towards the Gauls on the northern frontier—and with far greater justification—the Republic was much more severe. By a series of campaigns she overran their country and by 191 had them completely under heel. Their territory was annexed and turned into a province, though it differed from other provinces in that no tribute was demanded of it, and instead of receiving a governor of its own it was placed under the control of the consuls for each year. Fresh colonies were planted at Mutina, Parma, and even as far north-eastward as Aquileia, at the head of the Adriatic; and settlers, attracted by the fertility of the new province, swarmed thither in such numbers that it rapidly became Romanized. Meanwhile, to round off her dominion in the north, the Republic undertook in 180 the subjugation of the Ligurian mountaineers; and so dangerously intractable did she find them that no less than 40,000 were transplanted bodily to Samnium. Such treatment —smacking of the methods of Oriental despotism—was a significant indication of the new imperial spirit which was coming to the birth.

If the struggle with Carthage had thus served to strengthen Rome's domination of Italy, it equally served to strengthen the Senate's supremacy at Rome. The democratic movement, which before the war had showed so sturdy a growth, had been utterly discredited by the disastrous failure of popular favourites such as Flaminius and Varro. The Assembly, furthermore, could scarcely vote effectively when most males were under arms; and inevitably the Senate had assumed the direction of both campaigns and policy. Nor, when hostilities were over, did it readily relinquish the powers that it had gained. So, although the sovereignty of the people was still theoretically maintained, in practice the senatorial oligarchy continued to dictate to Assembly and magistrates alike. This oligarchy consisted of a narrow ring of families—perhaps two score all told—who managed to keep the more important offices in the hands of their own members. Time after time in the annual lists of magistrates we find the same names recur—father and son and grandson after him. In one way or another the voters of the poorer class were dependent on this 'nobility';[1] many even attached themselves as 'clients' to one of the big houses whose patronage they found useful in the law courts and elsewhere. The result was that at elections it was extremely

[1] The aristocracy were called 'nobles' or men of 'known' lineage.

difficult for any one to gain office who could not command through his family connexions the goodwill of this hereditary nobility; and the political upstart or 'new man', as he was called, was a very rare phenomenon.

To back this political power of the governing class came also an immense increase in their material wealth. It is true that by a law passed in 218,[1] when the popular movement was at its height, senators had been forbidden to engage in trade, and so were cut off from one obvious method of enrichment. But agriculture remained, as always, the staple industry of Italy; and, as a result of the war, great opportunities were opened for the larger landowners to increase the area of their estates. Thousands of yeomen farmers had been ruined through their long absence on campaign. Hannibal's depredations, especially in southern Italy, had left whole districts waste; and in Lucania and the Tarentine country large tracts of land had been confiscated to the State. So there was plenty of land to be leased or bought up cheap; and many aristocrats, who, having lent money to the State during the war, were now refunded, found abundant opportunity to reinvest it in this way. Consequently, large properties or 'latifundia', as they were called, became increasingly common, especially in the south; and this change had a profound effect not merely upon agricultural methods but upon the whole social condition of the country.

Living as they did at a distance from their estates, the large proprietors were no longer practical farmers; and all they cared was to see a good return for their investments. Hitherto the employment of slaves had been rather the exception than the rule; but now war-prisoners were flooding the market and the temptation to use servile labour was almost irresistible. So it became more and more the fashion for Roman landlords to work their newly acquired property with gangs of slaves superintended by a bailiff. The rough hill-country of the south was utilized for sheep-ranching. In Latium and its neighbourhood, where the competition of cheap supplies from Sicily or

---

[1] The *Lex Claudia*, which prohibited senators from owning sea-going vessels—the purpose of which was to prevent their political interest from being distracted by commercial operations.

Egypt had rendered corn-growing unprofitable, there was a tendency to develop vineyards, market-gardens, and above all olive orchards. Many small proprietors, unable to compete against the owners of such slave-plantations were driven off their farms and either went to make a new venture in the valley of the Po or else to swell the population of the already overcrowded capital. Thus the gulf between rich and poor grew steadily wider; and in their selfish pursuit of wealth, the senatorial oligarchy was unwittingly bringing into existence a mob of semi-idle and impoverished citizens which was to prove in later days one of the most serious complications of the government's task.

Meanwhile the introduction of slaves within the household as well as on the farm (for the well-to-do now began to keep large staffs of domestic menials) was another most unwholesome development. Nothing perhaps did more to brutalize the national character; for the Romans were not squeamish in their treatment of underlings. Flogging and even more brutal punishments were only too common; and Cato, living at this epoch, was not untypical when he declared that a slave incapacitated by age or sickness should be sold off like a useless animal. The average Roman possessed many sterling qualities. He had courage, self-control, thrift, a high sense of public duty, and, within somewhat narrow legal limits, of justice too. In business affairs, though he was grasping and close-fisted, his word was his bond. But, take him for all in all, he was a hard man—hard on others as he was hard upon himself, giving no quarter and expecting none. Even the members of the governing class were for the most part narrow in their outlook, splendid disciplinarians, but lacking the imagination and sympathy essential to the proper administration of a growing empire.

Such narrow-mindedness was natural enough in a country where education was still of the most rudimentary character. It is true that the practice of legal pleading and political debate was beginning to sharpen men's wits; but at a time when the Greeks had already produced their greatest masterpieces of poetry, drama, and philosophy the Romans still possessed no literature of their own; and it was not till their conquest of

Sicily had brought them into contact with Hellenic civilization that cultural influences began to take root among them.
During the period of the Punic Wars, accordingly, we find the
first beginnings of a Latin literature, modelled in every case
on the literature of Greece.   Livius Andronicus (brought as a
prisoner from Tarentum after the Pyrrhic War) had translated
Homer's Odyssey.   Plays adapted from Greek comedies had
been a favourite form of diversion during the stress of the
Hannibalic invasion.   Ennius composed a great epic on the
'Annals' of Rome; and Fabius Pictor wrote in Greek a prose
history on the same theme.   Above all, Hellenic masterpieces
themselves were beginning to arrive in Rome, where they were
studied with real enthusiasm.

This literary activity revealed an important change of outlook in some members at least of the aristocracy, to whose
patronage in fact it was chiefly due.   A small circle, headed by
the great Scipio and including such men as Flamininus and
Aemilius Paullus, were eagerly interested in all things Greek;
and, as we shall see, their interest led to a practical sympathy
with the country to which they owed their new enlightenment.
So in the coming years we shall find a curious internal struggle
—deeply affecting the foreign policy of the State—in which the
new spirit vies with the old, and the more enterprising and
even chivalrous liberalism of the Phil-hellenic party is pitted
against the inbred national habit of cautious conservatism.

CHAPTER IX

THE GROWTH AND THE PROBLEM OF EMPIRE

I. FIRST PHASE OF IMPERIAL EXPANSION

THE process by which in the next seventy or eighty
years Rome was to establish her overseas empire is a
fascinating study of conflicting impulses.   For it would
be an error to picture the Republic as setting out on a carefully
planned career of conquest.   It would be truer to say that, like
Great Britain, she won her world dominion in a fit of absence
of mind, and the acquisition of fresh territory was nearly

CARTHAGE

MAGALIA

Roman Works

Outer Walls

Inner Wall

BYRSA

New Outlet Harbour

Scipio's Mole

Lagoon

GULF OF TUNIS

GAUL

A

Arvern

Tolosa

Via D

Pyrenees Mts.

conqd 17 B.C.

Numantia
conqd
133 B.C.

R. Ebro

LUSITANI

conqd
60 B.C.

R. Tagus

CELTIBERI

NEARER SPAIN

Olisippo
conqd 138 B.C.

Valencia

Corduba

Baetis
R.
Hispalis
FURTHER SPAIN
Urso
×Munda

New Carthage

Gades

✗Carteia

MAURETANIA

NU

R.C.

SPANISH, GALLIC AND

NORICUM
Noreia

CISALPINE
Vercellae
GAUL
Genoa

Athesis

ILLYRIA

obroges
ALPINE

rausio

es Aquae Sextiae

Massilia

CORSICA

Rome
• Fregellae
Naples
Puteoli

Tarentum

SARDINIA

Enna
Former
King of
Hiero

Acragas
(Agrigentum)

Carthage

Utica

Carth.
Frontier
in 150 B.C

Cirta •

Zama Regia

A

Carth. Frontier in 201

Capsa•

TRIPOLI

S OF SECOND CENTURY B.C.

always the consequence rather than the deliberate purpose of her wars.

So it was, for example, with Spain, the first of her new acquisitions. Having originally sent her armies thither in the natural course of her struggle with Hannibal, it never occurred to her, when the war was over, to relinquish what she had won. So the long strip of southern coast which the Carthaginians had previously occupied was automatically annexed; and in 197 it was divided into two provinces—Hither Spain, which centred on the Ebro basin; and Further Spain, which lay round the Straits of Gibraltar and the valley of the River Baetis or Guadalquivir. To govern these, two additional praetors were created. A fixed annual tax was imposed as well as an obligation to provide military contingents; and it is not surprising that the natives soon began to resent the rule of their new masters. In 195 a general insurrection necessitated the dispatch of the consul Marcus Porcius Cato. His energy restored partial order. His firm but austerely just administration won respect; and his shrewd exploitation of the silver-mines—the most valuable asset of the province—opened up a fruitful source of revenue. A standing army was maintained in the peninsula, enlisted on terms of lengthy service; and so much did the Roman citizens dislike this dreary banishment that the troops of the Italian confederates were most unfairly employed for the purpose.

It would have gone hard indeed with Rome if in every land she conquered she had met with the same spirit of fierce independence as among the semi-civilized tribes of western Europe. But in the eastern half of the Mediterranean, where her next wars were to be waged, the situation was very different. Here, as we have seen, great dynasts ruled over the dismembered portions of Alexander's empire, but their appearance of power was deceptive. They commanded no heartfelt allegiance among their heterogeneous subjects. Their military strength, depending as it did on mercenary contingents, was apt after defeat to collapse like a card-castle. A victory here and a victory there and entire provinces would fall into the victor's hands. What to Rome at any rate made a still greater difference was that these potentates were, as a rule, sworn enemies. United, they might have proved most formidable antagonists; but their energies were wasted in interminable intrigues and the effort to increase their dominions at the other's cost. It was due in the first place to such territorial jealousies and ambitions that Rome herself was first drawn into the lists against them; but before we can proceed to consider these more closely, something must first be said about the three great principalities themselves.

The compact little kingdom of Macedon depended still, as in the days of Alexander, on its highly trained army; but, though this was more national in character than the armies of Syria and Egypt, its numbers and efficiency had shown a marked decline. The hegemony over the rest of the peninsula, which Philip had inherited from Antigonus Doson, was also going to pieces. Thessaly, though subject, was rebellious. The States of the Peloponnese, most of which were linked in a confederacy known as the Achaean League, were growing more and more unfriendly. But the worst thorn in Philip's side was the Aetolian League formed by the half-civilized mountain tribes lying north of the Corinthian Gulf. Among them was still to be found the virility which the remaining States had lost; for the rest of Greece was now in sad decay. Athens, for instance, once leader of Hellas, had declined into a university town where professors lectured to pupils from every part of the world. Even commercial prosperity had passed to the farther side of the Aegean, where the Kingdom of Pergamum in the north-west of Asia Minor and the island of Rhodes off its south-west shore still displayed considerable vitality.

Intellectual vigour had passed eastwards too; and the real centre of Hellenistic culture was now Alexandria, the capital of the Ptolemies in Egypt, where poets and grammarians, philosophers and scientists vied with each other in upholding the traditions of Classical Greece. As a commercial link between the Mediterranean and the East the realm of the Ptolemies had grown immensely rich; and a mercenary army, maintained on the resulting revenue, was a sufficient protection for its defensible frontier. But its outlying dependencies— Cyrene, South Syria, and Cyprus—were not so easily guarded. Still less so was a group of Aegean islands and seaboard

EASTERN MEDITERRANEAN, THE EMPIRES OF ALEXANDER'S SUCCESSORS

R. C.

A ROMAN GALLEY

POMPEY

States of Asia Minor, won by the naval activities of the early Ptolemies; and no prey could have been more tempting to the rapacious instincts of Egypt's two jealous rivals.

Of these the Seleucid realm remains to be described. Originally the most extensive of the Successor Empires, it had once stretched from the shores of the Aegean to the plains of the Punjab. But its remoter eastern dependencies had fallen away; and beyond the Euphrates had arisen the powerful native kingdom of Parthia. Equally too the Seleucids' hold on Asia Minor had gradually weakened. A wandering horde of Gauls, breaking across from Thrace about 280 B.C., had occupied the central district, henceforth to be known as Galatia. A little later Attalus of Pergamum (241–197) had carved out a kingdom for himself in the north-west of the peninsula, whilst Bithynia, Cappadocia, and Pontus had almost ceased to acknowledge any tie of allegiance to their former suzerain. Thus northern Syria and its immediate neighbourhood was all that remained to the Seleucid monarchs.

But in 223 there came to the throne a man of large ambitions and a fixed determination to recover the lost ground—Antiochus the Great. In 204, very aptly for his purpose, the death of Ptolemy IV left Egypt in the hands of an infant boy aged five The year before, as it so happened, Philip of Macedon had made his peace with Rome; and Antiochus, seizing the chance, arranged a secret compact with him to divide between the two of them the child Ptolemy's outlying provinces. Southern Syria and Cyprus were to go to Antiochus, Cyrene and the Aegean dependencies to Philip. But when in 202 the latter attempted to lay hands on his share, he found that unwittingly he had stirred up a hornet's nest. Pergamum and Rhodes headed a coalition against him; and what was his surprise when in the summer of 200 a Roman envoy, Marcus Lepidus, appeared at his headquarters with a peremptory order, 'Hands off the States of Greece.' Philip laughed aside the issue by replying that so pert a message could be excused in an ambassador so young and so good-looking. But not thus was Rome to be fobbed off.

The fact was that after Zama the Republic's military prestige had risen at a bound; and the victims of Philip's aggression now very naturally looked to her as a most desirable champion. Egypt, with whom she had long had treaty-connexions, appealed to her. Attalus appealed; and Rhodes appealed. But, coming as it did at a moment when the Roman people were enjoying their first respite after nearly twenty years of intolerable strain, the invitation to embroil themselves in a fresh war was most unwelcome; and among the mass of the citizens there was no enthusiasm for a crusade on behalf of these petty Greek States, with whom they had no tie of sympathy or interest. All therefore turned on the attitude of the Senate; and in order to understand this we must look more closely into the political situation at Rome. The great Scipio, now known by the proud title of Africanus, was at the height of his power. His popularity with the populace was immense. Members of his family filled in succession all the important offices of State, and the Senate could not but look with deference to his views. Now he and his friends, as we have seen, were keenly interested not merely in the literature of Greece, but in its political institutions too; and they felt that, if possible, a blow should be struck to save its liberties from extinction. Nor was this the only argument for intervention. When the envoys from the threatened States appeared before the Senate, we can well imagine with what flights of eloquence these glib diplomatists must have painted the perils of neutrality. The Romans, being still in comparative ignorance of foreign affairs, seem to have formed an exaggerated notion of the military strength of Antiochus and Philip; and, recalling perhaps the bitter experience of Pyrrhus' invasion, they may well have felt it wiser to stem these monarchs' aggression before it could threaten the west. So, though at its first session the Assembly refused point-blank to make a declaration of war, the Senate insisted, and in the autumn of 200 the declaration was made.

The Second Macedonian War, as it is called, was fought by comparatively small Roman forces, assisted at first by Athens, Rhodes, and Pergamum, and joined eventually by the Aetolian and Achaean Leagues and by Nabis, the royal leader of mercenaries who now ruled in Sparta. Operating from Illyria, the Romans began by invading the Thessalian plain, but progress

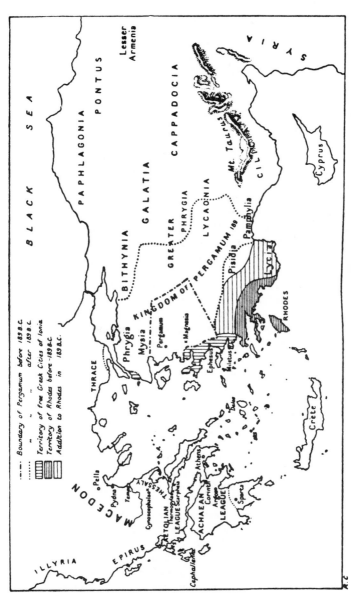

	Boundary of Pergamum before 189 B.C.
	" " " after 189 B.C.
	Territory of Free Greek Cities of Ionia
	Territory of Rhodes before 189 B.C.
	Addition to Rhodes in 189 B.C.

GREECE AND ASIA MINOR, MACEDONIAN AND ANTIOCHAN WARS

was slow until in 198 Titus Quinctius Flamininus, an ardent Phil-hellene, came out as *generalissimo*. He beat back the Macedonian army out of Thessaly and in the following year, when it returned to the attack, defeated it completely near Cynoscephalae or the Dog's Head hills. Philip capitulated and agreed to pay a large indemnity and abandon all possessions outside Macedon. But, not content with this, Rome now undertook on her own responsibility to redefine the frontiers of the distracted Greek world. It was a thankless task; for the mutual jealousies of these petty States and leagues were as violent as ever. For the moment, it is true, they were full of gratitude to their saviours; and when in July 196 Flamininus appeared at the Isthmian Games near Corinth to proclaim the 'Liberation of Greece', they gushed over him with excitable fervour and went home to erect temples in his honour. But no sooner was his back turned than they disputed the justice of his settlement. It was not that Rome had taken anything for herself; but, as is usual in such matters, she had failed to please all parties. Thus, instead of giving Thessaly to the Aetolians, she had there set up independent confederacies. Nabis of Sparta was equally annoyed at having to relinquish his hold on Argos. The truth was the Greeks were incapable of harmonious self-government. Carried away by his enthusiasm for their intellectual pre-eminence in the past, Flamininus had mistaken these glib intriguers for sagacious politicians. But how small was their sense of patriotism or even of gratitude was soon to be revealed.

Even before the Romans had had time to quit it, Antiochus of Syria entered the arena. After trying a bout or two with the forces of Egypt he had patched up his quarrel with the boy king Ptolemy, to whom he presently married his daughter. His covetous eye meanwhile turned towards Asia Minor, and with Ptolemy's leave he had coolly laid claim to the Greek States of the Aegean seaboard, which Philip had recently attempted in vain to filch. Undaunted by Rome's proclamation of the Liberty of Hellas, he calmly proceeded with their annexation, and in 196 with still greater audacity he had crossed into Thrace, which he claimed as a part of his ancestral realm. Thoroughly roused by his impudent manœuvre, Rome ordered him to withdraw. But Antiochus' ambitions were stirred. He had no intention of being brow-beaten, and, aptly enough, in the following year who should arrive at his court but Hannibal, freshly exiled from Carthage, but bitter as ever in his hatred of Rome and full of grandiose schemes for her overthrow. A swift blow aimed at Italy, so he urged his new patron, would bring Carthage, Macedon, and perhaps other States out against her. But, though he retained Hannibal's services, Antiochus determined on a more tentative policy. With the departure of the Romans, the ungrateful Greek States had resumed their old quarrels. In 193 Nabis of Sparta made a move to recover lost territory, and so set the flame alight. The Aetolians were soon up in arms, and with incredible fatuity invited Antiochus to assist them. In 192 he landed in Thessaly. Contrary to his calculations few other Greeks joined him, and Philip of Macedon hung jealously aloof. The troops he had brought with him were wholly inadequate; and when in 191 the consul Glabrio came out against him his position was hopeless. He was brought to bay at the famous pass of Thermopylae, and a detachment led by Cato, taking the same mountain-track by which three centuries before King Xerxes had turned Leonidas' position, closed in on his rear. Antiochus was lucky to escape across the Aegean with a small remnant of his force.

But once the Republic had succeeded in driving the king out of Greece she thought it wiser to suppress so dangerous a rival by driving him out of Asia Minor too. In 190, while the Roman and Rhodian squadrons cleared the Aegean of his war-fleet, an expedition was sent out overland under the joint command of the consul Lucius Scipio and his more celebrated brother Africanus. The two armies met near Magnesia in the west of Asia Minor. By this time all the native levies of the Seleucid realm had been summoned—camel-corps, scythed chariots, elephants, and a horde of light armed troops so numerous that the Romans could scarcely see the full extent of their deployment. Breaking in upon the crowded mass, they soon had it in indescribable confusion. It was a crowning victory. Hannibal, whose surrender was demanded, was forced to flee once more. Bowing to his defeat, Antiochus undertook to pay an indemnity of 15,000 talents, and, abandoning all claim to Asia Minor, accepted the Taurus mountains as the boundary of his domain.

It remained for the Romans to settle Asia Minor as they had settled Greece. In token of his recent assistance in the war, and with a view to counteracting future trouble from Antiochus, King Eumenes of Pergamum received vast territorial gains, so that his kingdom was extended northwards to the Hellespont, southwards into Pisidia and Pamphylia, and eastwards to the foot of the Mount Taurus range. Even the Galatian tribes in the centre of the peninsula were brought under his influence by a campaign undertaken by the new consul Volso. In Greece proper it remained to teach the Aetolians a lesson. Their League was overwhelmed, reduced to the status of a subject ally, and forced to cede the little island of Cephallenia. With this solitary reward for all her trouble Rome left the Greeks, as best they might, to work out their own salvation (189).

The influence of these eastern campaigns upon the Roman people was momentous. Not merely had they come to realize how hollow was the reputed strength of the Orient, but they had enjoyed a glimpse of its luxury and wealth. The Galatian campaign, in particular, had yielded enormous booty; and the city populace had gaped to see the wagon-loads of gold and loot brought home in the train of the army. So sudden an influx of wealth had a disastrous effect. It encouraged a new taste for extravagant expenditure, and a frantic craze for money-making set in. More demoralizing still was the introduction of vast hordes of Greeks into the capital. For whatever might be said for their intellectual heritage the Greeks were now a decadent race, loose in their morals and superficial in their tastes. Nor unfortunately did the Greeks who came to Rome belong to the best type. They included cooks and comedians, financial clerks and dancing-girls procured by Roman nobles or brought home by Roman officers from their campaigns; and the majority of them hailed from the Hellenized countries of the Levant, where they had added to their own national shortcomings the voluptuous habits of the East. The transformation wrought by such influences on the old-fashioned, puritanical morality of Rome is less easy to describe than to imagine.

II. SECOND PHASE OF EXPANSION

The introduction of Hellenism with its attendant evils and the foreign policy which had indirectly led to its introduction did not go unopposed. The traditional dignity of Roman life and manners found many champions among the more old-fashioned citizens, and of these by far the most stalwart and outspoken was Marcus Porcius Cato, one of the outstanding figures of the epoch. By no means a mere boor—for he was a practised litigant with a reputation for vigorous rhetoric, a voluminous writer, the author of a history of Roman anti-quities and a treatise on farm management, and in later life even a student of Greek itself—he was none the less deeply perturbed by the free thought and moral licence of the Hellenic movement, seeing with clear eyes what havoc it would work on the conventional fabric of Roman society. So he set himself heart and soul to combat the growth of this 'many-headed hydra'. To be 'a hundred-per-cent Roman' became the avowed object of his life and he strove to model himself on the soldier-agriculturist of the good old days. He drove the plough with his own hands, wore cheap clothes of coarse cloth, allowed no plaster or whitewash on the walls of his house, and observed the simplest diet. In his official capacities he practised a like austerity; economy of public funds was a downright obsession with him. As governor of Sardinia in 198 he made his circuits on foot, attended only by a single officer; and at the end of his Spanish campaign in 195 he left his war-horse behind him rather than burden the State with its transport. As censor in 194 he developed his wide powers over public morality into a formidable instrument of puritanical tyranny; and one man was actually struck off the senatorial roll for having kissed his own wife in public. Old laws against extravagance, passed at the crisis of the Hanni-balic War, were revived. Ladies' wardrobes and gentlemen's plate-chests were examined and mercilessly overtaxed. Rich folk who drew on the city fountains to supply their private houses were forced to demolish the pipes. Expenditure on public utilities, on the other hand, was not stinted, and a court of justice was built in the Forum and named after its author the Basilica Porcia. Thus in opposition to the growing spirit of individualism Cato endeavoured to uphold the sound old Roman principle that private interests must be subordinate to the State.

Between this bitter antagonist of Hellenism and the rival party of its supporters a clash was inevitable; and soon after the close of the war with Antiochus, Cato opened his attack. He arraigned Glabrio for misappropriation of booty and the commanders of the Galatian expedition for their encouragement of looting. Finally he assailed the Scipios themselves. Lucius was accused of having taken bribes from Antiochus and pocketed a part of the indemnity. The account-books were produced and the case looked black against him when suddenly his brother, Africanus, appeared in court and tore up the incriminating documents—a singularly un-Roman act. Lucius was condemned; but the vendetta ran on, and Africanus himself was to be the next victim. The second day of his trial chanced to fall on the anniversary of Zama. Turning to the populace, he reminded them of his great services; then, leading them off to give thanks on the Capitol, left the tribune who had brought the charge in an empty Forum. Nevertheless, the tide had begun to turn against him. Public opinion was perturbed at the dangerous growth in the political influence of such powerful personalities; and in 187, realizing his unpopularity, Scipio withdrew from public life. Three years later he died in his private house at Liternum, complaining bitterly of his countrymen's ingratitude.

Their victory thus won, Cato and his party brought their influence to bear upon State policy. They stood for an uncompromising nationalism. Towards the Italians they took a selfishly narrow view; and it must have been due largely to them that the extension of the franchise now ceased. With regard to the Empire, they desired to concentrate on the better administration and exploitation of existing dependencies rather than on the acquisition of new ones. Entanglements in other quarters they thought highly impolitic; and for the Greeks, who were not Rome's subjects, and whom they cordially despised, they would have preferred to undertake no responsibility. It was little in keeping with the national character to give something for nothing.

Yet the problem of Greece remained and the Roman Government found it impossible to wipe their hands altogether of this inconvenient neighbour. Shrinking from the trouble and expense of active intervention, they adopted the astute but discreditable policy of playing off one Greek State against another. Faction was fomented in the cities, and pro-Roman agitators, drawn from the richer class, were deliberately abetted. But, though it kept Greece constantly upon the rack of turmoil and intrigue, such a policy could not long postpone the necessity of renewed intervention. Again and again senatorial commissions crossed over, now to settle a quarrel between the Achaean League and Sparta, now to stop Philip of Macedon from extending his frontiers. But the situation, so far from improving, grew steadily worse.

So things ran on for a couple of decades, and meanwhile old figures were disappearing from the stage. Hannibal, who had taken refuge at the court of the King of Bithynia, was pursued even there by the long arm of Roman vengeance, and when threatened with extradition took poison. In 187 Antiochus too had died, to be succeeded first by Seleucus V, and then in 175 by Antiochus Epiphanes. In 179, on Philip's death, the throne of Macedon passed to his son Perseus, a notorious enemy of Rome, with more talent for organization and intrigue than real strength of character. He at once began to build up his army, to fill his Treasury, and, contrary to treaty stipulations, to draw some northern tribes into alliance. In the Greek cities he encouraged the nationalist aspirations of the anti-Roman democrats. By degrees the situation grew tense. In 172 Eumenes of Pergamum travelled to Italy to warn the Senate. On his journey home he was waylaid at Delphi, knocked on the head by a boulder, and left for dead. It was at once believed that Perseus was at the bottom of this outrage; and rumours said he had even planned to poison the Roman envoys. Late in 172 war was declared on Macedon.

At first the Senate, now shy of entrusting overseas campaigns to men of real ability, sent out commanders of indifferent quality, who allowed the troops to grow slack and alienated the Greek States by tactless looting. Perseus, for his part, held many good cards in his hand; for in 171 the Epirots joined him; and a little later the Rhodians, nettled by the interruption of their trade, took up an insolent attitude towards Rome. But when it came to action this master of intrigue lacked nerve; and in 169, when he had the enemy trapped near the Vale of Tempe, he lost his head and beat a hasty retreat. The chance did not recur, and in the following year a Roman general came out who was by no means a nonentity. This was Aemilius Paullus, a friend of the Scipios, and an ardent Hellenist, but retaining none the less all the old Roman qualities of piety, high principle, and devotion to the common weal. At the front he tightened up the lax discipline of the troops, and when in 168 he brought Perseus to battle he made short work of him. The Macedonian phalanx at first crashed through the more flexible Roman line, but, its order being deranged by rapid movement over broken ground, the maniples rallied and, fighting their way into the gaps, won within an hour a complete victory. Perseus fled, but was hunted down in the Aegean and taken a prisoner to Rome.

Even now the Senate shrank from the responsibility of annexing Macedon. But in order to render it harmless the country was divided into four separate States. The citizens of one State were forbidden even to intermarry with those of another. The monarchy was abolished, and in its place Aemilius and ten commissioners set up a federal council of representatives drawn from all four States, to which their individual magistrates were ultimately responsible. But this ingenious constitutional experiment brought no contentment; for the Macedonians were much attached to their kings and altogether unripe for self-government, and within twenty years the whole scheme was to crash to the ground.

Meanwhile Perseus' allies did not escape scot-free. His private papers proved that in many Greek cities the democrat leaders had been in correspondence with him, and a thousand of these were haled off as hostages to Rome. The Rhodians were punished for their rash self-assertion by being reduced to the status of *socii* or subject allies, and thus, like the Italian confederates, liable to furnish contingents in war. This measure marked an important step in Rome's imperial policy and she tended henceforward to treat her foreign satellites more as her vassals than her friends. The fact is that her forbearance with the Greeks was now exhausted; and as though to prove that she was tired of using the velvet glove, Aemilius, before quitting the country, fell on the Epirots, who had given aid to Philip, and destroyed seventy of their towns, selling 100,000 of the population into slavery.[1] It is small wonder if a settlement attended by so much harshness brought no lasting peace in Greece. Among the poorer classes especially there was grave discontent; for they resented the monopoly of political power which Rome had placed in the hands of her aristocratic partisans.

Two decades passed in apparent tranquillity. Then in 149 an adventurer called Andriscus appeared in Macedon, giving himself out to be the natural son of Perseus and a claimant to the throne. Thousands flocked to his standard. Thracian tribes came out for him and cut up a Roman detachment. In 148 an expedition was sent out under Metellus to stamp out the insurrection. It had been the last straw to Rome's patience. Macedon was now made into a province and garrisoned by Roman troops.

Meanwhile fresh trouble had been brewing in the Peloponnese. After long detention at Rome the Greek democrat leaders had been allowed to return home. The Scipios, urged by the historian Polybius, who was one of them, had sponsored their plea, and even Cato had admitted with characteristic candour that it made small odds whether these old fogies were to be buried by Italian undertakers or by Greek. But their repatriation proved ill-timed; for, seeing Rome preoccupied with Macedon, some of them began to stir up trouble in the south. In 149 the Achaean League fell foul of Sparta and in flat defiance of Rome's warning proceeded to attack the town. A senatorial embassy was sent to Corinth, the capital of the League; and instead of listening to their admonitions the silly mob hissed them in the theatre (147): Rome's answer to this

[1] At the same time Illyria was brought under direct Roman control and administered along with Cisalpine Gaul by the consuls for each year.

insult was to order Metellus down from Macedon; and near
Scarpheia in Locris he defeated a Greek army which had
crossed the Isthmus. Mummius, his successor, proceeded
against Corinth, and after a brief siege captured it. Then this
ancient and highly civilized city, once the leading mart of the
Aegean, was made a terrible example. Her inhabitants were
sold into slavery. Her splendid buildings were burnt to the
ground, and her matchless treasures of Hellenic art were
carted off in shiploads to Italy. The destruction of Corinth
was one of the blackest deeds of Roman imperialism; and
with it all semblance of Greek liberty vanished. The Achaean
League was broken up. Athens and Sparta were allowed to
retain their autonomy. The rest of the States were placed
under aristocratic governments favourable to Rome, and the
whole peninsula, though not as yet turned into a regular
province, was left under the surveillance of the Macedonian
governor. A blight settled on the country, and this people,
once so vehemently alive with wit and energy, sank into a
dull inertia of impoverishment and despair.

If Rome's dealings with Greece had brought her small credit,
still less excusable was her treatment of Carthage. For many
years she had watched, not without alarm, the gradual return
of her old rival's prosperity. Her most obvious means of
checking it had been to encourage the Numidian Massinissa,
whose independent kingdom, as we saw above, she had deliberately established as a counterpoise to Carthage. Massinissa,
for his part, was not lacking in ambition. By inducing his
restless tribesmen to settle down to trade and industry, he
had greatly increased the strength of his realm; and his chief
desire was to add to it a fertile strip of coast known in modern
times as Tripoli. Carthage, being its owner, naturally disputed
his claim; but by the terms of her treaty she was obliged to
accept the decision of Rome—and Rome allotted the disputed
land to Massinissa. Thus encouraged, the Numidian chief
continued his encroachments, and in 153 senatorial commissioners were sent out to investigate the situation. Cato, who
was one of their number, was profoundly impressed by what
he saw at Carthage—fleets of merchantmen, crowded docks,
and every evidence of sumptuous living. He returned home

convinced not merely that the commercial revival of Carthage was a menace to Roman prosperity, but also that the country, if annexed, would offer a splendid field for Roman exploitation. From Plutarch we have the story how he produced in the Senate a bunch of huge Libyan figs and bluntly intimated that the country which had grown them was but three days' sail away. But over and above this appeal to the national avarice Cato was voicing a still deeper national craving for a complete revenge. Henceforward in the Senate, whatever the subject of debate, he invariably wound up his speech with the celebrated slogan, 'In my opinion Carthage must be destroyed.' Scipio Nasica, Africanus' son-in-law, and other members of the nobility seem to have urged that the removal of all rivals from her path would spell decadence for Rome; but Cato's voice prevailed, and though in 149 death removed him from the scene the unhappy city's fate was already as good as sealed.

Meanwhile events within Carthage herself had precipitated the crisis. There two factions were at loggerheads—the aristocrats, who stood for peace at any price, and a patriot party, who wished to assert their country's independence from Rome. In 151, in flat defiance of the treaty stipulations, the latter party forced on a war with Massinissa, and, being handsomely defeated, fell from power. Apologies for their conduct were hastily sent to Rome; but it was too late. Rome now had her *casus belli*, and in 149 her armies set out for Africa.

While these were still on their way the Carthaginian Government made up its mind to surrender; and in their innocence delivered up all war-material in the city without even ascertaining what the Roman terms would be. What, then, was their consternation when they were told at last that the entire population must quit the city and build themselves a new one over *ten miles from the coast*. Such a sentence spelt irretrievable ruin to a commercial people and there was but one possible answer. They still had their walls, and behind these they prepared defiance. For a month the Romans dallied, expecting opposition to collapse; and during that month the garrison was somehow re-equipped, the men forging weapons and moulding bullets out of every available scrap of metal, the women plaiting their hair into strings for the new catapults. Meanwhile the craven authors of surrender had been put to death and patriot leaders took their place. A certain Hasdrubal commanded the garrison, and under Himilco and Hasdrubal the Fat other troops, operating in the open, so distracted the Romans that they failed to establish a complete blockade. By the end of 148 the slow progress of the campaign led to the appointment of a young officer named Scipio Aemilianus, son of Aemilius Paullus (the conqueror of Perseus) and an adopted member of Africanus' family. As a subaltern he had already distinguished himself at the front, and along with military qualities he combined a strong taste for letters and a marked skill in diplomacy. Under his leadership the siege at last moved forward. The city stood on a broad peninsula which could only be approached by a narrow neck of land. Across this neck Scipio erected a strong line of earthworks; but, revictualment by sea being still possible to the enemy, he proceeded further to block the harbour mouth by constructing a great mole over a hundred yards wide and many hundred yards in length. But scarcely was this completed when the Carthaginians were found to have cut a new exit from a small inner dockyard enabling their blockade-runners to slip out as before. These, however, were soon defeated, and starvation began in the city. The defenders still fought with all the fury of a Semitic people at bay; but their outer defences across the neck of the peninsula were carried, and they were driven back from the extensive suburbs (called Magalia) upon the inner town itself. They barricaded the streets and held house after house until the Roman storming-parties pushed them back on to the Citadel or Byrsa. The end came in a fearful scene of conflagration; and as the ancient city went up in flames it is said that Scipio wept. What remained of it was subsequently razed to the ground. Carthaginian territory was made into a province. Much of it was confiscated as *Ager Publicus* and sold or leased to Roman exploiters. Numidia was left to rank as a free allied State.

Macedon, Greece, and Carthage had thus all been conquered within a few short years, and Rome was left undisputed mistress of the Mediterranean world. Since her victory at Magnesia, it is true; she had made no further advance eastwards; but the opportunity had arisen to bring Egypt more closely under her influence. In 175 the Seleucid throne had passed to Antiochus Epiphanes, a crazy megalomaniac with an exaggerated passion for Hellenic culture. In support of his claim to Palestine he had gone to war with Egypt and followed up his successes to the gates of Alexandria. Here, however, he was met by a Roman envoy, Popilius, with peremptory orders to withdraw. Seeing the king demur, the Roman took a staff and tracing a circle in the sand around him defied him to step out of it before giving his reply. Nonplussed, Antiochus submitted and evacuated Egypt forthwith. By this diplomatic victory Rome assumed at a stroke the virtual hegemony of the East. Candidates for the Egyptian throne looked to her henceforward for official recognition. When Antiochus attempted to coerce the Jews, their patriot leaders, the Macabees, appealed for her assistance; and she gave them moral, though not military, support. Meanwhile the prestige of the Seleucid realm was dwindling, and the rising power of the new Parthian empire was beginning to threaten it from the Mesopotamian plains.

III. THIRD PHASE OF EXPANSION

Before we can complete the story of Rome's imperial expansion during the second century B.C. it will be well (even if it means anticipating chronology somewhat) to mention some important additions made in the next three decades.

In Spain, during the first half of the century, administration and exploitation had gone forward fairly smoothly. The most remarkable of its governors had been Tiberius Sempronius Gracchus, the father of the famous reformers, a friend of the Scipios, and one of the most enlightened type of Roman officials (179). He did much to conciliate the Spaniards by promoting their chieftains to command over native regiments, stimulating industry, and even founding several towns. A little later the first colony of 'Latin' rights outside the Italian borders was established at Carteia near Gibraltar for the half-breed descendants of Roman soldiers and Spanish women; and, what was even more surprising evidence of a sympathetic attitude, the natives' complaints against official extortions received a favourable hearing at Rome. But meanwhile the very success of the Republic's policy was causing considerable unrest among two great tribes of the interior which had never yet been conquered, and which acknowledged her suzerainty only in the loosest fashion—the Lusitani, who inhabited what is the modern Portugal, and the Celtiberians of the central plateau.

In 154 some Lusitanian freebooters made a raid across the frontier. War followed; and, other tribes joining in, the insurrection became general. At the end of four years the praetor Galba defeated the rebels and forced them to surrender; but he spoilt his triumph by an act of the meanest treachery, falling on their disarmed warriors and slaughtering thousands in cold blood (150). This outrage was much criticized at Rome; and Cato himself came forward to prosecute its author, though without success. In Spain, meanwhile, it roused the Lusitanians to a fresh effort. Under Viriathus, a young shepherd-soldier who had survived the massacre, bitter guerrilla warfare was carried on for years. At last in 141 the Roman governor Caepio made overtures for peace, and, while these were in progress, bribed Viriathus' followers to murder him in his sleep. After this the rebels weakened, and in 138 D. Junius Brutus succeeded in wearing them down. He transferred many of the mountaineers to lowland districts, where some were settled in a new 'Latin' colony at Valentia, and, pushing forward the frontier to the Tagus valley, fortified Osilippo (now Lisbon) as a strong defensive post.

Meanwhile in the Hither Province, and almost simultaneously with the Lusitanian outbreak, trouble had arisen with the Celtiberians over the fortification of their towns—a right which they declared had been granted them by Gracchus, but which the Senate denied. War followed; but it was not till 143, when the success of Viriathus encouraged greater efforts, that the revolt in this quarter became serious. So serious was it, in fact, that in 137 the consul Mancinus was cut off and surrounded with 20,000 men. Happily the young quaestor Tiberius Gracchus, son of the former governor, and for that reason popular with the natives, succeeded in procuring their release on terms. But at Rome it seems to have been the fashion to regard these uncivilized foes as outside the code of honour, and the Senate with incredible meanness refused to ratify the settlement. So the war ran on until in 135 things had come to such a pass that Scipio Aemilianus, the conqueror of Carthage, was sent out to the Spanish command. The struggle had long centred round the native stronghold of Numantia, which, try as they might, the Romans could not take. Scipio surrounded it with a double ring wall five miles in circumference; and in 133, after horrible scenes of cannibalism, the garrison were starved into surrender. The back of the resistance was now broken; and as a result of these bitter and protracted wars the greater part of the peninsula was brought under Roman rule. The natives settled down to peaceful habits. Agriculture thrived. Mining and other industries were developed, and the civilizing effects of town life hastened to complete the Romanization of the province.

In the same year as Numantia's surrender, though in another quarter and in a very different fashion, there came a fresh addition to Rome's provinces. In 133 Attalus, King of Pergamum, was dying. He had no heir to whom to leave his crown, but he was already in some degree a vassal of the Republic, and realizing perhaps the advantage of her civilizing rule, perhaps even more strongly the certainty of their ultimate absorption, he bequeathed the bulk of his extensive dominions to the 'people of Rome'. The bequest was of course accepted. The pretensions of Attalus' half-brother Aristonicus were swept aside, and the dead king's vast treasure was immediately transported to Rome. In 128 the consul Aquiieius proceeded to dictate the settlement of the Pergamene territory. Under the influence of bribes he made over its outlying districts to neighbouring princes—Phrygia to Mithridates of Pontus, and Lycaonia to the Cappadocian king. What remained became the Roman province of 'Asia'. The responsibilities for its government were taken lightly. Piracy, which the Pergamene and Rhodian fleets had suppressed, was allowed to break out again; and kidnapping for the slave-market became the scourge of the Aegean coasts. Worse still, the opportunity of extorting tribute from the prosperous inhabitants led to the most deplorable abuses; and during the next century these unfortunate folk were to suffer more perhaps than any other people from the oppression of Rome.

The truth is that the financial or commercial exploitation of the countries which came under her rule was becoming more and more a conscious motive of Rome's imperialism. There was one class of men in particular whose interest it was to push this policy farther. Ever since the Punic Wars it had been the fashion for rich men of the middle class to form syndicates or 'societies' for financial operations which lay beyond the resources of any single man. It was these syndicates which when Carthaginian territory was confiscated had taken up the lease of many large estates. It was these syndicates, as we shall see, which were given the privilege of farming the tax-collection of 'Asia'; and again a little later it was due partly to them that the first territorial annexation was made in southern Gaul. The leading power in that district, as has been stated above, was the Greek trading city of Massilia. It might have been expected that Rome would have felt jealous of this prosperous neighbour, but the fact was that the governing class of landowners was so little interested in trade that they seem never to have sought to impede the activities of their country's commercial rivals. With Marseilles, at any rate, they had always maintained the most cordial relations, and in 125 a military expedition was undertaken to protect her against two Gallic tribes of the interior, the Arverni and Allobroges. In return for this service the Massiliots agreed to cede a long strip of country along the rear of their own territory. Rome's primary motive in taking over this new province was undoubtedly the construction of a military high road linking Italy with Spain. But it was not the only motive, for a few years later a colony was planted at Narbo just north of the Pyrenees and the purpose of this settlement was to tap the trade resources of the Gallic hinterland. The spirit of commercial aggrandizement which this step displayed, was to lead in the next century to further conquests; but here for the time being the progress of Rome's expansion halted. She had already absorbed as much of the world as she could conveniently digest.

IV. THE ORGANIZATION OF THE EMPIRE

The problems and methods of the Empire's organization must now be briefly considered, and we will begin with its officials. When first faced with the necessity of sending out provincial governors, the Romans, as we have seen, adopted the expedient of electing every year a number of extra praetors. As time went on, however, it became more and more difficult to spare praetors from Rome, where with the growth of litigation their duties of administering justice grew every year more arduous;[1] and by the middle of the second century it was decided to employ, as provincial governors, ex-praetors or ex-consuls who had just completed their term of office at the capital. The powers of such provincial governors, as we have said, were comprehensive and arbitrary in the extreme. During their year of office, it is scarcely too much to say, they were responsible to no one. They commanded the garrison troops, preserved internal order, and supervised the administration of the local courts and the local finance. To assist them in these duties they took out with them a quaestor or financial secretary, a small military staff, some civilian *legati* or attachés, and a fair number of clerks. There was nothing resembling a permanent civil service such as Great Britain employs in India; and with this mere handful of assistants it was clearly impracticable for any governor—especially as in most cases he was entirely new to his job—to control every detail of local administration. The only course was to utilize, so far as possible, the administrative machinery already existing; and in the charter drawn up at the original foundation of each province this principle was clearly recognized. The terms of such charters differed widely according to the political development of the·province. Among backward peoples, as in Gaul and Spain, the tribal authorities were left to collect the quota of taxes in their own way, and, under some

---

[1] Even as early as 242, so many cases came up for trial in which foreigners were involved that an extra praetor called the *praetor peregrinus* had been appointed to deal with them.

supervision, to administer justice according to their own local law. Among the well-organized city states of Sicily or Asia, on the other hand, where the practice of self-government was well understood, a far greater measure of autonomy was frequently permitted. Some known as 'treaty States' were exempt from all burdens, save that of supplying a contingent in war. A very few, termed 'free States', enjoyed complete liberty, except, of course, in the sphere of foreign policy. Since, however, the original terms of the charters were drawn very loosely, the governor's powers of interference were ill defined, and in practice he was able to re-interpret or override them at will. The worst defect, indeed, of the whole provincial system was the absence of any real continuity of policy. Governors changed with every year, and few considered themselves bound by the acts of their predecessors. In general, however, their attitude was one of *laissez-faire*, and their reputation for tolerance was at bottom based on a contemptuous indifference to local issues. Like Gallio in the Acts, they 'cared for none of these things'.

On the other hand, the opportunities of making money out of their subjects were almost irresistible, and few could afford to neglect them. Political posts, it must be remembered, were unpaid whether at home or abroad. Electioneering expenses and the burden of providing official entertainments were a heavy charge upon a public career; and most men, being badly out of pocket by the time they obtained a provincial governorship, came to regard it as a legitimate means of recoupment. It would have needed a man of exceptional standards to do otherwise. From the very moment of his arrival he would be besieged by requests from individuals or communities, demanding exemption from such burdens as the billeting of troops or the entertainment of the governor's own staff, and such requests were always accompanied by the offer of a bribe. The more unscrupulous governor would even put on the screw by ordering, for instance, the delivery of army supplies at some inconvenient centre and then demand a *douceur* for changing it. The scandal of such malpractices did not, however, escape the authorities. The complaints of some Spaniards in the first half of the century had set men thinking, and in 149, by a

law called the *Lex Calpurnia*, a permanent court was set up
to deal with cases of provincial extortion. Though a praetor
presided, the actual verdict in this court was left to a jury
composed of senators;[1] and for this reason alone the opportunity of redress which the reform offered to the provincials
was not so great as might appear. For, since most members
of such a jury would probably at one time have been governors
themselves, there was little question which way their sympathies would lie. Nor was this the only obstacle in the way
of a conviction: it was difficult for the provincials to get good
Roman barristers to take up the brief; the visit to the capital
was expensive and often very prolonged; witnesses were shy
of coming forward to denounce a governor, knowing that by
doing so they would incur his successor's displeasure; last, but
not least, a prosecution could only be undertaken when the
governor's year of office was over, and the damage done
perhaps already irreparable.

Yet the Romans must have their due of credit for this
attempt to safeguard the interests of their subjects. Nor in
any case must we forget that their rule had its advantages
no less than its defects. There were good governors like
Gracchus as well as bad governors like Caepio. The taxation
was not on the whole excessive—in Macedon it only amounted
to one-half of what had previously been levied by the native
kings. Much of it too was spent in ways from which the
provincials themselves benefited—the upkeep of the garrison
by which peace and order was maintained; the improvement
of communications by the building of roads, bridges, and
harbours; the maintenance of the governor and his staff, which
made in the long run for higher standards of administration
and justice. Above all, there was an end to tribal feuds and
border-raids which had been the age-long habit of the primitive
west; and even in the Greek peninsula, that cockpit of interminable wars, the *Pax Romana* reigned.

[1] This court (known as *quaestio perpetua de rebus repetundis* or
'standing court for recovery of moneys') was, in fact, discharging functions which properly belonged to the Assembly; and the introduction
of jurors was due to the fact that they were acting as the Assembly's
representatives. As time went on and other standing courts were added,
the same procedure was also applied to them (see page 158)

V. THE IMPERIAL CITY

Rome at this epoch was a very different place from the Rome of the period of the Hannibalic Wars. She was now the wealthiest city in the world. From the provinces wealth flowed into her through many channels, tribute or tithes in the shape of corn or money, precious metal from State mines. and rents from confiscated territory, not to mention the enormous indemnities paid by defeated foes. After the successful campaign against Macedon in 167 the treasure brought home was so great that it relieved Italy from all necessity of raising a war-tax for a hundred years to come. Customs levied at the ports and a 5 per cent duty on the manumission of slaves were all that the imperial people were called upon to pay into a Treasury thus filled to overflowing. Private persons, too, drew wealth from the provinces no less freely than the State. Governors and their staffs went out poor and came home rich. Tax-farmers made handsome profits. Usurers lent money at exorbitant rates of interest to provincials who could only meet the tax-gatherers' demands by borrowing. Rome, in short, was living on the proceeds of her extortions. From an economic point of view she was a parasitic city, giving little or nothing in exchange for what she took. From the rest of Italy, it is true, wool, wine, and olive-oil were exported in some quantities, and iron implements went out from the Campanian metal factories. But in Rome herself no industries existed, except for local use. She consumed without producing; and the only reason why she did not completely exhaust the resources of her provinces was that the money she had wrung from them by her extortions went back to them in payment for the luxuries they supplied to her and so became available once more for a renewed extortion.

Meanwhile, the psychological effect of her prosperity was disastrous. A craze for financial operations had set in. Large syndicates were formed by middle-class capitalists and even senators invested in their funds. Immense fortunes were piled up, and the wealth thus accumulated could command a range of luxuries undreamt of in earlier days. High living became the fashion; and in the first half of the next century we have an amazing picture of the style kept by the plutocrat Lucullus —opulent mansions in town and country, galleries full of treasures of Greek art, terraced gardens with nooks for sun and shade, sea-water reservoirs to supply fresh fish for the table, costly sideboards studded with jewels and loaded with precious plate, banquets at which even the normal fare for a small party of friends cost £2,000 an evening. Not least of the new luxuries was the practice of employing large staffs of domestic slaves. A wealthy man's establishment would run into some hundreds, including, beside menial servants, secretaries, clerks, tutors, and copyists. The vast majority came, as we have said, from Hellenistic countries. The wars of eastern conquest had flooded the market. Kidnappers maintained the supply; and at the island of Delos, the chief centre of the traffic, as many as 10,000 slaves were once sold in a single day.

The population of Rome, as may well be imagined, was increasing by leaps and bounds.[1] Owing to the increase of large estates worked by slave labour, thousands of country-folk had found it impossible to maintain their homes and were seeking in the capital a livelihood equally precarious; for here, too, the aristocracy, clinging to the traditional Roman preference for a self-contained and self-supporting household, relied almost exclusively on their own domestic staff for the manufacture of clothes and so forth. The result was that the independent handicraftsmen and hucksters found business scarce; and a still larger number of men were without any regular job, living continually on the border-line of hunger. The free population was further swelled, as time went on, by emancipated slaves of Greek or Levantine origin; and though their nimble wits enabled them to make their way, these were no very wholesome addition to the citizen-body. The contamination of the pure Roman blood by this alien element was a grievous tragedy, and more than anything else it accounts for the unstable and grasping temper which was so marked a characteristic of the popular Assembly during the coming epoch.

---

[1] By the middle of the first century B.C. the total population must have been well over half a million, of which some 40 per cent were probably slaves.

The accommodation of this growing proletariat in itself presented a problem, for under the strictly limited conditions of space within the city walls the one-storied houses, which were usual in the ancient world, were quite inadequate. So superstructures were built, nearly always of timber—a fact which led to very frequent and disastrous fires. Enterprising capitalists, too, ran up enormous tenement blocks in which hundreds of families swarmed and bred, as though in some huge rabbit-warren. The further problem of keeping this over-swollen urban population fed was one of the most serious perplexities confronting the statesmen of the day.

Surrounded by the squalor of these hideous slums the centre of the city, where its public buildings lay, stood out with a new dignity. Not that Rome could vie in architectural magnificence or scientific planning with Alexandria or other great Hellenistic towns. For all that, a growing familiarity with these centres of Greek culture had begun to have its effect. The Forum was no longer a mere market-place, lined with tradesmen's stalls. During the Hannibalic War the destruction of its northern side by fire had cleared a space for the subsequent erection of several courts of justice which the growth of legal business now demanded.[1] They were called 'Basilicas'; and, as the name suggests, they were planned in imitation of Greek models. The garish features of the old Etruscan architecture were now replaced by the sober elegance of Hellenistic styles. The material used was a drab-coloured volcanic stone, which was the best that local quarries could produce; and for the sake of appearance and durability, this was normally coated with white stucco. The pillared porticoes or external colonnades of these Basilicas not merely lent an air of grandeur to the Forum, but served as a convenient shelter for the transaction of business. Here it was that the bankers carried on their trade, politicians exchanged views, and loungers foregathered to gossip.

Outside the Forum other public buildings had risen. The enterprising censors of 179 had not merely built a fish-market

---

[1] One was erected by Cato in 184, a second by the censors Aemilius and Fulvius in 179, a third by the Elder Gracchus (the Basilica Sempronia) in 170, and a fourth (called the Opimia) in 121 (see plan, page 39).

and a theatre, but had systematically laid out the Tiber-side with rows of quays and a colonnaded emporium, and had thrown the first stone bridge across the river. Architecturally, in short, Rome was beginning to live up to her proud position as an imperial capital. But to erect new buildings and to satisfy new needs is an easier task than to adapt old institutions to the solution of new problems. That all was not well with Rome seems clear enough. There was much that was rotten in the obsolete fabric of her conservative society; and the problems now confronting her—some imperial, some political, and some economic—were almost beyond the practical genius of even her citizens to solve.

CHAPTER X

THE CONSTITUTIONAL SITUATION

THE Roman constitution, like the British, was not a written or fixed code. When new circumstances arose, as we have seen, additions and readjustments were made to meet them, and many usages and precedents had grown up which had no positive sanction in law. It was thus that the Senate, which in origin had been an advisory body only, had won its ascendancy. A close corporation of several hundred life-members, recruited from ex-magistrates and so representing the best brains and experience of the community, it enjoyed a complete and overwhelming authority. By its motions or *senatus consulta* it instructed the executive officials, directed foreign policy, managed finance and controlled the recruitment and disposition of the army. It formulated legislation for the Assembly's acceptance. When opposition arose it could fall back on the appointment of a court of high treason; and, in the last extremity, it possessed or claimed to possess the power of proclaiming martial law.[1]

[1] Such a measure was known as the *senatus consultum ultimum* or 'ultimate decree', empowering the consuls to take action for the preservation of the State. As will later be shown, the Senate's right to make such a declaration was frequently challenged by its democratic opponents.

Against so weighty and influential a body the annual magistrates, in their brief period of office, were practically helpless. For a few years, it is true, the popularity and independence of the great Africanus had challenged its monopoly of power; but after his fall the Senate had been careful to see that his example was not followed. They had cut down provincial commands, which during the Hannibalic War had been frequently prolonged, to the normal term of a single year. By the *Lex Vilia* in 180 they had set a decisive check on the over-rapid rise of the young and self-assertive. An age-limit was thereby assigned for each successive stage of a political career. Thus, not till his twenty-eighth year, and after he had served his military apprenticeship as subaltern[1] in the legions, could a man make his début as quaestor, that is financial secretary either to the Treasury or to a provincial governor. At thirty-one he might take office as aedile, controlling the municipal buildings and food-supply and organizing public entertainments. At thirty-four he might become praetor and preside in the courts of law. At thirty-seven came the consulship, which meant command of the army, the presidency of the Senate, and supreme executive power. There remained the censorship, the crown of a Roman's ambition, with its wide authority to assign State contracts and regulate the composition of the Senate and the Assembly. Thus by the time a man had climbed to the top of the political ladder he was broken in, as it were, to the traditions and conventional courtesies of public life, which forbade the pushing of political disagreement to the point of violent extremes. For no body of men were ever more strongly united by mutual loyalty and *esprit de corps* than the governing caste of Rome. They consisted, as we have seen, of a small ring of families, bound together by ties of blood, intermarriage, and social intercourse. For outsiders, who did not belong to this intensely exclusive aristocracy, election to public offices was virtually impossible. The 'new man' in politics was a very rare phenomenon.

Yet election, it is important to remind ourselves, was still in the hands of the popular Assemblies, and in order to appreciate why the popular Assemblies had ceased to exercise their

---

[1] As *tribunus militum*, see page 137.

liberty of choice we must pause to say something about their character and composition.[1] In the first place, membership of the citizen-body was confined to a comparatively small fraction of the Italian people—that is, to the inhabitants of the fully enfranchised area which lay in more or less close proximity to the capital itself, perhaps a quarter of the whole peninsula. But even of these full citizens how many in actual fact would avail themselves of their privilege to vote? Except on occasions of critical importance, the farmers of the Sabine hills or the tradesmen of Campania would seldom spare the time and trouble to make the journey to Rome. The result was that in practice the Assembly was composed of members of the city-populace;[2] and by various methods—all more or less discreditable—this disreputable body of voters was induced to lend itself to the election of aristocratic candidates or the passage of aristocratic legislation.

One all too common method was bribery pure and simple. But there were others more subtle. It is a commonplace of statecraft that a mob is seldom intractable if kept tolerably well fed and amused. Since quite early times occasional distributions of free corn had been made by individuals anxious to ingratiate themselves with the populace. More lately, as we have seen, the importation of supplies from Sicily and Egypt had been used by the government to supplement the dwindling produce of Italian farms; and it was one of the aedile's duties to see that the supply was adequate and cheap. Aediles were also responsible, as we have seen, for providing free entertainments during the frequent holidays observed at religious

[1] One important change had been effected in the Assembly-by-centuries which elected the praetors, consuls, and censors. In 241 it had been reorganized so as to equalize the voting-power of poor and rich. But since it had apparently been divided into groups of seniors and juniors, men over forty-six commanded one half of its voting-power —a fact which continued to give it a strongly conservative trend.

[2] As the franchise had been gradually extended to outlying communities, thirty-one fresh 'tribes' or 'constituencies' had been added to the original four which composed the Tribal Assembly. In theory, therefore, the four tribes of residents at the capital should have been hopelessly outvoted. Actually, however, citizens migrating to the capital continued to be members of the tribe to which they originally belonged; so that in practice the urban voters were well represented in all the thirty-five tribes.

festivals, which sometimes lasted ten days or more at a stretch. Chariot-races and wild-beast shows were very popular; and, though gladiatorial combats were not as yet part of the official programme, candidates for office were already finding them a good form of advertisement. Thus by means of this dual bait of 'Bread and Circuses' the governing class found it easy to humour and control the mass of poorer citizens; and in very many cases, as we saw above, these were actually attached themselves as 'clients' to one noble family or another —a relationship which made independent use of their vote impossible.

There was, however, another class of the urban population, men of substance though not of good birth, who were beginning to make themselves felt in the State and who deeply resented the exclusive attitude of the aristocracy. These were the *bourgeois* capitalists whom the financial needs and commercial opportunities of a growing empire had called into existence. Romans, it is important to note, did not themselves engage directly in commerce; for seagoing was little to their taste, and the shipborne traffic had remained in the hands of the South Italian Greeks. But when trading operations required financial backing there were plenty of Roman capitalists ready to advance them money. Others engaged in usury and banking, arranging credits for officials or others who wished to travel abroad, making loans to spendthrifts or candidates for office, and, most lucrative of all, to provincials who were unable to meet the tax-gatherers' demands. The normal rate of interest was 12 per cent per annum, but as much as 48 per cent was sometimes charged. Side by side with these *negotiatores*, as they were called, were the *publicani*,[1] who undertook the financing of state-contracts for building, road-making, mining, or collection of taxes; and, since the magnitude of such contracts was beyond the resources of any single pocket, these men had formed large 'societies' or syndicates to provide the necessary funds jointly.

Now, though the capitalist, whether *negotiator* or *publicanus*, did not engage directly in the operations for which he

[1] These men must not be confused with the 'publicans' of the Gospels, who were their menial agents employed in the actual collection of tax.

supplied the necessary cash, he was regarded with contempt by members of the governing class; for senators' interests were almost wholly bound up in their agricultural estates; and, like the landed aristocracy of early nineteenth-century England, they considered the vulgar profession of business as wholly unfit for a 'gentleman'. Thus among the rich *bourgeosie* of Rome there was not merely a rankling sense of social inferiority, but a growing resentment at their enforced exclusion from the political stage.

So, although to all appearances secure in their monopoly of power, the governing class were in reality living on a suppressed volcano. Both in the swarming thousands of the populace and in the malcontent capitalists they had potential enemies; and at any moment one or both of these might become dangerous, if a man appeared to lead them. Now it was among the tribunes, if anywhere, that such leadership was most naturally to be found. The original purpose of their office had been to champion the lower orders against magisterial tyranny; though their proper function was rather to veto than to initiate action, they had come to exercise very considerable authority as presidents of the legislative Assembly-by-tribes. Of recent years, it is true, their tradition of popular champion-ships had fallen into abeyance. Bowing to the well-ordered etiquette of public life, they had become the tame agents of the ruling caste; and in practice they contented themselves with laying before the Assembly only such Bills as the Senate had approved and drafted. Nevertheless the democratic character of the Tribunate was not wholly forgotten; and as a safeguard against its possible misuse a tacit understanding appears to have grown up that no man should hold the office for two successive years. In other words, the Senate them-selves had recognized the danger—and, as the issue proved, a very real danger it was—that some day or other a tribune might arise who would turn traitor to his class and employ his opportunity of popular leadership to upset the comfortable security of their regime.

In a state so naturally conservative as Rome, such a con-tingency, it must be admitted, seemed unlikely—except for one significant fact. Blind submission to authority is the mark of an uneducated, or at any rate an unthinking, society; but once men begin to use their minds they will inevitably begin to question the validity and the efficiency of authoritative rule; and at Rome, as we have hinted, education in the highly critical literature and philosophy of Greece had already made much headway. The time could not now be long delayed before such influences would produce, in some minds at least, a new and challenging outlook on the problems of the day; and herein lay the seed of infinitely dangerous possibilities.

CHAPTER XI

HELLENISM AT ROME

I. EDUCATION

IN 155 some lectures on philosophy, given by certain Greek diplomatists who happened to be visiting Rome, aroused the indignation of the aged Cato, and he procured their abrupt dismissal from the city. This was perhaps the dying effort of his anti-Greek agitation, and at the close of his life even he himself appears to have recognized that Hellenism had come to stay. The leader of the movement was now Scipio Aemilianus, one of the noblest and most charming characters in Roman history, a perfect blend of the new intellectual culture with the high moral principle of the old regime. Into his society gathered not merely such Greek savants as Polybius the historian and Panaetius the philosopher, but all the ablest and most thoughtful Romans of the day, soldiers and politicians as well as orators and writers; and the vogue for free discussion which these ardent spirits set resulted in a general, though gradual, broadening of the Roman mind.

Under the stimulus of Greek influences educational methods, as was natural, were revolutionized. Familiarity with the wider world had emphasized the need for fuller instruction, and if fathers could no longer spare time to attend to their own children, there was no lack of professional teachers in the city. So in most aristocratic families it became the fashion to send their boys to school. From the age of six or thereabouts the lads would be placed in the charge of a slave-flunkey, called a 'pedagogue', and usually a Greek, whose business it was to conduct them to the class-room. There, too, the teacher would almost certainly be a Greek; and though the moral influence of these somewhat decadent aliens was a very poor substitute for the fine old traditions of a domestic upbringing, the intellectual gain was incalculable. Indeed, not merely were Greeks the best educationists in the world, but much of the school curriculum was inevitably concerned with Greek literature. For at the age of twelve, after mastering the elements a boy would pass on to the so-called Grammar School, where at least as much of his time would be given to the study of Homer, Hesiod, and other Greek authors as to the native works of Ennius, Plautus, or Terence. Long passages of poetry were learnt by heart, their grammar and meaning explained, and declamation practised. After three years thus spent, the next stage was to proceed to a school of rhetoric; for since a political or a forensic career was alone considered fit for a 'gentleman', oratorical instruction was in great demand. In the rhetoric schools, too, Greek models were almost exclusively followed; and during the following century it became the fashion for young men to pass on for a finishing course at one of the great university towns, Alexandria or Athens or Rhodes. Though philosophy was also studied, especially at Athens, the tendency to concentrate on rhetoric prevailed. The effect was unfortunate; for it cramped the development of Roman thought and encouraged a facility for plausible argument in preference to a genuine pursuit of truth. It also led to an over-emphasis on style and superficiality of ideas which characterized much Latin poetry as well as prose.

II. EARLY LATIN LITERATURE

Among the fragments we possess of primitive Latin writings there is a religious hymn comparable, one would say, to the cacophony of some Hottentot war-chant:

> ENOS, LASES, JUVATE:
> NEVE LVE RVE, MARMAR, SINS INCURRERE IN PLEORES
> SATOR FU, FERE MARS, LIMEN SALL. STA BERBER.

There is not much literary promise here; but by the time when Greek influences began to make themselves felt, there already existed a crude native metre called the Saturnian, which was based on a triple beat helped out by alliteration.[1] This metre Andronicus used in his translation of the 'Odyssey'; but his far greater successor Ennius, the true founder of Latin prosody, adapted the Greek hexameter to his own native tongue, and in his massive epic called the 'Annals' he attained a rich sonority of rhythm which was the peculiar virtue of all Latin poetry. The same process of adaptation was followed in other fields also. Thus, in the plays which he wrote in imitation of the Greek Menander, Plautus (254–184) employed a loose version of their original iambric metre. The entertaining plots of these borrowed comedies turned on the farcical adventures of lovers, the tyranny of parents, and the intrigues of witty and precocious slaves; but to suit the coarser tastes of his Roman audience Plautus contrived to spice them up with a good deal of broad buffoonery and jocular allusions to the crucifixion of slaves. His successor Terence (185–159), a far greater literary artist, kept more closely to his Greek models; and though he must have satisfied his educated patrons who were responsible for the official production of the plays, he won little popularity with the groundlings. Attempts to introduce a purely Roman comedy in which actors wore the toga instead of the Greek pallium were made by Afranius (c. 120 B.C.), but with little success; for contemporary drama with topical allusions and caricature of political personalities offended against the Roman sense of decorum and sound discipline.

The criticism of men and manners found, however, another form of expression. The one literary *genre* indigenous to Italy was a type of poem known as *satura*, or hotch-potch—a medley of comments upon contemporary life, loosely strung together without plot or form. An early exponent of this very artless literature was a certain Lucilius (180–102), a member of Scipio's *salon*, and an unsparing critic of the foibles and vices

---

[1] e.g. Andronicus' line 'tópper facit hómines | út priús fuérunt' (='straight she máde them húman | ás they wére afóretime'), which is stressed as 'the quéen was in her chámber | eáting bréad and hóney'

JULIUS CAESAR

A PROCESSION

of his enemies, but so rough and ready in his technique that Horace declares he would polish off 'a couple of hundred lines before lunch and as many more after it'.   In the literature of every nation prose is a later development than verse; and, as we have seen, the earliest Roman prose-writers composed in Greek.   But Cato used the medium in his Latin treatise on Farming, and he also set a fashion by publishing his speeches. Litigation was so popular among the legally minded Romans that it is not surprising that much attention was given to the study of law; and at the beginning of the next century we find eminent jurists such as Scaevola and Sulpicius who devoted great labour to the compilation of legal cases and precedents, thus founding a tradition which was to bear much fruit in later years.

III. PHILOSOPHY AND ITS INFLUENCE

What, however, for our present purpose is of primary importance is to understand the influence of Greek literature and Greek thought upon men's minds.   Hitherto being little given to thinking for themselves, the Romans had been content to follow blindly in the customs and institutions of their ancestors. As among all primitive peoples, these were largely concerned with religion.   The grossest form of superstition hedged their life on every side.   The flight of a bird or the colour of a sheep's liver had, in early days at least, affected the course of campaigns; and omens were still habitually consulted before political decisions were taken.   At the crisis of the Hannibalic War the terror-stricken populace even had recourse to strange foreign rituals; and after Cannae human victims were buried alive.   Men felt that, their old gods having deserted them, new protectors must be sought, and in 204 the government, anxious to allay their fears, had introduced from Asia Minor the cult of Cybele or the Great Mother.   Some twenty years later, too, the wild, ecstatic worship of the wine god Dionysus began to spread in southern Italy; at first the authorities were shocked, and, departing from their usual policy of religious tolerance, attempted to suppress it by the execution of its votaries.   But eventually this cult too was allowed to take its place alongside the other recognized forms of religion.

But, while the common folk thus continued to seek emotional satisfaction in the worship of alien deities, the aristocracy, now educated in the ideas of Greece, were growing
sceptical. But, though sceptical, they did not outwardly
abandon the religion of the State. Much as they realized the
fatuity of its unmeaning round of sacrifice and ritual, they felt
that such established institutions had a steadying influence
upon the masses; and, if only to keep things going as they had
always gone, the aristocracy continued as before to undertake
the functions of priests and augurs and to conduct a ceremonial
which had at least the virtue of teaching the lower classes to
know their proper place.

Some attempt, it is true, was made to explain ancient
religious beliefs along the lines of Greek rationalism, and there
was a certain vogue for the works of Euhemerus, who held that
the gods were merely the heroes of a bygone age, deified by the
superstitious fancy of posterity. But the Romans were not
greatly attracted by such speculation. More interesting to
their strictly practical minds were the problems of human
conduct and happiness. Now, among the Greek thinkers of the
day two main schools of philosophy held the field—the Epicureans and the Stoics. The two systems were based on
entirely different conceptions of the Universe. The Epicureans
believed that, all things being compounded by a purely
accidental conglomeration of atoms, it followed that there was
no law governing the world, and that the gods, if they existed,
could take no interest in mundane affairs. There was therefore no ultimate foundation for men's fears of divine displeasure, no ultimate sanction for the claims of State or family.
Right and Wrong, in other words, were simply man-made
conceptions based on practical experience of what is pleasant
or convenient; and it was therefore the business of each individual to discover for himself what makes for happiness—a
dangerously elastic creed; for while the finer natures might find
their happiness in contemplative study and a life immune from
cares, to the vast majority it would mean at best a life of pure
self-seeking and at worst of gross self-indulgence. By an ill
chance, too, the arrival of Epicureanism at Rome chimed in
with the prevailing temper of materialism, which resulted from

an over-rapid growth of wealth and luxury; and every young sensualist was able to find in its tenets an excuse for his own excesses and a reason for rejecting the claims of patriotism or even of moral law.

Fortunately, on the other hand, the Stoic doctrine, austere and uncompromising as the Epicurean was lax, provided an ideal more in keeping with the best traditions of the Roman character. According to that doctrine the Universe, so far from being the outcome of accidental forces, was a permanent organism governed by unalterable law. The basis of this law was a world-spirit of Reason, Right, and Justice, to live in harmony wherewith is the whole duty of man. The truly wise is therefore he who can discriminate between the solid substance of the genuine good and the empty husk of illusory desire. Such a man will remain virtuous in the midst of all temptations and happy even though he should suffer on the rack. It was a noble ideal, but terribly cold and inhuman, involving as it did, not merely indifference to pain but the suppression of all such softer emotions as pity or love, which might weaken or disturb the individual's self-sufficiency. Thus, in its purest form at any rate, it was a trifle too abstract for common-sense Romans, and happily its chief exponent among them, a Greek philosopher named Panaetius, and a protégé of Scipio, perceiving this defect, strove to interpret it in terms which were not merely more practical, but which gave a rational basis to the old-fashioned morality of the Republic. In other words, it was shown that the supreme claim of the State upon the individual, so far from being the outcome of mere human conveniences, originated in the divine principle of Reason and Justice. This conception of a world-law, applicable to all peoples, was to exercise a profound influence on the ideas of Roman jurists, and, inspired by it, they tried not merely to reduce conflicting legal formulae to a coherent system but to define the principles which underlay them. Still greater, however, was the influence of the Stoic creed on men's everyday behaviour. Its lofty conception of the great-souled hero unflinchingly faithful to duty and, though the very heavens should fall, indifferent to his fate, was exactly suited to a people who, as somebody has said, had always been unconscious Stoics; and in the troublous times ahead, when all that had made life worth living for free Roman citizens seemed lost, it was only by the aid of this grim philosophy that many remained able to possess their souls.

IV. PSYCHOLOGICAL EFFECTS

In estimating the general effect of Hellenistic culture at Rome the gain is obvious; for without the intellectual training which her citizens thus received the task of governing a Mediterranean empire—at least half of which consisted of Greek-speaking peoples—would have been impossible. Nor can we ignore the refining influence of Hellenism upon the Roman character. The leading personalities of the last century of the Republic were certainly great gentlemen, a trifle pompous perhaps, but dignified, courteous, and (as Cicero's letters show), astonishingly sympathetic. But there was loss as well as gain; and we have ample evidence of serious deterioration in both social and political standards. Divorce became increasingly common. Attendance to public duties grew slack, and in the next century the Senate House was often half empty. Under the veneer of culture too the coarser sides of the Roman's character remained. His taste for brutal spectacles and his inhuman treatment of slaves reveal it, and, worse still, as the events of the next hundred years were to prove, his readiness to carry political conflict to the point of the most bloodthirsty massacres and reprisals.

But, above all, we must recognize that the philosophy of Greece tended to make men critical of tradition and to give them a more individualistic attitude towards life. Even the Stoics, with all their insistence on duties, were mainly concerned with saving their own souls. The Romans were not by nature original thinkers, but they were ready to assimilate ideas at second-hand; and henceforward there can be no doubt that personal interests or ideals began to take the place of the old blind subservience to the common weal. It was just because the Romans had so long accepted without question the habits of their forefathers that the Republic had gone steadily forward for three hundred years without any serious break in its constitutional development. But now that men were arising who placed the dictates of their own conscience or ambition above the conventional claims of State, it was clear that revolution could not be far ahead. At first, as we shall see, the revolt against the existing order was to come from tribunes either voicing the grievances of malcontent elements or pandering to the selfishness of the mob. But this phase was to pass. The real menace to the senatorial regime lay in the fact that its chief executive officials were commanders of the legions as well. Military power is in most States held under control by subordination to civil authority. But if civil and military powers are combined in one person, the combination can only remain innocuous so long as the ambitions and aspirations of the individual are outweighed by his loyalty to the State. Hitherto such loyalty had been the invariable habit of the Roman mind; but it was beginning to be shaken now—and that meant that the end of the Republic was in sight.

CHAPTER XII

THE GRACCHI

I. TIBERIUS GRACCHUS

THE rock on which the Republican regime was ultimately to break was the difficulty of adjusting a constitutional machinery, originally devised for a small market-town, to meet the administrative and military problems of controlling a world-empire. But the first crisis in its long decline towards ruin arose over an economic trouble within Italy itself. At the close of the Second Punic War, as we then saw, the bulk of the country-side had passed into the hands of a comparatively small number of extremely wealthy landlords. Large estates lend themselves naturally to economical and scientific exploitation; and new methods of cultivation by the aid of manure and crop rotation had been carefully studied by Cato and others. A Carthaginian treatise, too, on the Libyan plantation system had been translated into Latin; and this served yet further to popularize the use of servile labour. On the sheep-ranches of the south, especially, large gangs of slaves were kept as herdsmen, housed in filthy barracks and treated with in-describable brutality. Even in the lowlands of central Italy the vineyards, olive orchards, and market-gardens were equally worked by servile labour under a bailiff in the interests of a rich absentee landlord. Only in the high dales of the Apennines and in the plains of Cisalpine Gaul did yeomen-farmers still struggle to maintain a livelihood, rendered the more precarious by the competition of cheap imported corn. Elsewhere, as we have seen, this type of men were driven to swell the population of a metropolis already overcrowded and rapidly becoming an economic problem in itself.

The extinction of its sturdy yeoman class was a serious matter for a State which depended for its very existence upon the steady recruitment of its army; and it needed no great perspicacity to see that the remedy lay in getting the sur-plus urban population back on to the land. Such an idea had already occurred to C. Laelius, the friend of the younger Scipio, but his proposals had come to nothing. The next man to study the problem was Tiberius Sempronius Gracchus, the son of the enlightened Spanish governor. He had enjoyed a sound Greek education, for his mother Cornelia, a daughter of Africanus, had procured him a Stoic tutor named Blossius of Cumae. His character was headstrong and impulsive; and, though he kept his emotions under an iron control, he had an obstinate conceit in his own infallibility. When faced with a problem he saw only the shortest cut to its solution, and was ready to ride rough-shod over all opposition to the attainment of his goal. On the way to his quaestorship in Spain he passed through Etruria, and the widespread evidence of rural depopu-lation made so deep an impression on his mind that when he came home he determined to tackle the problem. The diffi-culty was, of course, to find land available for the settlement of small-holders. One possibility alone presented itself. When Rome first conquered Italy she had, as we have seen, annexed large tracts of country as State lands (or *Ager Publicus*), and to these had been added further punitive confiscations made at the close of the Punic War. Some parts of this *Ager Pub-licus* were let out on annual leases; but over others the tenants —some noble and some poor—had established a claim to

permanent occupation legally known as *possessio* or 'squat-
ter-rights'.[1] Since very many of these 'squatter' occupiers
could point back to a tenure of a hundred years or more, it
would seem a gross injustice simply to turn them out. Technically, on the other hand, the State still had the power to
resume its rights; and a constitutional pretext was available
in the old Licinian laws—by this time a dead letter—which
limited an individual holding of public land to 300 acres.
The reinforcement of this limit would set free an area of
Ager Publicus fully adequate for the requirements of landless
citizens; and such accordingly was the proposal with which
Tiberius came forward when in 133 he entered on his famous
tribuneship.

Though he found a few supporters among the more enlightened aristocrats, Gracchus' proposal at once aroused the opposition of the vast majority; for, holding as they did large tracts
of *Ager Publicus*, they bitterly resented this attack on their
vested interests. The first outcry, however, was nothing to
their dismay when, against all precedent—for such a thing had
not been done within living memory—the impudent young
tribune proceeded to ignore the Senate's opposition and lay his
Bill direct before the *Sovereign Comitia*. But, though seriously
disconcerted, his enemies had their plan. The Clerk of the
Assembly was reading aloud the preambles of the Bill when
suddenly the blow fell. Another tribune, Cnaeus Octavius by
name, rose and interposed his veto on the whole proceeding.
The use of the tribunician veto to obstruct the legitimate expression of the popular will was certainly not in keeping with
its original institution; but it formed a dangerous precedent.
Tiberius' blood was up, and he proceeded to lay *his* ban on
all public business whatsoever. The machinery of government
came to a standstill. The law courts stood empty. The treasury
was closed. Gangs of roughs collected and free fights took place
in the Forum.

The situation looked critical, and Tiberius' next step did
nothing to improve it. In defiance of the rule that a tribune's
person was inviolable, he put forward a motion for Octavius'
deposition; and, after an undignified tussle, the unfortunate

[1] These squatter tenants still paid a nominal rent to the State.

man was dragged by main force from the rostrum. This obstacle removed, Tiberius proceeded to the passage of his Bill. Its enactments were as follows: (1) Occupiers of *Ager Publicus* were to relinquish all in excess of the 300-acre limit, with an additional allowance of half that acreage for each son up to two; (2) the land thus vacated was to be divided up into twenty-acre plots, to be the inalienable property of future lessees at a nominal rental; (3) a Commission of three was to be appointed to carry the reform through; and it was typical of Tiberius' tactlessness that he made the commission a family concern, consisting of himself, his younger brother Caius, and his father-in-law Appius Claudius. The scheme thus launched, it remained to provide the new settlers with stock and implements, and this would involve a large outlay. As it so happened, the enormous treasure, bequeathed to Rome by King Attalus of Pergamum, had just fallen in; and, though the disposition of such funds was by rights the Senate's prerogative, Tiberius insisted, with the Assembly's approval, on ear-marking the treasure for the Commissioners' use.

Meanwhile, however, the temper of Gracchus' opponents was growing more and more ugly. They began to put it about that he was aiming at a despotism. He had kept back, it was said, a gold crown and purple robe from the Pergamene treasure for his personal use. Much play was made of the violence done to a sacrosanct tribune; and, if one thing seemed certain, it was that on the day he laid down his office Tiberius would be impeached for high treason. What, then, was the consternation when suddenly came the news that he intended to stand for re-election. Whether technically illegal or no, such a step was contrary to past precedent; yet Tiberius seems to have been quite unconscious of taking a revolutionary step and went obstinately ahead. His electioneering programme offered attractive baits, for it included some relaxation of the terms of military service. The voting was, in fact, going in favour of his candidature when proceedings were suddenly interrupted on the question of its legality. From that moment Tiberius was convinced that his life was in danger. Friends rallied round him, and for the next few days he did not stir abroad without a bodyguard of supporters. When the interrupted election was at last resumed, plans were laid in anticipation of an attack. Presently came a message that the aristocrats were arriving and were out for murder. Gracchus raised his hand to his head—it was thought to be a signal; planks and benches were snatched up and his followers broke up the knot of the opposing faction. Meanwhile at a session of the Senate there had been hot discussion. The extremists, led by a certain Scipio Nasica, urged war upon the 'tyrant'. The consul Mucius Scaevola refusing, they determined to take the law into their own hands, and, arming their retinue, made for the Forum. In the affray that followed some 300 lives were lost; and Tiberius, clubbed on the head with a footstool, fell dead. Thus almost for the first time since Rome became a Republic blood had been spilt in a political quarrel—an ominous precedent.

II. SCIPIO AEMILIANUS AND THE ALLIES

Though Gracchus' death was followed by the execution or banishment of many of his supporters, his Land Commission, curiously enough, was permitted to continue its work; and on the evidence of the census lists it seems probable that as many as 80,000 persons were resettled on the land. At the same time, however, serious obstruction was encountered not merely from the big senatorial proprietors, but also from many Italian communities who were likewise 'occupiers' of much State land. These members of the Roman confederacy possessed, as we have seen, no civic privilege, and therefore, when threatened with a summary cancellation of their 'squatter' rights, they had no constitutional appeal against the Commissioners' decision. As it so happened, however, they had recently found a champion in Scipio Aemilianus. During his Spanish campaign he had come in close contact with their overworked regiments; and Rome's harsh treatment of these long-suffering allies had aroused the sympathetic interest of his philanthropic mind. Accordingly, on his return from Numantia, he had agreed to act as their legal representative; and now in 129 when they were hard put to it in resisting the Commissioners' attempt to deprive them of their lands he made a shrewd move in their favour; for he managed to procure that the decision of cases under dispute should be taken from the Commissioners and entrusted to the consuls; and since the consuls at this time seem deliberately to have absented themselves from Italy, the whole operation of land-settlement was interrupted.

What was even more remarkable, Scipio was apparently prepared to introduce legislation for the improvement of the Italians' political position. What his proposals were we do not know. But on the very morning when he was to have addressed the Assembly he was found dead in his bed. Foul play, though never proved, was suspected; and in any case it was a tragic close to a career so full of promise. Though called by circumstances to destroy Carthage and crush the Spanish revolt, Scipio Aemilianus was more of a student and a dreamer than a ruthless man of action; and, had he been spared, his broad-minded idealism might well have tided Rome through this period of bitter discord. His policy was clearly to hold the balance between the two opposing factions. He had little sympathy with the reactionary senators, and strongly denounced their provincial misgovernment. On the other hand, he disapproved of the unconstitutional tactics of the Gracchan democrats; and in 131 had successfully opposed the proposal of Tiberius' friend Carbo to legitimize re-election to the tribunate.

After the removal of his restraining influence the struggle was resumed. The democrats succeeded in carrying Carbo's measure into law, and, in order to placate the Italians' opposition to the Land Act, they actually proposed to offer them the franchise. Their opponents replied by expelling from the city a large number of Italian residents who might have supported this proposal; and its author Fulvius Flaccus was sent out of the way on a military mission to Liguria. But expectations had run high; and this frustration of the allies' hopes caused the town of Fregellae to come out in open revolt. Its courageous stand found no imitators; and the town was promptly destroyed. Charges of complicity were meanly levelled against the democrat leaders—Caius Gracchus amongst others. As he had only just returned from his quaestorship in Sardinia, Gracchus was able to clear himself with ease; and he was elected to the tribunate in 123.

III. CAIUS GRACCHUS

The situation which now confronted the new democrat leader was complicated in the extreme. If he tried to satisfy the needs of the urban mob (on whose votes his power depended) and continue the process of agrarian settlement, the Italians would take offence at the confiscation of their lands. If he sought to placate the Italians by an extension of the franchise, the mob, averse to sharing with others the advantages of citizenship, would equally take umbrage. Meanwhile the Senate, thoroughly scared by the recent blow to their prestige, had set their face against compromise in any shape; and between them and the would-be reformer there would clearly be war to the knife. Caius himself was not slow to fling down the challenge. He procured the banishment of Popilius, the consul responsible for the execution of his brother's partisans. He attempted to debar the ex-tribune Octavius from holding further office. It was made evident in short that he was not a man to be trifled with. A red-hot enthusiast for the cause he had at heart, he threw himself passionately into the conflict. Unlike his brother, he set no curb on his emotions. On the platform he would stride to and fro, gesticulating till the cloak fell from his shoulders and shouting till his voice rose to a shriek. It is even said that he kept an attendant with a pitch-pipe beside him as a warning to moderate his tone. It would be a grave mistake, however, to suppose him a mere excitable windbag. As an orator he had style as well as vigour. His powers of application were extraordinary, and at the height of his career he controlled half a dozen departments at once. He was, above all, a pastmaster of political strategy; and his various policies, as will be seen, were so comprehensive and so well co-ordinated that there was scarcely a single problem of the day for which they did not offer some solution.

His initial need, if he was to carry through his reforms, was to secure a permanent control over the city voters; and his method of achieving this was perhaps the most debatable measure of his whole career. Hitherto the administration of the corn-supply, being entrusted to young and inexperienced aediles, had been erratic and inefficient. Caius undertook to place it on a more scientific basis. He had large granaries built to hold a reserve, and he arranged for a regular distribution of five modii per month to every resident citizen who chose to apply in person—and this at only *half of the current market price*. This meant, on a rough estimate, a 2-lb. loaf *per diem* —a bare subsistence for a small family among folk accustomed to a purely vegetarian diet. Regarded in the perspective of history the defects of the scheme are obvious. It set a dangerous precedent which future demagogues were not slow to follow. It led to an unhealthy pauperization of the urban proletariat. It encouraged wastrels to flock into the city. The lowering of corn-prices, too, must have borne hardly on the agriculturists—not excluding the small-holders recently settled under the Land Act. Last, but not least, Caius miscalculated the charge on the Exchequer. For, though a large part of the supply came gratis from Sicilian tribute, the cost of transport and distribution proved a heavy drain on public funds. In any case, the corn-dole was at best a palliative; and, if Gracchus had nothing better than palliatives to offer, his claim to statesmanship would have been small.

Happily he had other more constructive and far-reaching schemes in prospect. First, he realized that, since self-contained agricultural communities were now a thing of the past, and town and country were with every year becoming more interdependent, an improvement of transport facilities was therefore essential to progress. We find him accordingly building roads of commercial rather than strategic importance, constructing bridges across rivers and causeways over marshes, and even modifying the gradient on the steeper hills. In the second place, he continued his brother's policy of moving the surplus population out of the capital; but, while the Land Commission resumed its operations, Caius recognized, as Tiberius had not done, that townsfolk make better merchants than farmers; and he determined to experiment with the alternative method of planting new colonies on sites favourably placed for commerce. One such colony was to be founded at Capua, still derelict since its destruction during the Hannibalic War, but conveniently close to the trade-centres of Puteoli and Naples;

another at Tarentum under the novel name of Neptunia; a third—and this was the most imaginative stroke of all, since it anticipated Rome's subsequent policy of extending her citizen-body overseas—on the desolate peninsula where once had stood the city of Carthage, now also to be re-christened as Junonia.

Of Gracchus' interest in commerce there is further evidence in the close relationship which clearly existed between him and the *bourgeois* capitalists; and, if anything were further needed to cement the alliance, it was provided by an opportunity which now presented itself of doing them a good turn. The system of taxation in Asia was proving unsatisfactory. Hitherto a fixed quota had been raised by the native authorities themselves, but in seasons of bad harvest the quota was difficult to collect; and it seemed better to substitute the tithe system, which had worked well in Sicily and which was liable to bear less hardly on the provincial farmers as well as to secure a prompter payment of their dues. Now, the contract for collecting the tithes was to be put up for auction in Rome, not in Asia; and, since only a large syndicate could possibly undertake such a contract, Gracchus was thus providing his capitalist friends with a highly lucrative opportunity for profit. To recoup themselves for their trouble by overcharging the provincials was regarded of course as legitimate; but to what scandalous lengths their extortions would be carried Gracchus can scarcely have foreseen.

Yet, whatever trouble in the future his various measures might entail, the young tribune was slowly but surely consolidating his own political ascendancy. He now held the Assembly in the hollow of his hand. The Senate, constitutionally unable to oppose its will, was forced to accept the unpalatable situation. Yet Gracchus was too great a statesman to be content with mere tactical triumphs. He clearly intended to remodel the State upon new lines and to render his regime secure against the risk of conservative reaction. Had it been possible, we are told, he would have liked to temper the aristocratic character of the Senate itself by a wholesale admixture of his middle-class friends. But so revolutionary a step would have involved a tremendous upheaval, and he was forced to fall back upon a more modest plan.   Perhaps the strongest point in the Senate's position lay in their monopoly of the jury-courts; for magistrates, looking forward as most of them did, to a profitable post in the provinces, were bound to defer to the body which might one day have to pass judgement on their use or misuse of it.   Gracchus' plan, therefore, was to transfer the jury-courts to his middle-class friends and so give them, instead of the Senate, the whip-hand over the provincial governors.   As a test of eligibility for the panel he had recourse to the old Servian classification, under which any man worth 400,000 serterces (or roughly £3,000) was ranked as an *eques* or Knight.   The title, of course, was by now an anachronism, for rich capitalists did not serve in the cavalry; but as a mark of official distinction it served Gracchus' purpose of introducing a new element into the political system.   For not merely did he intend that the new equestrian juries should act as a constitutional check on senatorial governors, but that the equestrians as a whole should serve as a rival order to the senatorial order itself.

It is clear, in short, that there was taking shape in Gracchus' mind a totally new and revolutionary conception of Rome's political future.   The popular Assembly, hitherto sovereign in theory alone, was henceforth to be sovereign in fact.   To it the Senate would be strictly subordinate and the magistrates directly responsible.   As for Gracchus himself, there can be little doubt for what role he had cast himself.   He was a student of Greek, and must have read how for nearly a generation that the great Pericles had led the Athenian democracy in the capacity of an elected magistrate.   Gracchus had no difficulty, it would seem, in securing his own re-election for the year 122, and there appeared no reason to set any limit to the perpetuation of his power.   In his hands the tribuneship, which had previously carried with it no executive powers, was completely transformed.   He was ruling Rome like an autocrat.   He had a finger in every pie.   He drew up the lists of the new jury panels himself.   Ambassadors from foreign States waited upon him.   His numerous administrative duties kept a throng of people perpetually dancing attendance.   Architects came to consult him about the plans for new granaries, engineers to discuss the building of roads, land-surveyors to report progress on the laying out of his colonies. Even the Senate listened attentively when he condescended to outline his schemes; and he did so, it would appear, with a disarming moderation.

To so far-sighted and broad-minded a statesman the scope of his political reforms could not stop short at the metropolis alone. Gracchus saw with clear vision that the true basis of Rome's prosperity must rest on a prosperous and contented Italy. Despite the agitation of previous democrat leaders the grievances of the allied communities were still without redress; and if hitherto he had made no move in this direction it was not from lack of sympathy. In his speeches, we know, he was at pains to quote disgraceful instances of their maltreatment at the hands of Roman officials—how an inhabitant of Venusia had been beaten to death for having jeered at a young Roman aristocrat's new-fangled sedan; or again how the mayor of Teanum had actually been scourged because the town bath had not been cleared quick enough to suit a consul's wife. There were good reasons, however, why Gracchus had hitherto postponed any attempt to tackle this most thorny problem; for the Roman mob, on whose support his own power was based, were extremely jealous of the material privileges which citizens, and citizens alone, enjoyed—a regular allowance of the corn-dole, preferential accommodation at public entertainments, and, last but not least, the lavish distribution of bribes by candidates for office. All these were advantages which would obviously be lessened, *if shared*; and it is little wonder that the Roman voters were opposed to a further extension of the franchise which might mean actual loss to their own pockets. Gracchus accordingly went warily to work. His proposals were twofold. First, *all* Italian allies were to receive the half-franchise, i.e. the legal privileges of citizenship in respect of their commercial transactions, bequest of property, and so forth. Second, those communities which already possessed the half-franchise were to be given a choice between receiving (1) full civic status, in which the privilege of voting would be set off to some extent by liability to the war-tax; or (2) in lieu of this, the right of appeal to the Assembly against flogging often inflicted by Roman army-officers.

The moderation of these proposals might very possibly have secured their acceptance, had it not been for the ingenious tactics of the opposition. For, though cowed, the Senate was not beaten. To make an open stand against Gracchus was more than they dared; but instead of this they slyly put forward another tribune, Marcus Livius Drusus, to act as a counter-demagogue, and, if possible, outbid Gracchus for the people's favour. Thus, as a set-off to Gracchus' three commercial colonies, Drusus proposed twelve of the old agricultural pattern in which the settlers were to receive their land rent-free. With regard to the Italians, he discarded altogether the idea of political enfranchisement, and proposed instead to abolish what had long been a grievance with their soldiery—liability to scourging at the hands of Roman officers. The appearance of this rival claimant for the mob's support put an entirely new complexion on the situation, and it would clearly have needed all Gracchus' eloquence to carry the day against him. Yet the extraordinary thing is that at this crisis of his career— a moment when, if ever, his presence was required at Rome —Gracchus chose to go off on a mission to Africa.

He was one of the Commissioners for the planting of the new commercial colonies. Those at Capua and Tarentum were somehow hanging fire; and, pinning his chief hope on Carthage, he had determined to attend its inauguration in person. The ceremonies were duly performed. The appointed area was marked out with boundary stones; according to ancient custom a plough was driven round it; a standard was flown—and then Gracchus came home again to find that during his absence his popularity had begun to wane. With his conservative opponents the Carthaginian colony was most unpopular. Many of them, it may be, had invested money[1] in syndicates which leased large plantations in Africa; and, resenting the prospect of this new competitor, they did their best to discredit the whole idea. Stories of bad omens were spread about—that Scipio had cursed the site, that hyenas had dug up the boundary stones in the night, that the standard-pole had broken more than once. More fatal still, the mob,

[1] The aristocracy used to invest in these concerns, though they abstained from handling them.

with a mob's ingratitude, was tiring of its benefactor. When his Franchise Bill came up for decision he failed to get it through; and worse was to follow. In the course of the summer came the elections for the next year's tribuneship. Harvest was in progress at the time, and Gracchus' rustic supporters could not leave their farms. He was not re-elected.

As soon as his term of office was over the attack on him began. The tribune Minucius Rufus moved in the Senate for the cancellation of the Carthaginian colony. A Bill was put before the Assembly. Feeling ran high; and, though Gracchus was for peaceful methods at all costs, some of his supporters, Fulvius Flaccus in particular, were in a hot mood. Supporters rallied from the country-side; and when the Assembly gathered many carried swords under their cloaks. During the ceremonial preliminaries, the consul Opimius' attendants insulted the Gracchans. A democrat stepped forward and struck the man dead, and only the breaking of a thunderstorm averted a riot. Nevertheless, this one rash blow played into the hands of the senatorial party.

By next morning they had armed their partisans, and these ostentatiously proceeded to parade the corpse of the murdered man in the Forum. When Gracchus attempted an apology he was accused of illegal interruption of the Assembly. Meanwhile Flaccus was concentrating his supporters on the Aventine. At a hurried meeting the Senate declared a state of emergency within the city and empowered the consul to take what measures he thought fit for the preservation of the Republic. A summons was then sent to both Caius and Flaccus to appear before the House. Parleys were begun, and when they broke down Opimius declared the two democrat leaders to be public enemies, set a price on their heads, and proceeded to the attack. After a fierce tussle the Aventine was carried and Flaccus killed. Gracchus was with difficulty persuaded to flee. Towards the Tiber bridge he fell and wrenched an ankle, struggled on amid cheering but unhelpful crowds, entered a sacred enclosure near the Janiculum Hill, and there persuaded a slave, his sole attendant, to run him through. When the pursuit came up his head was cut off and carried to the consul. It is said that its captor received its weight in gold. Opimius followed up his victory by executing three thousand democrats without trial. Women were even forbidden to make mourning for the dead.

So Gracchus' ideal of a thoroughgoing Roman democracy had failed; and perhaps from the outset its failure had been inevitable. For the truth is that this constitutional experiment which for a time had succeeded so brilliantly among the highly intelligent Athenians, was altogether inapplicable to the worthless Roman mob. Even if (as Gracchus himself had visualized) the citizen-body could have been enlarged and reinvigorated by the incorporation of the sound Italian stock, geographical difficulties would have made the working of such a democracy impossible without recourse to a representative system—an idea unknown to the ancients. Gracchus' scheme, in short, looked better on paper than it would have functioned in real life. In other words, as we might have expected from a man of his years and his training, it was the outcome rather of keen political study than of mature experience of political practice. Yet its effect was not wholly lost. His programme of reform outlived him. Parts of it were in time translated into fact; but not one of the democrat leaders who attempted to follow in his wake proved capable of initiating a comprehensive policy—until at length Caesar undertook the task in a very different role.

CHAPTER XIII

THE RISE OF MARIUS

I. THE JUGURTHINE WAR

THE Senate had won their victory, but the terrible circumstances under which they had won it had badly shaken their nerve; and it is significant that they did not dare to follow it up with any immediate or wholesale cancellation of Gracchus' various measures. Bit by bit, it is true, the operation of his Land Reforms was nullified. In 121 the holders of his allotments were empowered to sell their lands, which naturally soon passed back into the hands o

large proprietors. In 118 the Land Commission was dissolved
and the allotment of smallholdings thus brought to an end.
Finally, in 111 all 'squatter' tenants of *Ager Publicus* were
granted absolute possession rent free; so that henceforward the
aristocratic landlords could feel comfortably secure against
any further encroachment on their interests. In the year 106
an attempt was made to dispossess the knights of their
new judicial privileges, but it was soon repealed; and there
could be no more telling symptom of the Senate's loss of confidence than the fact that the powers of this rival order had
gone so long unchallenged. Henceforward, indeed, the knights
were to play an increasingly important role in the political
arena; and in the coming struggle against the senatorial
oligarchy the democratic leaders came more and more to rely
on the support of this wealthy middle-class.

For the Senate's troubles were not over. The spell of their
prestige had been so rudely shattered that Gracchus' revolt
against their authority could scarcely fail to find its imitators.
On the other hand, Gracchus' ultimate failure had proved once
and for all the political futility of the mob, and the real threat
to the constitution was no longer to come from tribune demagogues. It was to come from army chiefs, for, if the senatorial
oligarchy had proved themselves incapable of solving domestic
problems, still less was it capable of coping successfully with
the military responsibilities of a world-empire. Indeed, at the
very moment of which we have been speaking a campaign was
already in progress, their misconduct of which was destined
to raise an upstart soldier of the camp to the forefront of the
political struggle.

The origin of the campaign was as follows. In 118 Massinissa's son and successor Micipsa had bequeathed his Numidian
kingdom conjointly to three heirs—his two sons, Adherbal
and Hiempsal, and his nephew Jugurtha. Jugurtha—henceforward the villain of the story—was a handsome young dare-
devil with more than the usual Numidian talent for underhand
intrigue. During the siege of Numantia he had served, not
without credit, alongside with Roman officers; and on the
strength of what he had then heard of the corrupt state of
Roman politics he now laid his plans. He believed that, if

he could usurp the throne of Numidia, the Senate could be bribed to sanction his usurpation. To what extent his wire-pulling had a real influence at Rome[1] is not easy to tell, but the fact remains that when he murdered Hiempsal and drove Adherbal out of the country the Senate took no very strong line of action. They sent a commission, it is true, to reinstate the exiled prince, but when he was promptly attacked once more and laid under siege at Cirta, they merely sent an embassy to protest. This failing of any effect, they sent a second embassy, and Jugurtha's only answer was to sack the city and massacre a large number of resident Italian traders who had taken part in the defence. By this time the Roman public were growing restive. The capitalists no doubt resented the damage done to their commercial interests, and rumours began to pass that a large proportion of the Senate were in Jugurtha's pay. If only to silence criticism, war had to be declared; but after the briefest of campaigns Lucius Calpurnius Bestia, the general in command, patched up a feeble compromise. Then a storm of indignation burst at Rome. On a tribune's motion a full inquiry was voted, and Jugurtha himself was even summoned to give evidence in person. But while actually in the city he had the astonishing effrontery to procure the assassination of another rival claimaint, and the Senate sent him packing. He left the city, so the story goes, with the cynical farewell: 'A city for sale—to any man whose purse is long enough.'

The resumption of the war brought even worse humiliation to the Roman arms; for the legions were trapped in the desert and forced into ignominious surrender. The commander, Albinus, though absent from the front at the time, was made the scapegoat of a fresh agitation and sent into exile. There was a loud outcry for a more vigorous prosecution of the war, and there can be little doubt that underlying it was the big financiers' desire for the annexation of the rich Numidian estates. In any case, it had the desired effect, and in 109 the command was entrusted to a competent, incorruptible consul

---

[1] Our information comes from Sallust, an admirer of Julius Caesar, who was evidently anxious to blacken the character of the senatorial oligarchy, and is not too much to be trusted.

called Metellus. Jugurtha was now hard pressed; but he fell back on guerrilla tactics and despite every effort he could not be laid by the heels. The end of the war seemed as far off as ever, and Metellus' command was extended into the year 108.

In the summer of that year, and shortly before the date of the consular elections, a certain member of his staff called Caius Marius came forward with a request for furlough home. Though a capable soldier, he was a self-made man, and Metellus jeered at the idea of his candidature. But Marius persisted and succeeded in arriving at Rome a bare fortnight before polling day. As tribune in 119 he had already made his mark on the popular side; and now by a whirlwind campaign of blatant self-advertisement he carried all before him. For not merely did he secure his election to the consulship, but, in flat defiance of the Senate's right to assign the provinces, he insisted on his appointment to the African command.

The spectacular rise of this pushful upstart was a landmark in Roman politics. That Caius Marius was a man of the people, his very name declares; for he lacked the third name or cognomen which aristocratic families invariably adopted to distinguish them from the common herd of their clan.[1]

The son of a farmer of Arpinum, he was tough in fibre and capable, we are told of bearing a painful surgical operation without a tremor. Like many of his class, too, he possessed a shrewd head for business, in which he had done well. His education, on the other hand, had been rudimentary. He had no knowledge of Greek; and though his bluff outspokenness and coarse invective went down well with the mob, his faulty grammar drew the jests of high society, which deeply resented the rise of this pushful vulgarian.[2] As a soldier he belonged to the type of which good drill-masters are made, and showed considerable talent for organization. His first step, before setting out for the front, was to raise additional troops, and

---

[1] The three names were *praenomen* (personal), *nomen* (gens or clan), *cognomen* (family)—e.g. Marcus Tullius Cicero = Marcus of the Tullian 'gens' and the Cicero branch of it—(cf. John Smith-Dorrien).

[2] It was nevertheless a great feather in Marius' cap that he married a lady of the influential Julian family—an aunt of Julius Caesar himself.

here he at once revealed his characteristic contempt for convention. Hitherto, by immemorial custom, the Roman army had been conscribed from holders of property only. Yeoman-farmers, however, were becoming scarce, and long campaigns had tried their endurance to the limit. Marius, for his part, was determined to have an army of willing soldiers, bound by strong personal allegiance to their chief; and, as the hero of the city mob, he knew where to look for them. Among the pauper population of the capital were many thousands ready to enlist, including not a few discharged veterans of past campaigns; and, waving aside the rule of property qualification, Marius drew his recruits from this source. Out of the new material he soon succeeded in forging a highly efficient army. Meanwhile his quaestor, Lucius Cornelius Sulla, raised a troop of Italian cavalry; and together they soon counted on overcoming the enemy's resistance. With mobile columns they systematically ranged the country, penetrated deep into the desert, reached the oasis city of Capsa, and by the end of 107 had more or less secured the eastern half of Jugurtha's dominions. The next year was spent in a determined sweep westwards. Bocchus, the neighbouring chief of Mauretania, who had thrown in his lot with the rebels, grew alarmed and sued for peace. Sulla was accordingly dispatched on a diplomatic mission, and so adroitly did he perform it that Bocchus not merely agreed to make terms with Rome, but also to turn traitor to his ally. Jugurtha was lured into a conference, kidnapped, and delivered over captive into Sulla's hands. His kingdom was divided into two parts, the eastern half being entrusted to his cousin Gauda and the western half made over to Bocchus. He himself was eventually carried back to Rome to grace the triumphal procession of the victorious general.

But though the laurels of the campaign went to the *bourgeois* commander-in-chief, the real credit of ending it had lain with his aristocratic lieutenant. Hitherto Sulla had chiefly distinguished himself as a gay spark at the capital with a somewhat lurid reputation for loose habits and low companionship. The African campaign, however, had disclosed in him new talents both for soldiering and intrigue. He now made the most of the success of his great coup, even using on his official

seal a representation of Jugurtha's capture. Nor did he attempt
to conceal his jealousy of Marius; and between the two men
there sprang up a coldness which was to develop, as time went
on, into a ruinous political antagonism.

For the present, however, Marius was the hero of the moment.
He had been carried to power on the wave of an anti-senatorial
agitation; and his return with the added prestige of victory
seemed to offer exciting possibilities of political developments.
But Fate intervened, bringing him new and far more hazardous
tasks to perform upon the battle-field.

II. MARIUS AND THE CIMBRIC INVASION

One reason at least why in its opening stages the senatorial
government had treated the Jugurthine War so lightly was
beyond doubt the presence of a much more serious danger
nearer home. For many years there had been a fresh tide of
restless movement among the savage peoples of Northern
and Central Europe. One German tribe, the Cimbri, had
trekked south-west from the Baltic, carrying their families
in hooded caravans and moving by erratic stages in quest of
plunder or more congenial homes. They had marched into
Bohemia, crossed the River Danube at Belgrade, then
set out on their adventures into the unknown south—
a formidable host of fierce, fair-haired giants, well armed with
copper helm, mail coat, and long iron claymores, and accustomed to charge into battle in a serried mass linked man to
man by chains. Striking down into Noricum (the modern
Austria), they had seemed about to penetrate to the North
Italian plain. Papirius Carbo, the consul for 113, met their
host near Noreia and was heavily defeated. Yet instead of
following up their success the Cimbri swerved away; and two
years later were back again in Gaul, drawing bands of adventurers from the Tigurini and other tribes along with them, and
hanging threateningly above the valley of the Rhône. Tiring
at length of plunder, they requested from Silanus, the Roman
governor, a grant of lands for settlement. The Senate instructed refusal. Silanus attacked and suffered complete
disaster (109). Yet once again the Cimbri, after their aimless
fashion, had drifted off into the west.

Such a sequence of reverses was becoming serious; and in 105 the army of Caepio, the Transalpine governor, was reinforced by a second under the consul Mallius, an upstart from the ranks who promptly quarrelled with his aristocratic colleague. When the Cimbri came marching south the rift proved fatal; for, while Caepio stood on the defensive, Manlius sent his lieutenant Scaurus forward to the attack. This advance-guard was wiped out of existence; and several days later the rest of the army was overwhelmed at Arausio (now Oranges). The province was thus at the barbarians' mercy. The road to Italy lay open, and at Rome the unforgotten horror of three centuries before surged up into men's minds. Panic reigned; and then the Cimbri, lured by some tale of riches to be won in Spain, swerved west again and crossed the Pyrenees (105). So Rome was given a breathing-space.

It was at this very moment that Marius returned from his African campaign. All hopes now centred upon him; and being again elected consul for 104, he proceeded to take his measures for meeting the coming crisis. These measures involved nothing less than a complete reorganization of Rome's military system. As before, he was determined to recruit his troops from the lowest stratum of the population. To the unemployed of the city the prospect of regular pay, as well as of occasional plunder, offered obvious attractions. Such men were ready to enlist on lengthy terms of service, and there seems little doubt that henceforward legionaries were compelled to stay with the colours for sixteen or twenty years. Thus, instead of a militia raised (as in the past) at the beginning of a campaign and disbanded at the end of it, the reform of Marius created a standing army of professional soldiers—a system to which Rome clung throughout her succeeding history. Nor was this all, for simultaneously Marius also undertook a complete reorganization of its tactical formation. Hitherto, as we have seen, the legion was accustomed to fight in three successive lines, each formed of 'maniples' or sections widely spaced for free manœuvre. This flexible formation, though admirably adapted for offensive tactics against other enemies, had recently broken down before the reckless onrush of the massed barbarian hordes. So in place of the old maniples Marius now adopted a much more solid unit. It was called the 'cohort', each cohort consisting of six 'centuries,' that is, 600 men, and ten cohorts going to make up a legion.[1] The object of the change was not in any sense a return to the old close-knit phalanx; for open-order fighting—with a space allowance of about one yard per man —was still the normal practice. But the cohort gave much greater cohesion to the battle-front; and henceforward, since Marius also abolished the age-distinction previously drawn between the front, second, and third lines,[2] a greater homogeneity of personnel was obtained throughout the legion. Efficiency of drill and discipline improved accordingly. Regimental *esprit de corps* was encouraged by the introduction of a legionary standard—the famous *aquila* or 'eagle.' Last, but not least, a change was made (if not in the time of Marius, then certainly soon after) in the character of the higher command. The six military tribunes, young aristocrats who were attached to a legion and who in the past appear to have assumed the command in rotation, were so inexperienced that the main responsibility must always have fallen on the centurions or non-commissioned sergeants. But, although these centurions remained the real backbone of the service, some more intelligent officer was needed at the head; and it became the fashion for a *generalissimo* to place a *legatus* of his own choice in command of each legion, leaving the tribunes to perform routine duties of the commissariat and orderly room.

For our knowledge of Marius' reforms chronological data are unfortunately lacking; but the tactical reorganization which we have just described was almost certainly carried out during the two years of respite which preceded the return of the Cimbri from Spain. His head-quarters, we know, were placed near Arles above the Rhône-mouth; and since he relied on maritime transport for his supplies, he occupied the months of waiting in cutting a canal to the sea. Meanwhile his troops were

[1] Hitherto the number of a 'century' had been sixty men; and there were two centuries in each maniple of 120. The legion itself in early days had numbered roughly 4,000 men, but in the Punic Wars had been raised to something nearer Marius' figure of 6000.

[2] These lines were *hastati* consisting of the younger men; *principes*, men in the prime of life (both these lines being armed with the casting-spear or *pilum*); and in the rear the *triarii*, or older men armed with the thrusting *hasta*.

hardened by the discipline of long marches. These they performed in full equipment, carrying a pack which the general himself invented and utilising baggage-poles which were popularly nicknamed 'Marius' mules'. Thus the long delay, though tedious, was not without its value. At Rome public confidence in Marius was well sustained; and he had been re-elected to a fourth year of consulship when in the spring of 102 the barbarians reappeared.

In striking contrast to their previous haphazard movements the enemy now adopted a strategic plan of campaign. The Cimbri and Tigurini were dispatched round the north of Switzerland to push through the Tyrolese passes upon the plains of Lombardy. Their allies, the Teutones and Ambrones, were meanwhile to march direct through the Transalpine province. Their blow naturally fell first; and, failing to make any impression on the Roman camp, they took the road for Italy. Marius followed them at leisure, caught them at Aquae Sextiae (now Aix) and by skilful encirclement accomplished their complete destruction. The butchery was tremendous, and the fields were so drenched with blood that for many years, it is said, they produced a bumper corn-crop (102).

Presently came bad news. The other consul, Catulus, who had been sent to meet the Cimbri, had been forced back from the River Athesis (or Adige), and thus most of Cisalpine Gaul was left at the invaders' mercy. Not caring, however, to cross the Po they had moved vaguely westwards, anxious to meet their confederates, of whose fate they were still ignorant. Marius returned to Rome where for a fifth time he had been elected to consulship; and in the spring of 101 he marched north with fresh reserves to reinforce the army of Catulus and his own legions from Provence. The Cimbri, who were still searching for the Teutones, seemed in no haste for battle, but at last in August they were brought to a decision on the Raudine Plain near Vercellae between Milan and Turin. Their enormous battle-line, a good three miles in breadth, threatened at one moment to break the Roman front; but the heat of the Italian summer had sapped their vigour; the dust-clouds of the plain choked their throats and they were overwhelmed. It is said that 120,000 were slaughtered on that day.

So Italy was saved, and Marius was ready to come home again. At his back was the army which had just fought two victorious campaigns under his command, and which, having received from him the promise of suitable rewards, was naturally devoted to the person of their chief. The populace of Rome was wild with enthusiasm and gratitude, and what would be the political upshot of his return was the question of the hour. But before we can understand the political situation awaiting him at the capital we must first glance back at the events which had occurred during his three years' absence.

III. MARIUS' POLITICAL FAILURE

The senatorial government, needless to say, had fallen under a cloud. The failure of its representatives, first against Jugurtha, and then (more serious still) against the barbarian menace, had badly shaken its prestige. During Marius' absence, moreover, other troubles had served to emphasize its incapacity for dealing with the growing complication of its imperial responsibilities. In the East the scourge of piracy which the independent navies of Pergamum and Rhodes had previously done much to check had once more become intolerable. Corsairs from the coasts of Pamphylia and Cilicia swept the seas, interrupting commerce, kidnapping ships' passengers, and raiding coastal towns to supply the slave-market on which Roman capitalists drew for their plantation-gangs. Torn between the conflicting interests of the peaceful trader and the plantation owners, the Senate had long sheltered itself behind the traditional policy of naval inaction. At last, however, in 103 M. Antonius was sent out to suppress the nuisance. After reducing the pirate strongholds, he seems to have annexed the southern seaboard of Pamphylia, Pisidia, and Cilicia; and thus temporarily at least the activities of the kidnappers were kept within bounds.

Meanwhile in Sicily there had been another and more tragic issue to their horrible traffic. Here, as in North Africa and Italy itself, the large estates were worked by servile labour imported mainly from abroad. In numbers and virility the slaves were far superior to their pampered masters, and brutal ill-treatment had hardened their nerve. Already in 134 one terrible uprising had occurred. Huge bands of desperate fellows had broken loose and ranged the island, 200,000 strong, and it had taken a full three years before the trouble was got under. And now in 104 an even worse revolt had broken out. A mere spark lit the flame. A vassal prince of Bithynia had excused himself from sending a contingent to the Cimbric War on the ground that half his available soldiers were in bondage on Roman territory. The Senate ordered an inquiry, and hopes of liberation spread among the Sicilian slaves. But on the owners' protest the governor discontinued the execution of the order and with that the explosion came. Under a leader called Tryphon the slaves broke out once more. They collected arms enough to defeat the local garrison, and in so doing captured more. The Greek and Roman inhabitants cowered helplessly behind town walls; and Rome, preoccupied with the barbarian peril, was slow to act effectively. In 103 Lucullus was sent out, but failed. His successor fared no better. At length, in 101, the Teutones being mastered, superior forces were brought to bear in Sicily, and the revolt was fought down. It had cost, it is said, 100,000 lives; but nothing was done to remedy the conditions which had caused it; and its suppression was a triumph not so much for the cause of order and justice as for the material interests of the capitalist party, who by this time had gained the upper hand at Rome.

For the discrediting of the senatorial oligarchy had given the democratic party its chance. The knights had used their control of the jury-courts to wipe out political scores against their aristocratic opponents, and, what was more ominous, two worthless demagogues, Saturninus and Glaucia, had gained complete ascendency in the *comitia*. They had played up to the mob by a further cheapening of the corn-dole, and they had made a shrewd bid for Marius' support by proposing to find land-allotments in Africa for the veterans of his Numidian campaign. Nevertheless, if one thing seemed certain it was that they would be completely overshadowed when the great man himself came home from the war.

There could have been no more melancholy anticlimax than that home-coming. Though acclaimed the saviour of his country and elected for a sixth time to the consulship, Marius completely failed to make good his leadership of the democratic cause; for this rough soldier of the camp was incapable of planning or expounding any large constitutional measure. Even his platform speeches lapsed into stammered incoherence, till he was forced to get others to compose them for him; and the best he was able to do was to drive a bargain of alliance with the two glib demagogues. When he entered his consulship for the year 100, Glaucia as praetor and Saturninus as tribune were to be his recognized spokesmen. Their programme was the debased imitation of the old Gracchan policy. There were to be land-allotments for Marius' veterans in Cisalpine Gaul, transmarine colonies in Greece, Macedon, and Sicily; and, to establish beyond dispute the sovereignty of the *comitia*, a measure was appended rendering liable to impeachment any one guilty of 'impairing the majesty of the Roman people'. Furthermore, every magistrate and senator was obliged to take an oath to support this legislation—a monstrous attempt to stereotype the constitution which Marius himself at first resisted. Eventually he took the oath, but his old rival Metellus retired into exile rather than yield. Feeling ran high. Riots were frequent; and, when by an irregular subterfuge the whole group of measures was put to the vote *en bloc*, it was only carried by ruthless methods of intimidation.

The crisis came to a head at the summer elections of 100 B.C. Glaucia was standing for the consulship; and when a rival candidate, Memmius, was clubbed to death by democrat roughs, the aristocrats in turn began to arm. As though in preparation for a *coup d'état*, the two demagogues seized the Capitol. Then, nerving itself to action, the Senate passed the ultimate decree, empowering the consuls to save the State. It was an awkward dilemma for Marius, for to obey the Senate was to destroy his friends. Yet he obeyed; and with a strong retinue of senatorial partisans proceeded to do his duty. The water-pipes which supplied the hill were cut, and the democrat defenders forced into surrender. Then, contrary to Marius' orders, a massacre ensued; and both Glaucia and Saturninus were among the victims. Sick at failure, embittered and utterly discredited, Marius decided for the time being to abandon the struggle; and when the motion was passed for the recall of Metellus, his inveterate foe, he left Rome and set out for a tour in the East (99 B.C.).

CHAPTER XIV
THE RISE OF SULLA
I. DRUSUS' FAILURE

MARIUS' departure from Rome cleared the air for the moment; but, though the antagonism between the Senate and the knights had been temporarily forgotten at the recent crisis, the permanent source of friction remained. For nearly a decade there was indeed no open conflict, but each side scored where it could. The Senate secured the passage of a Bill forbidding block-legislation such as the democrat leaders had lately employed. The knights, through their control of the jury-courts, attacked senatorials, even condemning to exile a certain Rutilius Rufus who had tried to secure fair play for Asiatic provincials against the extortion of the capitalist-companies' collectors. Things were clearly moving towards a fresh crisis when a certain Marcus Livius Drusus[1] came forward with a proposal for compromise. Though a stiff, puritanical fellow with strong aristocratic connexions, he saw the necessity of moving with the times and as tribune for 91 set out to capture the support of the mob. He promised fresh distributions of land. He further cheapened the corn-dole, and this on so lavish a scale that before the year was out he was compelled to make two ends meet by debasing the currency. But such demagogic proposals were a mere stalking-horse. Drusus' main design was to compose the quarrel between the rival orders, and in pursuance of this end he proposed to restore the senatorial control of the jury-courts and simultaneously to promote 300 knights to the Senate. His compromise pleased neither party. The more reactionary senators disliked the concession to the despised *bourgeoisie;* the knights were suspicious of anything which might break

---

[1] Almost certainly the son of Caius Gracchus' opponent.

the solidarity of their order. But with characteristic obstinacy Drusus persisted. Lumping all his various proposals in a single Bill, he got the Assembly to pass it; but on the strength of the recent enactment against such block-legislation the Senate promptly declared it null and void.

Nothing daunted by his failure to solve one thorny problem, Drusus plunged headlong into another; and during the few months of office which still remained to him he undertook to champion the unpopular cause of Italian enfranchisement. No question of the day was indeed more urgent. After their frequent rebuffs and disappointments the patience of Rome's long-suffering confederates was well-nigh exhausted. For their various grievances—the subordination of their troops to Roman commanders, the exposure of their persons to the arbitrary violence of Roman officials without opportunity of either appeal or redress, their inability to enter upon legal action save througn the friendly offices of a Roman patron—there was but one adequate remedy, the franchise. Yet their attainment of the franchise seemed farther off than ever. Even their chance of migrating to the capital and so worming a way on to the civic register had again been recently cancelled. For in 95 a large number of Italian residents had been struck off the lists and many packed off to their original homes. This high-handed act aroused great anger throughout the length and breadth of Italy; and secret societies had begun to form in many townships, prepared, if peaceful methods failed, for a recourse to arms. There can be little doubt that the ring-leaders of this revolutionary movement appealed to Drusus; and as his own schemes of constitutional reform began to fail the greater grew the temptation to set himself at its head. He must have known that a majority not merely of the Senate but even of the urban voters would be against the project; but he was growing desperate now. The Italians, it was said, were sworn on oath to back him to the death. None could tell to what appalling crisis things were tending. Then one evening, as he was making his way home from a mass meeting in the Forum, he was struck by an unknown assassin and fell mortally wounded with a knife deep in his groin.

This fatality sounded the knell to the Italians' hopes.

Activity was redoubled in the centres of disaffection. Drilling was rumoured to be secretly in progress, and the Senate dispatched officers to various parts of the country to control the situation. Before three months were out the explosion came. One of these officers was murdered at Asculum and all Romans resident in the town were massacred. In a twinkling half Italy was up in arms. The revolt had begun (91).

II. THE GREAT REBELLION (90–89)

The momentous upheaval known to history as the Social War was no unpremeditated affair. The rebels' plans were well laid; and as soon as their formal demand for the citizenship had been rejected by the Senate they constituted themselves into a new federal State under the name of Italia. Its capital was to be at Corfinium, due east of Rome. Here were to meet its federal councils or senate of 500 representatives; and, as executive officers, two consuls and twelve praetors were to be chosen—presumably by this senate, since to convene an assembly of the scattered dalesmen was clearly impracticable. The secessionist area included eight tribes of the central or southern Apennines—the Marsi, Paeligni, Marrucini, Frentani, Samnites, Lucanians, and the unenfranchised portions of the Vestini and Picentes. The Apulians at first hung back; and, still more important, the Etruscans and Umbrians never joined effectively—so far were these northern peoples still divided from the south by differences of dialect and local custom. Rome for her part was able to command the loyal support not merely of the central enfranchised area and of the widely scattered Latin colonies, but also of the semi-privileged Greek cities of the south. The troops she could draw from such sources, though not equal to her opponents in either numbers or virility, were at least superior in training and equipment. Her hold on the seaports of south and west gave her access to supplies and reinforcements from abroad. Her practised methods of organization, the incomparably greater experience of her generals, and, above all, the strategic advantage of her central position, all these combined to save her against almost overwhelming odds; and, last but not least, her governing class showed at this crisis a shrewd instinct of moderation

POMPEII—HOUSE OF THE SILVER NUPTIALS

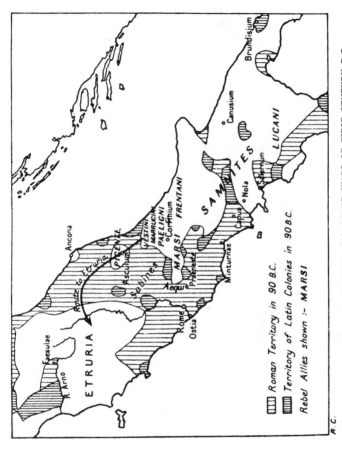

ITALY, THE GREAT REBELLION AND OTHER WARS OF FIRST CENTURY B.C.

R.C.

which led, as we shall see, to timely concessions, and availed in the upshot to weld the disgruntled peoples of the entire peninsula into a truly national State.

When the campaign opened Rome found herself compelled to a war upon two fronts, for her enemies' strategy was directed towards driving a wedge westwards to the coast upon either flank of Latium. Of these two offensives the southern was so far successful that Campania was deeply penetrated; and first Nola then the coastal town of Salernum were captured. In the north equally things at first went ill for Rome. Her army was overwhelmed by the Marsi and the consul Rutilius was killed. Marius, however, who was appointed in his place, restored the balance and the town of Asculum—a key position, the capture of which would have cut off the rebels from the waverers of Umbria and Etruria—was laid under siege. While the issue thus hung in the balance, and before the year 90 was ended, the wisdom of some form of compromise was recognized at Rome. The consul Lucius Julius Caesar, returning from the Campanian front, proposed and carried a measure offering the franchise to all allied communities which had either never taken up arms at all or were prepared to make immediate surrender. Etruria accepted the offer. The resolution of many other tribes was visibly shaken; by the spring of 89 Rome had the situation in hand.

The new year's changes in the high command were important. Marius, who was no favourite with the powers at home, was retired. Pompeius Strabo, well known to be sympathetic to the rebels' demands, took over the northern front, where Asculum was presently captured. Meanwhile, the other consul having been killed in battle, the southern command was entrusted to Sulla. His military powers had greatly developed since the Jugurthine War; and striking into the heart of Samnium he succeeded in cutting in two the remaining centres of disaffection. The real danger was soon past, and the reduction of scattered strongholds such as Nola in Campania remained only a matter of time. Already, too, by a fresh concession all real reason for continued resistance had been removed. Earlier in 89 a law had been passed on the motion of two tribunes, Plautius Silvanus and Papirius Carbo, offering the citizenship to all *individual* Italians who should appear before a Roman magistrate and register their names within sixty days. The offer was not disregarded. Men flocked in by thousands to enrol; and by the end of 89 the Samnites and Lucanians alone remained obdurate. Otherwise south of the Po every freeborn inhabitant (not even Gauls excluded) became a Roman citizen with full legal and political rights. In the townships which thus, as a natual corollary, were incorporated in the Roman State, municipal self-government appears to have been instituted, placing the control of local affairs in the hands of a Senate and elective magistrates. As for military service, the allies were now eligible for enlistment in the legions, and henceforward all auxiliary troops—more especially cavalry— were invariably recruited from provincial sources. Thus, from every point of view, Italy became at length a homogeneous whole; and, terrible as had been the cost of the bitter internal struggle—involving losses comparable only to those of the Hannibalic War—the issue was undoubtedly worth while.

The satisfactory nature of the settlement was, however, somewhat marred by the renewal of the old feud at Rome. Dispute arose over the method of distributing the newly enfranchised citizens among the 'tribes' or constituencies by which the Assembly voted. The reactionary party with whom Sulla was identified wished, by confining them to eight tribes only, to minimize their political influence. The progressive party led by a young tribune, Sulpicius Rufus, wished to spread them in such a way as to give them a real voice in the Assembly's decisions. The latter was obviously the fairer course; but unfortunately, to win Marius' support for his measure, Sulpicius took a most ill-judged step. At the moment, as it happened, the Roman province of Asia was threatened by invasion from Mithridates, King of Pontus. It was indeed their knowledge of this impending danger which, as much as anything, had hastened the Senate's surrender to the Italians' claim; and it had already been settled that Sulla, the consul elect for 88, should undertake the campaign in the East. Marius, however, still smarting under the slights of the aristo-cratic party, was determined to get the command for himself; and against all constitutional practice Sulpicius agreed to incorporate the transfer in his legislative programme. Feeling ran high. There were rowdy scenes in the Forum; and by dint of much intimidation Sulpicius' laws were passed.

At the heat of the crisis Sulla had quitted the capital and rejoined his army, which was still engaged in besieging some rebel diehards in the Campanian town of Nola. Here the news reached him that his Asiatic command had been transferred to his rival. His decision was soon taken. He told his legions bluntly that their chances of winning rich spoils in Asia Minor were in jeopardy; and with their enthusiastic approval he proceeded to march on Rome. The city was utterly unprepared for defence. By long constitutional custom no military force had ever been allowed to enter its sacred precincts; and it is not difficult to picture the horror of the citizens when Sulla's men came marching through the gates. After some hot street-fighting the democrats were scattered. Sulpicius' bloody head was nailed up on the Rostrum. Marius fled and was declared an outlaw. He sailed from Ostia, but was driven by winds on to the coast of southern Latium. He swam out to a passing ship, but the crew refused to carry him. He then sank himself up to the neck in a marsh, but was discovered by his pursuers and haled before the magistrates of Minturnae, who condemned him to death. When the executioner entered his cell, he cried out defiantly, 'Wilt thou slay Caius Marius?' and the man fled. Released, he took ship for the African coast, where he took refuge on an island and was soon joined by his son. We shall hear of both again.

Meanwhile at Rome Sulla had everything his own way. He repealed the recent laws of Sulpicius, and then, as the acknowledged champion of the aristocratic party, proceeded by various measures to strengthen their position. He created 300 new senators, chosen for their conservative tendencies; and he enacted that 'for the future no Bill should come before the Assembly without first securing the assent of the House. He further attempted to secure the election of his own nominees to the next year's consulship; but the populace, regaining something of its spirit, chose Lucius Cornelius Cinna, a patrician turned democrat and a wire-puller of dangerous ambition.

To leave such a man behind him at the head of affairs was no pleasant prospect for Sulla; but, since his own power depended on the loyalty of his troops, he could scarcely afford to disappoint them by remaining in Italy. So early in 87 he set sail for the East.

Sulla's career, and indeed his whole character, was a compound of strange contradictions. By every association of birth and party he was closely identified with the old Republican tradition; and yet by his march on Rome he had dealt a serious, perhaps even a mortal, blow at the Republican constitution itself; for he had shown that a general at the head of his troops could override the recognized machinery of political authority and dictate his wishes as an autocrat. Then, again, this champion of the old regime was very far from being a disciple of its austere moral code. He was a shameless debauchee, varying his bouts of abnormally hard work by orgies of intemperate self-indulgence. Wine and women were his favourite pastime; and, as he advanced in years, a blotched purple complexion like 'mulberry spotted with meal' became the notorious symptom of his gross excesses. The influence of a shallow Epicurean philosophy had reinforced these natural tendencies. For, though scarcely a serious thinker, Sulla affected Hellenism, admiring Greek art and collecting rare Greek books; and the sceptical outlook which he thus came to adopt made him utterly contemptuous of all conventional restraints. He was, in fact, a law to himself, completely callous of human life or suffering, cruel or merciful at whim. Yet, strange to say, he had a deeply superstitious conviction that he was under the gods' patronage. He assumed the name of Felix, the 'Lucky', wore a figure of Apollo under his cuirass, and believed in the significance of dreams. Certainly he did nothing by halves. He was thorough in his work and thorough in his pleasures. Yet he was a man of moods, quick to laughter and moved easily to tears. A whimsical humour seems to play round all his actions; and it is hard to believe that there was much in life which he took quite seriously. He tasted its vicissitudes as a connoisseur tastes wines, enjoying their variety; and even on his death-bed, we are told, he was visited by visions of a most reassuring character.

III. SULLA AND THE MITHRIDATIC WAR

That the movements of a King of Pontus—hitherto a quite insignificant State—should suddenly have become one of the most anxious preoccupations of the Republic's foreign policy seems to call for some explanation. The truth is that after the humiliation of the Seleucid monarchy there had remained no preponderant power in the Near East. Apart from her acceptance of the Pergamene domain in 133 and her seizure of the Cilician seaboard just thirty years later, Rome had not actively interfered in the affairs of Asia Minor, and the field had thus been left clear for the rivalries of its small principalities. Of these Pontus had, at first, little claim to importance. It did not even possess an outlet on the Black Sea, till Mithridates V (156–121) had occupied Sinope, an ancient Greek colony, and made it his capital. His son and successor Mithridates VI was a man of most commanding personality, a wiry athlete of extraordinary endurance, a skilful organizer, no mean tactician, and (unlike most of his neighbour princelings) a profound admirer of Hellenic culture. When he came of age in 114 he set to work at once to increase his hereditary domain. The Greek cities of the Tauric Chersonese (or Crimea) having invited his aid against the Scythian marauders, he had won the hegemony of this important trading centre and therewith resources of timber for the construction of a fleet. Once master of the Euxine he had turned to the task of inland expansion. First Lesser Armenia had fallen to him, then part of Paphlagonia. Finally he laid hands on Cappadocia too, and, though ordered by Rome to withdraw in favour of a native claimant, Ariobarzanes, he had persuaded Tigranes of Greater Armenia to turn this princeling out. In 92 Sulla himself had been given a commission as governor of Cilicia to bring Tigranes to book, and had actually penetrated inland as far as the upper Euphrates. Finding himself foiled in this direction, Mithridates then had turned westwards and attacked Bithynia. Once again a Roman envoy gave him orders 'to withdraw, and with very ill-judged zeal incited the Bithynians to invade his territory. The challenge immediately put Mithridates on his mettle. Calculating shrewdly upon Rome's

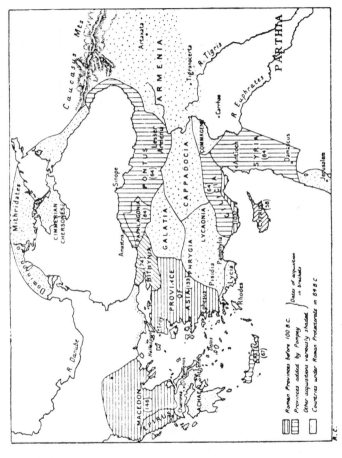

ROME'S EASTERN CONQUESTS IN FIRST CENTURY B.C.

PARTHIA

R. Tigris

R. Euphrates

Caucasus Mts

Artaxata

ARMENIA

Tigranocerta

Carrhae

Lesser Armenia

Sinope

PONTUS

PAPHLAGONIA (64)

Amasia

COMMAGENE

CAPPADOCIA

Antioch

SYRIA (64)

Damascus

BITHYNIA (74)

GALATIA

CILICIA (64)

LYCAONIA

Jerusalem

Dominions of Mithridates

CIMMERIAN CHERSONESE

PROVINCE OF ASIA (133)

PHRYGIA

Pisidia

Pamphylia

(58)

Ephesus

Lycia

R. Danube

Troy

Halicarnassus

Cos

Rhodes

MACEDON (146)

ILLYRIA

Chaeronea

Delphi

ACHAEA (67)

Megalopolis

Sparta

R.C.

Roman Provinces before 100 B.C. }
Provinces added by Pompey } Dates of acquisition in brackets

Other acquisitions variously shaded

Countries under Roman Protectorate in 54 B.C.

preoccupation with the great Italian Rebellion, he proceeded at once to his most cherished ambition—the conquest of her province of Asia.

In 88 he struck. His army swept aside the weak forces of the Roman governor and occupied the town of Pergamum itself. By the provincials themselves he was welcomed as a saviour. Fifty years of oppression had taught them to regard their Roman masters with implacable loathing; and this was their opportunity for a horrible revenge. The province was swarming with Romans and Italians—tax-collectors' agents, moneylenders, and merchants; and nothing could save these miserable creatures now. Eighty thousand were butchered in cold blood. Meanwhile Mithridates' fleet had broken through the Bosphorus and the Aegean lay at his mercy. At Delos, an important trading centre, another massacre of Italian merchants took place. Athens, seeing the spectacular collapse of her suzerain's forces, was seized by a sudden fit of insubordination; and under the leadership of Aristion—a philosophy teacher turned tyrant—she threw in her lot with the victor. A Pontic army under Archelaus came over, and most other Greek States joined the revolt. Meanwhile Mithridates' son was rousing the Thracians to an invasion of Macedon, and it looked as though the entire peninsula would be lost to Rome. Such was the critical situation when in the spring of 87 Sulla landed with five legions on the Epirot coast.

Having no naval force to pit against the powerful Pontic fleet, he at once dispatched his quaestor, Lucullus, to collect ships from Rhodes, Egypt, and elsewhere. Then he himself proceeded to lay Athens under siege. Its fortifications were strong, and it was not till the spring of 86 that famine and disease reduced the garrison to impotence. A terrible sack ensued, and Aristion was killed. It remained to deal with Archelaus' army, which moved away from the neighbourhood of Athens to join further reinforcements arriving from the north. At Chaeronea on the Boeotian plain Sulla won a resounding victory, in which (no doubt with an eye to propaganda at home) he reported his own losses at no more than fifteen men. Next spring (86) a fresh Pontic army arriving by sea was defeated at Orchomenus. The fickle Greek States had meanwhile returned to their allegiance. Lucullus, now at the head of a considerable naval contingent, was regaining command of the seas; and in Europe at any rate it was clear that Mithridates' effort had failed.

But now an awkward complication arose in Sulla's task. His departure from Rome, as he must have foreseen, had been followed by a democratic reaction. Of this more shall be told presently; here it is sufficient to say that Sulla himself had been declared an outlaw, his command of the Mithridatic campaign had been cancelled, and Valerius Flaccus was sent out to take his place. Flaccus' troops, however, were badly out of hand. His advance-guard deserted to Sulla, and rather than risk a further clash of loyalties he made off towards the Hellespont and crossed over to Asia. There he had the misfortune to quarrel with his hot-headed lieutenant Fimbria and was murdered. Fimbria, assuming command, drove Mithridates to evacuate Pergamum and take refuge on the island of Lesbos, where, with co-operation of Lucullus' squadron, he might easily have been captured. To share the honours with a democrat was not, however, to Sulla's liking. He opened negotiations with Mithridates, and, moving up to the Hellespont, summoned the king to a rendezvous near the site of ancient Troy. All things considered, the terms offered were surprisingly light— the surrender of the Pontic fleet, the evacuation of all territory outside the old Pontic frontiers and the payment of a comparatively small indemnity; and Mithridates was glad to accept them. As for Fimbria, he committed suicide; and on the approach of Sulla's troops his men obligingly surrendered. It merely remained to settle accounts with the now penitent provincials. Quickly as they had tired of Mithridates' extravagant conduct, they could not escape the penalty of having rendered him assistance. Sulla punished them with exactions so intolerable that they were forced to borrow heavily, and the Roman moneylenders once more got them into their clutches. The fact was that Sulla needed funds for his coming operations against Italy; and in his preoccupation he lost all interest in the settlement of Asia. He left a terrible condition of affairs behind him when in the autumn of 84 he took ship to Greece. He spent the winter collecting rare manuscripts and drinking waters for the gout; and then in the following spring he landed with his army at Brundisium.

IV. SULLA AND THE DEMOCRATS

During Sulla's four-year absence much had occurred in Italy. It had not been long before Cinna, the democrat consul, had come out in his true colours. Reviving Sulpicius' programme, he had rallied to his side a large band of hooligans. Street-fighting had broken out, and in the upshot he was driven from the capital by Sulla's partisans. Nothing daunted, he had set to work to gather adherents in Campania. The army of the south took up his cause. So also did many Samnites and Lucanians, who had never laid down their arms. The younger Marius joined him. Soon, too, came the elder Marius, now well over seventy, a horribly sinister figure, farouche, revengeful, his mind still harping on his late privations, his beard and hair studiedly unkempt. With a few ships he seized Ostia; meanwhile Cinna from the south and his lieutenant Sertorius from the north closed in on Rome. Thus cut off from provisionment by sea and land alike, the city was soon on the brink of starvation. Plague broke out among the senatorial troops, and there was no choice but surrender. Cinna had promised mercy, but Marius' pent-up passion for revenge now found its opportunity, and he saw red. For five days there followed a reign of terror which outran all precedent—parties of ruffianly freedmen patrolling the streets, killing ferociously at Marius' least nod, and hunting down the victims of his will; mutilated corpses littering the roadway; more heads set to decorate the Rostra; properties and houses confiscated wholesale and knocked down to the highest bidder. Of the conservative section in the Senate scarcely any survived. No wonder Sertorius, a man of real character, was disgusted. Even Cinna quailed; and eventually they engaged a company of Gauls to fall on the murderers in their sleep and put an end to them.

For the year 86 no consular elections were held. Marius and Cinna nominated themselves; and when on the thirteenth day of office the old man died, Valerius Flaccus took his place and, as we have seen, went out to challenge Sulla in the east. For the next three years Cinna remained at the head of the

State, posting his nominees to the chief offices and packing the Senate with his partisans. No attempt was made at constitutional reform; but all Sulla's arrangements were annulled, and he himself was declared an outlaw.

To the men who had thus dealt with him the prospect of his return became more and more alarming as the day approached. Many, too, were ready to back them—the Italians, who, remembering Sulla's conduct during the Great Rebellion, felt nervous for their new-won liberties; capitalists and others who had acquired properties and houses through the recent confiscations. Confident in such support, Cinna and Carbo, his colleague for the year 84, resolved on armed resistance. An advance-guard was actually sent on to Greece to forestall Sulla's embarkation; but before more could follow Cinna was murdered by the mutinous troops. Meanwhile, the moderate democrats were working hard to effect a compromise; but the hot-heads prevailed and on the eve of Sulla's landing Cornelius Scipio and Junius Norbanus, the two democrat consuls, took command of the troops, while Carbo went northward to raise reinforcements in Cisalpine Gaul.

Sulla was as much a diplomatist as a soldier, 'fox and lion rolled into one'; and when he landed at Brundisium in the spring of 83 he made no sudden dash on Rome. His enemies' numbers were overwhelmingly superior, and advancing slowly northwards he set himself to allay or conquer opposition. By promising to respect the political rights of such Italian communities as would treat with him, he secured the neutrality of all save the Etruscans and the Samnites. Norbanus he drove back and shut up in Capua. Scipio's troops deserted to his side; and by autumn all the south, except Samnium, was won. In the spring of 82, after driving the younger Marius into Praeneste, Sulla advanced on Rome and entered it without a blow. Meanwhile in the north his two able lieutenants, M. Licinius Crassus and Cnaeus Pompeius, managed to disperse the enormous levies which Carbo had enlisted, and it now merely remained to reduce the young Marius in Praeneste. As Sulla moved south, however, a force of Samnites under Pontius swept in behind him and reached the walls of Rome before he could come up with them. Though his men had marched all night, he gave battle that same afternoon; and outside the Colline Gate, under the very eyes of the horrified citizens, was fought the fiercest conflict of the Civil War. Sulla won a complete victory, and the prisoners taken in the battle were butchered in cold blood in the Circus Maximus. When the startled Senate overheard their shrieks Sulla grimly ordered the debate to continue. 'It is merely some male-factors suffering for their crimes.' With the fall of Praeneste and the suicide of Marius hostilities were virtually at an end (82).

From first to last these wars and political massacres had accounted in all for half a million lives; and a new and hideous feature of the conflict had been the readiness of the troops to turn their sword against their fellow-citizens. Partly perhaps this was due to the demoralizing effect of professional soldiering abroad. The army, we must remember too, was now largely recruited from the riff-raff of the urban proletariat, and was full of half-breed adventurers, often of servile extraction, who had never learnt the national habits of decency and self-restraint. From the same source also were drawn the ruffianly retainers who backed the heady violence of successive dema-gogues. Many of the freedmen class had even risen to influen-tial positions in the households of the nobility; and in the still more horrible excesses which were now to follow these scheming rascals played a notorious part.

V. THE SULLAN SETTLEMENT

Sulla had a long score to pay off against the defeated party for their ruthless massacre of his senatorial friends. It was not his habit to do anything by halves; and he set out to exter-minate all equestrians and democrats who had taken sides against him. At first he proceeded by promiscuous slaughter. Then, on request, he drew up lists of proscribed persons whose lives and properties were thereby forfeit and their murderer entitled to a handsome reward. 'Those,' he remarked with a chuckle, 'are all I can remember *at present*.' No one could feel safe. His favourites continued to insert on the lists the names of men whose property they coveted. 'My· Alban villa pursues me,' cried one blameless citizen on reading his name. Fortunes changed hands with bewildering rapidity;

and we hear of a sergeant acquiring an estate worth a hundred thousand pounds. The worst elements of society profited at the expense of the best, and the foulest passions of revenge were aroused. One of Marius' sons was flogged through the streets and then put to death by torture. Altogether 50 democrat senators, 1,600 knights, and 2,000 other persons lost their lives. The experiences of the Terror left an indelible imprint on the memories of every class at Rome.

Sulla's treatment of Italian communities which had opposed him was scarcely less stern. Local leaders were hunted down. In Volterra and elsewhere the inhabitants were disenfranchised. Much land was confiscated especially in Etruria and Samnium and a large part of it distributed as small-holdings among Sulla's veterans. Since many of them were provincials from Spain or Gaul this measure did little to consolidate Italian unity; but so little did Sulla care for this that he proceeded further to enfranchise the slaves of proscribed persons over 10,000 in number, presumably for the sake of gaining their votes. Such political props, in reality, were wholly needless. By virtue of his victory Sulla was absolute master of Rome. He caused himself to be appointed Dictator, not for the normal period of six months, but for an indefinite period and with unlimited power to amend the constitution at will.

Sulla's reform was perhaps the most thoroughgoing piece of reactionary legislation known to history. He undertook to put back the clock by a century at least and restore to the Senate the political supremacy of its prime. First, he struck at the sovereignty of the Assembly by curtailing the power of the tribunes. Their veto was limited to its original purpose of protecting individuals against summary arrest. The corn distributions, on which so much of their popularity rested, were discontinued; and the further to discourage ambitious politicians from undertaking the office, its tenure was made a disqualification for all higher magistracies.

Finally it was laid down that no Bill might come before the Assembly without the Senate's approval. Thus the House was to be endowed henceforward not merely with absolute control of administration and policy, but also with a decisive voice in legislation as well. Three hundred new members of known senatorial sympathies were again drafted into it; and the better to ensure that it continued to be a thoroughly conservative body, the censors' powers of personal selection were abolished in favour of a new method of recruitment. Twenty quaestors were to be annually elected and on vacating office were automatically to enter the House. In other words, the personnel of the Order was to be continuously replenished by men in the prime of life; and thus from the outset of their careers subjected to its mellowing influence. Rapid promotion up the official ladder, moreover, was to be checked by strict application of age-limits[1] and it was made illegal to attain the higher offices without first passing through the lower.

Perhaps the most important, and certainly the most permanent, of Sulla's reforms was concerned with the administration of the Empire. Consuls and praetors after the conclusion of their terms were to pass on automatically to provincial commands; and the number of praetors was raised from six to eight in order to furnish the complement necessary for the ten existing provinces. In one respect the military importance of these provincial governorships was considerably enhanced; for, since troops were no longer to be quartered in Italy, the consul ceased to be the national commander-in-chief, and the control of the legions henceforth belonged exclusively to provincial governors, especially to the governor of Cisalpine Gaul, now the recognized guardian of the Italian frontier. On the other hand, this decentralization of the military executive was intended to simplify the Senate's task of controlling it. Not merely were provincial governors assigned to their posts at the discretion of the House, but without its leave they were forbidden to move outside their appointed frontiers. Last, but not least, at the expiration of their command they were henceforth liable to prosecution before a senatorial tribunal. For, naturally enough, it was the cornerstone of Sulla's dispensation that the Order should resume control of the jury-courts. Nor were these courts now limited to cases of extortion alone. New courts for 'high treason' and for 'riot' had recently come into existence; and Sulla himself

[1] According to Sulla's revised scheme, a man could not become quaestor till thirty, praetor till thirty-nine, consul till forty-two.

seems to have established four others—for 'embezzlement', 'electorial corruption', 'assassination', and 'fraud'. Such systematization of judicial procedure was long overdue, and it is striking evidence of Sulla's genius for organization that he recognized the need for it.

System was certainly the keynote of his whole constitutional reform. What had previously been based upon unwritten custom, precedent, or etiquette he attempted to set down in a fixed and logical code. But it was beyond the power of codes or logic to restore the old spirit of political loyalty whereby alone the various elements of the Republican constitution had worked harmoniously together in the past. Sooner or later a fresh clash was sure to come between individual ambition and the oligarchical interest; and, when it came, all rules and regulations, however carefully framed, would inevitably be swept aside—as Sulla himself had swept them. The truth is that by the example of his own career he had destroyed the very basis of the constitutional system which he was attempting to restore. Strive as he might to observe the regular forms of procedure—and he seems to have sought the Assembly's approval for most of his measures—no one could forget that behind the legislator stood the all-powerful soldier. His dictatorship itself was no more than a thin disguise for a rule of sheer terrorism; and it was significant that even in the year 80, though elected to the consulship, he did not relinquish his extraordinary powers.

For all that his mind was made up. He had put the Senate into the saddle and it remained to see if it could ride. In 79 he refused re-election to the consulship, and scarcely had his successors entered office than he suddenly announced his intention of throwing up the dictatorship also and retiring into private life. He dismissed his retinue of lictors and walked quietly to his home. Such an act exposed him at once to the vengeance of his enemies. Yet nobody dared touch him; and the story is told how, when some ribald fellow threw an insult at him in the streets, he even took it in good part.

So the curtain was rung down upon the penultimate scene of Sulla's strange career. His spell of hard work was over and it was the turn for pleasure now. Retiring to his villa

near Puteoli in Campania, he devoted himself to a life of unwholesome debauchery. The tale that he contracted a particularly loathsome disease may well have been due to the
malice of his enemies; but he was clearly failing. One day in
78 he summoned a local official who had defied the claims of
the Treasury and in a fit of passion had him strangled before
his eyes. The excitement was too much for him and he broke
a blood-vessel and within twenty-four hours was dead. Rome
gave him a public funeral, and over his monument was written
the epitaph composed by his own hand: 'No friend did him a
good turn nor enemy a bad, but he was repaid in full.' It was
no bad summary of his career. Had his aims been as lofty as
his methods were thorough, he would have been a great man.

CHAPTER XV

THE RISE OF POMPEY

SULLA had no doubt been right in regarding a complete
restoration of senatorial government as the sole possible
alternative to autocracy or mob-rule; and his constitutional code was at least a thoroughgoing attempt to fit
that government to the chief administrative needs of the day.
Nevertheless, at his death he left Rome in a state of uncertainty and bewilderment probably unique in her history.
The terrible events and kaleidoscopic changes of the past few
years had created an atmosphere of nervous suspicion, mean
cupidity, and reckless despair. In the frantic effort to preserve
their skins or replenish their pockets men seem to have lost
their bearings, and the old divisions of party alinement were
becoming hopelessly confused. The senatorial conservatives,
it is true, still hung together against the factious agitations
of a heterogeneous opposition. But there were an increasing
number of aristocratic adventurers who had lost all sense of
allegiance to the old regime; and who in the selfish pursuit
of personal interests were prepared to plunge headlong into
the exciting opportunities of popular leadership. For not
even Sulla had dared to deprive the Assembly of the right to

elect magistrates, and so long as office could be won by pandering to the mob there was no lack of competitors for its favours. Democrats after Gracchus' style such men certainly were not. They simply made use of the conventional democrat programme to further their own ends. So for a quarter of a century and more there was to run on this unedifying yet intensely fascinating struggle—on the one side the ruling oligarchy increasingly helpless and yet not the less intransigent; on the other side the mob swayed by the skilful manipulation of political adventurers and bribed by the long purses of their capitalist backers; and meanwhile, emerging into greater and greater prominence, the threat of intervention by the armed forces of the State, which at length, under the leadership of a democrat turned soldier, were destined to settle the quarrel of the parties by destroying once for all the power of both.

I. LEPIDUS, SERTORIUS, AND SPARTACUS

That under such circumstances Sulla's constitution would not go long unchallenged was obvious enough; and in 78, the very year of his death, the attack was begun. One of the consuls, M. Aemilius Lepidus, made a bid for mob leadership by proposing a restoration of the corn-dole and the reinstatement of the victims of the Sullan proscription. When temporarily thwarted by the opposition of his colleague Catulus, a stalwart senatorial, Lepidus determined on a *coup d'état* for the following year. With a motley army of malcontents enlisted in Etruria he proceeded to march on Rome, but was defeated by Catulus and forced to flee the country.

The task of rounding up the remaining rebels was entrusted to Cnaeus Pompeius, formerly one of Sulla's most brilliant lieutenants. This ambitious young man made shrewd use of his commission. While he had troops at his back he was in a strong position to get what he wanted; and he was careful not to disband them till the Senate had granted him the province of Spain (77).

The importance of this command requires some explanation. In 83 the democrat government had sent out Sertorius to secure Spain in their interest. When Sulla's troops drove him out he had taken refuge on the African coast. Three years later he accepted an invitation from the Lusitanian natives to assist them in an insurrection against Rome. His presence among the natives worked like magic. They obeyed him like children, and he even played on their superstitions by keeping a snow-white fawn, which he assured them could impart to him the gift of second sight. Thousands flocked to his standard, swearing an oath of fidelity to the death. Soon he had material for a formidable army, which he equipped and trained after the Roman model; and despite the efforts of the official governors his influence spread rapidly over the whole peninsula. The use he made of his ascendancy was extremely enlightened; for he possessed a constructive genius very rare among his countrymen; and first perhaps of any before Julius Caesar he made it his policy to Romanize the provincials, encouraging their nobility to wear the toga, and even organizing a school where their sons might learn Latin and Greek. So far from wishing to detach Spain from the Empire, it was his object to make it a rallying-point whence the defeated Marians might recover their hold on Italy. Many prominent refugees joined him, and of these he actually constituted a mimic senate. Finally in 77 his cause was reinforced by the arrival of Perpenna with a remnant of Lepidus' army which had eluded the vigilance of Pompey.

Next year Pompey himself came out. He had been given proconsular powers conjointly with Metellus Pius, the existing governor; but since jealousy prevented the two from acting in harmony little headway was made against the guerrilla tactics of the insurgents. Sertorius had, meanwhile, been acquiring allies among the enemies of Rome. He was in league with piratical commanders, and in return for the loan of some Roman officers he got Mithridates of Pontus to lend him a fleet. Nevertheless, his star was slowly on the wane. The Spaniards were beginning to resent his arbitrary discipline; and among the dissolute Marian officers there was a tendency to challenge his leadership. Perpenna, for his part, was playing a traitor's game, and one night in 72 Sertorius was assassinated by the tipsy diners at the head-quarters' mess. With his death the rebellion lost cohesion. Perpenna was captured and killed, and the province was swiftly reduced. The example of Sertorius' enlightened policy was not wholly wasted, for citizen-rights were conferred on many loyal Spaniards, Caesar's friend Balbus among them. But the settlement of the province had no longer much interest for Pompey. His ambitions were now thoroughly aroused, and by the autumn of 71 he was hurrying back his army overland to Italy; for there momentous and terrible events were once again in progress. The slaves had risen in revolt.

As we have frequently hinted, the employment of servile labour on Italian estates had grown to alarming proportions. On the sheep-ranches of the south especially slaves of the more savage and intractable type were utilized in large numbers. They were housed in horrible barracks called *ergastula*, where they were brutally maltreated and at nights often kept in chains. Roaming the hills by day they often robbed passing travellers; and being armed for the defence of their herds against wild beasts they were a potential menace even to the State itself. In 73 a Thracian slave named Spartacus, assisted by a band of fellow-gladiators, broke out of Capua and began to lead a bandit's life on Mount Vesuvius. The news of their success spread rapidly; and slave herdsmen from the farms and slave-workers from Campanian factories trooped out to join them. Before long South Italy was at the mercy of these desperadoes, villagers were plundered, travellers killed. Spartacus did what he could to restrain the worst excesses of his followers; and since many hailed from Central Europe—some taken in the Cimbric War, some on the Macedonian frontiers—he planned to march north and cross the Alps. When, however, it reached Mutina, the rebel army abandoned the project and swept back into Lucania. It was now well over 100,000 strong and included a troop of cavalry. The Roman public was at last thoroughly scared, and Marcus Licinius Crassus (another of Sulla's officers) was appointed to take the field at the head of six legions. He drove Spartacus back into the tip of the peninsula and pinned him to the coast by a line of strong entrenchments. The bandit chief cut his way through; but after a series of engagements was defeated and killed in 71. Crassus celebrated his victory by crucifying 6,000 of the prisoners along the Appian way between Capua and Rome. He had delivered his country from a nightmare as hideous as any it had known, and by rights he should have been the sole hero of the hour. But at the last moment the unique credit of his triumph was partially obscured. A forlorn hope of the insurgents, while making its escape northwards, fell in with Pompey's returning army and was of course cut to pieces. On the score of this success Pompey coolly put forward the claim that, whatever Crassus might have done to break the back of the rebellion, he himself had stamped it out.

The two generals were now face to face. Crassus was nominally the Senate's champion, Pompey the favourite of the populace. Both were hungry for power; and there was no love lost between them. Once again civil war seemed imminent; but saner counsels prevailed, and the two rivals were persuaded to compose their differences and combine in a joint-candidature for the consulship. Both were elected and entered office for the year 70 B.C.

II. THE CONSULSHIP OF POMPEY AND CRASSUS

In character these two men were a complete contrast. Crassus was a born schemer, quick-witted, persuasive, and perfectly unscrupulous. During the Sullan proscriptions he had bought up property cheap, and when prices resumed their normal level found himself possessed of prodigious wealth. He thus became a leading financial magnate and chief controller of the tax-collecting syndicates; and by advancing loans to young men of promise—Julius Caesar amongst others —he gained a political influence out of all proportion to his intrinsic worth. Statesmanship he had none; he was but a mediocre speaker; and his military reputation was based on little more than a ruthless enforcement of discipline. Pompey, on the other hand, was a soldier pure and simple, and a soldier of a very high order, immensely popular with the troops and as an organizer second to none. But there his claim to greatness ended. A blameless, well-meaning, unimaginative soul, devoted to his home, generous even to his enemies, and universally respected for the good fellow that he was, he was intellectually no match for the cynical society in which his lot was cast. Though ambitious to the point of sheer vanity, he lacked the nerve for great decisions. Knowing his weakness, he affected in public a pose of inscrutability, but in private relied on others to make up his mind for him. The result was that at various periods of his career we find him now against the Senate, now for it; at first the friend and associate of Caesar, then finally his mortal foe. No wonder that in his portraits Pompey wears the puzzled look of a man for whom life has been too difficult.

As consuls for the year 70 both Pompey and Crassus owed their position to the democratic vote; and, though Crassus was characteristically anxious to keep in with the Senate, he could scarcely resist the wishes of his equestrian friends. The repeal of the Sullan constitution was therefore a foregone conclusion. Some of its provisions had already gone by the board. In 75 the rule disqualifying tribunes from election to further offices had been disannulled; and two years later the corn-dole had been revived. The main strength of the system was now to be undermined by a fresh series of reforms. First the tribune's right of initiating legislation was restored; then the censor's power of suspending senators—a power which was promptly used to remove notorious opponents of the democratic cause. It remained to deal with the jury-courts; and here a compromise was effected, more as a result of disagreement between Pompey and Crassus than of any statesmanlike desire for an equitable settlement. On the motion of Cotta, Julius Caesar's uncle, a Bill was passed whereby in future the juries were to be drawn conjointly from three different orders—senators, knights, *tribuni aerarii*, a class probably composed of men whose assessment rated next after the knights. This arrangement was permitted to stand until the end of the Republic.

Thus the result of the year's legislation was a more or less complete restoration of the earlier Republican system. Beyond this neither Pompey nor Crassus possessed any constructive policy; and when their office expired neither chose to take up any provincial command. Pompey, acutely conscious that he could only shine in a military capacity, preferred to await some opportunity truly worthy of his salt. Crassus, for his part, was in his element at Rome. His animosity against his late colleague was as vigorous as ever; and he knew that he could play his cards most effectively by remaining on the spot.

Nor was Pompey the only man who needed watching. Others were coming to the fore who were soon to play important roles on the political stage. There was the young Julius Caesar, for example, intellectually a far more dangerous rival. Though a member of one of the oldest families in Rome, he was nephew by marriage to the great Marius, and a partisan of the democrat cause. During the Terror he had defied Sulla's order to divorce his wife, Cinna's daughter, and had narrowly escaped death by flight. After serving a campaign in Asia Minor he had returned to Rome, where he made himself conspicuous by the extravagance of his hospitality. After another period in the East, where he studied rhetoric at Rhodes and saw further service in the Mithridatic War, he was back again in the capital and had joined the reformers in their attack on the Sullan constitution. His ambition was self-evident; and, though barely turned thirty, he had already secured election to the distinguished life-office of pontiff. Yet Caesar was nothing if not shrewd. He had no desire to compromise his future by premature self-assertion; and in 68 he was content to go off as quaestor in Further Spain.

Slightly more to be reckoned with as being by some years Caesar's senior was Marcus Tullius Cicero. The son of a knight of Arpinum, he had no aristocratic connexions; and when election to the quaestorship won him a seat in the Senate he was entirely dependent, as a 'new man' in politics, on his personal efforts alone. By his brilliant forensic gifts—in particular by his plucky defence of a young farmer called Roscius against the intrigues of Sulla's freedman Chrysogonus —he had already made his mark. Study at Rhodes had further developed his powers; and in the very year of Pompey's consulship he found matchless opportunity to display them in a *cause célèbre*. From 73 to 71 Sicily had been suffering under the administration of the notorious Caius Verres; and on the expiration of his tenure the provincials, deciding to prosecute, placed the case in the hands of Cicero, who had formerly served among them as quaestor. Since at this date the jury still consisted of senators, the odds were clearly in Verres' favour. A hurried visit to Sicily, however, armed Cicero with much damning evidence—of extortionate manipulation of the corn-levy, of thefts of innumerable works of art from temples and private houses, of hideous acts of personal revenge and official cruelty culminating in the summary crucifixion of Roman citizens. Some of Verres' victims, it is true, were probably Italians turned pirate and richly deserved their fate; nevertheless, the indictment was so overwhelming that before the trial was half over Verres threw up the sponge and retired from Italy. After this unprecedented triumph over the forces of senatorial corruption Cicero was a made man; and seeing what was then the power of eloquence to determine the greatest issues and sway even the destinies of nations, it was not difficult to prophesy for him a brilliant political career.

It remains to mention one other outstanding figure—Sulla's old lieutenant Lucullus, not merely as being among the staunchest champions of the senatorial cause, but because at this moment he was in command of a campaign of primary importance—the Second Mithridatic War. Before more can be said of Lucullus, however, it will be necessary to describe the origin and course of this struggle.

III. THE SECOND MITHRIDATIC WAR

On his death in 75 Nicomedes of Bithynia had bequeathed his kingdom to Rome. Mithridates had long coveted this neighbouring territory and, denouncing the will as a forgery, he had led an army into Bithynia, professedly in support of an alleged son of the dead king. He had chosen his moment shrewdly. Rome he knew to be exhausted by the Civil War. Sertorius, as we have seen, was ready to offer him assistance. He was in close touch with the piratical commanders who were at this time sweeping the seas; and, above all, he had a powerful ally in his own son-in-law Tigranes of Armenia, now the most powerful monarch of the Orient. Such a strong combination of forces was a threat to which the Republic could not be indifferent; and in 74 Lucullus was sent out in command of five legions, with Cotta as his naval assistant. At first they found some difficulty in overcoming the Pontic forces, which had by now completely recovered from their defeat at the hands of Sulla. But by 72 the situation was mastered, and Mithridates himself driven to take refuge at Tigranes' court. Well aware that there could be no lasting peace in Asia until these two troublesome monarchs were effectively suppressed, Lucullus now determined to carry the war into Armenia. In 69, accordingly, he undertook a long march up country and captured Tigranocerta, a new and sumptuous capital which Tigranes had founded in the southern part of his realm. An honourable peace might now have been had for the asking; but Lucullus' ambitions were aroused, and in the following year he prepared to proceed against Artaxata, the old Armenian capital, far away in the north-east. He had counted, however, without his men. The rank and file were sick of campaigning; many of them had been absent from Italy for nearly twenty years. Political agitators from Rome were spreading disaffection in their ranks; and, appalled at the prospect of spending the winter among the Armenian wilds, they flatly refused to march. Lucullus was obliged to call the expedition off. An enemy force, collected by Tigranes, threatened his rear; and failure stared him in the face.

The ultimate cause of Lucullus' undoing, however, was the animosity of his political enemies at home. Since the democratic revival under Pompey and Crassus it was only natural that he should have fallen from favour; but, as it so happened, there were special reasons why he should have been singled out for attack. In the intervals of campaigning he had by no means neglected the provincial administration of Asia. There Sulla's exactions had produced an appalling condition of financial chaos. In the endeavour to pay, the native communities had been forced to borrow at the most exorbitant interest from Italian bankers and syndicates. Their indebtedness had mounted from five million pounds to nearly six times that sum. Private individuals were in no better case; and many were even compelled to satisfy their creditors by selling their children as slaves. It must have required high courage on Lucullus' part to attack the vested interests of the big capitalists; but philosophic and literary studies had bred in him an independence of outlook uncommon in a Roman, and he did not flinch from drastic measures. Two-thirds of the public debts were written off, and the remainder to be paid in four yearly instalments, while in case of private liabilities the creditor had to be satisfied with one-quarter of the debtor's annual income. Thus Asia was saved from bankruptcy; but against the man who had saved it a vigorous agitation was begun among the capitalists at Rome; and, as soon as his Armenian failure exposed him to attack, the blow fell. In 67 Lucullus received the news that he was to be superseded. He came home a disappointed and disillusioned man, and abandoning politics retired into a life of refined but self-indulgent ease, keeping open house to his friends with an elaboration of luxury and splendour which made his name a byword among Roman plutocrats.

There can be little doubt that on Lucullus' recall Pompey would himself have taken over the Asiatic command, had he not at this very moment received an even more urgent and important commission. Of recent years piracy, which had long been a nuisance, had become a positive menace. For, after suppressing one by one those maritime States which had previously kept it in control, the Roman Government itself had made no serious effort to patrol the trade-routes. The consequence was that piracy, going unchecked, had become a thriving profession. Men of all countries, including even political exiles from Italy, had taken to the seas. Large, well-organized flotillas with regular bases and arsenals in Crete, Cilicia, and elsewhere had received encouragement from Mithridates and other enemies of the Republic. From the Levant their activities spread to western waters. Roman troops had been prevented from crossing the Adriatic. Roman squadrons had been defeated, and peaceful Roman travellers had been made to walk the plank. Ostia had actually been entered and its shipping burnt. The more audacious marauders even ventured inland, and travellers scarcely dared proceed along the Appian Way. Worst of all, the corn-supply had been frequently interrupted, and the populace of the capital more than once half starved. From time to time, indeed, action had been taken. In 79 Servilius Vatia had suppressed some Cilician strongholds. In 69 Caecilius had done the same in Crete. But such piecemeal efforts were foredoomed to failure.

For, when driven from one base, the pirates could always find another; and since Roman governors might not act outside their particular province effective co-operation was impossible. What was needed was that the task of suppression should be entrusted to some single commander; and Pompey, though the Senate shrank from committing such powers to one whom they so much mistrusted, was clearly the man for the job. In 67 a tribune named Gabinius brought forward a Bill conferring on some person unnamed the sole and extraordinary command of the whole Mediterranean basin. The commission was to last three years and entitled its holder to operate with full proconsular powers in any province up to fifty miles inland from the coast.

Pompey's nomination followed as a matter of course; and he obtained leave to raise 500 warships, 120,000 infantry, and 5,000 horse. Actually, he found such numbers quite unnecessary. He divided the Mediterranean into thirteen districts, placing a lieutenant over each. Then, closing the exits at Gibraltar and the Bosphorus, he began a methodical sweep of the seas. Within forty days he had cleared all waters west of Sicily. Most of the pirates retreated to the Levant, and, after a brief visit to Rome, Pompey set out in pursuit, defeated a strong concentration of the enemy off the Cilician coast, and then one by one reduced their strongholds in that region. Within seven weeks from his departure from Brundisium his task was completed.

At Rome he was naturally the hero of the hour; and, though he did not return in person to dictate his wishes, it is clear that his agents were well primed. Since Lucullus' recall from the Asiatic command various officials had been sent out to complete his unfinished work; but public opinion was dissatisfied with such makeshift appointments, and it was felt that for a successful termination of the Mithridatic War some stronger hand was needed. Accordingly, in 66 another tribune named Manilius proposed that Pompey should be given sole command in the east, including control of the three provinces, Cilicia, Bithynia, and Asia, and coupled with the right to declare war or conclude peace at his own discretion. Never in all Roman history had power so tremendous been conferred upon one individual. The senatorial diehards protested in vain. Caesar and Cicero both backed the Bill, and it was duly passed.

It can scarcely be doubted that, underlying this extraordinary appointment was the desire of the capitalist class for a new policy of eastern expansion, bringing with it not merely more tribute for the Treasury, but also fresh fields of exploitation for themselves. In any case there now followed a campaign of deliberate conquest unprecedented in the annals of the Republic. It was more, indeed, of a parade than a campaign. Besides Lucullus' troops, Pompey took with him several legions of his own; but material resources were of far less consequence than the immense prestige of his name. Mithridates scarcely stayed to put up a proper fight. After a series of rear-guard actions he fled first to Armenia, then, finding Tigranes did not want him, to the Crimea. There he maintained himself for two years more, still acting with furious energy (though he was nearly seventy), planning even to march on Italy by way of the Alps, and struggling desperately against the disaffection of his army and the treachery of his sons. At last, in 63, from utter weariness, he ended his own life—so stout of frame to the end that the poison he first took proved ineffectual, and he was compelled to get a Gallic officer to slay him.

Meanwhile Pompey, after following in his tracks as far as the Caucasus, had turned back to gather the fruits of his tremendous triumph. Tigranes appeared at the Roman camp, and, after making abject submission, was allowed to retain his kingdom as a vassal prince. Pompey clearly intended it to serve as a buffer State against the growing power of the Parthians. To have come to definite terms with them would have been a wiser policy; but when their king, Phraates, asked that the Euphrates should be recognized as a frontier between himself and Rome, he was put off with an evasive reply. 'I will do what is just,' said Pompey, and turned to carry out the grandiose imperialist schemes which his supporters at home were expecting of him. No more serious fighting was needed; and his next three years were spent in annexing, settling, or repartitioning the lands of the Near East.

In Asia Minor itself the southern province of Cilicia was

greatly enlarged, while in the northern province of Bithynia were incorporated Paphlagonia and Pontus. Galatia in the centre was allowed to retain its native organization of independent cantons, under the suzerainty of a pro-Roman chief, Deioteirus. Lycia and Cappadocia were similarly left as free client States. Far more important was Pompey's treatment of Syria. This district, once the proud centre of the Seleucid Empire, had latterly fallen into sad decline. For a while it had even passed under the sway of Tigranes of Armenia, until Lucullus had restored its independence. Now, however, Lucullus' policy was to be reversed; for, though the Syrians were guilty of no hostility against Rome, Pompey's mind was made up. In 65 he sent ahead his lieutenant, Gabinius, to keep watch on the country. Next year he followed himself, and, taking up his head-quarters at Antioch, proceeded to dictate the terms of annexation to the helpless Seleucid monarch. The only serious trouble arose over Palestine, a former dependency of Syria which nearly a century before had achieved its liberation under the gallant leadership of the Maccabees. Their successors had sadly degenerated, and bloody disputes had arisen over the high-priesthood, now the sovereign position at Jerusalem. Hyrcanus, the legitimate holder of the office, after having been ejected by his brother Aristobulus, had returned with the aid of an Edomite prince named Antipater, and was now blockading his rival on the Temple Hill. In 63, when Pompey marched on the city, he was admitted by Hyrcanus' supporters; but Aristobulus held out and a regular siege followed. At the end of three months the walls were breached and many priests were massacred around the temple altar. Pompey, though forbearing to touch the sacred treasure, insisted on entering the Holy of Holies; and Jewish omen-mongers noted with satisfaction that from that moment his luck turned. Hyrcanus was left to rule as high-priest over a somewhat diminished Palestine; and Antipater's son, the famous Herod, eventually succeeded in his place. Jewish independence, however, was merely nominal. The country was placed under the supervision of the governor of the Syrian province; and, what was peculiarly obnoxious to this freedom-loving race, an annual tribute was levied.

The imposition of financial burdens, even upon autonomous allies who were normally immune, was a significant feature of Pompey's settlement; and as a result the revenue from the East was multiplied as much as five-fold. Apart from this he seems to have followed the traditional policy of *laissez-faire* and interfered very little in existing methods of government. Backward States were left under their native kings. Cities with democratic institutions were permitted to retain them. Much, however, was done to encourage rural populations to concentrate in towns; and no less than thirty-five new foundations were officially ascribed to Pompey himself. The motive of this policy was no doubt to promote the commercial advantage of his capitalist friends rather than to spread Roman ideas; for the culture of the new towns—as of the old—remained essentially Greek. In most there were Greek schools. In many, lecture-halls, gymnasia, and theatres. Above all, the debased Greek lingo called the *Koiné* was spoken throughout the Levant. Roman governors used to translate their edicts; and Pilate, writing the superscription of the Cross, wrote in Greek as well as Hebrew and Latin. Thus, for better or for worse, the eastern half of the Empire was destined to remain intellectually, morally, and to a large extent politically distinct from the European half.

Pompey's work was now complete and he began his homeward journey. It was a sort of leisurely rehearsal for the triumph he was to celebrate with unprecedented splendour when he reached the capital. He was bringing with him enormous quantities of booty wrung from the nine hundred cities which he boasted to have captured, together with a train of hostages said to have included one hundred and sixty-two princes. On his voyage he put in at Rhodes, Athens, and other Greek cities, where he listened with patronizing condescension to complimentary poems and addresses. The slowness of his progress roused expectation in Italy to a fever-pitch. Whether he would lay down his tremendous powers with equanimity or, like Sulla, assume an autocratic authority, no one could tell; but, before we can fully appreciate the situation we must survey the events which had taken place at Rome during the great man's lengthy absence.

V. THE SITUATION AT ROME

Though the political situation at Rome was as confused as ever, one or two tendencies were now more or less clearly defined. Sulla's attempt to stereotype the oligarchical regime had completely broken down. With every year that passed the Senate was losing its grip upon affairs; and the violence of the mob and its demagogic leaders was becoming more and more of a menace. The result was that decent folk, both among the senatorial nobility and the equestrian *bourgeoisie*, had come to feel that if revolution was to be avoided they must forget the old party quarrel and close their ranks. The idea of such a 'Union of the Orders' made a special appeal to Cicero, who threw all the ardour of his idealistic temperament into the cause; and in particular it became his object to enlist the absent Pompey in its support. Pompey's political views, as we have said, were a very uncertain factor. He had begun his career as a Sullan. During his consulship he had turned democrat; and it was now the desire of every party at Rome either to win his adhesion or else to fortify its own position against the unpredictable consequences of his return. Of such parties or political groups three can be distinguished—first, the conservative majority in the Senate, led by the stalwart reactionary, Catulus; second, the knights, sometimes inclining under Cicero's direction to the senatorial side, sometimes swayed by the shifting opportunism of their great magnate Crassus to continue their traditional support of the Marian democrats; third, the Marian democrats themselves, now beginning to rally round the leadership of Caesar, and normally backed by the voting strength of the mob. Such groups were neither clear-cut nor exclusive; for the individuals which composed them might hang together on one issue and part company on another. Nor, of course, did there exist at Rome anything which in our modern sense could be called a party-organization. Political leaders gathered what following they could by various methods. Aristocrats could normally count on the votes of poor retainers; ex-generals on the loyalty of their discharged veterans. In recent years, too, there had been attempts to make political use of the working-men's clubs or guilds—associations formed between men of a common craft for purposes of religious worship or to defray the funeral expenses of their needy participants; but in 64 the Senate, foreseeing the danger of their exploitation, had suppressed all but a few. Still more undesirable was the now prevalent habit of hiring gangs of idle hooligans who patrolled the streets and intimidated the electorate by the rough and ready method of knocking their employer's opponents on the head.

In such a condition of anarchy and violence lay the opportunity of political adventurers, who, in the hope of retrieving their own personal fortunes, were prepared to plunge the whole State itself into the throes of revolution. Among the most dangerous of these was a certain Lucius Sergius Catilina, an aristocrat by birth and regarded even by Cicero himself as a respectable person, yet utterly unscrupulous and hopelessly in debt. In 66, on returning from the governorship of Africa, he found himself threatened with prosecution for maladministration, and thus baulked of standing for the consulship on which he had set his heart. In reckless desperation he planned (or is said to have planned) a secret coup for the following year. On January 1st of 65 the incoming consuls were to be assassinated and the whole country plunged into chaos. The Senate, however, got timely information, and nothing came of the plot. Indeed, the likelihood is that the whole tale was a mare's nest. For though Piso, his chief lieutenant, was sent out of harm's way to govern Hither Spain, Catiline himself remained at large;[1] and both Crassus and Caesar, whom rumour declared to have been privy to the plot, continued openly to support him.

In the following year, when the magisterial elections for 63 came round, Catiline stood for the consulship. With aid of his two powerful backers his chances seemed good; but Cicero was now in the lists against him, and after a hot contest Catiline was defeated, Cicero and Mark Antony's uncle, Caius Antonius, heading the poll.

The leading figure in this critical year 63 is better known to us than any character in antiquity. Besides his speeches and

[1] Even Cicero continued on good terms with him and thought seriously of defending him in the extortion trial.

philosophic treatises we have much of Cicero's private correspondence; and it reveals a very charming personality—
courteous, considerate, dignified, and witty. Deeply imbued
though he was with the influences of Greek thought and letters,
he nevertheless retained the old Roman qualities, now more
common in the middle-class stratum of Italian society from
which he had sprung than among the aristocracy proper—a
high moral standard of life, an earnest devotion to duty, and
an unswerving fidelity to the Republican tradition. On the
other hand, he laboured under the parvenu's weakness of
regarding those above him in the social scale with exaggerated
respect. He never seems—even in his letters—to have been
quite at his ease with the great hereditary nobles. It may be
that his tiresome habit of harping on his personal achievements
was nothing more than his method of concealing a latent
self-distrust; and certainly in a man so naturally sensitive
it is the more creditable that he should have braced himself
to acts and decisions requiring the highest degree of moral
courage.

Even at the outset of his year of office it was clear that
there was trouble ahead. For the rebuff of Catiline's defeat
had by no means damped the democrats, and in the last days
of 64 a scheme had been launched by a young tribune called
Rullus, which plainly had Caesar behind it. It was proposed
to set up a new Board of Land Commissioners with five years'
tenure of office and far-reaching powers. All the remaining
public land in Italy was to be parcelled out among needy
citizens, and more, if necessary, was to be purchased from
private owners. Funds were to be found for the latter purpose,
partly from the tribute of Pompey's new provinces, partly
from the plunder of his wars; and, as a sop to the great commander, his veterans were to receive their due share of allotments. Since, however, Pompey himself was debarred by
absence from election to the Board, the credit for this generous
provision would go not to him but to its democrat authors.
The subtlety of the manœuvre was not lost on Cicero, who
desired above all things to avoid giving Pompey offence. He
threw all the weight of his authority and eloquence against
the proposal, and in the upshot it was dropped.

AUGUSTUS

VESPASIAN

The democrats' next move was less ambitious. With a view to testing the legitimacy of the Senate's ultimate decree—a weapon which they feared might one day be used against themselves—they proceeded to impeach an old man called Rabirius for having killed Saturninus forty years before on the strength of it. The antiquated form of trial they adopted led to an entertaining sequel. It was held in the Campus Martius before the Centuriate Assembly, and in the course of proceedings the red flag, which was still flown at its sessions, was suddenly lowered—a signal which in ancient times had given warning of an enemy's approach; and the mystified Assembly broke up. Caesar and his democrat following took the jest in good part and abandoned the trial. But as the year wore on it became more and more evident that their agitations were making no headway. The seal was set on their failure when the autumn elections came round. Catiline was once again a candidate for the consulship. More deeply in debt than ever, he was desperate now. He had gathered round him a group of associates in no better case; and there was wild talk of cancelling all debts and proscribing the rich. Cicero's authority appeared their chief obstacle, and there were threats against his life. On polling day he appeared with a cuirass under his cloak. The electors were impressed; and, though Catiline posed as the champion of the poor, the votes once more went against him.

Catiline's mind was made up. Sending his lieutenant, Manlius, to raise troops in Etruria preparatory to open revolt, he himself began to arrange for a simultaneous *coup d'état* in Rome. The city was to be fired at various points, Cicero assassinated, and the reins of government seized. On the night of October 20th Crassus handed Cicero an anonymous warning. On the 22nd, at Cicero's request, the Senate passed the 'ultimate decree', which, in the absence of a regular police or standing army, was essential to the organization of national defence. The outbreak was expected on October 28th; but nothing occurred. Was it possible that the danger had been exaggerated? On November 6th came another warning of an attempt on Cicero's life. Two days later he summoned the Senate. Before a crowded house—in which Catiline sat haggard and aloof in gloomy isolation—he unfolded the story of this latest plot in the first speech of his famous series. That night, leaving Lentulus and Cethegus to continue preparations in the city, Catiline set out to join Manlius in his camp at Faesulae in the hills above Florence. Both men were proclaimed public enemies and large rewards offered for information against them.

Conclusive evidence of their guilt was still lacking. But in early December this came. At the moment there happened to be in the city two representatives of the Allobroges who had been sent from Transalpine Gaul to obtain redress against the Roman governor. During their visit they had been secretly approached and advised to engineer an insurrection in Catiline's support. Their hearts misgiving them, they communicated the fact to one of Cicero's friends. They were told to get the treasonable proposal in writing and set off quietly homewards. At the Mulvian bridge outside the city they were waylaid and brought back under guard. The Senate was hurriedly called. Lentulus and Cethegus were summoned. Confronted with the incriminating letters, they were dumbfounded. Denial was useless. Arms had been found at their houses, and they and their accomplices were laid under arrest.

Two days later (December 5th) a full-dress debate was staged in the Temple of Concord. On Cicero's instructions the speeches were taken down in shorthand. The general verdict of the speakers was for execution of the prisoners. Caesar, who, as Catiline's old supporter, was in a delicate position, took the ingenious line that the death-sentence might provoke a dangerous reaction, and it would be wiser to keep the prisoners in custody for life. The House was visibly impressed. Then Cicero rose. He was prepared, he said, as consul to do his duty. Cato, an uncompromising champion of the old regime, wound up the debate with a vigorous demand for the death-penalty. The motion was carried by a large majority.

Cicero was resolved to leave no loophole for an escape or a rescue. Though the winter daylight was fading when the House broke up, he gave orders for immediate execution. Under his own escort the prisoners were conducted to the

State dungeons at the foot of the Capitol and there strangled. A huge crowd was waiting in the dusk when he emerged and with simple dignity pronounced the single word *Vixerunt* ('They have lived'). It was the proudest moment of his whole career. He had saved the State. But, as his critics lost no time in pointing out, he had put Roman citizens to death without a formal trial; and this was by no means the last he was to hear of it.

VI. POMPEY'S RETURN

In January of the following year (62) the forces of Manlius and Catiline were overwhelmed at Pistoria; and, both leaders being killed, it merely remained to round up a few surviving members of the gang. The emergency therefore was over; but the democrats, wishing to discredit the Senate's handling of it, put forward a proposal that Pompey should be immediately recalled. The Senate was justifiably indignant, and when Caesar, now praetor, gave his support to the idea they decided to depose him from office. The mob, enthusiastic in his defence, surrounded his house and clamoured for him to lead an insurrection. But with characteristic dislike of mob violence Caesar would have nothing to do with them; and his self-restraint was rewarded by a withdrawal of the decree.

The rest of the year passed in an atmosphere of anxious suspense. What would happen on Pompey's return remained Pompey's secret; but it was ominous that he sent home a request for the postponement of the annual elections—a request which no ordinary magistrate would ever have ventured to make, and which was accordingly refused. The interval of waiting was enlivened by an unsavoury scandal in high society which, indirectly at least, was to have important consequences. Caesar had recently been elected High Pontiff and in December a festival of the Bona Dea was held at his official residence. During its rites, which women alone might attend, a notorious young rake named Clodius was discovered in the building disguised in female clothes. As tongues naturally wagged, Caesar divorced his wife, declaring (in the famous phrase) that 'she should have been above suspicion'. Meanwhile, on the score of sacrilege, an inquiry was held at which Cicero's evidence came near to upsetting Clodius' fabricated alibi.   The offence which he thus gave to the young scoundrel was one day to cost him dear.

On the eve of the year 61 Pompey and his army landed at Brundisium; and the enigma of his intentions was at last to be resolved.   Every one was expecting him to set himself at the head of his legions and march on the capital.   But he did nothing of the sort.   He quietly ordered them to parade before him, addressed them in a few gracious words of gratitude, and then—told them to disperse to their homes.   The motives of his great refusal are unknown to us.   Good-nature no doubt played its part; for Pompey was not the man to 'wade through slaughter to a throne'; but it is probable too that with characteristic vanity he overrated his powers and imagined that by his prestige alone he could carry all before him.

If such were his calculations a bitter disappointment was in store; for, his troops once disbanded and his uniform doffed, Pompey was incapable of holding his own in the intricate manœuvres of the party struggle.   His triumph indeed was celebrated with unprecedented splendour; but men who had so recently angled for his favour went out of their way to belittle his achievements.   At his first appearance in the Senate Crassus, while lauding Cicero to the skies, never even so much as mentioned them.   The conservatives, led by Cato, did all they could to thwart his wishes.   His scheme for providing his veterans with land-allotments was talked down in the Assembly.   His provisional settlement of the Asiatic provinces was debated clause by clause, and after much dilatory debate was left without official ratification.   Meanwhile Caesar, the one man whose assistance might have been invaluable, was no longer on the spot.   Since the Catilinarian conspiracy his position at Rome had been distinctly embarrassing.   Electioneering expenses had left him heavily in debt; and the best way out of his difficulties was to undertake a provincial post. It may well be, too, that he was jealous of Pompey's prestige and reckoned that, if left to fend for himself for a while, the 'Great Man' would come to set a higher value on his own co-operation.   However that may be, in the summer of 61 Caesar set out to take up the governorship of Further Spain.

CHAPTER XVI

THE RISE OF CAESAR

THERE was clearly in Caesar's personality some unique quality of magnetism. Few even of his opponents were wholly insensible to the spell of it. Among his friends he could count men of every type and station, winning subordinates in particular by his generous loyalty. The mob idolized him. To soldiers his mere presence at their side was a guarantee of victory. His way with women was irresistible.

He himself was conscious of his power and used it to the full. Mastery of men was a necessity of his nature. He would rather, he said, be head of a small country town than play second fiddle at Rome. At what stage of his career he consciously aimed at the monarchy is nevertheless hard to determine. For he was a realist rather than a dreamer, living much in the moment and content to concentrate on the immediate task in hand. His political conceptions, moreover, developed very gradually; and he does not seem to have troubled his head much over problems until it was within his power to deal with them effectively. In short, unlike Alexander, he reserved his strength and cultivated his natural powers by a lifelong habit of self-discipline. The very style of his writings reflects the quality of his mind; for he goes straight to the point, wasting no words on effect or embellishment. It was perhaps no unimportant factor in the formation of his character that, though later trained in the full Hellenistic culture, he began his studies under an Italian tutor, a native of Transpadane Gaul. For, take him for all in all, he was a true son of Rome. He possessed the old Roman abstemiousness in food or drink; and though this was in part a precaution for a health not too robust (for he was subject to some sort of fit or seizure) he was capable, on campaign, of extraordinary fatigues, taking his sleep in travelling coach or litter in order to waste no moment of the journey. Like most Romans, too, he was not scrupulous or squeamish about the means of attaining his ends. He would slaughter or mutilate rebellious Gauls as a warning to their fellows; and to satisfy a political grudge he abandoned Cicero to the mean vengeance of his minion Clodius. Where clemency, on the other hand, seemed more repaying, his generosity was notable, and he never followed Sulla's example of massacring political opponents. During the early stages of his career he was undeniably canny, feeling his way forward with deliberate caution and careful to compromise his future by no false step. Yet, once he was resolved upon his goal, nothing could equal the swiftness of his decisions, the lightning rapidity of his movements, or the reckless audacity of his initiative. Confidence in his own star gave him a moral ascendancy over a more timorous foe, and in the event his calculations, however rash, were seldom falsified. It was this singular combination of cool judgement and fearless enterprise, of patience and impetuosity, self-control and self-assertion, opportunism and statesmanship that won for Caesar not merely the mastery of the Roman world, but the claim to have laid the foundation of the greatest imperial experiment in history.

I. CAESAR'S CONSULSHIP, 59 B.C.

Spain was not unknown to Caesar. He had served there as quaestor, and among his intimate friends was a Spanish engineer named Balbus, now a member of his staff. Sympathy with the natives was therefore to be expected of him, and he not merely took their part against the extortionate methods of Italian moneylenders, but also improved the political institutions of the great trading city of Cadiz. On the other hand, in undertaking a campaign against the Lusitanian tribes his motives were probably less creditable. The chance of testing his powers of military leadership can scarcely have been unwelcome to a man of his ambitions, and of even greater importance to his future career was the replenishment of his pockets.

He left Spain shortly before election time in the autumn of 60 B.C.; and having set his heart on the consulship for the following year he forwent his title to a triumph in order that he might enter the city in a private capacity and so comply with the rules of candidature. His twelve months' absence had done much to smooth his path. For one thing, the coalition between the knights and the Senate had almost broken down over a financial disagreement. In making their bid for the right to collect the revenues in Asia, one of the big equestrian syndicates had overestimated the probable yield. They therefore asked for a rebate on their original bargain, and Crassus, as their spokesman, deliberately named a sum to which the more conservative senators could not possibly agree. Despite Cicero's efforts at compromise the rift had rapidly widened; and the knights were now looking round for some anti-senatorial who, if elected to office, would implement their demand. At the same time Pompey too was disgusted with the Senate's refusal to provide for his veterans or ratify his eastern settlement; and only an inveterate dislike of Crassus prevented him from making common cause with the knights. Here then was Caesar's chance to unite the divided forces of the Senate's opponents by pledging himself to redress their respective grievances. Negotiations were undertaken as the result of which both Pompey and Crassus agreed to back Caesar for the consulship, and thus was formed a coalition of the three great political 'bosses', which is known to history as the First Triumvirate.

Caesar was duly elected, and in January 59 entered on his office. Though his colleague Bibulus was a stupid, short-sighted, and extremely obstinate senatorial, he himself with ᵗhe full democrat vote at his back was so strong that sweeping ιeforms seemed in prospect. But Caesar was not the man to waste his effort. With only twelve months of office ahead of him he was in no position to secure permanence for revolutionary measures; and most likely he did not as yet see his way clearly to the solution of the political problem. So apart from a minor change in the procedure of jury-courts, a strengthening of the laws against provincial extortion, and a new and salutary innovation of posting a daily summary of senatorial business in the Forum, Caesar made no use of his opportunities for statesmanlike reform. His only important legislation was concerned with making good the bargain with his two powerful backers. First, a Bill was put forward—much on the lines of Rullus' abortive proposal—to furnish land-allotments for Pompey's veterans and impoverished citizens generally. In the Senate the terms of the Bill were bitterly contested; and Bibulus, finding argument useless, announced that he would 'watch the sky' for unpropitious omens, and so bring all public business to a standstill. Caesar, ignoring this farcical abuse of an obsolete superstition, proceeded to submit the Bill directly to the Assembly's vote. There were ugly scenes in the Forum. Bibulus had a bucket of filth poured over him and was knocked off the rostrum. There was no regular police force at Rome; and the city being full of his ex-soldiers, Pompey held the whip-hand. If the opposition took the sword, he significantly remarked, he would take both sword and buckler. The threat had its desired effect. Resistance collapsed. Many prominent senators, including Cicero, left Rome. Bibulus, shutting himself up in his house, spent the eight remaining months of office in his futile vigil. For all the impression he made he might just as well have abdicated; and wags, who saw the humour of the situation, dated their documents 'in the consulship of Julius and Caesar'.

For the rest of the year Caesar's position was virtually that of an autocrat. Acting through the Assembly alone and without further reference to the Senate's authority, he satisfied the grievance of the equestrian syndicate by remitting one-third of their contract. In similar fashion he carried through the ratification of Pompey's eastern settlement; and, the requirements of his two great partners having thus been loyally fulfilled, it remained for him to take steps to secure his own future position. The Senate had of set purpose allotted to the consuls of this year two provincial posts of minor importance. Such an arrangement would have suited Caesar but ill; and he insisted on receiving nothing less than Illyria and Cisalpine Gaul conjointly, with a tenure of five years. But an opportunity of active campaigning was what he most desired. At this moment, as we shall later see, Transalpine Gaul was in a condition of great unsettlement; and here, therefore, seemed to lie a golden chance of emulating in Europe the conquests which Pompey had achieved in the East. Either because they knew refusal would be useless or else because they hoped thereby to keep their arch-enemy well employed, the Senate yielded, and Caesar's command was extended to cover the existing province of Narbonensis—and in his own mind at least the whole unconquered hinterland of Gaul.

The prolongation of his official status gave Caesar welcome security against political attack; but, what was less satisfactory, it also involved three years' absence from the capital, and it was essential to find a lieutenant to represent his interests there. His choice fell—oddly enough after the Bona Dea affair—upon no other than the notorious Clodius. Caesar's wishes were the wishes of his two great partners also; and with such powerful backing this scoundrel found no difficulty in obtaining the tribuneship for the year 58. He at once embarked on a reckless programme of demagogic legislation. The law for the suppression of workmen's clubs was to be repealed, the corn-dole distributed gratis, and the repetition of Bibulus' obstructive methods rendered illegal. But the real purpose of Clodius' elevation to power was to hold the lists against his great employers' senatorial opponents. Of these Cicero and Cato were by far the most dangerous; and there can be little doubt that he was given a free hand to deal with them both.

Clodius himself had by no means forgotten his old grudge against Cicero, and the prospect of revenge was sweet. In the early spring of 58 he produced a Bill whereby any one responsible for the execution of Roman citizens without trial should be declared an outlaw. Cicero, realizing at once that the Bill was aimed at him, lost his nerve completely and went round making abject appeals for sympathy and protection. The Senate was impotent. Many of the knights donned mourning as a token of their sorrow; but all knew that the orator's fate depended on the Triumvirs, and the Triumvirs made no move. In the middle of March came a further Bill outlawing Cicero specifically by name. On friends' advice he had already fled to southern Italy, and now he crossed over into Macedonia, where the friendly governor gave him a refuge. The helplessness of the Senate seemed to set a seal on their political bankruptcy; and meanwhile their other most stalwart champion had been got out of the way in a more legitimate manner. The annexation of Cyprus had recently been decided on, and Clodius proposed Cato's name for the governorship. Cato was most reluctant to go, but his Stoic principles permitted no disobedience to the State's demands, and he went.

The senatorial party was thus left without effective leadership, and Clodius remained undisputed master of Rome. Armed gangs of hireling ruffians paraded the streets, and for the remainder of the year the city was subjected to a rule of sheer terrorism. Even Pompey was powerless; and meanwhile Caesar had plunged into a task of military conquest which for the ten succeeding years was to occupy the greater part of his thoughts and energies.

II. CAESAR IN GAUL, 58–55 B.C.

There can be little doubt that Caesar undertook the Gallic command, in the first instance, as a means of obtaining a large body of troops and of acquiring some greater experience in the art of handling them. But there is also much to show that he envisaged from the outset a deliberate scheme of conquest. Such unprovoked aggression was something new in the history of Roman imperialism (for even Pompey's annexations had been in some sense a natural sequel to the Mithridatic War); and in publishing an account of his campaigns Caesar was clearly anxious to justify this new departure. What were his real motives, beyond a desire for personal distinction, is difficult to say. It is noteworthy, however, how careful he was to pose as the champion of the Gauls against the menace of German encroachments; and it is at least possible that on his journeys to and from his Spanish province he had gained a favourable impression of the Celtic peoples and foresaw how much the Empire might gain by the incorporation of so virile a stock. What remains certain is that, having once his hand to the undertaking, he realized to the full the importance of completing it; and instead of returning to Rome to reap the advantage of his first spectacular achievements, he was prepared to spend a second spell of five years in consolidating the vast area which he had won for the Roman realm.

When in the year 58 he first assumed control of the Transalpine province, its frontier still ran, as in the previous century, from Tolosa in the west to the upper waters of the Rhône

TRINOBANTES
CATUVELLAUNI
Verulamium
USIPETES
TENCTERI
SUGAMBRI
MENAPII
EBURONES
MORINI ATREBATES NERVII
Portus Itius ADUATUCI Aduatuca
Coblentz
BELGAE UBII
R. Somme
AMBIANI TREVERI
Samarobriva Ardennes Mts. R. Rhine
R. Aisne
BELLOVACI SUESSIONES REMI R. Meuse
R. Marne SUEBI
CARNUTES R. Seine
AREMORICA SENONES Agedincum LINGONES
Cenabum
VENETI
R. Loire Alesia
Noviodunum AEDUI
Avaricum Bibracte
Gorgobina SEQUANI HELVETII
BITURIGES L. of Geneva
Gergovia ALLOBROGES
ARVERNI
R. Rhone
Uxellodunum

AQUITANI
Tolosa
Massilia
Pyrenees

☐ Area of Province in 58 B C
---- Route taken by Helvetii

CAESAR'S CAMPAIGNS IN GAUL

in the north-east, where it included the powerful, but somewhat disgruntled, folk of the Allobroges. North of these
again, the Aedui, though lying outside the province proper,
had long cultivated friendly relations with Rome; and in the
year 61 they had appealed for assistance against their neighbours the Sequani and Arverni. Pressure from this quarter
had recently been intensified by the arrival of some German
adventurers called the Suebi, who under their chief Ariovistus
had crossed the Rhine at the invitation of the Sequani, and,
having once arrived there, had insisted on settling in the plains
of Alsace. The Romans temporized, and Caesar during his
consulship had actually recognized Ariovistus as a 'friend' of
the Republic. The fact was that a still more urgent menace
required to be dealt with first. In Central Europe a westward
movement of barbarian peoples was once again in progress;
and driven by the pressure on their rear the Helvetii of North
Switzerland decided to migrate into Gaul. Two years had
been spent in making their arrangements. Wagons were
procured, supplies of corn got ready; and finally in the spring
of 58 they set out—an enormous host nearly 400,000 strong,
including women and children—upon their adventurous
march. After making a formal request for leave to do so,
they were preparing to traverse the north-east corner of the
Roman province when suddenly Caesar struck. Setting out
from Italy and covering the distance of nearly 700 miles in
little over a week, he arrived in time to beat them back
from the crossing of the Rhône. When, however, they turned
to take an alternative route through the country of the Aedui
he made no attempt to stop them; and it was not until they
reached the neighbourhood of Bibracte, the Aeduan capital,
that he followed on their tracks, and there cut them up
decisively. The remnant, scarcely more than a quarter of
their number, was shepherded back into Switzerland.

The incident had served Caesar's purpose to perfection. It
had enabled him to move into the very heart of Gaul and
(what was still more important) to appear there as champion
of the Celtic population against the menace of an alien invasion. The grateful natives implored him to complete the
good work by crushing Ariovistus and his Sueban warriors.

A brief campaign sufficed to drive these intruders back beyond the Rhine. But at the approach of winter, though Caesar himself returned to his administrative duties in Cisalpine Gaul, he left his legions quartered in the country of the Sequani—an ominous decision which the northern tribes of the interior noted with unconcealed alarm.

Beyond the line of the Seine and the Marne Rivers lay a large group of tribes, some of Celtic and some of German blood, but all known under the common title of Belgae. Among these, preparations were at once begun for the expulsion of the Roman invader; and with the return of spring (57) Caesar decided to take the offensive. A pretext was once again provided by the friendly overtures of the Remi, who hoped with Roman aid to get the better of their neighbours. Crossing the Aisne, Caesar found himself faced on the northern bank by an enormous Belgic host nearly 300,000 strong. He succeeded in driving them back; and inter-tribal jealousies—which now, as so often, were to prove the undoing of the Gauls—enabled him to conquer them piecemeal. Quickly pushing north-westwards towards the English Channel he received the submission of the Suessiones, Bellovaci, and Ambiani. He had thus driven a wedge between the remaining Belgae on his east and the tribes of Aremorica (now Normandy and Brittany) upon his west; and he chose to deal with the Belgae first. Their strongest tribe, the Nervii, gave him a tough fight, surprising his legions during the construction of a camp; but the characteristic clemency with which he treated the survivors of this Celtic tribe stood in marked contrast to the severity meted out to their neighbours the Aduatuci. These were reputedly the descendants of the Cimbric warriors who had settled in the district half a century before when their comrades marched away south; and when Caesar followed up his victory over them by selling their entire population into slavery the act was clearly a broad hint that Germans were Rome's enemies and Gauls her friends. Meanwhile the in-activity of the central and south-west tribes afforded proof that such a policy was bearing fruit. In Aremorica the younger Crassus with a single legion had won the submission of the Veneti and others; and winter quarters for the legions were selected in the neighbouring valley of the Loire. Thus by his masterly strategy Caesar had almost completed the encirclement of the central districts, which he had hitherto left untouched; and their surrender now seemed merely a matter of time.

The work of subjugation, however, had been too rapid to be permanent; and in the spring of 56 the Veneti, assisted by two Belgic tribes, the Menapii and Morini, came out in revolt. It was no easy matter to hunt down this ·maritime enemy among the creeks and islands of the Loire mouth; and the organization of a fleet, already begun during the winter months under Decimus Brutus' supervision, proved a timely aid to their suppression. Meantime Caesar himself had marched up across the Seine and overawed the Belgic rebels, while the younger Crassus made a south-west sweep along the Aquitanian seaboard as far as the Pyrenees; and with this the conquest of Gaul might be regarded as more or less complete.

At Rome the significance of Caesar's triumph had been fully realized. That a decisive check had been set to the dreaded incursions from across the Rhine was a source of very genuine relief; and after his brilliant campaign of 57 the unprecedented compliment of a fortnight's celebrations had been decreed in his honour. Meanwhile, however, the effect of his withdrawal from the centre of affairs had proved disastrous. The party struggle had been revived in all its bitterness; and before we pursue the further fortunes of Caesar's Transalpine campaign we must pause to consider the political events which had been occurring at the capital.

III. ROME DURING CAESAR'S ABSENCE

On Caesar's departure for Gaul in 58 the unofficial Partnership of Three had not, of course, been dissolved; and during his absence it was understood that the other two great bosses should keep the political situation in control. Clodius' excesses, however, had so disgusted all decent folk that there was a marked reaction in the Senate's favour and an agitation was begun for Cicero's recall. The consuls chosen for the year 57 were favourable. Publius Sestius, one of the tribunes, went to Gaul to procure Caesar's sanction; and another tribune named Milo collected a gang of roughs to combat the violence of Clodius, who even after vacating office continued to parade the streets. Meanwhile public sympathy for Cicero was growing, and when in August a Bill was brought up for his recall men poured in from all parts of Italy to vote. Soon after, Cicero himself landed at Brundisium, and as he travelled up to Rome he received a regular ovation from the towns along the route. His vanity was flattered; and though disappointed at the compensation paid for the damage done to his various properties, he greatly enjoyed the luxury of harking on the retrospect of his year's martyrdom. The only thing to qualify his satisfaction was the pledge which Caesar had extracted from his brother Quintus that he himself would support the cause of the Triumvirate.

Meanwhile riots were no less frequent than ever; and perhaps the most deplorable feature of the situation was Pompey's complete failure to fulfil the role assigned to him of keeping order in the city. The rough-and-tumble of party politics was in fact too much for him, and only in some executive capacity could he hope to make himself felt. Soon after Cicero's recall, it is true, he had been given a commission, with proconsular power, to reorganize the food-supply of Rome; but the proposal to entrust him with a fleet and army had been quashed, and he was looking round for some alternative employment. Now it so happened that for some years past relations with Ptolemy Auletes, the ruling King of Egypt, had been greatly strained. Rumour declared that he had fraudulently suppressed his predecessor's will bequeathing the country to Rome; and it was only in return for an enormous bribe that Caesar during his consulship had accorded him official recognition. In the attempt to raise the money, Ptolemy had alienated his subjects; and in 57, being driven out from his kingdom, he had taken refuge at Rome. The task of restoring him would have suited Pompey's requirements perfectly, but with characteristic reticence he would not openly declare that he coveted the post. Demonstrations against his appointment were organized by Clodius, and, if tales were true, financed by Crassus himself. So the restoration of Ptolemy was indefinitely postponed, and Pompey's hopes were frustrated.

In short, not merely was the authority of the Triumvirate rapidly dwindling, but even the harmony between its members was more than a little strained. Without Caesar's moderating influence Pompey and Crassus were sure to fall out; and meanwhile the brilliance of Caesar's military achievements made Pompey doubly impatient at his own enforced inaction. Nor can it be seriously doubted that his approval had been given when in the spring of 56 Cicero came forward with a proposal for the repeal of Caesar's Land Act. This open affront was more than Caesar could brook. He was wintering, as usual, in his Cisalpine province and he acted swiftly. By the rules of his proconsular office he might not go to Rome; but he could make Rome come to him. In April accordingly there assembled at Lucca, the most southerly town within his jurisdiction, all the prominent politicians of the day— two hundred Senators, many magistrates, two proconsuls and, above all, Pompey and Crassus themselves. At a secret interview between the three great bosses their differences were settled, and they arranged to divide the administration of the Empire between them. Caesar's Gallic command was to be prolonged for another five years. Pompey and Crassus were to become consuls for 55, and thereafter were each to receive a similar term of proconsular power, Pompey in Further and Hither Spain and Crassus in Syria, both of which provinces involved the command of an army. Meanwhile Cicero, though not summoned to Lucca, was given a blunt reminder of his brother's pledge. He took the hint, and retired from politics and henceforth immersed himself—a disappointed man—in literary studies.

IV. CAESAR IN GAUL, 55–49 B.C.

The campaigns of 56 had completed, as we have seen, Caesar's mastery of Gaul, and the following year brought him a fresh opportunity of posing as the protector of its inhabitants against the German menace. For in the course of the winter a body of Tencteri and Eburones crossed the lower Rhine and pushed into the territory of Usipetes. Rebel Gauls joined them, and the critical situation seemed to call for drastic measures. An act of treachery on the part of the

Germans gave Caesar his excuse; and, trapping their leaders under cover of a parley, he proceeded to exterminate their entire company, putting even women and children to the sword. A small remnant, escaping to the east bank of the Rhine, found shelter among the Sugambri, and on the latters' refusal to surrender the fugitives Caesar bridged the river near Coblenz and ravaged their country. He then returned to organize an expedition into Britain.

Among the various motives which brought Caesar to this island a desire for exploration may well have played some part; for his writings bear witness to his observant interest in the customs of foreign folk. From Gallic traders, too, he must already have learnt something of the country's resources, and an exaggerated estimate of these may have suggested possibility of loot and tribute. In any case a pretext for invasion was provided by the suspicion that British chieftains had lent aid to rebel Gauls; and Caesar, for his part, was able to turn the tables by employing a loyal Belgic noble called Commius to sow dissension among the British tribes. In the campaign of 55, however, the lateness of the season prevented more than a bare reconnaissance. Landing near Deal in the face of severe opposition he advanced little more than ten miles inland before autumn compelled his return. But experience had been gained, and the havoc wrought by a gale upon his transports prompted the construction of flat-bottomed boats for the next year's campaign.

Owing to trouble in Illyria it was not till midsummer of 54 that he was able to rejoin his fleet at Portus Itius (now Wissant near Boulogne). Many merchant adventurers made the voyage with him; and his military force comprised five legions besides loyal Gallic auxiliaries. At the landing no enemy was to be seen; and the first resistance was encountered near the River Stour. Caesar's victorious pursuit was interrupted by news of a fresh disaster to his fleet and much time was wasted in beaching and entrenching the surviving vessels. Meanwhile Cassivellaunus, King of the Catuvellauni, the most powerful tribe in the island, had concentrated a formidable host; and a battle was again fought in the neighbourhood of the Stour before advance could be made to the Thames valley.

The Trinobantes of Essex, who had been won by Commius'
overtures, now tendered their submission; but the rest of the
Britons stood firm, and dogged the marching column with
guerrilla tactics. Still they failed to prevent the fording of
the Thames at Brentford and the territory of the Catuvellauni
(Hertfordshire) was entered. After a diversion into Essex
Caesar turned to assail their capital at Verulamium (now St.
Albans), and upon its fall Cassivellaunus sued for terms.
The situation in Gaul was causing Caesar anxiety and the
offer of hostages and tribute was gladly accepted. Payment,
however, was soon discontinued; and the expedition, if not a
failure, had no permanent results.

On his return to Gaul, Caesar found the country seething
with discontent. Bad harvests had rendered his corn-requisi-
tions exceedingly burdensome to the natives; and as a result of
the shortage he was himself obliged to distribute his troops in
widely scattered camps. Feeling somewhat uneasy, he delayed his usual departure for Cisalpine Gaul; and it was well
he did so. For Indutiomarus, chief of the Treveri, was secretly
stirring up revolt among the neighbouring tribes; and, as a
result, the Eburones under Ambiorix suddenly attacked the
camp of Sabinus and Cotta at Aduatuca. Finding themselves
cut off, the Romans rashly accepted an offer of safe conduct to
the nearest legionary post, some fifty miles away, but on the
march they were surrounded in a wooded valley and all but a
few wiped out. Encouraged by this success, the Nervii laid
siege to the camp of Quintus, Cicero's brother; and only by a
forced march did Caesar himself arrive in the nick of time to
save it. But the blow to Roman prestige was so serious that
he decided to winter in Gaul. The next twelve months were
spent in crushing out the revolt. Its ringleader, Indutiomarus, lost his life during an attack on Labienus' camp near
the modern Sedan; Ambiorix was hunted into the wooded hills
of the Ardennes; and Caesar harried the lands of his tribesmen,
the Eburones, with such brutal ferocity that thousands must
have starved.

The severity of such measures, though apparently successful
in restoring tranquillity, had in reality awoken a new spirit
of resistance in an unexpected quarter. Hitherto tribal

jealousies had played into Caesar's hands, and more than anything else the dissension of his enemies had made their subjugation possible. But now there arose a leader capable of organizing resistance on something like a national scale. In the early months of 52, while Caesar was still busy in Cisalpine Gaul, a young noble of the Arverni, Vercingetorix by name, was secretly laying his plans. Many tribes of the south and centre, which had hitherto remained inactive, entered into league with him; and one winter day the Carnutes struck the first blow by attacking the Roman trade depot at Cenabum (now Orleans) and massacring every foreigner in the place. By the time that Caesar reached the area of revolt he found that the Bituriges of central Gaul had also joined it; and he proceeded to lay siege to their capital, Avaricum (the modern Bourges). In the attempt to relieve it Vercingetorix adopted the most ruthless tactics. He was a stern disciplinarian, torturing and even mutilating to enforce his authority; and realizing the superiority of the Romans in the field, he compelled the Gauls to burn homes, barns, villages, and everything in the hopes of starving them out. Thus the siege of Avaricum was carried on in the centre of a smoking wilderness; but Caesar's men insisted on pressing the assault, and, when it succeeded, not a human being found within the walls was spared.

Caesar's next move against Gergovia, the almost impregnable stronghold of Arverni, failed; and, seeing this, fresh tribes came out for the rebel cause. Amongst them were the Aedui, who, though Rome's traditional allies, were weary of the heavy strain of supplying corn to the legions. It was at Alesia in their territory that Vercingetorix chose to form his base; and thence he continued by well-planned raids and wholesale destruction of grain-stores to wear the Romans down. Never perhaps had Caesar stood in a more critical position. For even his communications with Italy were interrupted, and his infantry were ill-adapted to meet these guerrilla tactics. But he rose to the emergency, enlisted German cavalry from beyond the Rhine, and with their aid drove back his elusive enemy into Alesia. As the approaches to this hill-top fortress were too steep for direct assault he decided to draw vast lines of circumvallation round it and so starve the garrison out. They had already reached the end of their resources and had actually driven their noncombatants from the town when an enormous host of confederate Gauls arrived to its relief. After a desperate struggle upon two fronts the Romans forced the capitulation of the garrison, and to save his fellows' lives Vercingetorix delivered himself up. With this the back of the revolt was broken, and in the year 51 it merely remained for Caesar to stamp out the resistance of the Bituriges and Bellovaci, and capture one last fortress at Uxellodunum. When this town surrendered he ordered the survivors to be turned adrift with their right hands amputated.

Of the details of Caesar's settlement of Gaul we unfortunately know little; nor had he now many months in which to complete his work. Beyond question, however, his policy was liberal and conciliatory. There were no confiscations of land. The tribute demanded was moderate, and the tribes were left to manage their local affairs. Roman citizenship was conferred on many chiefs and other loyal individuals. A legion of Gallic warriors, raised during the war, was similarly rewarded; and every encouragement was given to the wilder spirits to enlist in auxiliary regiments. From all we know of him, in short, it is clear that Caesar meant Gaul to be absorbed into the imperial organism, rather than treated as mere material for commercial exploitation; and, if it was left to his successors to develop the civilization of this most valuable province, it is significant of the success of Caesar's pacification that even during the turmoil of the ensuing Civil War the Gauls made no effort to recover their lost liberty.

V. EVENTS AT ROME, 56–50 B.C.

The day when Caesar's Gallic command would come to an end was now looming close ahead, and what would happen when he should come home from his wars was an issue upon which unquestionably hung the Empire's fate. But before we can consider this prospect more closely we must first turn to see what had been happening at Rome since the conference at Lucca.

At the elections of 55, amid scenes of great disorder and in the teeth of strong senatorial opposition, Pompey and Crassus had been duly elected consuls. Their next step, in accordance with the Luccan programme, had been to secure for themselves the allotment of proconsular commands in Spain and Syria respectively. When it came to the point, however, Pompey showed small desire to go to his province. No laurels were to be won there, and when his consulship expired he lingered on indefinitely in Italy, as though thinking by virtue of his very presence to keep what remained of his old authority and waiting in his muddle-headed way for something to turn up. Crassus, on the other hand, hurried off to Syria even before the proper terms of his proconsulship began. As a set-off to Caesar's exploits he had dreams of Eastern conquest; and to this prince among financiers the fabulous riches of Parthia seem to have offered a tempting bait.

It had been more than a century earlier that the Parthians, a tribe of Scythian marauders hailing from the shores of the Caspian, had wrested Mesopotamia from the Seleucid realm. Through contact with the Greek cities, long since founded there by Alexander, they soon came to adopt a debased form of Hellenistic culture; but they had lost none of their ancestral quality as fighters and their mounted archers were accounted the best cavalry in the world. The aggressive policy of their monarchs was a menace to which Rome would have been wise to attend; but Phraates' offer of an agreed frontier had, as we have seen, been rejected by Pompey. The opportunity of conciliation did not recur. His successor Orodes had begun to encroach on Armenia; and Gabinius, the recent governor of Syria, had planned punitive measures. On private instructions from Pompey, however, he had undertaken the alternative task of restoring Ptolemy Auletes to Egypt. Thus Crassus was provided with a ready-made pretext for hostilities against Parthia, and immediately on his arrival in the spring of 54 he set out into Mesopotamia.

During that year he crossed the Euphrates and ravaged much of the country beyond it. No serious opposition was encountered, and after a winter spent in Syria he returned to the attack in 53. Crossing the Euphrates once more he pushed east across the plains, till in the neighbourhood of Carrhae he was suddenly attacked by immense hordes of Parthian horsemen. His own cavalry was inadequate to protect the hollow square into which he formed his infantry; and the enemy archers, cantering round at a safe distance, rained a terrible shower upon their helpless ranks. Retreat through the night exposed the struggling column to fresh persecutions. Only a tiny remnant, under Cassius the quaestor, escaped, and Crassus himself was treacherously cut down at a parley. When the messengers of the victory reached King Orodes' court, the *Bacchae* of Euripides was being performed; and in place of the dummy head of the mythological Pentheus, the actor—with a horrible touch of realism—substituted the head of Crassus himself, winning the reward of a silver talent for his bright idea. Meanwhile Cassius, having rallied what troops he could for the defence of Syria, succeeded in beating the Parthians back. There for the time being the situation rested; and though Rome had lost an army she was fortunate to lose nothing more.

The removal of Crassus had an important influence on the political situation at home. For, if the harmony of the Triumvirate had been precarious, a partnership of two, in which the two were obvious rivals, was more precarious still. In the autumn of 54, moreover, Caesar's daughter Julia, whom Pompey had recently married, died in giving birth to a child; and from this time onward a marked coolness sprang up between the two. It was ominous that, though Caesar offered to marry Pompey's daughter, Pompey declined the arrangement and himself married young Crassus' widow.

Meanwhile Pompey's political position showed little sign of improvement. The growing disorder in the city seems to have given him some idea of assuming the dictatorship, but, as always, he lacked nerve for the plunge. As the election of magistrates for 52 drew on matters went from bad to worse, and such was the state of anarchy that polling had to be postponed. In January of 52 occurred an untoward incident which brought the crisis to a head. Milo, backed by Cicero in the conservative interest, was standing for the consulship, Clodius, his old rival, for the praetorship. Clashes between their retinues were frequent; and one day a chance encounter on the Appian Way near Bovillae led to a sharp scuffle. Clodius was dragged into an inn hard by and killed. His body was carried back to Rome; and the indignant mob, making a pyre for it in the Senate house, burnt the whole building down. Popular feeling against Milo ran so high that the Senate passed the ultimate decree, empowering Pompey to levy troops. Soon afterwards, in the absence of elected magistrates, he was appointed sole consul, and he proceeded to make arrangements for Milo's trial before a special court. During the trial the Forum was lined with troops, but so menacing was the attitude of Clodius' supporters that Cicero, in making his speech for the defence, altogether lost his nerve. Milo went off into exile in Transalpine Gaul, and when Cicero sent him a copy of the speech he had meant to deliver, the ruffian sarcastically remarked that he felt no regrets—the mullets of Marseilles were so tasty.

In spite of this set-back the senatorial party were fortified by the certainty that Pompey was now theirs, for even Pompey himself was shrewd enough to see that it would serve him best to assume the role of a constitutionalist and so force upon his rival the unpopular counter-role of the revolutionary. For a constitutionalist it was indeed a curiously anomalous situation to be holding simultaneously the consulship at Rome and the proconsulship of Spain; but the time had long gone by for political niceties, and Pompey further proceeded to strengthen his position by obtaining a prolongation of his Spanish command for another five years.

The issue was now immensely simplified. On the one side stood the Senate, upheld by their new champion Pompey; on the other stood their arch-enemy Caesar, with the armies of Gaul at his back. But before the issue was pressed to its terrible conclusion, there was much manœuvring for position, and the constitutionalist party, being on the spot, naturally had the absent Caesar at a considerable disadvantage. His situation was in fact extremely delicate. The additional five years' term, which had been voted him in 54, was due to expire *in March of 49*. From that moment he would become a private person, until at the elections in the latter half of the year he might hope to secure once more an official position. The interval, though not long, would be long enough for his enemies to impeach him and so crush him out of hand. One loophole remained. Governors were allowed to stay in their province till the arrival of a successor; and, since in the normal course of events Caesar's successor would be one of the magistrates of 49, none of these would be free to relieve him till the end of that year. He would therefore be entitled to prolong his command past the period of the autumn elections, and so all might yet be well. Absentee candidature, it is true, was technically illegal; but, in accordance with arrangements made at Lucca, Pompey had passed a Bill waiving the rule in Caesar's favour. The awkward thing now was that after his change of front in 52 Pompey was beginning to waver on this point; and under the influence of his new senatorial friends he sponsored a new measure even more fatal to Caesar's plans. This measure enacted that henceforward provincial commands should be assigned only after a lapse of five years from the holding of a magistracy. This meant that posts now falling vacant would have to be filled up by magistrates of five or more years back.[1] It also meant—and here lay the rub—that, in March 49, when Caesar's command expired, there would be plenty of successors available and no excuse would be left for the prolongation of his term.

These intrigues were bad enough, but there was worse to follow. For one of the consuls of 51, Claudius Marcellus by name, proved to be an out-and-out opponent of Caesar, and in September he proposed in categorical terms that his Gallic command should terminate at the appointed date. Pompey, still nervous of pushing the issue to extremes, objected, and the question was put off for decision until March of the following year.

Meanwhile the atmosphere at Rome was growing tense with fear and suspicion. Men knew the tried prowess of Caesar's legions. They knew the ruthlessness with which he had conducted his Gallic campaigns. The memory of the Sullan Terror was still vivid in their minds; and it is little wonder that his opponents were determined to snuff out Caesar's career at the first opportunity. Cato made no secret of his intention to prosecute for high treason. Should, therefore, the proposal

[1] Incidentally the rule compelled Cicero, much against his will, to go out and govern Cilicia.

of Marcellus become law, trial, conviction, and exile stared
Caesar in the face; and, if previously undecided what policy
he should pursue, he must have begun to realize that there was
no room in Rome for an independent Senate and for Caesar too.
The course before him seemed plain enough. He had at his
back an army of devoted troops. His rival's legions were far
away in their Spanish province. Italy was practically undefended, and nothing seemed simpler than to concentrate his
forces in Cisalpine Gaul, march down and impose his will—
perhaps even without a struggle. Nevertheless, it was not
Caesar's habit to be hasty where patience might yet serve;
and while continuing to manœuvre for position he still strove
to achieve his goal through constitutional channels, and was
prepared to go almost any length to avoid an appeal to arms.

CHAPTER XVII

CAESAR'S TRIUMPH AND DEATH

I. THE DIE IS CAST

WHEN the critical year 50 opened—the year in which
was to be made the fateful decision about the termination of his Gallic command—Caesar needed
above all a spokesman who should represent his interests at the
capital. His choice fell on one of the tribunes, C. Scribonius
Curio by name, an unscrupulous young adventurer of remarkable debating powers who had hitherto taken the senatorial
side. Like many of his class, this man had enormous debts (said
to have amounted to the fantastic figure of half a million pounds).
On Caesar's undertaking to pay them a bargain was struck;
and, though posing at first as an independent demagogue,
Curio watched his chance to play the game of his absentee pay-
master. Confident in this arrangement Caesar made no overt
move. He acceded to the Senate's request for the use of one
of his legions in a forthcoming campaign against Parthia. He
even returned another legion which Pompey had previously
lent him. Meanwhile, on the motion of the consul Aemilius
Paulus—who as likely as not had received a *quid pro quo*—

the critical decision, which was to have been taken on March
1st, was once again postponed.

During the next few months several proposals were made, but
none gave Caesar adequate immunity against the threat of
prosecution, so Curio blocked them all, and himself suggested
as a compromise that both Caesar and Pompey should resign
their commands simultaneously. At the beginning of December a motion to this effect was actually adopted by a majority
in the Senate. That Pompey would obey it, however, seemed
in the last degree unlikely; but, as its ingenious author had
foreseen, he could only defy it at the cost of breaking with
his senatorial friends. The more reactionary members of the
House were determined to forestall so disastrous an issue; and,
making the most of a scare that Caesar was preparing to march,
they proposed that Pompey should be entrusted with the defence of the State. On the defeat of their motion, they rushed
off to his house and melodramatically thrusting a sword into
his hands commissioned him then and there to take command
over all forces in Italy. This unauthorized gesture could carry
no real sanction. Yet Pompey immediately gave orders for a
general levy. War, he told Cicero, was now inevitable.

On December 21st, on the expiration of his tribuneship,
Curio fled to his chief at Ravenna, expecting to find him ready
to march. Caesar, however, refused to be rattled. Civil war
was still the last thing he wanted. So he sent Curio back to
Rome and repeated an offer previously made to surrender most
of his legions, on condition of retaining either Illyria or Cisalpine Gaul till the date of the autumn elections. The offer was
ignored, and in the first days of 49, after a series of stormy
debates, a motion was passed declaring that, unless Caesar
retired on the appointed day, he should be declared a public
enemy. Two tribunes, M. Antonius and Q. Cassius, who had
now undertaken Curio's role, promptly vetoed the measure;
and on January 7th, having no other means whereby to override their veto, the Senate passed the ultimate decree. This
violation of tribunician privilege gave Caesar the chance he
needed. He could now pose as the champion of the constitution, and he hesitated no longer. He had by now been declared a public enemy; and on January 11th he crossed the

frontier at the River Rubicon. Though at the moment he had only a single legion with him, he hoped that the two others, which he had recently surrendered and which were still on Italian soil, would take his side. By the rapidity of his movements, too, he counted on forestalling his enemies' preparations and in this he was right A body of troops raised by Domitius —his successor-elect to Transalpine Gaul—was easily reduced at Corfinium. Pompey, who had meanwhile withdrawn into the south with whatever forces he could muster, despaired of resistance and decided to cross into Greece. Caesar was hard on his heels, and, when in March his last transports set sail from Brundisium, was hammering at the gates of the town. Along with Pompey went most of the leading senatorials; so that the capital submitted without a blow being struck and Caesar's unexpected clemency did much to placate all who remained. He lost no time in assuming the reins of government. He seized the State Treasury, assigned to Marcus Lepidus the control of the city, to M. Antonius the defence of Italy, and to Curio and other lieutenants the task of securing the vital corn-provinces of Sicily and Sardinia. His own hands were thus left free to prosecute the coming campaign against the military forces of his foes.

II. THE CIVIL WAR TO PHARSALIA

The strategical outlook was decidedly problematic. In addition to the ten legions he already possessed Caesar had, of course, ample means of recruiting as many more as he wanted; and his financial resources enabled him to undertake immediately the construction of a fleet. On the other hand, Pompey held the command of the seas, and was thus in a position to concentrate where he chose. Indeed, apart from Italy and Sicily, the whole Mediterranean lay at his disposal. Spain was held by his legions. Marseilles had declared for him, and his lieutenant Domitius (though generously released by Caesar at Corfinium), was thence endeavouring to assert his command over Gaul. In Africa the loyalist governor, Atius Varus, succeeded in beating off Curio's attack. And, most important of all, the provinces of the East—Pompey's special preserve, the scene of his earlier triumphs, and an almost inexhaustible

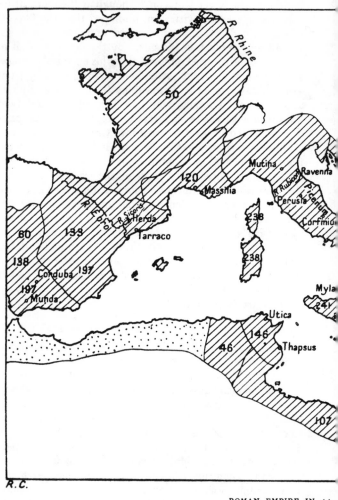

ROMAN EMPIRE IN 44

Sinope

64

Zela

Heraclea

74

Philippi

146

Via Egnatia

ssus

chium

Apsus

Thessalonica

133

Apollonis

64

Antioch

64

Corcyra

Pharsalus

Laodicea

Actium

58

67

Alexandria

CYRENAICA

74

CAMPAIGNS OF THE CIVIL WAR

reservoir of men, money, and ships—were solidly at his back. Under such circumstances, and because it offered the most convenient base for the recovery of Italy, Pompey very naturally selected Macedonia for the concentration of his troops. But such concentration was bound to take time. The raw levies brought from Italy would require some training. The undisguised jealousy of his senatorial associates impeded Pompey's efforts, and progress was slow.

For Caesar, therefore, time was a vital factor; and speed, as we have seen, was his strength. The central position of Italy too enabled him to strike either east or west; and he chose first to make certain of Spain. He left Rome on April 5th. A fortnight later he appeared before Marseilles. Not wishing to leave behind him so serious a threat to his communications, he told off Trebonius and Decimus Brutus to invest the town and himself proceeded across the Pyrenees. The Pompeian forces under Afranius and Petreius were concentrated at Ilerda, on the west bank of the Sicoris, a tributary of the Ebro. After some initial reverses, Caesar presently mastered the situation; and the enemy, finding themselves cut off from supplies by his cavalry-patrols, determined on a retirement. Making their escape across the town bridge eastwards, they counted on getting some hours' start on the pursuit, for Caesar's only available bridge lay many miles upstream. His engineers, however, succeeded in splitting the swollen stream into several fordable channels, and the infantry, wading across breast-high, raced ahead of the fugitives and cut them off in a defile, where they were compelled to surrender. The troops of the Further Province then threw in their hand, and by the end of September Caesar was back at Marseilles, which was just on the point of yielding to his two lieutenants. He treated the town with clemency; and, though confiscating some territory, permitted the retention of its old autonomous rights.

The summer's campaign had thus won the west for Caesar, and in December he returned to Rome. He assumed the consulship for 48, took measures to avert a financial crisis in the city, and after sending twelve legions ahead to Brundisium, arrived there in person on the last day of 49. All this time the concentration of Pompey's troops had been steadily proceeding. In addition to the five legions originally transported from Italy he had drawn four from the Eastern provinces, to say nothing of a motley host of auxiliary contingents—Cretan bowmen, Thracian slingers, Syrian horse-archers, and (what was to play a highly important part in the coming campaign) a large number of cavalry from Asia Minor. At the beginning of 48 he set out along the great Egnatian high road from Macedonia for the Epirot coast. Meanwhile his naval squadrons, under the command of Bibulus, were patrolling the Adriatic; and Caesar's chances of eluding them seemed small. The sheer improbability of a winter crossing, however, had somewhat lulled their vigilance, and on January 5th Caesar landed seven legions some twenty miles north of Corcyra. His next objective was Dyrrhachium. This important key position formed the terminus of the high road by which Pompey was approaching; and Pompey won the race. A temporary stalemate resulted, and for the next three months the two armies faced each other across the River Apsus, some thirty miles south of the town. Delay suited Pompey's plans well; but for Caesar, cut off as he was from provisionment by sea, the position grew intolerable. His reinforcements, too, failed to arrive, and at one time, so the story goes, he actually set out in a rowing-boat to fetch them over in person, till the crew, scared by a rising gale, insisted on putting back. Then suddenly towards the end of March sails were sighted. It was the long-awaited transports from Brundisium; but, the wind being high and a disembarkation impossible, they sailed past in full view of both armies and disappeared into the north. With this the stalemate ended. Pompey cautiously withdrew to the neighbourhood of Dyrrhachium. Caesar made a detour inland and, joining his reinforcements which had landed farther north, prepared for a decisive action. But Pompey knew his own limitation. He realized that he himself was no match for the genius of his opponent, nor were his raw troops for the veterans of the Gallic campaign. So, rather than be drawn into fighting he sat still on the coast somewhat south of Dyrrhachium, and actually allowed Caesar to close in and invest him. The audacity of this move was the more astonishing since Caesar's force can have numbered scarcely half of the Pompeians, and whereas they could revictual from sea, he was forced to depend upon the country-side, which was constantly swept by their cavalry. It was largely in order to put an end to these cavalry raids that Caesar undertook to surround the enemy's camp with a vast semicircle of double entrenchments. The length of line to be covered was a good fifteen miles, but despite sallies and countervallation the system was completed by midsummer, except at its extreme southern tip. At this point, where the double ring of earthworks ran down to the shore, a cross wall still remained to be built; and here one day early in July the Pompeians landed troops in the gap between the earthworks, which they simultaneously assaulted from the flank. The defence was thus rushed; and after a bitter struggle Caesar was compelled to recognize defeat. His whole system of invest-ment having been rendered untenable, he drew off his army to Apollonia, some forty miles down the coast.

Pompey was now free to move again; and, learning that some Caesarian troops under Calvinus were blocking the arrival of his reinforcements from Macedonia, he set out along the Egnatian road eastwards to deal with them. On the news of this, Caesar marched too. He crossed the mountain passes farther south, and, joining hands with Calvinus, descended into Thessaly. The fertility of the district assured him of ade-quate supplies, which had been seriously lacking on the western coast, and, if Pompey should follow him, there seemed here a better prospect of forcing a decision on the level plains. Pompey followed sure enough, and took up his position on a hill-top near Pharsalia. But his plan was still to wear his opponents down by the harassing tactics of his vastly superior cavalry; and though day after day Caesar persistently offered battle, the offer was no less persistently refused. So things would have continued had it not been for the impatience of Pompey's senatorial associates. They expressed open con-tempt for his dilatory strategy. Even Labienus (who at the outset of the war had come over to his side and was now one of his most trusted advisers) presently added his voice to the chorus; and at length such pressure had its effect.

On the 9th of August it was observed that Pompey's army

had ventured much farther than usual from the shelter of its camp, and Caesar made his dispositions swiftly. Noting that the enemy's cavalry was heavily massed against the meagre squadrons of his own right wing, he placed eight infantry cohorts in reserve behind the threatened flank. All fell out as he foresaw. His cavalry was forced back by overwhelming pressure. The reserve cohorts charged, and, using their javelins to stab instead of throw, checked, held, and finally routed the Pompeian horsemen. It was now Caesar's turn to outflank his opponents. He ordered up his third line supports and threw them into the wavering battle-line; and the day was won. The enemy camp was carried the same afternoon; and on the morrow a wholesale surrender of the defeated army followed. Pompey fled to the coast, and, embarking on a merchant ship, escaped to Egypt.

III. THE CIVIL WAR—SECOND PHASE

Some years before, Pompey had used his influence to restore Ptolemy Auletes to his throne, and he now expected a welcome in Egypt. But Ptolemy was dead, and his son and daughter, Ptolemy XII and Cleopatra, had fallen to quarelling. Cleopatra had been expelled and had returned with an army; and the issue still hung in the balance when Pompey appeared off Pelusium. Her brother and his advisers had no wish to embroil themselves with Caesar and decided to encompass his defeated rival's death. So Pompey was invited ashore, and, as he stepped out of the boat, was stabbed in the back.

Meanwhile Caesar was hard on his tracks. Perhaps he still hoped for a reconciliation with the man who, after all, had been his son-in-law; and when he landed and an obsequious Egyptian presented him with Pompey's mummified head, it is said that he wept. Once in the country, he decided not to hurry away. He was in sore need of money, and a large part of the sum which Auletes had promised him was still owing. But, having undertaken to adjudicate between the two royal claimants, he soon got into trouble. He fell in love with Cleopatra and so alienated her brother. The mob of Alexandria, too, resented his interference, and there were ugly demonstrations. Then an Egyptian army was brought up from Pelusium; and

Caesar, whose forces numbered at most 4,000 men, was blockaded in the palace. All winter fierce fighting continued in the
streets; but gradually reinforcements began to arrive—first
a legion from Asia Minor, then a further contingent brought
overland from Syria by a son of Mithridates; and with the aid
of these Caesar gained the upper hand. Ptolemy, whom
he had long kept prisoner, but recently released, was killed in
the fighting; and it remained to settle Cleopatra on the
throne. It was no doubt a congenial task, for Caesar was
very human; and he spent three precious months in arranging
the settlement of the beautiful girl's kingdom before he could
tear himself away.

It was high time for him to go; for during his nine months'
stay in Egypt the world had not stood still. The most pressing
danger was in Asia Minor. A certain Pharnaces, a son of
Mithridates who had inherited his realm in the Crimea, had
seen a chance to take advantage of the Civil War. He had
invaded Pontus, overrun Cappadocia, and defeated Calvinus,
who was there in charge. In July 47 Caesar left Alexandria,
and marching through Syria encountered Pharnaces at Zela,
where he won a crushing victory. The famous dispatch he sent
to the Senate, 'I came, I saw, I conquered', was a not inappropriate summary of the campaign; and it conveyed no doubt
a hint that he was not to be trifled with. By September he was
on his way home.

The situation in Rome was far from satisfactory. On the
news of Pharsalia the Senate had voted Caesar unlimited
dictatorship, and Mark Antony, in the capacity of his Master
of Horse, undertook the control of the city. But his authority
was soon challenged by political adventurers. Financial chaos
reigned, and first one magistrate and then another attacked the
regulations which Caesar had laid down for the settlement
of debts. Rioting broke out, till Antony was obliged to interfere and much blood was spilt in the Forum. Meanwhile
the troops, which had been brought back from Thessaly, were
clamouring for their prize-money and discharge. Antony
could do nothing with them; and when towards the end of
September (47) Caesar landed at Tarentum he came not a day
too soon.

The scene of his meeting with the mutinous legions is historic. They were in no very pleasant temper as they crowded round him in confident expectation that he would accede to their requests. But never was the magnetic quality of his personality more convincingly displayed. He told them curtly that they were dismissed the service; and in an instant they were on their knees imploring him to take them back. He relented, knowing well enough that their swords might soon be needed; for the Republican cause, though defeated at Pharsalia, had by no means been extinguished. When Caesar went off to Egypt in pursuit of Pompey he had left his lieutenants to deal with the survivors of that stricken field. But many had escaped. Scipio and Afranius had taken ship to Africa—the one province still unshaken in its old allegiance. Cato and other diehards, after first sailing eastwards in Pompey's wake, had joined them; and the Pompeian fleet, being severely handled in the Adriatic, had made its way there too. King Juba of Numidia had furnished them with cavalry; and thus a formidable, if miscellaneous, army was awaiting Caesar when he chose to cross.

Realizing the weariness of his sorely tried veterans, he took with him new regiments in the main, when in the last days of 47 he set sail from Lilybaeum and landed at Hadrumetun some distance south-east of the enemy camp at Utica. At first he could do little more than hold his own; and had the Pompeian fleet fulfilled its function his communications with Italy would have been in serious danger. In spring, however, his veteran troops came over, and, marching on Thapsus, which lay east of Utica, he drew down Scipio, the Republican *generalissimo*, to its assistance. Outside the walls was fought the decisive battle of the campaign. The enemy was routed and in the fierce pursuit thousands were butchered, including most of the leaders. Labienus and Varus escaped to Spain, where we shall hear of them again. Meanwhile Cato, who had been left in charge of Utica, despaired of further resistance. With a philosophic composure, he first read and re-read Plato's dialogue on the Immortality of the Soul and then stabbed himself mortally in the breast. He was not a great man; for in his pedantic adherence to the Stoic creed he made a parade of independence, which often took the form of boorish incivility. He positively enjoyed shocking public opinion; and, as an exponent of the simple life, used actually to appear on the judicial bench without either shoes or shirt. Nevertheless, in an age of flux this staunch upholder of the old regime stood like a rock, and his name came to be identified in a peculiar degree with the Republican cause; so that freedom-loving Romans of a later epoch looked back with sentimental admiration to his self-sought martyrdom.

The victory of Thapsus, though deciding the issue, did not end the unhappy struggle. Africa, it is true, was cleared of the enemy; and Numidia, which Juba by his treachery had forfeited, was divided into two parts, one going to a Roman adventurer named Sitius, the other being constituted as a province. But meanwhile in Spain, as we have said, the surviving Pompeian leaders had secured a refuge. The Further Province, as it so happened, was in a restless state. Quintus Cassius, whom Caesar had left in charge, had set every one by the ears through his gross mis-government. There had been a mutiny among the troops, and not even Cassius' removal had availed to quieten things down. The result was that, on their arrival, the Pompeian leaders found many adherents, not merely among the troops but among the discontented provincials; and, his lieutenants on the spot having failed to cope with the situation, it was clear that Caesar's own presence was needed. In July 46 he had returned to Rome, where he had set to work on his vast schemes of reform, but in the following December he was forced to interrupt his labour and to set out for the last of his wars.

That winter's campaign was of the bitterest. The weather was severe, supplies were hard to come by, and the enemy, with the ruthlessness of despair, committed horrible atrocities which were duly repaid in kind. The fortified cities of the south and west were nearly all in Pompeian hands; but, when Caesar's successes began to win over the townsfolk, the end was plainly near. In a final effort to decide the issue the enemy accepted battle at Munda near Corduba and were completely overwhelmed. Labienus fell in the fighting. Of the other leaders, Sextus, one of Pompey's sons, alone eventually survived.

There was in fact no one left to raise a finger against Caesar, now the undisputed master of the world.

IV. CAESAR'S REFORMS

The all-powerful dictator who undertook on his return from Africa—and resumed after the interruption of the Spanish campaign—the task of remodelling the entire fabric of imperial government was a very different man from the consul of 59 whose year of office had proved so singularly barren of constructive reform. During the course of his Gallic campaign Caesar had not merely developed new powers of action, he had also had time to think. At a distance from the capital and its absorbing party politics, he had been able to study the vast problems of the world with clear-sighted detachment, so that, when the time came to undertake their solution his plans seem to have been ready; and in a few short months he effected changes for which many men would have needed years. His powers of work were certainly extraordinary. During his last journey to Spain he found leisure to compose a grammatical treatise, a pamphlet in criticism of Cato, and a poem on the journey itself. This intellectual fertility was furthermore controlled and strengthened by a disciplined habit of concentration; and, though the strain of his campaigns had told on his health and he himself was apparently conscious that he had not long to live, there were no visible signs of deterioration in his creative powers. Fortunately, too, for him, political obstruction was at an end. Not merely was he dictator and consul, but censorial powers, which had been voted him for life, enabled him to pack the Senate with his partisans; and when he chose to submit his legislative reforms to either the House or the Assembly they were accepted as a matter of course. Unhappily our knowledge of them is fragmentary and their chronology largely conjectural; but that they all were part of a well-planned whole seems certain; and we need scarcely attempt to distinguish between those which belonged to the interval between his African and Spanish campaigns and those which belonged to the last seven months between his return to Italy in September 45 and his death in March 44.

It was significant of the precision and thoroughness of

Caesar's mentality that one of his first reforms was a reorganization of the calendar. The ancient system, based on the religious tradition of an agricultural people, was clumsy in the
extreme. By its reckoning the year consisted of twelve lunar
months, totalling 355 days, an extra month being added at the
end of February in every second year. Even so the reckoning
was faulty and needed frequent adjustments by the College
of Pontiffs. Since the Pontiffs had recently neglected their
duty endless confusion had arisen; and the consequent dis-
location of business called for some drastic change. With the
assistance of Sosigenes, a Greek astronomer from Alexandria,
was produced the calendar, which, with a slight modification
introduced by Pope Gregory in 1582, survives to the present
day. Amongst other changes the official year, which had
previously begun with March, henceforth began with January;
and the month Quintilis, in which Caesar himself was born,
was renamed July in his honour.

In dealing with other and more important problems Caesar
displayed the same instinct for systematization; and instead
of tinkering with what was past repair he struck at the very
root of the mischief. One of the most urgent needs, as we have
frequently shown, was the restoration of a healthy tone to the
demoralized society of the capital. The self-indulgence of
the rich has baffled most reformers, and Caesar was indeed no
exception. He adopted an expedient—common enough in
ancient times—of promulgating sumptuary laws, limiting the
cost of funerals, ostentatious attire, or luxuries of the table;
but such legislation very soon became a dead letter. More
successful was his attempt to curb the abuses of the corn-dole.
From a return supplied by tenement landlords Caesar found
that 320,000 persons were in receipt of free allowances. He
cut down the number to 150,000; and henceforward vacancies
caused by the death of recipients were filled up by praetors,
no doubt on proof of genuine need.

Such a system of poor-relief—though necessary to avoid
starvation—was no real cure for Rome's maladies; and by more
genuinely constructive measures Caesar endeavoured to furnish
productive occupation for the surplus populace. Within the
capital itself he planned an ambitious scheme of architectural

construction. In addition to a new Basilica,[1] which had already been built during his governorship of Gaul, there was now to be a new Senate House, a Temple of Mars, a theatre on the slopes of the Capitol, and some public libraries. In the Campus Martius, outside the walls, even larger works were in prospect. Here a vast enclosure, surrounded by marble colonnades over a mile in length, was to be provided for the Tribal Assembly, for whose accommodation the old Forum was no longer adequate. As a connecting link between the old Forum and this new political centre there was to be another colonnaded square or Forum at the centre of which stood a temple of Venus Genetrix, the patron goddess of the Julian family. All these works promised employment for a huge army of labourers; and outside the city other operations were planned for the draining of the valuable Pomptine marshlands and of the Fucine Lake.

As these last measures indicate, Caesar was fully alive to the necessity of reviving Italian agriculture, and it is noteworthy that in order to encourage the employment of free labour he enacted that on ranches one citizen should be engaged for every two slave-herdsmen. But it is clear that he did not pin his faith on an agrarian revival alone. Like Caius Gracchus, he saw that trade was the true basis of Italian prosperity and that the Roman people must play an active part in the commercial organism of the Empire. To this end various measures were undertaken. First, the harbour at Ostia was to be deepened, and a ship-canal dug through the Isthmus of Corinth. Next, overseas colonies were planned on a vast scale; and 80,000 citizens drawn from the surplus population of Italy were planted at sites well placed for trade, and ranging from Tarraco and Hispalis (Seville) in Spain to Heraclea and Sinope on the south shore of the Black Sea. Corinth was to be resettled with freedmen. Carthage was to be rebuilt, and there were to be several new colonies in Africa. Nor did even the death of its promoter prevent this vast scheme of emigration from being largely carried out.

That such settlements should serve to spread Roman ideas

[1] The Basilica Julia, remains of which are still extant on the south side of the Forum.

and customs among the provinces of the Empire was no doubt Caesar's intention; but it was an even more important part of his programme that the provincials themselves should be gradually absorbed into political unity with Rome. The extension of the franchise was, in fact, begun on a scale hitherto unattempted. Caesar was, for a Roman, extraordinarily free from racial prejudice. Already, as we have seen, he had begun the practice of making special grants of citizenship to deserving individuals of non-Italian birth, not least to doctors, teachers, and other professionals whose services to culture had won his approbation; and he now even went so far as to promote Gauls and Spaniards (and in some cases freedmen's sons) to the Senate House itself. More remarkable, however, was the wholesale enfranchisement of many provincial communities. Spanish towns, which had supported him during his last campaign, were thus rewarded. Most towns of the old Transalpine Province, too, received full citizenship; and Sicilian towns were given the 'Latin' or half-franchise. Caesar's death, unhappily, cut short his plans; but we can scarcely doubt that this process was to have been continued, and that step by step the Empire would have been converted into a homogeneous political whole.

How far the municipal institutions of these newly enfranchised cities were definitely to be modelled upon Roman lines is difficult to determine; but a brass tablet unearthed at Heraclea in South Italy suggests that Caesar had such intentions. Among the regulations therein contained is one clause providing for a census of free inhabitants on the same basis as the census held at Rome, another defining the qualifications for municipal office and membership of the municipal senate, a third allowing for subsequent amendment of the municipal statutes, presumably in harmony with those in operation at Rome. If such regulations were applied to Italian townships, it is reasonable inference that they would have been applied to provincial townships too; and it is almost impossible to doubt that a cautious but steady advance towards political unification would have been the guiding principle of Caesar's imperial policy. What at any rate seems clear is that he viewed the provinces no longer as mere vassals of Rome's rule, but in some real sense as partners of the Roman Commonwealth.

In this, as indeed in very many respects, Caesar was striking out a line of policy which other emperors were subsequently to follow; and it may be said in passing that among his unfulfilled projects was a codification of the laws—a reform long overdue, since the age-long accumulation of formulae and precedents had inevitably resulted in much overlapping and even contradiction. There was, however, one still more vital point in which Caesar's statesmanship served to determine the future character of the imperial system; for by concentrating all the reins of government in the hands of a single man it set an example of autocracy which, despite Augustus' experiment of sharing his sovereignty with the Senate, remained the fundamental principle of the new order of things. The Republican regime, it is true, was never formally repealed, and its ancient institutions continued for the most part to be outwardly observed. But its essential spirit—the spirit of freedom—was dead. The Populus Romanus, was, in short, dethroned; and henceforward, in fact if not as yet in theory, the ultimate appeal in all things was to 'Caesar's judgment-seat'. We have already shown how the legislative functions of both Senate and Assembly were reduced to a mere formality, and though the *comitia* still voted at the election of annual magistrates, Caesar's 'commendation' of candidates permitted no real liberty of choice. He appointed men at his own discretion to provincial posts, often with complete disregard for the traditional sequence of offices. The actual constitutional titles under which he chose to veil his wholly unconstitutional power were scarcely of real consequence, except as a concession to the Roman's passion for political formalism. After rejecting the Senate's offer of a ten-years' consulship, he accepted life-tenure of the dictatorship with full censorial and tribunician powers, and, even more important, with proconsular authority throughout the Empire.

This last function was indeed the keystone of Caesar's whole position, for it gave him control over the armed forces of the State. Nor can there be much doubt that his own conception of his sovereignty was based in some degree on those military despotisms which had been so striking a feature in the history of the East. It may well be that the example of Alexander, whose career he greatly admired, appealed to him as a suitable precedent to follow. For, after all, nearly one-half of the Empire consisted of Levantine countries which had once been part of Alexander's realm, and in many of which a military despotism was the only form of government that the inhabitants really understood. What seems certain is that Caesar's eyes were closely fixed on the East. The problem of the frontiers was evidently much in his mind; and we know that at the beginning of 44 he was mobilizing an unprecedented force of sixteen legions for a campaign against Parthia. Some even think he intended to remain for many years in the East; and, making his head-quarters at Alexandria or elsewhere, to rule there with a pomp and majesty such as might well befit his new conception of world-monarchy, but would very ill consort with the freedom-loving atmosphere of the old imperial capital.

How far a certain element of megalomania was beginning to reveal itself in Caesar's plans we can scarcely gauge with certainty, since those plans never matured. One circumstance, however, suggests that unlimited power was disturbing in some degree the balance of his judgment—his desire to be regarded as a god in his own lifetime. To ourselves such a claim seems almost incomprehensible; but in ancient times, we must remember, it was not without precedent, especially in the East. The Ptolemies, for example, were considered gods by virtue of their royal office; and Alexander himself had demanded divine honours even from his Greek subjects. In Italy, moreover, the *numen* of the deity had always been conceived as dwelling in material objects; and in every family cult the father was held to personify the 'genius' of the home. The idea that a human being could thus represent the 'genius' of a group or race was to play an important part in the later development of Emperor worship; and it doubtless inspired Caesar to erect his temple to Venus Genetrix, who, as mother of Aeneas and so grandmother to Iulus, might be held to have transmitted some portion of her divinity to her descendants—of the Julian gens. But Caesar went farther than this. He allowed one image of himself to be carried in procession with the statues of other gods. He had a second placed in the shrine of Romulus, the deified founder of the Roman race. Finally, if one authority is to be trusted, he intended to assume the title of Jupiter Julius. In all this it may well be that he was consciously following Alexander's example; and from a practical point of view the idea of thus consolidating his political supremacy cannot be dismissed as wholly fantastic. Roman society, however, was ill prepared for the acceptance of so unfamiliar a doctrine. The extravagance of the claim clearly came as a shock to the more conservative minds; and it must in some degree have accounted for the revulsion of feeling which led to the formation of the fatal conspiracy.

V. CAESAR'S MURDER

It would be ridiculous to suppose that Caesar's autocracy was generally unpopular at Rome. He was a master of statecraft and had taken much pains to placate opposition. His singular generosity towards political opponents came as a surprise even to his worst enemies; and meanwhile the favour of the urban mob was easily won with the aid of the vast financial resources which his victories brought him. After the campaigns of Thapsus and Munda he held celebrations of unprecedented splendour. Largess was distributed with lavish prodigality to every member of the proletariat. Twenty thousand tables were laid for citizen diners. Plays and other spectacles were organized. Wine flowed freely; and bullion was brought in wagon-loads for distribution to the veterans of the legions. But, great as was the enthusiasm which such liberality aroused among the common folk, there remained a small section of society who could neither forget nor forgive; and beneath the fulsome adulation of both Senate and officials a careful observer might have noted an undercurrent of bitter resentment.

Nor, once his power was well established, did Caesar pay much heed to the susceptibilities of those around him. There were signs of annoyance when, on the death of a consul on the last day of the year, Caesar appointed one of his nominees for the few remaining hours. 'No one lunched while Caninius was

consul,' wrote Cicero to a friend.   'Think it funny or no, it
brings one near to tears.'   One day, when holding an audience
of the Senate, Caesar received them seated, and again tongues
wagged.   Towards the end of January two tribunes were deposed for arresting a man who instigated a crowd to greet
Caesar as 'king'.   A fortnight later Antony made his famous
offer of a crown, and though Caesar rejected the offer feeling
against him grew.   Yet, when friends warned him that his life
was in danger, he resolved to make a gesture and dismissed his
bodyguard.

One of his chief problems in establishing his power was to
find subordinates whom he could really trust.   Most men of
decent character had taken the Republican side in the Civil
War and had suffered either death or disgrace.   Of his own
followers the greater part were bankrupts or adventurers, men
of small repute.   So in making his appointments Caesar was
often forced to choose between men whom no one respected
and men whose loyalty was dubious.   In one important
instance he had preferred the latter alternative.   Marcus
Junius Brutus belonged to one of the oldest and most highly
honoured Roman families.   After Pharsalia he had submitted;
but he was no friend of Caesar's, and it was mainly to enlist
upon his side a man of such illustrious and influential standing
that Caesar had made him governor of Cisalpine Gaul.   Brutus
was of a harsh, uncompromising nature, and, like Cato (whose
daughter he married), a student of philosophy.   As evidence
accumulated that the Republic was being destroyed past all
prospect of recovery, he began to associate with others who
were working for Caesar's death.   Amongst the confederates
was Trebonius, Caesar's governor in Asia, Decimus Brutus a
relative of Marcus, Casca, Cimber, and C. Cassius Longinus,
the chief engineer of the plot.   Cicero, though not consulted
or committed, had expressed his approval of tyrannicide.

On March 15th—the famous Ides—a meeting of the Senate
had been arranged in a hall adjoining the Pompeian Theatre in
the Campus Martius.   It was nearly noon when Caesar himself
arrived.   As he entered some one placed in his hands a scroll
containing full information of the plot.   Owing to the throng
at the doors he could not unfold the scroll, and passed in with

it unread. When he was seated Cimber approached him with a petition for the recall of an exiled brother, and, as though in supplication, seized his hands. The other accomplices pressed round, and, when Caesar tried to rise, Casca stabbed him in the back. Then all in a frenzied scuffle drove their daggers home. The murdered man wrapped his cloak about his head and fell, pierced by no less than three and twenty wounds, at the foot of Pompey's statue.

One fact remains to be recorded. It would not seem to have been Caesar's purpose that his constitutional experiment should die with him; and by his will, the contents of which were not disclosed until after his death, he bequeathed his name and his vast fortune to a great-nephew, Octavius, the grandson of his sister Julia. Octavius (or Octavianus as he became on entering upon his heritage) was only eighteen years of age and physically, at least, very far from strong. The odds against him were enormous; but in spite of them all he survived to re-establish, under his more famous title of Augustus, the autocracy which his great-uncle almost certainly intended to bequeath to him. Thus the precedent of a hereditary monarchy was not the least contribution which Caesar made to the building up of the Imperial System.

CHAPTER XVIII

THE TRIUMPH OF OCTAVIAN

I. FROM CAESAR'S MURDER TO PHILIPPI

NO sooner was their blow struck than the conspirators discovered to their surprise that it aroused no popular enthusiasm; and, alarmed by the symptoms of public disfavour, they retired into the security of the Capitol. The state of general uncertainty offered a golden opportunity to any man bold enough to seize the initiative; and here lay Antony's chance. He was not, it is true, a man of steadfast character. He was notoriously self-indulgent, an associate of loose livers, much given to strange fits of indolence and stormy outbursts of passion. But he had an abundant, if somewhat erratic, energy, diplomatic skill, a ready tongue, and much military experience; and, what mattered even more, he had been Caesar's right-hand man and was now in occupation of the consulship. Though badly scared at the moment of the murder, he soon came out of hiding and took over from Caesar's widow her husband's papers and his fortune in ready cash, said to have amounted to many hundred thousand pounds. With a show of conciliation he induced the Senate to vote a general amnesty to the murderers. Then at the dead man's funeral on March 20th he threw down the gage by the famous harangue which Shakespeare has immortalized. There was a riot in the Forum. Attacks were made on the houses of the chief conspirators, and Brutus and Cassius fled into the country.

Antony now had the game well in his hands. The conspirators were discredited. The Senate was cowed. The provinces were held by Caesar's nominees; and none of these, with the exception of Decimus Brutus, who now controlled Cisalpine Gaul, was likely to give trouble. To secure an army of his own was, of course, Antony's first requirement; and, while getting his fellow-consul Dolabella appointed to Syria, he himself procured the command of Macedonia and thus of the legions which had been concentrated in that province for the coming Parthian campaign. Meanwhile, in Italy itself he was voted a bodyguard, and busied himself in collecting a formidable host of veterans. Thus, when in September of 44 Brutus and Cassius took ship for the East, Antony seemed complete master of the situation and in a strong position to deal faithfully with Decimus Brutus.

But, though at first Antony can scarcely have taken him seriously, a rival had already appeared in the field. At the moment of his uncle's murder the young Octavian had been with the Macedonian legions, and friends had advised him to place himself at their head for a march on Italy. But he refused. Young as he was, he was already possessed of extraordinary astuteness, and he saw that until he could make himself better known, and so win a following, he must walk with extreme wariness. Returning to Rome in April 44. he claimed the bequest to which he was entitled under Caesar's will. Antony refused the demand; but by selling property which came to him under the will Octavian was able to pay out of his own purse the donations which Caesar had bequeathed to the Roman populace. In this shrewd bid for popularity Antony must have perceived a challenge; but, though their relations were strained, no open breach between the two occurred as yet. Octavian, for his part, went to raise troops in Campania; and by promise of higher pay actually enticed to his side two of the four legions which Antony had summoned from Macedon for use against Decimus Brutus.

Meanwhile, in exchange for Macedon itself, Antony had received authority to take over Cisalpine Gaul. In autumn he formally demanded its surrender, and on Decimus Brutus' refusal proceeded to blockade him in Mutina. The departure of Antony from Rome let loose all the forces of latent opposition. The Senate, hitherto cowed, recovered its independence. The aged Cicero emerged from his retirement to resume the leadership; and in a powerful series of speeches (which, in imitation of Demosthenes' orations against the King of Macedon, he entitled his 'Philippics'), he inveighed with increasing violence against 'that monster' Antony. This senatorial revival gave Octavian his chance. He encouraged Cicero's overtures, and, accepting the role of constitutional champion, was given formal commission to enlist more troops. Early in 43, accompanied by one consul and soon to be followed by the other, he moved to the relief of Decimus Brutus at Mutina. This combination of forces was too much for Antony. In a preliminary engagement near Forum Gallorum, he was severely handled; then, a week later, suffered complete defeat. Escaping westwards across the Apennines, he joined Lepidus, formerly Caesar's Master of Horse and now governor of the Narbonensian province; and Plancus, governor of northern Gaul, threw in his lot with them.

While Decimus Brutus was engaged in following up the fugitives Octavian struck out upon a different tack. He saw that, whichever way the campaign might end, his own services would be of little account to the victor; and in the interval he proceeded to play his cards with characteristic subtlety. Both consuls having fallen in the recent fighting, he demanded his own election, and by a sudden march on Rome left the Senate no choice but to comply. Thus for the moment he was master of the city, and, though he could scarcely hope to hold it, he had at any rate made himself a political force with which even Antony and Lepidus would be bound to reckon. The result was that when in autumn 43, finding Decimus Brutus dead they re-entered Cisalpine Gaul at the head of seventeen legions, he was able to strike a bargain. The three leaders met on an island in a tributary of the Po near Bononia; and there they resolved to constitute themselves a new Triumvirate, 'for re-establishing the commonwealth'. A motion confirming them in this title—thus giving it the character of an *official* appointment in contrast to the personal coalitions of the preceding decade—was passed through the *comitia*. It was further arranged that Antony and Octavian—the one as governor of Transalpine and Cisalpine Gaul, the other of Sicily and Africa—were to undertake the campaign against Brutus and Cassius. Lepidus, while technically to be governor of Spain, was to control Italy in their absence.

The standards of public life were by now so degraded and his own position so perilous that we can well excuse Octavian for this cynical *volte-face*—to which indeed there was no alternative but retirement. It is not so easy to excuse its sequel; for with his acquiescence, if not with his approval, a proscription was decided on. The outlawry of his uncle's assassins had already been proclaimed at his own request when he assumed the consulship; but what his two colleagues now demanded was the wholesale destruction of political opponents. This hideous barbarity—even more cold-blooded than Sulla's Reign of Terror—was partly dictated by financial needs; for the sale of confiscated properties was intended to meet the Triumvirs' lack of ready cash. But among the 300 senators and 2,000 knights whose names were on the lists many owed their death to nothing more than motives of revenge. Such a one was Cicero, whose 'Philippics' had drawn down on him the special wrath of Antony. The old man had quitted Rome, and, when the news arrived, was in his country-house at Tusculum. He made his way to the coast and had embarked for Greece when winds drove him back on the Campanian

THE ROMAN WALL IN NORTHUMBERLAND

POMPEII-- FRESCOED HALL

POMPEII—SHOP WITH ELECTION POSTERS

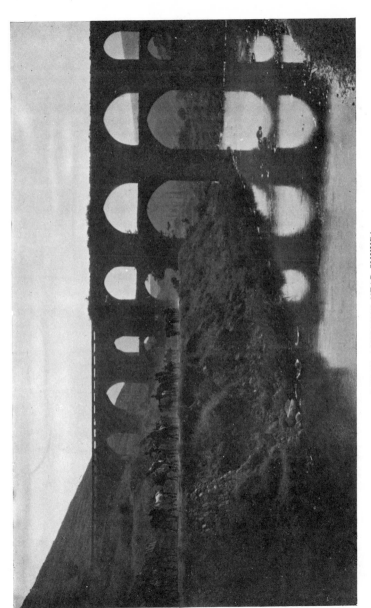

ROMAN AQUEDUCT NEAR SMYRNA

ARLES THEATRE AND AMPHITHEATRE

coast. At Formiae, where he had another house, Antony's minions found him, and his slaves' attempt to save him by flight was in vain. His head and the right hand with which he had penned the obnoxious speeches were carried back to Antony, who had them nailed to the Rostrum.

What meanwhile Brutus and Cassius had been doing in the East must now be briefly considered. After leaving Italy in the Autumn of 44 Brutus had proceeded to northern Greece. The Illyrian troops were made over to him by the sympathetic governor, and in 43 the Senate further sanctioned him to take charge of Macedon. Meantime in the Further East Cassius had been equally successful. He went first to Syria. There he defeated Dolabella, who, as Antony's colleague, had been assigned the province; and as a result of his victory assumed control of Asia Minor too. Thus, when Brutus presently joined him, they could boast that the whole eastern half of the Empire was again in Republican hands. Their land forces, the bulk of which were now concentrating in eastern Macedon, amounted to nineteen legions. They had collected, too, a formidable fleet; and, what was a valuable asset, they were able to count on the co-operation of Sextus Pompeius, the old Republican leader. After Munda, this man had turned buccaneer; and on the renewal of Civil War had re-enlisted his services in the senatorial cause. Overrunning Sicily, he had attracted to his standard a large number of piratical adventurers, and when Octavian sent an expedition against him had succeeded in beating it off.

Thus, when the forces of the Triumvirs were ready to move, they found the Adriatic patrolled by enemy squadrons; and even when they made the passage to Greece in the summer of 42, they were under the constant threat of having their communications cut behind them. It was their obvious policy therefore to force a battle with all speed; and marching along the Egnatian Way they confronted the armies of Brutus and Cassius in the neighbourhood of Philippi. The first engagement proved inconclusive, but in the course of it Cassius, prematurely despairing at the rout of his own contingent, committed suicide. Brutus was thus left in sole command; and in mid-November, yielding to the impatience of his officers, he at

length accepted a decisive test. It ended in the crushing
defeat of his army, and, realizing that the end had come, he
induced a comrade to kill him. The noble sincerity of his
character has been somewhat obscured by the erroneous idea
that, having been a real friend of Caesar, he was guilty of
black treachery in joining the conspirators. The truth is that
patriotic motives alone dictated his course; but he was too
much of an idealist to compete on equal terms with men like
Antony or to understand the mentality of the Roman mob.
His dream of a restored Republic was scarcely more practical
than Cato's; and had it come into being he was certainly not
the man to have saved it from inevitable shipwreck.

II. FROM PHILIPPI TO ACTIUM

A partitioning of the Empire between the Triumvirs was a
natural sequel to their victory. Lepidus the weakest of the
three partners, was now thrust into the background and
eventually relegated to the unimportant province of Africa.
The other two reshuffled the provinces to suit their own convenience. Antony was to take control of the East, and moved
to Asia Minor, where, by an accident which altered his whole
career, he fell in with Cleopatra, and, being captivated by her
charms, followed her to Alexandria. Meanwhile Octavian,
who had been suffering much in health, returned to Italy and
there undertook to deal single-handed with the manifold problems of the West. Chief among these was the settlement of
the discharged legionaries, who insisted on receiving lands in
the richest parts of Italy. Thousands of yeomen were driven
from their farms, amongst others the three young poets
Horace, Propertius, and Virgil, and the unpopularity of these
evictions fell of course on Octavian. His embarrassment was
unscrupulously exploited by Antony's wife Fulvia and his
brother Lucius, who, alleging that the land measures had not
received Antony's sanction, pushed the quarrel to open war.
Lucius actually seized Rome, but was driven out by Octavian's
lieutenant, Agrippa, and then blockaded in the Umbrian
fortress of Perusia, where at the beginning of 40 B.C. he was
compelled to surrender.

These complications apart, relations between the two great

partners were now becoming strained. Report said that Antony was secretly in correspondence with Sextus Pompeius, whom it was Octavian's business to crush; and when later in the year 40 he landed at Brundisium it looked almost as if the final clash was to come. Saner counsels, however, prevailed. By now all the best men in Rome were rallying round Octavian; and it was largely through the intervention of Maecenas and others that the widening breach was temporarily healed. By the convention of Brundisium their separate spheres of East and West were definitely assigned to the two Triumvirs; and to cement the agreement Antony, whose wife Fulvia had just died, took in marriage Octavian's sister Octavia.

While Antony sailed off to take up his head-quarters at Athens Octavian resumed the interrupted task of resettling the West. The most urgent part of it was the suppression of Sextus Pompeius. It was an extraordinary sidelight on the naval weakness of the Imperial Government that, in order to keep this impudent corsair quiet, the Triumvirs had actually ceded him in 39 not merely Sicily and Sardinia, but the Peloponnese too. The truce did not last, however, for he soon broke his bargain, and regaining control of the seas proceeded to cut off the corn-supplies of Rome. The situation was critical, and Octavian undertook preparations on an enormous scale. Hundreds of ships were built; and, to provide a secure harbour for the training of the crews, Lake Avernus near Naples was connected with the sea by a canal. Additional ships were lent by Antony; and in 36 Octavian and Agrippa, assisted by Lepidus from Africa, descended on Sicily and eventually succeeded in defeating Sextus off Mylae. The pirate chief himself escaped to eastern waters, and next year was caught and killed by Antony's lieutenant. Meanwhile Lepidus, who on the morrow of the battle attempted to seize Sicily for himself, was formally deposed from his place in the Triumvirate; and Octavian was at last left to pursue his policy of reorganization unimpeded. His veterans were settled on the land. Brigandage in Italy was suppressed; and a regular police force for the first time instituted. Agrippa was sent to arrange affairs in Gaul; and the consolidation of the north-eastern frontier was begun by a campaign against the Dalmatians in 35. By such measures Octavian was, in fact, laying the foundation of a vast imperial policy which he was later to consummate as Emperor.

Meanwhile Antony was for once shouldering his responsibilities with something like a sustained effort. His main trouble lay with the Parthians, who had taken advantage of the Civil War to cross the Roman frontier. They had overrun Syria; then, finding a leader in Quintus Labienus, son of Caesar's old lieutenant, they had even pushed beyond the Taurus mountains into Asia Minor itself. To meet this serious threat Antony sent Ventidius Bassus, a remarkable man who had started life as a slave, then become a mule-contractor, and finally, thanks to Caesar's patronage, risen by swift promotion to the consulship. He swept the Parthians first out of Asia Minor, then out of Syria too; but such rapid success awoke his chief's jealousy, and Antony decided to take personal command of the campaign. Feeling that the disgrace of Carrhae had not been sufficiently avenged, he began to contemplate a vast scheme of Oriental conquest; and with a force of eighteen legions advanced through Armenia into the valley of the upper Tigris. Once again the audacious adventure nearly ended in disaster, and the army was obliged to retreat, harried by the pursuit of the dogged enemy and suffering terrible privations among the Armenian snows. One further expedition was undertaken to punish the defection of the Armenian king; but by now the spell of Cleopatra had taken a firm hold on Antony. He settled down in Alexandria, yielding himself to the luxurious habits of the Egyptian court and lavishing domains on his mistress and her children after the style of some Eastern despot. The climax came when, before even divorcing Octavia, he married Cleopatra. Such an affront to Octavian was unforgivable; and when it became known that Antony had made a will bequeathing portions of the Empire to Cleopatra's sons, feeling at Rome rose high. Men realized that before this threat of an Orientalized monarchy the whole fate of Italian supremacy was at stake, and that it must be resisted to the death. In 32 the Senate declared war on Cleopatra.

Antony was not slow to take up the challenge. By the autumn of 32 he had already advanced with his queen as far as Greece, in preparation for the invasion of Italy. Finding the home ports strongly held, he elected to winter on the Aetolian coast. His great armada of 500 galleys considerably outnumbered the smaller, though swifter, vessels which Octavian could bring against him; and on land he could count on an enormous army over 100,000 strong. When, however, in the spring of 31 Octavian and Agrippa crossed the Adriatic against him, a distinct lack of cohesion revealed itself in his unwieldy host; and several of his vassal allies went over to the enemy. He made the fatal mistake, too, of allowing his fleet to be blockaded inside the Ambracian Gulf behind the promontory of Actium. His supplies ran short. His land forces were immobilized; and eventually he decided to fight his way out of the gulf for a retreat on Egypt. On September 2nd 31 the two fleets met in the final struggle of the Civil War. The impatient Antonian captains were drawn out into the open, where Agrippa's swifter vessels were able to encircle them. Foreseeing defeat, Cleopatra ordered her personal squadron of sixty galleys to run for it; and so the rout began. Antony and a few ships escaped in the wake of the queen; but the rest were either destroyed or captured, and the land army soon surrendered.

Some trouble over the disbandment of his legions necessitated Octavian's return to Italy, and it was some months before he followed the fugitive pair to Egypt. Outside Alexandria Antony still showed fight, but the defection of a part of his army led to the surrender of the city. A message falsely reporting Cleopatra's death drove the unhappy man to make away with himself; and despite an interview with Octavian, in which he promised her good treatment, the queen also resolved to die. It is said that she had been in the habit of making experiments with various poisons on condemned criminals; and as a result of her investigations she chose the bite of an asp as the least painful form of death. It stands to Octavian's credit that she was laid, according to her wish, in the tomb with her great lover.

CHAPTER XIX

LIFE AND LETTERS DURING THE DECLINE OF THE REPUBLIC

I. WOMEN AND FREEDMEN

AN epoch that witnessed the collapse of an ancient political system could hardly fail to bring with it a corresponding change of thought and manners. During these years it is not too much to say that the Roman character was thrown into the melting-pot. The conventional standards of conduct and belief had almost completely broken down. Individuals were thus compelled to strike out for themselves; and it is scarcely surprising that the generations which saw the last of the Republic and the beginning of the Empire should have displayed a liberality and even an originality of outlook unique in the history of Rome.

Among the many developments which occurred during this period not the least interesting concerned the status of women. From the earliest times, as we have seen, women were more highly respected in Italy than in Greece, and often exercised a considerable influence even beyond the family circle. In the eyes of the law, on the other hand, they enjoyed no independent status; and throughout her life a female always remained under the tutelage of some male. By the most ancient form of religious marriage (known as *confarreatio*) a bride passed automatically under the power of her husband; and his authority over her was so complete that in theory at least he was entitled to put her to death. Side by side with this, however, there existed alternative forms of non-religious marriage, which involved no such complete subjection to the husband's authority, and under which the wife's property could be retained at her own disposal subject to her father's tutelary powers. After the Punic Wars, when so many males were killed, women had frequently become owners of considerable estates; and owing to a natural reluctance to allow such property to pass out of the family the non-religious forms of marriage became increasingly popular. The strength of the tie was thus weakened; and towards the end of the Republican era the widespread relaxation of all moral standards led to frequent divorce. Husbands discarded their wives without apology or pretext. Even Cicero himself, after thirty years of apparently harmonious marriage, divorced Terentia to marry a rich young heiress, and his only reason seems to have been that during his absence at the time of the Civil War she had been insufficiently attentive to his interests.

It was a natural counterpart to such behaviour that women themselves tended more and more to assert their own independence; and so a step was taken, though not perhaps a very salutary step, in the direction of female emancipation. During this epoch, accordingly, we encounter ladies of good family, such as, for instance, Clodius' sister Clodia, who formed the centre of a 'fast' society, keeping young men, like the poet Catullus, dangling round her and playing fast and loose with their affections. Wits and scandalmongers were drawn into the circle of such women. Sempronia, the mother of Decimus Brutus, wrote poetry and danced—an accomplishment very ill suited to the stern old notions of female decorum. Politics were discussed and plots hatched in her *salon*, which included many of Catiline's satellites. The unwholesome influence of such charmers did much to debase the moral and social standards of the day, and under the Early Empire the ladies of the court were to exercise power which in earlier times would have been unthinkable.

Another element in society, though scarcely so prominent, produced an effect even more undesirable. During the period of imperial expansion the population of the metropolis, as we have noted, had steadily grown more cosmopolitan; and it now included perhaps 200,000 persons of servile status, a large proportion of which were either Greeks or Hellenized Orientals indispensable to the financial, educational, or cultural activities of a Roman aristocrat's household. For such nimble-witted folk the process of emancipation or promotion was normally swift; and many freedmen or their sons had quickly risen to positions of some importance. We have already seen what dangerous powers were wielded by Sulla's favourites; and the names of such upstarts now begin to figure more and more frequently in history. They were freely admitted to the social entertainments of the great, at which their ready wit and varied accomplishments were considered a valuable asset. But the vulgarity of their manners and conversation is amply attested by the literature both of this and of the succeeding period.

II. LIFE AT ROME

A strange contrast indeed it was between the gay, busy, many-sided life of these Late Republican gentlemen and the staid, stolid community of farmers who had been their ancestors. Business and pleasure had become complicated to a degree undreamt of even a few generations back. The city itself was full of noise and bustle; and the traffic nuisance was so serious that Caesar prohibited the passage of wagons through the streets at night. Escape into the peace of the country-side was welcomed by those who could afford the luxury of a country-house. Cicero possessed half a dozen 'villas' in various parts of Italy, and in addition he had numerous lodges at which he could break his journeys; for the fastidious tastes of the cultured class was ill satisfied by the rude hospitality of the squalid local inns.

A great elaboration of domestic comfort was another symptom of the growing luxury. The town-house of the Roman, as of the Greek before him, presented a blank wall to the street.[1] and was unlit by external windows. Its rooms were grouped, however, not, as in most Greek houses, round a colonnaded courtyard, but round a spacious hall or 'atrium,' the roof of which sloped down inwards to a central aperture. This in early days had served as a vent-hole for smoke as well as for skylight and rain-water drainage. For in more primitive times the atrium was the living-room, eating-room, kitchen, and domestic chapel all rolled into one. At the period of which we are speaking it retained only the first and last of these functions; for in it were placed the altars of the Lares and Penates, the gods of the home. Meanwhile, under the influence of Greek customs, the additional rooms which convenience demanded were grouped round a colonnaded courtyard or

[1] Sometimes little shops were built into these wall-spaces and hired out to trades-folk.

'peristyle'. Between this and the atrium was placed the dining-room. When space was available there were often several courtyards, with flower-beds in some. Upper stories were coming into use; and, though heating arrangements were as yet almost unknown, bathrooms were attached to the more important houses.

A Roman's day started at dawn; for, though lamps fed with olive-oil were used in large numbers, the illumination they gave was far from good, and a busy man could ill afford to waste a moment of daylight. His clothes, like the Greeks', were simple. Over a woollen shirt or tunic he draped the voluminous folds of his toga—a garment more fitted for slow, dignified movement than for strenuous work or exercise. His fast was broken by a frugal meal of bread dipped in wine or eaten with cheese and olives. Meanwhile visitors were gathering. For at this hour duty-calls were paid. Poor dependents came to pay their respects, some to crave assistance or favours. Such interviews over, our friend would normally make his way to the Forum—the hub of social and commercial as well as of legal and political life. With him would go a regular retinue of slaves and other attendants, friends, and clients, so that any man of importance marched about at the head of a formidable procession. If election day were looming near and he himself a candidate for office, he employed an agent to keep him posted with the names of all folk he encountered in his progress.

By this time the Forum would be thickly thronged; and the forenoon would be passed in the transaction of business of one sort or another. There were bankers to be visited and perhaps arrangements made for a loan or a money-draft to be paid to a son studying in Athens. A lawsuit might be in progress in one of the adjoining basilicas, and, even though not himself engaged, our friend might have undertaken to support the defendant by his presence in court. Under any circumstances there was much time to be spent in gleaning the gossip of the day, political rumours, and news from the provinces.

Lunch of a light character was taken at noon and a siesta normally followed. More business might occupy the interval before dinner—the chief meal of the day, which took place in later afternoon. It was preceded, as a rule, by some exercise and a bath. The Romans were not so much addicted as were the Greeks to athletic sports, but a game of ball was thought good for health. By the close of the Republican era, as we have said, most large houses possessed a suite of bathrooms. In one the bather would undress and leave his clothes. In the next the atmosphere would be heated by hot air issuing through subterranean flues from an underground furnace. In this Turkish bath he sweated heavily, then entered a room of more tepid atmosphere, was anointed all over with olive-oil, and scraped down with a metal instrument which removed grease and dirt together. In some houses it was possible to have a plunge-bath; otherwise more simple methods were employed.

Dinner was a serious affair. The Romans were sociable beings, and as a rule many guests were invited. All lay down on couches—a custom adopted from the Greeks—and tables laden with food were brought in by slave attendants. As compared with the Greeks, the Romans were heavy eaters, and the menu was lengthy and extravagant. Drinking followed; and a 'master of the feast' was usually appointed to dictate the proportions in which water and wine should be mixed. Tongues wagged freely and tipsy brawls were not uncommon. But various forms of entertainment were provided; and in the more cultured houses there was plenty of good talk and discussion on serious topics. Such diversion ran on well into the night.

III. LITERATURE

In the foregoing sketch of a Roman's daily life no mention has been made of literary pursuits, yet in the age of which we are speaking they bulked large. Nothing indeed is more astonishing than the enthusiasm with which this once most unliterary people took to writing. Most leading men tried their hand at it. Many were virtually bilingual; and Lucullus once undertook for a jest to compose a history of the Marsi alternatively in Latin or Greek verse. On the whole, however, it was characteristic of the period that men wrote because they had something to say rather than because they simply wished to write; and as compared with the studied lucubrations of the

Imperial epoch, the Republican literature is fresh in ideas and spontaneous in expression.

A notable example of these qualities was Lucretius'[1] masterpiece on *De Rerum Natura*, or, as we might say, *The Universe*. In it he set out to explain—on Epicurean principles—the atomic composition of all existence and hence to establish the certainty that souls no less than bodies must be dissolved with death. Such a theme was at many points more suited to a scientific treatise than to poetry; and crabbed or even cacophonous lines are inevitably frequent. Yet Lucretius had the soul of a true poet, and his similes and other descriptive passages serve to flood the whole work with a quality of beauty astonishingly vivid and romantic. Most of all does he rise to heights of real sublimity when, with all the vehement earnestness of a preacher, he strives to expose the disastrous illusions of superstitious belief:

Wherefore man made shift to ascribe unto gods the dominion
Over all things create. Then said he, their seat is in Heaven
For that in Heaven he saw the Sun to roll and the Moon roll,
Sun, Moon, Night and Stars in the Night, grim constellations
Flames in the night-sky wandering, and wingèd fiery cressets,
Cloud-wrack and Sunshine, Snow, Rain, Hailstorm, Whirlwind and
    Thunder,
Crash of the rending bolt and muffled moan of the Tempest.
Woe for the pitiful sorrows of man who herein hath discernéd
God's hand, and tokens withal, saith he, of a baleful displeasure.

Beside the relentless march and solemn splendour of such passionate outpourings even the melodious cadences of Virgil's verse are apt to sound a trifle artificial and unreal.

Equally refreshing, though infinitely less serious, were the lyrics of Catullus (87–54). The young man's life was not a very reputable one, and he wasted much misplaced affection on the notorious Clodia, the 'Lesbia' of his poems. Yet there is a sweet simplicity about his pieces which no writer of any age has surpassed, and the playful tenderness of his celebrated elegy on Lesbia's dead sparrow has few rivals:

Weep, Loves! Weep, Lovers, for my dear!
For her poor sparrow's dead—

[1] 97–53 B.C.

The sparrow that was more to her
Than the eyes out of her head.

So sweet he was to her; more fond
Toward mother maid was none;
For in her lap he'd hop around
And pipe to her alone.

Now down the Dark Way past reprieve
He's journeying. Out upon ye
Ye dark and dismal Shades of Death,
Which ravish all things bonny.

So bonny is the bird ye've sto'en!
Foul deed, and birdie sad!
'Tis all for thee my pretty one
Has wept her bright eyes red.

In Catullus, as in Lucretius, we feel indeed that the true Italian genius was bursting at last from its sheath of Hellenic pupildom into a blossom of rare native loveliness. Both express their ideas and feelings with a spontaneous freedom which no subsequent Latin poet was quite able to recapture. For with the passing of the Republic and Liberty there comes a sense of constraint; and it is as when a stream gushing and sparkling in its earlier reaches falls into the more deliberate and unadventurous course of a well-canalized river.

In prose, still more than in verse, most writers of the age had a practical rather than a literary aim. Varro (127–116 B.C.), a prominent leader during the Civil War, wrote various treatises, on 'Agriculture', on the 'Latin Language', and above all on 'Roman Antiquities'. Even busy men, like Sulla, found time to compose a record of their own achievements. Caesar, besides his Gallic *Commentaries*, published a history of the Civil War; and the strictly practical spirit in which he undertook the work produced a restrained, lucid, and logical style which, perhaps more than any other, displayed the essential qualities of the national tongue. Sallust (86–35 B.C.) was more consciously an artist; and in his histories of the 'Jugurthine War' and the 'Catilinarian Conspiracy' he is inclined to place effect before accuracy; but his gift for telling epigram exercised a considerable influence over the style of Tacitus and other later writers.

In the Rhetoric of the day there were similarly two tendencies. Politicians, who had to address themselves to the limited intelligence of the popular Assembly, followed the severely simple style of the old Attic speech-writers. Others, who pleaded before educated jurors of the upper class, preferred the more florid model taught in the Rhodian schools of oratory. Cicero, though he himself studied at Rhodes, struck a mean between the severity of the one style and the verbosity of the other. No more powerful instrument of rhetorical appeal has ever been devised than the Ciceronian 'period', with its steady rise and fall of resounding cadences and the nicely calculated rhythm of its triumphant close. His private letters too are a pattern of graceful style, reflecting a personality of exceptional refinement and charm. Nor must we forget the numerous philosophic treatises written in his retirement—on 'Friendship', 'Conduct', 'Religion', and other kindred subjects. In these he endeavoured to bring the best principles of Greek philosophy into line with the practical problems of a Roman citizen's life; and in the process he evolved a precise terminology such as the Latin tongue had not hitherto possessed and which was destined to form a basis for the work of subsequent philosophers. Thus Cicero's role in language as well as in thought was to remodel the heritage which Rome received from Greece into something essentially Roman in its quality; and he represented, as perhaps no other man did, the cultural union of the two racial characters, blending the intellectual agility of the Hellene with the moral earnestness of the native Italian stock. Henceforward the Roman mind was to run no longer in leading-strings. It had attained to the independence of maturity.

IV. ART AND ARCHITECTURE

The Italians were not by instinct an artistic people; and any chance of a natural development was greatly impeded by the fact that, when, under Greek influence, a taste for artistic objects arose, it was easily satisfied from other than native sources. For the houses of Roman aristocrats were commonly adorned with statues imported from Greece, and when the supply failed replicas were turned out in large numbers by

Greek copyists. Craftsmen from Alexandria and elsewhere poured into Italy to decorate the walls or carve the furniture of rich Roman patrons. But unfortunately the standard of taste was too crude to encourage good workmanship. Such frescoes as have survived are for the most part of a cheap vulgarity. The replicas of Greek statues were often mere travesties of the exquisite originals; and only in the field of sculptured portraiture was any real skill maintained.

Architects too came from Hellenistic centres; but in building, at any rate, the artistic achievement was more considerable. The first century B.C. saw a great renewal of activity. Sulla, employing the resources won on his eastern campaigns, spent enormous sums on new monuments. His chief work was a reconstruction of the Temple of Jove on the Capitol. The quaint old Etruscan building had been destroyed by fire during the Marian anarchy, and on its site he erected a far more splendid edifice in which marbles brought from Greece were employed to great decorative effect. Besides other temples in various parts of the city, he also built on the slopes of the Capitol an enormous block (still extant) called the Tabularium, in which were kept the public records and other official documents of the State. Sulla's precedent was followed by other victorious generals. Pompey utilized the spoils of his Oriental conquests to construct a temple and a theatre in the Campus Martius. But all these works paled into insignificance before the splendour of Caesar's conceptions, of which we have spoken above. Their chief feature was systematic planning, in imitation of the methods employed in Hellenistic cities. In all his buildings, too, as in those of the Late Republic, the Greek styles were freely used. But already perhaps, as in Sulla's Tabularium, the characteristic Roman taste for dignified mass and solid masonry was beginning to assert itself; and thus was laid the foundation of an architecture appropriate to the enduring genius of the national character.

During this transitional period, then, we may conclude, the national character itself, though profoundly modified, was not fundamentally changed. In other words, the Roman, when Hellenized, remained the Roman still. His debt to the new culture was, it is true, incalculable; and without the intellectual stimulus and discipline, which Greece opportunely supplied, he would have lacked the mental equipment whereby alone he was enabled to govern successfully the Mediterranean world. Nor was it the least part of his historic task to hand on to western Europe the precious cultural heritage which he had thus acquired. On the other hand, his own contribution to that culture was by no means negligible; and, having taken from Greece her styles of writing and building, he was able, as we have seen, to evolve from these a literature and an architecture essentially his own. What was more important, though he experienced to the full the disturbing influences of her critical philosophies, his morale was not fatally undermined; and in the coming era, along with much that was brutal, coarse, and unpleasing in his character, he preserved also in large measure those same sterling qualities which had been responsible for his greatness in the past. He retained, for instance, his extraordinary tenacity, which, through all the strain and stress of internal dissensions, had never allowed him to lose either a war or a province. He retained, in relation to the subjects of his rule, his old instinct for tolerance and adaptability; and he retained, above all, his high tradition of loyalty to the common weal, upon which, far more than upon anything else was to be based the efficiency and permanence of the vast imperial system that Octavian was now destined to inaugurate.

PART II
THE ROMAN EMPIRE

CHAPTER XX

AUGUSTUS

I. THE NEW ORDER

FOR two years after his crowning victory at Actium, Octavian, now undisputed master of the world, remained in the East. He organized Egypt, treating it as a domain personal to himself and placing it under a prefect of his own appointment. He even found time to attend to its irrigation system. He paid a visit of inspection to the other Eastern provinces; and then in the autumn of 29 he returned at last to Rome. The splendour of his triumphal celebrations was phenomenal. On three successive days the spoils and prisoners of victories won in three continents were paraded before the eyes of an enthusiastic populace. Games and gladiatorial combats were held in the Circus Maximus; and for the first time since the conclusion of the First Punic War in 241 the gates of the Temple of Janus were closed. Peace had come at last. After twenty years of recurrent anarchy, bloodshed, and bankruptcy men breathed again. A new hope had dawned upon the weary world; and towards the young man in whom that hope was centred all eyes turned with a fervour of hero-worship that was little short of idolatry.

Octavian was as yet not half-way through his thirties, but in experience he was old. He had learnt life in a hard school; and events had taught him to watch the men about him, to beware of pitfalls, and to bide his opportunity. So now, though the most extravagant of compliments were showered upon him, his head was never turned. Limitless power lay within his grasp; but the lesson of his uncle's fatal megalomania had sunk home and he was little minded to risk a second Ides of March. He gave himself no airs. In his household the standard of living which he set (and which he maintained to the end of his long life) was studiously simple. He walked about the streets of Rome like a private citizen. As for authority, he was determined to hold none but what he could hold constitutionally. Octavian, so far as we can judge, was a conservative at heart. In the struggle with Antony, we must remember, he had stood forth as the champion of Roman Society against the threat of an Oriental despotism; and it seems clear that he himself had a profound belief in the traditions and institutions which had made his country the mistress of the world. Somehow or other, therefore, his own power was to be fitted into the existing framework of those institutions. In January of 27 B.C. he came forward in the Senate House with a startling pronouncement. The Republic, he said, should be restored. The consulship, to which (as on half a dozen previous occasions) he had been elected for that year, he would retain. All other powers he would lay down forthwith. The Senate were dumbfounded. What were they to do? Could they dare to take his words seriously? And, if so, could they dare to hand over once more the armed forces of the State to a variety of jealous captains and watch their rivalry once more make havoc of the world? It was not to be thought of. They at once insisted that Octavian should resume his command over the legions, and therewith of the frontier provinces in which the legions were necessarily quartered—Gaul, Hither Spain, Syria, and Egypt. So, besides the consulship to which he was to be annually re-elected, he was given a grant of proconsular power for the period of ten years.[1] Finally, as though to set the seal upon his pre-eminent position, the name of Augustus was conferred upon him—a title hitherto reserved for the very gods themselves.

His position thus regularized, Augustus proceeded to leave Rome for a prolonged tour of inspection in the Western provinces. Did he wish to give the Senate a fair chance of carrying on without him? Did he expect them to succeed, or hope that they would fail? Such speculation is useless. Already events had proved the senatorial oligarchy incapable of governing a world-wide empire; and events, as time went on, were to compel the transference of more and more responsibility on to the shoulders of the one man who was capable of sustaining it. That Augustus, who from his earliest years

[1] For this dual arrangement there was the precedent of Pompey, who in 52 B.C. had been concurrently governor of Spain and consul at Rome.

had striven and schemed for power, should have been eager to relinquish it the moment it was won seems, on the face of things, improbable. But the secret of this mysterious man's real thoughts was closely guarded. The emblem he wore upon his signet-ring was characteristic. It was a figure of the Sphinx.

From 27 to 24 B.C. he was absent from Rome. In Gaul he organized the financial system. In Spain he subdued the wild tribes of the extreme north-east, hitherto unconquered. But Augustus' health was never strong; the strain of incessant work and heavy responsibility had told; and in June of 24 he fell dangerously ill. He actually made arrangements in event of his decease. At Rome the public was aghast. Happily he recovered; but once again, and this time perhaps with more sincerity, he threatened to resign. The upshot was the same, and he resumed control, but this time in a somewhat altered form. His annual term of consulship had proved unsatisfactory. It imposed certain inconvenient duties at Rome, and it gave him, still more inconveniently, a colleague. Henceforward he abandoned it and fell back on a vaguer but equally constitutional grant of tribunician power for life. This gave him the right to initiate legislation and to override opposition at home. Abroad it was now definitely understood that his proconsular authority should entitle him to interfere even in senatorial provinces; and it was renewed for further terms throughout his life.[1]

Thus was launched one of the most ingenious constitutional experiments known to history. Nominally the Republic was restored. The republican magistrates, consuls, praetors, and the rest, were annually elected. But their powers were only a shadow of what they once had been. The consuls' duties, for instance, were mainly ceremonial, and soon, in order to furnish an adequate supply of recruits for governorships of senatorial provinces, it became customary for several pairs of consuls to hold office in one year, each serving for a few months at a time. Under Augustus the magisterial elections

[1] This so-called *majus imperium* actually extended over the city of Rome itself, thus giving the *princeps* supreme authority at home, even when not holding the consulship.

were still, as in the past, submitted to the Assembly's vote; but his successor Tiberius discontinued the practice of consulting the worthless rabble and transferred the function to the Senate. In either case, however, it was a mere formality. The list of candidates contained no names of which Augustus disapproved. Some he appointed directly as his own nominees. It is all-important to remember that by thus controlling the elections he was also able to control the recruitment of the Senate, which, as in the past, was composed of ex-magistrates. So far as appearances went, the House recovered much of its old authority. Its motions (or *senatus consulta*) had virtually the force of law; for ratification by the assembled people was henceforth but rarely sought. It discussed all important business. It sat as a supreme court in important judicial cases. The administration of Rome and Italy were under its special care, as well as of those non-military provinces which had not been assigned to Augustus.[1] The old senatorial aristocracy had, in short, been taken into partnership. Its members were not ungrateful to the man who treated them with so much deference; but for those who had eyes to see its position was no longer what it had been. For if it was the Senate which passed the laws it was Augustus who framed them. He was often present in the House. Without his approval nothing could be done. Even in the provinces he had the power to interfere over the heads of the senatorial governors. Above all, as commander-in-chief of the imperial forces, he held the whip-hand. Constitutionally, it is true, he was no more than First Minister of the Republic. Men called him the *princeps*, or leading citizen of the State; but call him what they might, he was the State's master. The theoretical partnership between the *princeps* and the Senate, which many historians have termed the dyarchy, was, in fact, a hollow thing. In the first place, it concerned administration alone; for in the direction of policy the Senate had no share. In the second place, the compromise could only last so long as the reigning *princeps* was at pains to keep up appearances; and

[1] Africa, which contained a garrison, was, however, left to the Senate. Its other provinces were Illyria, Greece (or Achaea), Asia, Bithynia, Crete, Cyrene, Sicily, Sardinia, and Further Spain.

by degrees, as the successors of Augustus grew careless, their power was to stand revealed for what it was—a legalized military autocracy.

It was the old tale of the superior efficiency of a single ruler as compared with the more casual and dilatory methods of an oligarchical or democratic regime. In our own day we have seen parliaments replaced by dictators; and at Rome the *princeps* was bound gradually to encroach upon the senatorial sphere. The process began early. In 22 B.C., when Augustus was setting out for a tour of the Eastern provinces, a severe food shortage brought the population of the capital (nearly a quarter of a million of whom were still in receipt of the dole) to the brink of starvation. The mob got out of hand and clamoured for Augustus to become dictator. He refused, but agreed to take over the management of the corn-supply, which he placed at first under *curatores* or commissioners and later, in A.D. 6, under a prefect. In 20 B.C. he appointed similar commissioners to superintend the roads of Italy and organize a post system, with relays of horses at various stages along the important routes. During his absences abroad he appointed a prefect[1] to keep order in the capital—an official who under his successors attained a permanent and highly influential position. In A.D. 6 he further took over and reorganized the fire brigade or 'watch', which he likewise placed under a prefect of his own appointment. Thus step by step duties which had devolved on annual magistrates responsible to the Senate were transferred to permanent officials who were Augustus' nominees.

Most significant perhaps was the revolution in the financial system. The expenses of the State, especially for the upkeep of a standing army such as the Empire required for its defence, were very great. The *aerarium* or public treasury, which was fed by the revenues of the senatorial provinces and which continued, as in the past, under the control of the home government, was quite inadequate to meet them. Augustus, on the other hand, had vast resources. Besides what came to him from the frontier provinces (in each of which apparently

---

[1] This 'urban prefect' must not be confused with the prefect of the Praetorian Guard.

he created a separate fund or *fiscus* for the payment of the
legions) he possessed in Egypt, his own personal domain, a
source of almost incalculable wealth. Furthermore, it must
be noted, he was beyond comparison the richest man in Rome.
He had an enormous private fortune, which was fed by the
income from his personal estates and swelled by the addition
of frequent legacies. Out of this privy purse or *patrimonium*
he was occasionally obliged to assist the public treasury which
found much difficulty in making two ends meet; and it is obvious
that his control of finance, scarcely less than his control of the
legions, formed a prime foundation of Augustus' power.

Such control implied, of course, an elaborate organization;
and not the least important of Augustus' tasks was to set on
a new footing the whole administrative system of the Empire.
It involved nothing less than the institution of a permanent
civil service. In the first place, for the management of his
privy purse and personal bureau he employed a large staff
of subordinates, ranging from highly gifted confidential secretaries down to menial clerks, copyists, and messengers. To
undertake such service in a private household, even were it in
the household of the Emperor himself, was beneath the dignity
of free-born citizens. So almost inevitably even the most
responsible members of the Emperor's staff were drawn from
the despised class of freedmen or *liberti*. The arrangement had
its drawbacks; but in point of fact, being often of Greek
extraction and Greek education, such men were often extremely
capable administrators, and their complete subordination to
their master's authority was perhaps essential to the efficiency
of the bureau.

Then, again, in the administration of provincial finance big
changes were necessary, which involved the creation of a still
more extensive service of 'procurators' or revenue officials.
True, the old Republican system of farming out the tax-
collection to private companies of contractors was not swept
wholly away; for Augustus left to these *publicani* the control
of the harbour dues levied on goods passing in and out of
ports throughout the Roman world. But he took away from
them the collection of the two main direct taxes, the *tributum
soli* or levy on land, and the *tributum capitis* or levy on houses,

slaves, animals, and other forms of property.[1] To afford a fair basis for assessment a census was necessary. During his visit to Gaul in 27 B.C. Augustus, we know, instituted a property census; and the mention of an 'enrolment' in the Gospel story of the Nativity suggests that something similar took place in the East. The actual collection of revenue was controlled by the procurators; and by a wise provision these procurators were made responsible directly to the Emperor and not to the provincial governor.

As for the provincial governor himself (styled *legatus* in a large imperial province like Syria, *procurator* in a small one like Judaea), his position was regularized in two ways. His term of office was extended, normally to three years, and sometimes even more—a rule which allowed much greater continuity of policy than the old republican system of annual replacement. In addition to this he was now paid a salary— at first perhaps in the smaller provinces only, but eventually, too, in the larger; and though under later emperors governors were by no means immaculate, the temptation to make money out of the natives must henceforward have been greatly diminished. Even on the proconsuls of senatorial provinces, though not technically his servants, Augustus kept a watchful eye; and any guilty of misdemeanours were sure to be hauled before the courts on their return to Rome.

The governor of an imperial province, it must be remembered, was generally, though not always, the commander of the troops quartered therein; and any account of Augustus' organization would be incomplete without some mention of these. His victory at Actium had left him commander-in-chief of some sixty skeleton legions. More than half of these he pretty soon demobilized, settling the discharged soldiers upon farms in Italy, for which he wisely paid due compensation to the owners thus dispossessed. The remaining legions— twenty-eight in number—must have numbered in all about 140,000 men (for 5,500 was now the complement of a legion).

---

[1] Augustus also instituted two new forms of taxation (*vectigalia*), a 1 per cent tax on sales and a 5 per cent inheritance duty, both of which were paid into a new military chest (*aerarium militare*), used mainly for the payment of soldiers' pensions.

They were citizen troops recruited by voluntary enlistment for a term of twenty years and drawn mainly from the Italian peasantry or (failing these) from the inhabitants of the Romanized provinces of the West who, if not citizens already, would automatically receive citizen-rights on enrolment. Alongside of these first-line regiments was an approximately equal number of so-called auxiliary troops, which were recruited from the less civilized portions of the Empire, and of which a regular complement (either of cavalry or infantry or both combined) was brigaded with each legion. Such, then, was to be the army of the Empire—what in principle at least the Republic had never admitted—a standing professional force. Its size, somewhat over a quarter of a million, was by no means over-large for the purpose which it served; and Augustus, as we have seen, deliberately posted the legions in those outlying provinces where trouble might be anticipated either within or without the frontier. Four were in Syria, one in Macedon, six or more in the Danubian districts, eight on the Rhine, three in Spain, one in Africa, and two in Egypt. In Italy itself no legions were retained; but three cohorts, known as the Urban Guard, were concentrated at Rome under the command of the city prefect; and a special force, known as the Praetorian Guard, 9,000 strong and commanded by two prefects of high authority, was quartered at various points throughout the country. These men were a picked corps recruited from the townships of Italy and receiving much higher pay than the legionary soldiers. In time to come, as we shall see, the Praetorians and their commanders were to play a very decisive part in imperial politics.

That Augustus chose to recruit this privileged corps—and to a large degree the legionaries too—so exclusively from the home country was highly significant. Caesar would have followed a very different policy. His aim had been to extend the privileges of citizenship to the provincial populations, merging ruler folk and subject folk in one homogeneous political whole. He had conferred the franchise broadcast on deserving members of the Western provinces. He had even promoted Gauls to the Senate House. Antony, from less reputable motives, had followed the same ideal and filled his legions with the riff-raff of the East. To the Italians, who wished to retain their monopoly of civic privileges, such a state of things was most distasteful; and Augustus' popularity was largely based upon his championship of their narrow nationalism. So his policy was a reversal of Caesar's. The distinction between citizen troops and provincial auxiliaries was to be rigorously maintained. The extension of the franchise, though not wholly discontinued, was kept within narrow limits. The Senate was purged of its alien elements; and in the assignment of administrative posts true Romans born were given all the plums. Two classes of society were officially recognized as fields of recruitment for the public service. First there was the aristocracy proper—consisting of senators, senators' sons, and men specially promoted into it at the Emperor's discretion. From these 'senatorials' were drawn not merely the consuls, praetors, or other annual magistrates, and, as naturally followed, the governors of senatorial provinces, but also the governors of imperial provinces and the commanding officers of the legions. In the second place, the *bourgeoisie* was not forgotten, for Augustus gave to the equestrian order, as to the senatorial order, an official status. From its members he drew the governors of the smaller imperial provinces; and from them too the commanding officers of the auxiliary troops. Finally, as the summit of an equestrian career, there was reserved a much coveted post—not safe presumably to entrust in senatorial hands—the captaincy of the Pretorian Guard.

It is not to be supposed that nobody grumbled at the passing of the Republic. Many of the old families felt the degradation bitterly. Some retired from public life and sulked in philosophic seclusion; some diehards were still found under succeeding emperors eager to strike a blow for liberty. But the majority acquiesced; and by his skilful statecraft Augustus soon succeeded in diverting their thoughts and energies into useful channels of imperial service. It was perhaps the greatest part of his achievement that he inspired his fellow-countrymen with a new sense of public duty. Psychologically, no less than politically, his reign marked a turning-point. For the past hundred years and more the Roman character had been subjected to the disintegrating influences of Hellenistic culture and individualist philosophies. But now at last the sterling moral qualities of that character, strengthened rather than weakened by its new intellectual development, began to re-emerge. The regeneration was timely for the progress of civilization; for in the coming days, under the gross misrule of some of Augustus' successors, it was the conscientious zeal and cool efficiency of the average Roman official which alone availed to hold the Empire together.

II. THE AUGUSTAN REVIVAL

Augustus was far too shrewd a man to consider it sufficient to keep his fellow-countrymen well occupied. Like more than one European statesman of to-day, he saw that after the widespread demoralization of the preceding era it was essential to restore pride and self-respect to the national character; and there can be no doubt that a moral, artistic, and religious revival played an important part in his programme of reform. Of the need for some moral improvement it is scarcely neces-sary to speak. The over-rapid growth of wealth and luxury, together with the sudden influx of free-thinkers and often of loose livers from Greece or the Levant, had worked sad havoc on Roman society. Among the aristocracy divorce was widely prevalent. Unsettled conditions had discouraged marriage and the raising of families, and the birth-rate was declining. Every form of vice and extravagance was rampant. Now in Augustus' nature, as we have hinted, there was a strong vein of conservatism. A return to the old-fashioned sobriety of early days made a strong appeal to him. His personal habits were extremely simple; and it is not surprising that he attempted by legislation to impose a similar austerity on others. At one time he tried (as others had done before him) to limit the sum which might be spent on private banquets. He made adultery a public offence to which severe penalties were attached. He forbade the attendance of women at athletic displays. But his most famous measures were those by which he sought to regulate divorce and encourage a return to larger families. By the *Lex Julia* of 18 B.C. bachelors were forbidden to receive legacies at all, while married men who had no children were forced to pay a heavy inheritance duty. Subsequently by the *Lex Papia-Poppaea* of 9 A.D.[1] the parents of three children and over were rewarded by exemption from certain taxes and by preference in promotion to certain offices. Such legislation, however, was very unpopular and could have but a passing effect. The young dandies of Rome were incorrigible. The emancipated ladies of the day were no better. Even within the circle of the court itself there were sad goings on; and, as we shall see later, a scandal in which his own daughter was involved cast a gloom over the Emperor's life.

But whatever the frivolity of some sections of society, Augustus could count on carrying the more serious-minded with him. Among his special intimates two stood out— Agrippa, the soldier who had fought his battles at Actium and elsewhere, and whom during his absence in the Eastern provinces he left in charge of Rome; and Maecenas the refined and courtly diplomat who was always ready at his master's elbow to discuss a point of morals or offer sage political advice. It was thanks chiefly to the discrimination and encouragement of Maecenas that the reign of Augustus became an age of culture second to very few in the history of the world. For he gathered round himself, and so introduced into the Emperor's entourage, a circle of literary genius which included amongst others Propertius, Horace, and Virgil. To their patron some of these owed everything. Virgil, when evicted from his farm during the early days of the Civil War, had recovered it through Maecenas' intervention. Horace for his part received the grant of a small estate among the Sabine hills. The facilities for publication, too, which the great man's staff of copyists must have afforded, would mean much to poor writers in days when all books had to be written out by hand. But the effect of patronage is double-edged. The spontaneous vitality which characterized the poetry of Lucretius and Catullus seems somewhat lacking in the literature of the Augustan Age. It is as though with the loss of political liberty a sense of constraint and artificiality crept in. Men had to watch their words; and not daring to express their innermost thoughts

[1] Introduced, significantly enough, in the names of two consuls who themselves were *bachelors*!

freely, they contented themselves with an elaboration and perfection of style. Many, like Propertius and Tibullus, were mainly occupied in writing elegiac odes to their mistresses; or, like Ovid, in his *Metamorphoses*, in retelling the fairy-tales of Greece in mechanical Latin hexameters. But even Ovid, popular as he was with the gayer sparks at court, paid dearly for it when he overstepped the bounds of propriety, and found himself exiled to the shores of the Black Sea. Flattery of Augustus was only to be expected from the recipients of his bounty; and quite certainly it was in part the purpose of Maecenas' patronage that his protégés should help to glorify the new regime. The Emperor must have approved though he did not dictate; and from an historical point of view the most important feature of Augustan literature is unquestionably its patriotic tone.

Under a ruler who aimed at a restoration of Rome's past greatness, the glorification of that past was a congenial theme; and the most notable prose work of the period was the monumental history of Titus Livius. From his native town of Patavium in Cisalpine Gaul Livy moved to the capital; and being there admitted to Augustus' favour, he proceeded with the compilation of his prodigious narrative. Of its 142 books scarcely a quarter now remain to us; but in its original scope the history began with the foundation of the city in 753 B.C. and continued right down to the middle of Augustus' reign.

It remained for Virgil to sing the glories of an even remoter past in a still more famous work. He too was a native of Cisalpine Gaul, but despite his obscure origin his earliest poems attracted the notice of Maecenas. These were the *Eclogues*, written in imitation of Theocritus' *Idylls*, charming and wistful dialogues in highly artificial language between highly imaginary rustic folk. The choice of his next theme was due to Maecenas' suggestion. A revival of Italian agriculture was ardently desired; and the good cause might, it was thought, gain popularity and dignity by a poem written in its praise. The result was astonishingly successful. In the *Georgics*, which dealt with such subjects as the culture of olives, the making of a plough, and the care of cattle or bees, Virgil's intimate knowledge of the country-side and his gift for melodious word-painting found abundant scope; nor did he neglect the opportunity of representing Augustus as a god-like figure presiding over a world miraculously restored to prosperity and peace. But it was, as we have said, in a remoter past and the mythical story of Rome's antecedents that Virgil found his noblest inspiration. The *Aeneid*, which even at his death in 19 B.C. still lacked its final polish, is an epic in twelve books, ranking beside the *Iliad* and *Paradise Lost* as one of the greatest poems of all time. It told of the adventures of the Trojan hero Aeneas, how after the downfall of his city he took ship and after many wanderings was driven on to the coast of Africa; how there he fell in love with the Carthaginian queen Dido, but left her in obedience to the call of destiny, which required that he should refound the fortunes of his race upon Italian soil. The last books tell how this destiny was accomplished, but not before Aeneas, led by the Sibyl of Cumae, had made a descent into the Underworld and there had witnessed, as in prophetic vision, the line of Rome's great sons in ages yet to be. This episode, like many another passage, is aglow with patriotic pride; and since Aeneas' son Iulus was regarded as the original founder of the Julian family (to which, through his uncle, Augustus himself belonged), the complimentary character of the whole poem could scarcely fail to please. Had Virgil's genius been of a lesser order, its popularity would never have outlived his age; but the lofty perfection of its measured diction, the haunting music of the melodious lines, and above all, perhaps, the unforgettable touches of melancholy pathos have won for the *Aeneid* more admirers than any other poem of antiquity can claim.

The lyrics of Virgil's close friend Horace, though very different in tone and manner, have also a peculiar appeal for many modern minds. Apart from the faultless felicity of his highly studied versification (he adapted many Greek metres with inimitable skill) there is a singular charm about the author's genial personality. He is not very profound; but he is extraordinarily sane and well-balanced; and whether he enlarges upon the pleasures of friendship, the frailty of mortal life, or the advantages of temperate self-restraint, he always has something to say abundantly well worth saying and says it with a wit, brevity, and precision that give many of his lines an almost proverbial ring. In the days when the classical tradition was at its height in England, no ancient poet was more frequently quoted.

To Horace himself the crowning success of his career came in 17 B.C. In that year Augustus determined to celebrate—as though in solemn inauguration of the new regime—the Secular Games, a festival which by ancient tradition was due to be held every 110 years; and since Virgil was dead he selected Horace for the task of writing the Secular Hymn to be sung in procession by a chorus of girls and boys. Thus by a shrewd touch of statecraft the skill of a sceptical poet and the ritual of an obsolete ceremony were enlisted in the cause of a national religious revival. It was a cause which most certainly lay very near Augustus' heart. Already on his return after Actium he had made a point of restoring the temples of the gods—no less than eighty-two in number—which had fallen into ruins or disrepair during the Civil Wars. He built a new temple to Mars the Avenger, in memory of the vengeance taken on his uncle's murderers; and sedulously maintained the cult of Venus Genetrix, by tradition the patron goddess of his uncle's family. He took a pleasure in reviving primitive rites of augury and such like. He bestowed special honour on the Vestal Virgins; and finally in 12 B.C. he himself assumed the role of Pontifex Maximus the official president of the orthodox State cults. Here, as elsewhere, we can detect the conservative instinct which underlay Augustus' policy; and it is only to be supposed that he genuinely hoped to re-vitalize men's interest in such things. The pomp and circum-stance of public religion had no doubt its influence upon the mob; for, superstition apart, they would be impressed by the mere spectacle. But most educated men were weary of the threadbare make-believe and had long since turned to the consolations of philosophy; some, as Stoics, holding themselves aloof from politics in a somewhat puritanical pose of conscious rectitude; others, as Epicureans, abandoning themselves with a sort of fatalistic insouciance to the enjoyment of leisure or vice.

Nevertheless, beneath this mood of widespread scepticism there lurked an uneasy craving for something more satisfying than mere crude materialism. Many attempted to find it, as we shall later see, in the Mystery Cults of Greece or the Levant. But the superstitious impulse took one peculiar form of which more must be said here, for it led to the worship of the very Emperor himself.

Nothing in antiquity appears to us more inexplicable than the narrowness of the dividing line which men then drew between the human being and the god. Julius Caesar, like Alexander before him, had apparently courted divine honours during his lifetime. He certainly had been deified after he was dead; and now there seems to have sprung up throughout the Empire a spontaneous desire to thrust the same honours on the man to whom it owed so much. In the Eastern provinces, long accustomed to pay to royal personages the homage, if not the actual worship, due to gods, the idea spread rapidly. The most extravagant titles were conferred upon Augustus. In an extant Greek inscription he is described as 'God, Son of God, Augustus the Benefactor'; in Egypt he was 'Son of the Sun, Eternal Lord of the Diadem'. Temples and altars were set up in his honour; and seeing, no doubt, the political advantages of such a step, he allowed his image to be worshipped in conjunction with the goddess Roma, a personification of the imperial city. The cult soon extended to the Western provinces, and, after some hesitation on Augustus' part, was even admitted to Italy. Here, however, it was rather his 'genius'—the divine element which according to the old Roman belief was held to reside in every home and family—that was to be the object of men's veneration; and a special order of priests—drawn chiefly from the freedman class and known as 'Augustales'—was established both in Italian and provincial townships to superintend its rites. At Rome no actual temple was allowed; but by a characteristic compromise Augustus sought to graft the new cult on to an old tradition, the worship of his 'genius' being associated with the shrines of the 'Cross-road Lars' or protective spirits which stood in every ward of the city. Deification proper was to follow after Augustus' death; and it became the almost invariable practice to bestow the same honour upon each successive emperor. When the recipient was manifestly unworthy, the sceptics at Rome might crack their jokes over the anomaly; but from the point of view of imperial policy the cult had real importance. The worship of the Emperor became a symbol, uniting the heterogeneous population of Rome's dependencies in a common loyalty and encouraging a superstitious belief that the rule which they obeyed was somehow rooted in the divine order of things.

One result which followed from Augustus' religious revival —and a result which he himself no doubt intended—was the beautification of the capital. Not merely was he responsible for the reconstruction of old temples and the erection of several new ones, but also for a very marked improvement in the lay-out of the city. During the last two generations the influence of Greek art had been steadily growing at Rome. Artists and architects had come over in large numbers; and an increasing familiarity with the great Hellenistic cities, such as Alexandria, produced its effect. Like Julius Caesar before him, Augustus borrowed from these the conception of a spacious and symmetrical planning which contrasted well with the irregular, haphazard development of Republican building. Like Caesar, he too laid out a forum or open square which was called after his name and which contained the Temple of Mars above mentioned. In the Campus Martius— a site which till Caesar's time had been little used for building —there now arose a magnificent series of monuments. First of all there was the huge circular tomb or mausoleum sixty feet in height and three hundred in circumference, which was intended to form the resting-place of Augustus and his family. Then there was a theatre built in memory of Marcellus, Augustus' favourite nephew. Agrippa was responsible for a large public bath, and, still more splendid, for the great temple known as the Pantheon, which, in the altered form that the Emperor Hadrian gave to it, remains one of the outstanding achievements of Roman architecture.

The style of these buildings, as indeed of all Roman buildings, was adapted from Hellenic models, the Doric, Ionic, and Corinthian orders being employed, often in combination with each other. Though in the finish of their detail they were vastly inferior to buildings of the best Greek periods, they often attained great magnificence of scale and proportion. Their huge mass was in itself imposing; and the frequent use of arches, vaults, and even soaring domes[1]—the characteristic feature of Roman architecture as compared with the rectangular style of the Greeks—gave an added sense of height and dignity. The great Roman masterpieces were in fact achievements of engineering even more than of artistry; and their construction owed much to the discovery of a building material far more durable than the sun-dried brick or the porous local stone which had hitherto been largely employed. This was the famous concrete—a compound of volcanic ash with lime and powdered stone which was now coming into vogue. Its texture was almost indestructible; and its value for constructing a solid arch or vault is obvious. But the ugly brown surface needed covering. Normally a coating of white stucco was used; but in public buildings and in the richer private houses a veneer of marble slabs was preferred. Thus Augustus' well-known boast that he had found a city of brick and left one of marble was, in a superficial sense, justified. In any case he had given his countrymen a capital to be proud of and a capital at last fully worthy of its position at the head of a world Empire.

III. ECONOMIC PROSPERITY

The reign of Augustus is rightly reckoned as one of the Golden Ages of history. Contemporary poets hailed it as such. Yet despite the magnificence of its architectural achievement and the brilliance of its literary output the keynote of the age was not so much intellectual or artistic activity (as had been the case in Periclean Athens). but rather material prosperity. For the first time within human record the whole Mediterranean world enjoyed peace. Under Rome's rule the less civilized of her subjects in Spain, Gaul, and Africa abandoned their age-long feuds. The conflicts of kings and empires which had so long racked the East were a thing of the past. Piracy—that ever-recurrent scourge of the middle seas—was completely suppressed; for now a regular fleet—another innovation which must stand to Augustus' credit—was permanently maintained in two squadrons based one at

[1] The dome of the Pantheon was due to Hadrian's reconstruction.

Misenum near Naples and the other at Ravenna near the mouth of the Po. Men felt a new sense of security, immensely welcome after the turmoil and hazards of the preceding epoch. As was natural, both trade and industry began to flourish on an unprecedented scale; and it will not be inappropriate to say something here concerning the economic development of the world under the Early Empire.

The outstanding fact of the Empire's economic life was the dependence of Rome and, to a lesser degree, of Italy upon the products of the provinces. In the first place (as has often been noted), the home-country was far from self-supporting in the matter of food. Agriculture, it is true, was improving. Land, which for nearly two centuries had been under grass, was now ploughed up again and was found to have recovered its fertility. Unfortunately, however, many yeoman-farmers were displaced by the discharged veterans of the Civil War; and as the latter were generally lacking in both agricultural tastes or experience, the farms soon reverted to the ownership of large proprietors. Meanwhile except in the south the culture of vines, olives, and vegetables remained more profitable than corn-growing; and the population of the capital, as perhaps of other towns, continued to be fed from the granaries of Asia Minor, Egypt and North Africa.

When we turn to consider the products of Italian manufacture, the situation was better, but was scarcely conducive to the maintenance of a vigorous native population. There were still of course a large number of small craftsmen—smiths, cobblers, carpenters and their like—who made goods to sell to their neighbours; but their number was dwindling. The attractions of a military career drew into the legions many who found it impossible to make a living as independent artisans; and the healthy development of large-scale industries was rendered almost impossible for two reasons. The first was lack of leadership. Among the upper classes of Roman society there was a rooted prejudice against engaging in industrial enterprise.[1] The professions proper for an aristocrat

[1] A curious exception was the manufacture of bricks, which, being reckoned part of the normal work of a landed estate, was considered respectable. The Emperor Marcus Aurelius inherited a vast fortune from this source.

were soldiering, the bar, or a political career; for an equestrian banking or trade. In either case the Roman 'gentleman' felt a snobbish contempt for the artisan class; and the idea of organizing manufacture seems therefore to have been distasteful to him. Secondly, when the rich man did employ labour, it was almost invariably slave-labour. Slaves now drove the plough on his farms. Slaves minded the sheep on his ranches. Even the clothes on his back were woven from the wool, which those ranches supplied, by the female slaves of his domestic staff. It was therefore inevitable that when manufacture on any large scale did take place, slaves and not free-citizens should be almost exclusively employed.

There were two main centres of manufacture in Italy which were now, however, of some real importance; but neither of them, be it noted, was in the neighbourhood of Rome. Round Arretium (the modern Arezzo in Umbria) beds of fine red clay were being utilized for making a good glazed pottery, decorated, as a rule, with delicate embossed patterns. This ware was very popular even outside Italy and enormous quantities of vessels were turned out on stereotyped patterns for export to the Western provinces. Then again in Campania the proximity of the Elba mines had led (as we have seen) to a vigorous metal industry. Iron instruments of every kind were wrought in the smithies round Puteoli and Naples, also for the export trade. The bronze ware of the Capuan factories too was famous throughout the world; and immense numbers of slaves must have been there employed on a system of mass-production. In these commodities, indeed, Italy held for a time a definite lead in world trade.

On the other hand, the goods thus exported were more than offset by what came into Italy from overseas. There was by now a vast accumulation of wealth in Rome—acquired partly as income from property owned abroad, partly as the proceeds of moneylending or commercial enterprise; so that the cost of the adverse balance was not difficult to meet and the produce of East and West alike poured into the luxurious metropolis. From the Western provinces, as yet half-civilized, came chiefly raw materials such as wool, leather, and minerals, and to some small extent the coarser kinds of cloth. The

East, on the other hand, long skilled in many handicrafts, supplied manufactured goods. Glass came from Sidon; rugs and tapestries from Asia Minor (as they still come to-day); linen from Egypt, and silk from the Far East. The caravan trade with Arabia, India, and even China brought spices, incense, jewels, and all manner of luxuries to the Levantine ports for shipment to Italy. By this time Italian merchants were coming more and more to control the actual processes of purchase, packing, lading, and so forth; but the carrying trade still remained, as before, principally in the hands of Greek and Syrian mariners. More or less regular services seem to have been developed along certain well-defined trade-routes. As a port of disembarkation in Italy, Ostia, though nearest to Rome, was little favoured, since the unproductive metropolis offered small chance of a return cargo. Puteoli, on the other hand, not merely possessed a better harbour, but was admirably placed to serve the Campanian export trade. So here, as we may read in the Acts of the Apostles, ships from the East were wont to unload their wares which were then transported overland to Rome.[1]

Though Rome was thus still a parasitic capital and though the ruling race continued to be—in Tacitus' famous phrase— the 'exploiters of the world', yet it would be quite wrong to suppose that the provinces did not share in the new prosperity. On the contrary, they profited in innumerable ways. The *Pax Romana*, as we have said, conferred an enormous boon. Not merely was the scourge of perpetual war removed, but even domestic faction and disorder were suppressed. The reforms of Augustus secured the natives against some of the worst forms of official tyranny. Administrative methods grew sounder. The machinery of local government, which was still left in the hands of the provincials themselves, was regularized by supervision and, in the less orderly districts, reinforced by the presence of imperial troops. So, too, the more important legal cases could always be referred to the

[1] If Italy itself was not self-supporting it is important to realize that the Empire as a whole contained all the resources necessary for a prosperous standard of living, so long, that is, as those resources were properly exploited.

governor's tribunal and native codes of law became gradually assimilated to the Roman model of jurisprudence. In the pages of the New Testament we can find abundant evidence of the beneficent influence of Roman rule. We read how a governor of Achaea would not permit the Christian missionaries to be bullied by a pack of jealous Jews, how a town clerk at Ephesus was seriously troubled at the prospect of being brought to book for a day of uproar, how St. Paul was rescued by Roman soldiers from the fury of the Jerusalem mob, and how finally, when in dissatisfaction at his treatment by local governors, he appealed to Caesar's judgment-seat, there was scarcely a question but that to Caesar he must go.

Nobody in truth benefited more by the change from the Republic to the Principate than did the inhabitants of the provinces. The Senate's concern had been merely for the welfare of the small section of Roman society. The Emperor was ruler of the Empire as a whole. Even Augustus, as we have seen, spent many years on tours of inspection in both East and West. The best of his successors did the same. The example of an Emperor's zeal, moreover, could scarcely be lost on his subordinates. There were still, of course, good governors and bad governors; but the progressive aim of provincial administration is attested by the rapid spread of culture in every form. The primary motive was not philanthropy, but the twofold urge of military efficiency and trade. Both purposes were served by the construction of roads, bridges, and harbours. Towns sprang up where Roman garrisons were quartered or where Roman traders desired a centre of exchange. But, as Tacitus later remarked, comfort is the best civilizer of backward peoples; and knowing this the more far-sighted governors even sought to foster a local pride among the natives. The construction of municipal buildings was encouraged and schools were started. The Roman toga replaced the trousers of the Gaul or (when conquered) of the Briton; and gradually the provincial townships became, as it were, little replicas of Rome. Such were to be the ultimate fruits of imperial rule; but this achievement was naturally not accomplished in a day. Nor must we forget that its peaceful development depended first and foremost, on the security of

the frontiers; and to this, which more than any was the
Emperor's special sphere, we must now turn.

IV. THE FRONTIERS EAST AND WEST

Almost continuously throughout its history the problem
of the frontiers was to tax the military resources of the Empire
and exercise the minds of its rulers. As time went on, in fact,
the problem became a question of life and death for Roman
civilization; and since in these pages we shall have to recur
again and again to wars fought in those frontiers' defence, it
will be well to say something here about their character.

Of the three main frontiers—the African, the Asiatic, and
the European—the African presented few difficulties. To the
old province which roughly corresponded with Carthaginian
territory, Caesar had added the new province of Numidia;
and though Mauretania was still left in the hands of client-
princes, the whole coastal strip was now in the process of
rapid Romanization. So the task of the one legion quartered
there was simply to safeguard the trade-routes and keep at
bay the nomad tribes of the interior; and for this occasional
raids into the desert appear to have sufficed.

In the East the problem was very different. The province
of Syria indeed was well protected by a great expanse of well-
nigh impassable desert on its eastern borders; but the Roman
territory in Asia Minor (which; beside some client principalities,
now included the provinces of Asia, Bithynia, and Cilicia,
and after 25 B.C. Galatia and Pamphylia) was defended by no
natural barrier of river or mountain-range; and through the
rugged hill-country of Armenia or the still easier passage of
the upper Euphrates valley, the way lay open for the Parthian
enemy. This people had long since been recognized as a
formidable menace; and since their destruction of Crassus
and his legions in 53 B.C. their ambitions had not abated. Their
subsequent invasion of Asia Minor had in 38 B.C. been checked
by Antony's lieutenant Ventidius Bassus; but Antony himself,
in attempting to turn the tables, had narrowly escaped disaster.
It was expected of Augustus that he would undertake a
campaign to wipe out the disgrace of Carrhae. Horace in
delighted anticipation predicted that he would 'add the dour

THE EASTERN FRONTIER

Parthian to the Roman realm'. But such a crusade had no attractions for the Emperor himself. He was not by instinct or ability a soldier. He had reduced his army to a minimum, and all available troops which could be spared were to be needed on the European frontier. He preferred to try what diplomacy could do.

Now the best safeguard perhaps which Rome possessed against Parthian aggression was the Parthians' own tendency to internal dissension. The succession to the throne was endlessly disputed by claimants and counter-claimants; and about this time, as it so happened, one such quarrel was in full swing. A certain Tiridates, being ejected by Phraates, whom he himself had previously dispossessed, had taken refuge in the province of Syria. Incidentally, too, he had managed to get into his power an infant son of Phraates, and the indignant parent approached the Romans with a demand for his extradition. Negotiations were begun, and in 20 B.C. Augustus himself arrived in the East in time to conclude an honourable settlement. It seems clear that Phraates was eager to buy off any danger of Roman intervention; and in exchange for his child he restored the standards captured at Carrhae and (to quote Augustus' own words) 'begged for the friendship of Rome'. The *entente* was sealed by the dispatch of young Parthian princes to be educated in Italy (just as young oriental princes come to England to-day); and, conveniently enough for the Eastern frontier's security, the faction in Parthia which supported these pro-Roman candidates for the throne, showed small inclination to compromise with their more nationally minded opponents.

Meanwhile the problem of the Eastern frontier further involved the consideration of the intervening State of Armenia. There was little to be said for attempting the conquest of this mountainous principality, which it would have needed a large army to conquer and a considerable garrison to hold. There were obvious advantages, too, in avoiding a direct abutment of the Roman upon the Parthian frontier; and Augustus decided to treat Armenia as a 'buffer-State'. In 20 B.C. the accident of the murder of the ruling prince enabled him to place Tigranes—another oriental at that time quartered at

Rome—upon the vacant throne. After Tigranes' death, however, fierce quarrelling broke out between the faction which favoured Rome and the faction which favoured Parthia; and though in A.D. 2 diplomacy procured the Parthian King's recognition of Augustus' nominee, the policy of the 'buffer-State' left, as it so frequently does, a somewhat uneasy situation. Within a few years Armenia was in fact to relapse under Parthian influence.

If on the Eastern frontier natural barriers were lacking, it was not so in Europe. The merest glance at the map suggests that the two great divergent rivers, Rhine and Danube, would form a good defensive line for an Empire covering not only Gaul, but most of the Balkans; and, inasmuch as since Caesar's conquest the Gallic frontier had already marched with the Rhine, strategical considerations seemed to dictate a corresponding advancement of the Illyrian-Macedonian frontiers[1] to the Danube. The need for some such co-ordination of the defensive system was urgent. Even in the intervals of the Civil War Augustus himself had been compelled to conduct a campaign against the Dalmatian tribesmen at the head of the Adriatic. Wild mountaineers, descending from the Alpine passes, were still liable to harry the peaceful plains of Cisalpine Gaul; while beyond the Rhine and Danube in the forest lands of Central Europe the savage German peoples were predatory and restless. The terror of the Teuton and Cimbric wanderings barely a century before was still a hideous memory at Rome, and if more was wanted to prompt a resolute policy, it was provided by an incident which occurred in 17 B.C. In that year the Sugambri, Tencteri, and other German tribes broke across the Rhine, cut up a legion under Marcus Lollius, and carried its standards away home. Augustus himself hurried north. His stepson Tiberius was given the military command of Gaul, and the forward move was begun.

Tiberius' first step—since punitive measures against the Germans were postponed—was to effect the subjugation of

[1] The Macedonian frontier had in fact been already secured by a campaign conducted by M. Licinius Crassus in 29 B.C. This had resulted in the creation of a 'military area' in Moesia which was placed under a *legatus*, Macedonia becoming at the same time a senatorial province.

the Alpine tribes which formed a hostile salient inconveniently projecting inside the intended frontier line of Rhine and Danube. Assisted by his younger brother Drusus, who marched up from Cisalpine Gaul, he reduced the districts of East Switzerland and the Tyrol, and formed of them a new province called Raetia. Simultaneously the kingdom of Noricum (the modern Austria) was annexed by the Illyrian governor, Publius Silius. Both Raetia and Noricum bordered on the upper reaches of the Danube; and when three years later Tiberius was transferred to the Illyrian command he pushed the frontier forward to the middle reaches also, by creating the new province of Pannonia (12 B.C.).[1] It was probably in the following year that Moesia was also formally annexed, and since Thrace was already under the protectorate of Rome, the River Danube thus became from source to mouth the official frontier of the Empire.

While Tiberius was engaged in the conquest of Pannonia, Drusus, his younger brother, and his successor in the Gallic command, was undertaking a far more adventurous task. The motives which led to the attempted subjugation of Germany are not difficult to guess. From a strategic point of view the angle formed by the lines of the Rhine and Danube was no ideal frontier. Far shorter and more easily defensible would be the *straight* line formed by the Elbe and the middle Danube. Much, of course, would depend on the possibility of permanently pacifying the uncivilized German folk. But the ease of Caesar's Gallic conquest suggested an encouraging parallel; and traders no doubt had already done something to familiarize the nearer tribes with Roman habits. In any case the project, when once decided on, was pursued with extraordinary tenacity for over a quarter of a century.

It was indeed a troublesome business. The absence of roads in that wild forest country prompted the use of river valleys not merely for commissariat but also for the movement of troops. Flowing into the North Sea, and roughly parallel with the Rhine, are three rivers—the Ems (or Amisia), the Weser (or Visurgis), and the Elbe (or Albis). By these a

---

[1] Henceforward Illyria, enlarged by additional territory at the head of the Adriatic, was known as Dalmatia.

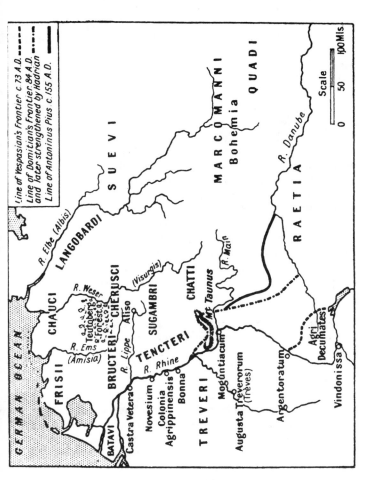

Line of Vespasian's Frontier c. 73 A.D.
Line of Domitian's Frontier 84 A.D. and later strengthened by Hadrian
Line of Antoninus Pius c. 155 A.D.

GERMAN OCEAN

R. Elbe (Albis)

LANGOBARDI

SUEVI

CHAUCI

MARCOMANNI

Bohemia

QUADI

R. Weser

CHERUSCI

(Visurgis)

BRUCTERI

Teutoberg
Forest

Aliso

R. Ems
(Amisia)

R. Lippe

SUGAMBRI

CHATTI

R. Main

Mt. Taunus

TENCTERI

R. Rhine

Moguntiacum

R. Danube

RAETIA

FRISII

BATAVI

Castra Vetera

Novesium

Colonia Agrippinensis

Bonna

TREVERI

Augusta Treverorum
(Treves)

Argentoratum

Agri
Decumates

Vindonissa

Scale

0   50   100 Mls.

THE GERMAN FRONTIER

Roman force, working from the coast, might penetrate the interior stage by stage; and, if communications by sea were maintained, might similarly be fed with supplies. As a preliminary, therefore, a canal was dug, opening a short-cut from the lower Rhine into the Zuyder Zee. Through this passage in 12 B.C. Drusus set out with a flotilla of ships. Coasting along the shore, he easily won the adherence of the Frisii, and, though he reached the River Ems, he appears to have been content with a mere cursory exploration of this northern coast. The Romans were not much accustomed as yet to a scientific consolidation of their conquests. In dealing with other wild peoples, especially in the East, they had usually found that a powerful demonstration of military strength was sufficient to ensure submission. Drusus therefore made no attempt to hold the districts he had overrun; but led his troops back to winter on the Rhine.

Meanwhile he had begun to fortify the Rhine frontier with a series of strongly entrenched camps, including Castra Vetera, Bonna (Bonne), Moguntiacum (Mainz), and Argentoratum (Strasbourg); and the additional security thus afforded enabled him to concentrate a considerable striking force for the next year's campaign. Starting from Castra Vetera on the Middle Rhine, he marched up its tributary the River Lippe, struck across country past the sources of the Ems, and so through the territory of the Cherusci to the upper waters of the Visurgis or Weser. This thrust into the centre of Germany attained three ends. It advanced the Roman pioneer posts from the Ems to the Weser. It completed the encirclement of the area previously attacked from the sea; and by the planting of a great forward base at Aliso on the Lippe a wedge was driven between the tribes of this northern area and the tribes of the south. Chief among the latter were the Chatti, and the following year (10 B.C.) seems mainly to have been spent in their subjugation.

All was now ready for the final advance which in 9 B.C. was to carry the frontier forward from the line of the Weser to the Elbe itself. Drusus led his army in triumph to the coveted objective, and proudly set up a trophy on the river-bank. Not long afterwards he fell from his horse, broke a leg, and died in agony within the month. The loss of his favourite stepson was a grievous blow to Augustus; and though he replaced Tiberius in the vacant command, there was little love lost between them. A couple of years later Tiberius was again transferred. This time his mission was to be in the East; but he threw it up in disgust and retired to sulk in the island of Rhodes. During his absence Domitius Ahenobarbus was given the German command; but, since Augustus was unwilling to entrust full control of the armies to any but members of his own family, there was a lull in active campaigning. In A.D. 4, however, Tiberius was restored to favour and resumed the German command, and it then seemed as though only the finishing touches were needed to complete the pacification of the conquered country. Everywhere Roman officials were busy with the work of organization. Military roads were being built eastwards from the Rhine. In the country lying between the Weser and the Elbe a rebellion of the Chauci was put down. The Elbe itself was navigated by the fleet; and in order to carry the frontier from its upper waters to the line of the middle Danube nothing more was now required than the reduction of the Marcomanni, a formidable tribe who under the vigorous rule of their king, Maroboduus, had occupied Bohemia. All preparation had been made for this crowning campaign. The Rhineland army under Saturninus was to descend from the north-west. Tiberius, with the Illyrian troops, was to cross the Danube from the south. Then suddenly all went wrong. In A.D. 6 a terrible revolt broke out in Pannonia and Dalmatia. At Rome the public completely lost their nerve. The wildest rumours were afloat. But luckily Tiberius kept a cool head. He made terms with Maroboduus; then returned to Pannonia and settled down to a systematic reduction of the guerrilla insurgents. It took him, however, the better part of three years; and before he could resume the task of conquering Germany a thing happened which destroyed all real hope of achieving it.

The truth is that to conquer Gaul and to conquer Germany were two very different things. National unity may have been equally lacking in the one case as in the other; but the primitive savagery of these wild German tribesmen did not offer such favourable soil for Roman cultural influences as did the settled and comparatively civilized communities of Gaul. They were daring huntsmen and ferocious fighters; and Tacitus tells us how some of their warriors were accustomed to wear an iron bracelet which they vowed not to lay aside until they had slain their man. So now, under an appearance of tranquillity, the fierce spirit of their independence was smouldering still. The ringleader of disaffection was a young chief of the Cherusci, Arminius by name, who, while maintaining the friendliest relations with the Roman staff at whose mess he frequently dined, was all the while hatching schemes of revolt with the Chatti, Bructeri, and other tribes. The command of the Rhine armies was now in the hands of Publius Quinctilius Varus. He was a man of no military distinction; and having come recently from the East, where he had served as governor of Syria, he now set to work with singular fatuity to tax the Germans as though they had been submissive Levantines. While his collectors were busy, he spent the summer on the Visurgis, and, as autumn drew on, he set out to lead back his three legions into winter quarters at Aliso. They were making their way through the Teutoberg Forest in the territory of the Cherusci when they were suddenly assailed. Beating off the attack, they abandoned their baggage and plunged on through the thickets and swamps. Rain beat down on them in torrents. The wind rose to a hurricane. Broken branches descended on their heads and fallen trees blocked their path. For three days they struggled desperately on; but they could not shake the enemy off. At length Varus committed suicide. Many followed his example. The remainder surrendered. Most were massacred then and there; some were put to death by torture; hardly a man escaped (A.D. 9).

The news fell like a thunderclap on Rome. Fresh troops were hastily levied and the safety of the Rhine front secured. But all attempt to recover the lost ground was postponed; and though, after Augustus' death, Drusus' son Germanicus was to lead the legions into the interior once more, the Rhine remained henceforward the permanent frontier of the Empire. In some ways this line was actually more convenient than the

TIMGAD

TRAJAN

more distant Elbe; for its army of defence could also act as garrison over the provinces of Gaul. But for the future of Europe the defeat of Varus had the most momentous consequences; and it is scarcely too much to say that had Germany been Romanized, as Gaul and Spain were Romanized, the whole history of civilization might have been altered.

How complete had been Augustus' confidence in the success of his great venture is proved by the terrible nature of the shock its failure dealt him. From that moment he appears to have been a broken man. 'Varus, give me back my legions,' he was heard to mutter again and again in his distress. The long years of responsibility had told; and it was plain that he could not now be very far from his end. There remained the crucial question: What would happen when he died?

V. THE PROBLEM OF THE SUCCESSION

To a man who like Augustus had built up an autocracy based in a large degree on popular approval there could be no more anxious preoccupation than the choice of a successor fit to carry on his work; and under the circumstances it was a natural instinct as well as sound policy to limit the choice to members of his own family or kin. Now it was one of the bitter disappointments of Augustus' life that he never had a son. His first marriage brought him no issue. His second wife Scribonia bore him a daughter, Julia. His third wife Livia— a beautiful and accomplished woman, to marry whom he had divorced Scribonia in 38 B.C.—brought him no children; but by her former husband Tiberius Claudius Nero this lady had two sons, Tiberius and Drusus; and, as every one knows, it was in the eldest of these two stepsons that Augustus was forced eventually to find his heir.

At first, however, his ideas had centred round his daughter Julia, or rather round Julia's husbands one after the other in unpleasantly fatal succession. In 25 B.C. he married her to his sister's son Marcellus; and it was a bitter blow when two years later this favourite nephew was taken ill and died. Next, in 21 B.C., Julia was married to Agrippa, the capable commander on whom Augustus had so frequently relied and whom he now marked out as his consort and successor by a special grant of tribunician and proconsular powers. In 12 B.C., however, Agrippa also died, and Julia was thus left once more a widow, but this time with three sons, called Gaius, Lucius, and Agrippa Postumus. Looking round for a man who might make a fresh husband for his daughter and a suitable guardian for these infant grandsons, Augustus' choice fell upon his own stepson Tiberius.

To Tiberius himself marriage with Julia was exceedingly distasteful, for it meant that he must divorce his own much-loved wife, who, by a curious irony of fortune, was Agrippa's daughter by an earlier marriage. He complied, but with great bitterness at heart. A coolness sprang up between him and Augustus; and, though he too was invested with tribunician power, he soon began to realize that his two young charges, Gaius and Lucius, took precedence of himself in the Emperor's favour. In 6 B.C. he retired, as we have seen, to the island of Rhodes. But fate still continued to thwart Augustus' plans. First in 2 B.C. he discovered to his horror that Julia had been playing fast and loose with young dandies of the court. The scandal of his daughter's immorality was a bitter pill for the moral reformer to swallow. He struck out savagely—put one of her lovers to death, banished others, and sent her into permanent exile on an island.

Then in quick succession both his favourite grandsons died, Lucius in A.D. 2, and Gaius in A.D. 4. Agrippa Postumus was an impossible creature; and there was nothing for it but to fall back on Tiberius. Augustus adopted him as his son, and in A.D. 13, a year before his death, invested him with pro-consular power equal to his own. Of the wisdom of this final choice there could be no question. Apart from his military experience and ability, Tiberius was a man of sterling character, and if not possessed of his stepfather's brilliant powers of improvisation, he was at least fully capable of following the lines of policy which his stepfather had laid down.

As with all else in his life, Augustus had made arrangements with systematic care for the time when he himself should pass from the stage. He had drawn up a simple, but dignified record of his own achievements, copies of which were placed not merely in his great mausoleum on the Campus Martius, but also in various provincial centres where the cult of his 'genius' was observed. One of these copies, inscribed on stone, has actually been discovered at Ancyra (or Angora) in Asia Minor. More important still, Augustus left behind him a Breviarium or Survey, which included a statement of the population of the Empire, statistics of its military resources, a balance-sheet of his imperial exchequer, and finally, at the end, a legacy of advice to his successor, warning him against either an enlargement of the frontier or too free an extension of the franchise. Tiberius was almost certainly at his bedside to receive his last instructions when in A.D. 14 he died, a worn-out and, in many ways, a disappointed man, in the seventy-seventh year of his age. As he lay dying he quoted to his friends these lines from a Greek drama:

> Have I played well my part? Then clap your hands
> And blithely so dismiss me from the stage

—strange sentiments for a man who beyond all question had saved the civilized world!

CHAPTER XXI

THE JULIO-CLAUDIAN DYNASTY

I. TIBERIUS, A.D. 14–37

AUGUSTUS might nominate a successor, but he had no power to impose him upon the Roman State. Nevertheless, the awkward transition was accomplished with surprising smoothness. On his stepfather's death Tiberius acted with decision by immediately assuming the duties of commander-in-chief. The only rival claimant, Augustus' half-crazy grandson Agrippa Postumus, was murdered by his jailer—on whose orders no one knew. A few hot-heads talked wildly of a return to liberty; but the vast majority of Roman society accepted the new ruler almost as a matter of course. The armies took the oath of allegiance. The Senate voted the necessary imperial powers. The only note of hesitation was struck by Tiberius himself, who declared that he was unequal to the burden thus thrust upon him. Tacitus the historian, with his habitual cynicism, sets down this modest utterance to pure hypocrisy; but it is by no means certain that his interpretation is correct. There are few more fascinating studies in history than the character of Tiberius. Naturally austere, self-contained, and sensitive, he had been deeply embittered by the circumstances of his early career, first the enforced severance from his beloved wife, then by marriage with the frivolous and faithless Julia, and finally by the repeated snubs with which Augustus had rewarded his exemplary obedience and unswerving devotion to public duty. As a military commander he was both popular with the troops and successful in the field; but he was somewhat lacking in imagination and too proud to ingratiate himself by acquiescing in the shifts and shams of statecraft. The cult of emperor worship, for example, was extremely repugnant to his downright nature. Thus, when the Spaniards proposed to build a temple in his honour he refused. 'Think of me as a mortal,' he said, 'and (if you would honour my memory) as one who was worthy of his ancestors, steadfast in adversity, scrupulous of his subjects' welfare, careless of his own popularity.' It was characteristic of him that he dismissed as futile the attempt to curb luxurious extravagance by legislation, and refused to re-enact measures which Augustus had instituted, but which had never been observed.

Tiberius, in short, was conscious of his own limitations; but his genuine diffidence is best proved by the fact that he followed almost slavishly the lines of policy which Augustus had laid down for him. Above all he aimed at maintaining that appearance of partnership with the Senate which had been the foundation of Augustus' success. He treated them with courteous deference, attended their debates, deprecated flattery and even invited criticism. As a further compliment he transferred to the House the Assembly's function of electing the annual magistrates. Often he went out of his way to avoid any encroachment on its proper sphere, and when asked to nominate a governor to the senatorial province of Africa he suggested two names, but refused downright to make the final choice. On the other hand, there can be little doubt that it suited Tiberius to place upon his 'partners' the responsibility for actions which might have brought odium on himself. When cases came up for trial in which aristocrats were implicated he let the Senate try them. The House became, in fact, a court of high treason; and the consequences of this development, however well-intentioned, were most unfortunate. In the first place, unscrupulous persons, seeking either to satisfy a private grudge or simply to curry favour with the Emperor, came forward with charges which must often have been totally unfounded. In the second place, the Senate, feeling the Emperor's eye to be upon them, showed themselves only too ready to listen to such charges. So a treason trial usually led to a conviction. In A.D. 21 a man was put to death for no worse crime than reading aloud a poem which he had composed in mistaken anticipation of the death of Tiberius' son. Tiberius himself disliked such judicial abuses and did his best to check them; but the fact remains that both in this and the succeeding reigns the activities of these informers or *delators* became a regular scourge; and thus was bred an unwholesome atmosphere of insecurity and suspicion which reacted seriously not merely, as we shall see, upon the Emperor's nerves, but also upon Society's attitude towards him. Men came to regard him in the light of a tyrannical monster—which he certainly was not; but the tradition grew, and Tacitus' somewhat jaundiced vision led him to ascribe many of Tiberius' actions to motives of fear and jealousy of which he was probably quite innocent.

The first and perhaps least justified example of such misconstruction was concerned with the career of Tiberius' nephew Germanicus, the son of his dead brother Drusus. At the beginning of the reign this brilliant young man was in command of the Rhineland armies. Both here and in Pannonia[1] the military crises, which had occurred a few years previously, had left their mark on the troops. Recruits from the riff-raff of the capital had been drafted into the legions, thus lowering their quality; and it had been found necessary to

---

[1] Simultaneously with that meeting of the Rhineland Legions, there was unrest among the Pannonian troops which were tactfully pacified by Tiberius' son, Drusus.

retain with the colours many veterans who were due for their discharge. At the news of Augustus' death the smouldering disaffection blazed up into mutiny, and there was wild talk of marching on Rome and making Germanicus emperor. The young man, who was engaged at the moment in holding a census in Gaul, hurried back to the Lower Rhine; and the influence of his winning personality had its effect on the troops. He indignantly repudiated their disloyal suggestion and promised them certain concessions of service and pay. These, however, Tiberius refused to ratify, and the ugly temper reappeared. Then, feeling that the best remedy would be a bout of active service, Germanicus proceeded to a fresh invasion of Germany. The emperor must have approved the campaign; but in making this apparent departure from Augustus' instructions he seems to have intended not so much a serious attempt at reconquest, but rather a demonstration of Roman power. Prestige demanded that the disgrace of Varus' defeat should be wiped out and the Germans taught a wholesome respect for the imperial arms. Once the attack was launched, however, Germanicus' ambitions were stirred and the war assumed very formidable dimensions. In the first year, since the season was well advanced, he had to content himself with a march up the Lippe. In A.D. 15, however, adopting the same strategy as his father Drusus, he transferred his army by sea to the mouth of the Ems and pushed up it to join hands with another army which had marched overland. Then spreading devastation far and wide he paid a visit to the scene of Varus' disaster in the Teutoberg Forest—a ghastly spectacle of bleached skeletons and mouldering carcases. The Cherusci, still led by Arminius, proved, however, a dangerously elusive foe, and on the return march the overland column under Caecina was very nearly cut off. The main force under Germanicus also got into trouble; for, as it marched along the northern coast, a high tide, lashed by the equinoctial gales, caught it unawares and destroyed immense quantities of stores. Nothing daunted, Germanicus redoubled his efforts; and in A.D. 16 he once again transported his troops to the Ems, and advancing thence to the Weser fought and defeated Arminius in a pitched battle at Idistaviso and actually pushed on to the banks of the Elbe. Though the advance was only achieved at the cost of enormous bloodshed, no attempt was made to hold the ground thus won, and Germanicus returned to the Rhine, which remained, as heretofore, the official frontier. As a further protection a wide strip of country upon the eastern bank was cleared of inhabitants and kept in a state of semi-desolation useful only for pasturing cattle. The real safeguard against aggression, however, was the internal disunion of the Germans themselves. Within a year or two the Marcomanni were actually appealing to Rome for aid against their neighbours the Cherusci; and she was thus able to play off tribe against tribe, most advantageously to herself. Sometimes, as in the East, she even succeeded in slipping a nominee of her own into a vacant chieftainship.

Meanwhile seeing that Germanicus' zest for military adventure was becoming an almost excessive tax on the imperial resources, Tiberius very wisely recalled him (A.D. 16), and after allowing him to celebrate a triumph at Rome dispatched him on a mission with wide powers to the East. Here there was much diplomatic work for the young man to do. He superintended the formal annexation of Cappadocia. He visited Artaxata, the capital of Armenia, where he established a fresh pro-Roman prince on the throne; and finally on the Upper Euphrates he held an interview with Artabanus, the King of Parthia, thus cultivating better relations with that great oriental power. So far the success of his mission had been complete; but friction now arose with a certain Gnaeus Calpurnius Piso, a conceited and self-assertive aristocrat, whom Tiberius—with malign intent, if Tacitus is to be believed—had recently appointed to be governor of Syria. There was a difference of opinion concerning the movement of troops; and though on technical grounds Germanicus' special powers entitled him to override the decisions of a provincial governor, he obligingly withdrew to make a tour of sightseeing in Egypt. On his return, finding that his instructions had been completely disregarded, he ordered Piso out of the country. No sooner had he done so than he fell mortally ill. The ancients, in their extreme ignorance about internal maladies, jumped readily to conclusions; and Germanicus, before he died,

declared that he must have been poisoned by Piso's agents
(A.D. 19).

The dark suspicion caught the imagination of Roman
society, for the dead man was universally popular. Feeling
ran so strongly against Piso that, though acquitted of murder,
he committed suicide. Worse still, as the Emperor had failed
to shed tears at the State funeral, men's tongues began to wag;
and from this time on Tiberius was continually haunted by
a growing sense of hostility among those around him. His
soured, distrustful temper grew irritable under the strain, and
eventually a vein of cruelty, perhaps always latent in him, was
aroused by fears for the security of his throne. Already in
A.D. 16 one plot to murder him had been unmasked. Informers
were ready with denunciations of others, often more imaginary than real; and Tiberius' nervousness was yet further
increased when in A.D. 23 there occurred the death, from
some mysterious cause, of his only son Drusus. The sudden
removal of the Emperor's heir—for Drusus' infant child could
scarcely now reach maturity before Tiberius died—left the
stage clear for rival claimants and the opportunity of endless
intrigue. As so often during the Early Empire, the atmosphere
of the court was poisoned by female influences. There was
Germanicus' widow Agrippina, herself a daughter of the ill-
starred marriage between Julia and Agrippa, an impetuous
virago, intensely determined that nothing should stand between her sons and the succession to the throne. There was
Tiberius' own mother Livia, the ex-Empress, a still more
formidable figure, whose relations with her son were anything
but cordial. Under such circumstances life became well-nigh
intolerable for the aging Emperor, and in A.D. 27 he quitted
the city to take up his permanent residence on the beautiful
island of Capri in the Bay of Naples. The man who apparently
suggested this course and who, as events were to prove, had
certainly the best reasons for desiring it, was Lucius Aelius
Sejanus, the Prefect of the Praetorian Guard. Step by step this
ambitious upstart had been maturing a deep-laid scheme.
First he had greatly increased the importance of his command
by concentrating the scattered detachments of the Guard in a
great barrack outside the capital. He had wormed his way

into Tiberius' confidence until he became his almost indispensable lieutenant; and on his master's retirement to Capri he was left in undisputed control of the situation. But Sejanus aimed higher still. Young Drusus being out of the way, the succession to the Principate seemed hardly beyond his grasp. Eager, as a suitable prelude, to become a member of the imperial family, he proposed himself for the hand of Drusus' widow, Livilla. Permission was refused him; but it remained at least in Sejanus' power to remove all rival candidates for the throne. After Livia's death in 29 there was no one left to shield Agrippina and her children; and they were consigned to prison from which Agrippina at any rate never emerged alive. Feeling himself now secure of success, Sejanus assumed the airs of an autocrat. He actually had the audacity to ask for tribunician power as though he had been the heir designate. For a while, though something of what was going on must have filtered through to him, Tiberius made never a sign. Then at last he struck. One day a messenger arrived in the Senate with a letter from Capri. It began by touching on matters of general import, then came a passing reference to Sejanus; then generalities once more. The House was on tenterhooks of suspense. Then suddenly at the close came an order for the punishment of the hated favourite. Members who had been crowding round him left Sejanus' side. He was haled off to prison, and that same evening an order was given for his execution. His body was torn in pieces by the infuriated mob. After his death evidence came to light that the fatal illness of the heir-apparent Drusus had been due to his poison agents (31).

Tiberius' nerve now failed him utterly. He struck out with hideous savagery at any against whom the least suspicion might be breathed. Executions followed thick and fast; and the reign of terror was long remembered at Rome. What added a crowning touch of horror was the persistent rumour that during the remaining years of his life Tiberius' seat at Capri was the scene of the grossest debauchery and vice. It must be admitted that at most periods of history similar gossip had been circulated about unpopular despots. On the other hand, a complete moral break-down would seem no improbable climax to the tragic degeneration of Tiberius' character.

The news of his death was hailed with joy at the capital; but if it was thought that the Empire would profit by a change of masters, the error of such an opinion was soon to be revealed.

The truth is that, so far as the provinces were concerned, Tiberius' reign had been exceptionally peaceful and prosperous. There had been, it is true, a rebellion in Gaul, where resentment against commercial exploitation had led to an ugly massacre of Roman traders. The movement was put down by the use of the Rhineland legions—an important reminder that Gaul required a garrison more closely on the spot than troops posted on the more distant Elbe would have provided. In Africa too there was trouble with a nomad leader named Tacfarinas, who for nearly seven years defied the Roman efforts to round him up. But, these minor incidents apart, the better conditions inaugurated by Augustus were well maintained. Tiberius, it would seem, was particularly severe on the malpractices of governors; and several convictions for extortion are recorded. Even more to his credit was the readiness with which he came forward to assist the victims of natural catastrophes. Thus, in A.D. 17, when a large district in Asia Minor was devastated by earthquake, he not merely allowed the inhabitants five years' immunity from taxation, but provided a special fund for the relief of the stricken cities. He made a similar grant to the people of Fidenae when in A.D. 27 a large amphitheatre collapsed during a performance and fifty thousand spectators were either killed or injured. Even as late as A.D. 33 when a serious financial crisis took place in Italy he advanced the then enormous sum of a million pounds in loans, free of interest, to men who were threatened with bankruptcy. Thus even in his declining years it must be admitted that Tiberius set a fine example of philanthropic paternalism; and whereas the strictures of Tacitus and other historians reflected the views of a small social clique, men outside Rome continued to see in the Emperor a genuine custodian of the interests of every class. Loyalty to the established order remained, in fact, unshaken by the events of this reign; and even in Jerusalem, that hotbed of disaffection, the Jewish priests could declare with apparent sincerity, 'We have no King but Caesar'.

II. GAIUS (OR CALIGULA), A.D. 37–41

In his will Tiberius had nominated two joint-heirs, his grandson Tiberius Gemellus still scarcely of age, and Gaius, the only son of Germanicus and Agrippina. The latter was popular, especially with the army. As a child he had been brought up among the Rhineland legions of which his father was then commander; and, his mother having made it a practice to dress him up in a miniature uniform, the soldiers had nick-named him in jest Caligula or 'Little Boots'. The support of Macro, now Prefect of the Guard, easily secured his accession, which all Rome hailed with joy. At the outset he behaved in an exemplary fashion. He clearly intended that his rule should mark a happy reaction from the terrible conditions of the previous reign, proclaiming an amnesty to those who had suffered exile under Tiberius and sending all *delators* away with a flea in their ear. But this phase did not last long. There would seem to have been a taint of madness in the blood of Julia's descendants, and soon after his accession Gaius was attacked by an illness which left his mind more or less unhinged. It must be remembered, too, that, unlike most of the early Emperors, he had received no training whatever to fit him for his task or even accustom him to the habit of command. The consciousness of possessing unlimited power was altogether too much for him, and he became the prey to the most fantastic delusions. He imagined himself to be in very truth a god on earth; and on his instructions not merely were statues of various deities imported from Greece and furnished with new heads in likeness to his own, but a bridge was built connecting the Palace with the Capitol, in order that he might more readily hold converse with 'his brother' Jupiter. Dignity, however, he had none. As a boy he had been brought up in the company of some oriental princelings who were being educated at Rome and he had picked up the coarsest of habits. He scandalized even the court by appearing in female costume. His reckless extravagance soon dissipated the fortune which Tiberius had left him; and he resorted to the most barefaced extortion to replenish his empty treasury. New taxes were imposed; and with whimsical caprice he had the schedules written so small and posted so high that no one could read them. Confiscation of property was another of his methods; and informers now once again claimed many victims. The senators were singled out for special persecution; and it amused this crazy bully to play on their fears by summoning them to the Palace at dead of night, where he would scare them by weird noises, sing songs to them and then—pack them off to bed. Many lost their lives on various charges; and so, despite his services, did Macro the Prefect of the Guard. There was at least one serious conspiracy against the Emperor's life, and though it came to nothing, the marvel is that his reign lasted as long as four years.

Not even the provinces were spared his folly. Finding that his bodyguard needed some Batavian recruits from the Rhine mouth,[1] he decided to conduct a campaign into Germany. According to that story, the credibility of which seems highly doubtful, he crossed the Rhine, ordered a night-attack against an imaginary foe, and sent home a dispatch describing his victories. Then next year, inconsequently changing his objective, he marched to the English Channel, as though for an invasion of Britain, and when he got there, ordered the soldiers to collect shells as trophies of war. In the East he reversed the policy of Tiberius by reconverting the newly made province of Commagene into an oriental principality, while Herod Agrippa, who had been a boon-companion of his boyhood, was presented with Samaria and other adjacent territory. Among the Jews he raised a violent commotion by threatening to place his image in the Holy of Holies at Jerusalem. An embassy of protest, headed by Philo the theologian, waited on the Emperor in Italy. He received them while inspecting a country house near Naples, and as he moved from room to room poked fun at their perplexity. 'Why did they not eat pork?' he asked, then inconsequently adding, 'They were quite right too; for it was tasteless stuff.' Finally he dispatched them with the remark that they were 'more to be pitied than blamed for not realizing that he was a god'. Happily his death averted the intended sacrilege. For the farce was now played out. Stung to action by the tyrant's insults, a

[1] See page 315.

certain Cassius Chaerea and other officers of the Guard waylaid him one day in a subterranean corridor of the Palace, as he was on his way to the bath, and struck him down in cold blood.

III. CLAUDIUS, A.D. 41–54

On Gaius' death Rome was suddenly left without a master, for no successor had been nominated. In the Senate some babbled of a return to the Republic; but while the issue hung undecided, the soldiers clinched it. While engaged in looting the Palace, some members of the Guard discovered a middle-aged man hiding behind the curtain, and dragging him out found him to be a brother of Germanicus named Claudius. They carried him off to their barracks, and, as he imagined, to execution. Next day they proclaimed him Emperor (for after all he was of the 'blood royal'), and the Senate accepted their choice. And a strange choice it was. For Claudius was a gawky, unattractive creature. He had a sickly body and spindle shanks. He stammered and slobbered. Though uncle to Caligula he had been the joke of the court, and had deliberately sought obscurity in the low company of slaves and freedmen. Nobody could have suspected in this vulgar glutton even the makings of a ruler; and yet Claudius had his points. He was a great student of books. He wrote a history of Carthage and interested himself greatly in Roman antiquities. As Emperor he indulged his hobby by raking up obsolete customs and institutions. He resuscitated the order of priests known as *haruspices* whose business it was to foretell the future by inspecting the entrails of sacrificial victims. He revived the censorship and busied himself, to everybody's amusement, in that antiquated capacity. By some juggling with the Calendar he contrived another celebration of the Secular Games nearly a generation before they were properly due. His historical researches had, however, one more practical result; for they seem to have given him a great admiration for Julius Caesar; and in many of his measures we can trace a desire to emulate his illustrious predecessor. Amongst the many public works which stood to his credit were the improvement of the harbour at Ostia and the reclamation of land around the Fucine Lake, both of which had been projects of Caesar's.

Indeed, there is much to be said for the view that Claudius' whole policy was in the main a reversion to Caesar's more autocratic and at the same time more liberal methods rather than a continuance of Augustus' conservative compromise.

For, strange as it may appear, the reign of this middle-aged pedant was an important landmark in the development of the imperial system; and the new departures, if made on his personal initiative, would suggest that Claudius was not the fool he appeared. A much simpler explanation lies, however, to hand. All the evidence goes to show that he was much under the influence of his private staff of secretaries; and an enormous growth in their power was one of the outstanding features of the reign. Ever since Augustus' institution of it, the imperial secretariat, we must remember, had handled a large variety of highly important functions. There was a Finance Minister who controlled the revenues of the imperial exchequer and was responsible for the pay of the army, the corn-supply of Rome, and the department of public works. A Secretary of Correspondence dealt not merely with reports from provincial governors, but also with commissions and promotions in the army and the grant of citizenship to individuals and communities alike. A third minister had to do with 'petitions', and since there was a constant flow of such appeals to the Emperor, the answers given upon knotty points of law or administration might play a vital part in the formulation of future policy. There was also a secretary who looked after the imperial archives and libraries. Now under Claudius, as under Augustus, all these posts were held by freedmen. The finance minister was a certain Pallas, obviously of Greek extraction. So too was Narcissus the secretary of correspondence, and Polybius the librarian. It must have been easy for these men to flatter the Emperor's vanity by giving him the credit for ideas they had previously put into his head; and they allowed him to fancy he was ruling, while they themselves quietly 'got on with the job'.[1] But the influence which they exerted was a

[1] The estimate here given of the Emperor's character has been disputed by high authorities, partly on the evidence of the personal style of Claudius' extant rescripts. None the less, the known subservience of his domestic relationships is hard to square with the belief that he had real moral strength.

great scandal to Roman society; for it was a bitter pill for aristocrats to see the reins of power gathered into the hands of men who half a century before might have been performing menial offices as common clerks. Not unnaturally the most discreditable stories were told against these upstart ministers. That they were corrupt is not improbable. For they must have had endless opportunities for jobbery, and it is certain that they grew immensely rich. Pallas, we know, had a fortune of over three million pounds. Nevertheless, it is beyond doubt that these men were of very high ability; and many, if not all, of the Emperor's policies may well have been the product of their brains. One thing is certain. The process of administrative centralization was now carried a big step forward. The management of the imperial fiscus, for example, a branch of which seems hitherto to have existed in each separate province, was henceforth concentrated in Rome under the direct control of the Emperor's secretariat; and by a law passed in A.D. 53 the procurators or revenue agents were empowered to make decisions and even inflict penalties in cases of financial dispute— a serious infringement on the rights of the ordinary courts.

Such concentration of power in the hands of the Emperor and his subordinates served no doubt to promote efficiency; but it carried with it a corresponding curtailment of liberty; and in the judicial sphere particularly this tendency began to make itself felt. Claudius' scholarly instincts led him to interest himself greatly in jurisprudence, and he was never so happy as when sitting on the bench. What, however, was particularly obnoxious to Roman ideas of justice was his habit of hearing important cases *intra cubiculum*, as the phrase ran, —that is, in his own private chamber. This smacked too much of despotism to please a public which could still remember Augustus' more constitutional methods.

Another point in which Claudius appears to have deliberately departed from the line of policy which Augustus had laid down, and which Tiberius had obediently followed, was concerned with the extension of the franchise. For here too he reverted to the more liberal outlook displayed by Julius Caesar. The number of citizens which in 8 B.C. had been little over four millions rose to nearly six millions in A.D. 48, and the philosopher

Seneca, with a touch of ironic exaggeration, declared that 'the whole barbarian world would very soon be wearing the toga'. There were of course several ways in which the franchise could be extended. First it could be granted to individuals in recognition of special services. They could also obtain it for cash down, like the officer in the Acts of the Apostles who boasted to have paid a 'great sum' for it; and there is little doubt that under Claudius not merely the imperial exchequer, but also the freedman secretaries must have reaped a considerable harvest from this source. In the second place, citizenship could be bestowed upon the inhabitants of some community or district as a whole. An inscription has been found telling how Claudius enfranchised an Alpine tribe called the Anauni on the Upper Adige. Frequently, too, an existing township, such as Verulamium in Britain, received the status of a self-governing *municipium* which automatically gave its burghers civic privileges, whether in full or half measure. Where, on the other hand, settlers were specially planted or a town properly organized for the first time, the title given was not *municipium*, but (on the old Republican analogy) *colonia*. One famous instance of such a 'colony' founded by Claudius was Camulodunum in Britain, where a large number of discharged soldiers were settled. Another was Colonia Agrippinensis or Cologne, so named after Agrippina, Claudius' wife, and inhabited largely by members of a German tribe, the Ubii, who had been transferred from the farther bank of the Rhine nearly a century before. What is still more remarkable (seeing how unpopular the step had been in Julius Caesar's day) Claudius actually promoted Gauls to the Senate. Both from Tacitus and by an odd coincidence, from an inscription lately discovered, we have versions of the speech which he delivered in defence of this measure; and there seems little doubt that he (or his advisers) had grasped the important principle that Rome needed to assimilate her subjects and so draw fresh blood into the dwindling stock of the national citizen-body.

Most astonishing of all, perhaps, is the vigour with which foreign policy was conducted by this Emperor, who could boast neither military capacity nor even normal physical courage. Here again there was a reversion from the programme of Augustus to that of Julius Caesar; and Rome's commitments were deliberately enlarged by the conquest of a new province —Britain. The motives which led to this step are uncertain. Since Caesar's abortive invasion of 54 B.C. Britain had been left to itself. Roman traders had, however, pushed their activities, and it is not unlikely that the prospect of further commercial exploitation and, in particular, of lucrative mining operations played a part in commending the project. From a military point of view some uneasiness about the security of Gaul must always have been felt so long as the kindred Celts across the Channel remained still unsubdued. On the other hand, Britain was at this moment extremely disunited. After a reign of thirty years death had just removed Cunobelinus (or Cymbeline) King of the Trinobantes in Essex, who had built up a powerful hegemony over the south-eastern districts. Quarrels had arisen about the succession to his throne and one of his sons had fled for protection to Rome. The moment seemed to offer a golden opportunity for attack, and Claudius may well have coveted the glory to be gained by a cheap victory. His own part in the campaign was trifling. Though he came over in person, he liked the experience so little that he stayed barely a fortnight (A.D. 43). The forces employed seem to have amounted to about 50,000 men; and for spectacular purposes included some elephants. After landing in Kent, where they apparently made Canterbury their base, the Romans moved up to the Thames, across which they pushed in the teeth of a fierce resistance, and occupied Camulodunum, capital of the Trinobantes and the most important town in Britain. Thenceforward the invasion was continued by at least three separate columns, one working up into East Anglia to overcome the Iceni, another north-westwards through the Midlands, a third under Vespasian (the future Emperor) overrunning the district south of the Thames as far perhaps as Somerset. The commander-in-chief of the whole campaign was Aulus Plautius, one of the most capable generals of the day. On his recall in 47 his place was taken by Ostorius Scapula, who pushed the occupation forward to the line of the Trent and Severn, marking the frontier by a low embankment which ran from Lincoln to the neighbourhood of Exeter and was accompanied by a track still known as the Fosse Way. This was part of the elaborate network of military roads—that indispensable factor in Rome's organization of a newly conquered country; but of these the majority radiated outwards from Londinium or London a city now founded for its obvious commercial advantages and henceforward by far the most populous in all the island.

Throughout the story of the occupation the systematic handling of the military problems is very notable. Whoever chose the officers chose well; and it is clear that the imperial service was bringing to the fore a plentiful supply of highly trained and competent commanders. Another such, named Corbulo, was engaged about this time in carrying war once more into Germany. There had been unrest among the coastal tribe of the Frisii, who though lying beyond the frontier was kept under the surveillance of the Roman fleet and compelled to pay a tribute of hides. In 47 Corbulo conducted a punitive expedition against them, and was proceeding farther afield against the Chauci beyond the Weser. At this point he was recalled; for the extension of this frontier clearly played no part in Claudius' plans, largely no doubt because the military resources of the Western provinces were already sufficiently strained. What, however, is worthy of special remark, was his consistent pursuit of the policy of incorporating within the Empire dependencies previously left under the control of native princes. Mauretania in 42, Lycia in 43, Thrace in 46 were definitely annexed and placed under a governor. Such was the process whereby the Empire, which had at first included, alongside of its directly subject States, a heterogeneous miscellany of autonomous cities, client kingdoms, and protectorates, was gradually assimilated to a uniform pattern of provincial government.

Thus under Claudius' rule there occurred several developments of far-reaching importance—a considerable concentration of power in the hands of the Emperor and his personal ministers, a broadening of the political basis of the Empire by the liberal enfranchisement of non-Italians, and, last but not least, a rapid extension of the provincial system and the addition of the one *permanent* territorial gain made subsequent to Augustus. When from these achievements we turn again to the private life and character of Claudius himself the paradox is extraordinary. If he was under the thumb of his secretaries, no less was he the victim of continual female intrigues. One of the least pleasant features of the Early Principate was (as we have said) the unwholesome influence exercised by the emancipated ladies of the court; and of these few won for themselves a more lurid reputation than the young Empress Messalina. This abandoned coquette was married to her middle-aged husband at the age of fifteen. Her beauty cast its spell on him, and, egged on by her jealous temper, Claudius became the willing instrument of hideous revenges against her possible rivals. Amongst those who were put to death at Messalina's instigation was Julia, one of Germanicus' surviving daughters. Her cruelty was abominable. She stuck at nothing to attain her ends. One of her victims was Valerius Asiaticus, whose luxurious gardens she coveted; and the summary execution of many other leading men began to recall the horrors of Tiberius' reign. Meanwhile this profligate girl encouraged a whole series of lovers behind her husband's back; and eventually, while he was absent at Ostia, she agreed to go through a public ceremony of marriage with one of the Roman beaux called Caius Silius. The whole town was buzzing with the scandal, and the minister Narcissus determined to enlighten his master. Claudius decided to act. Silius and many of his friends were put to death, and Messalina herself was murdered. The choice of a new Empress was eagerly canvassed among Claudius' chief confidants, and the selection of Agrippina, who, being a daughter of Germanicus, was actually his own niece, was forced on him by the persuasions of the unscrupulous Pallas. But Claudius, as it proved, was out of the frying-pan only to be into the fire. For Agrippina was a domineering female whose one object in life was to secure the succession for her son by an earlier marriage—Nero. The natural and proper heir to the throne was Claudius' own son Britannicus, but step by step this amazing woman pushed her boy towards the goal of her ambition. First, at 'her instance, Nero was adopted as a member of Claudius' family. Next, though he was only thirteen, he was given proconsular power; at fourteen he was appointed prefect of the city. At fifteen he was married to Claudius' daughter Octavia. Meanwhile the philosopher Seneca was brought back from exile to act as tutor to the lad; and, more important still, Afranius Burrus, who apparently was ready to support Agrippina's plans, was made Prefect of the Guard. Finally, fearing the counter-influence of Narcissus, who favoured Britannicus, she decided to put Claudius out of the way. He was taking the waters at Sinnuessa at the time; and a professional druggist named Locusta was hired to prepare a dose of poison, which was administered to the old man in a dish of mushrooms, his favourite delicacy. So at least the story ran; and in any case the fact remains that he died on October 13th, A.D. 54. At noon next day, Nero, accompanied by Burrus, appeared at the door of the Palace and was hailed as Emperor by the detachment of the Guard then on duty. Agrippina's triumph was complete.

Few regrets were felt in Rome at the old Emperor's death. For he had estranged the aristocracy by his high-handed measures; and the curtain was presently rung down on the tragi-comedy of his life by the publication of a singular treatise. It was composed by Seneca, and the form it took was a parody of the late Emperor's deification. It described how a bald little old man with a top-heavy head and a lisp in his speech arrived in heaven only to find himself denounced by the shade of Augustus and to be consigned to the nether regions, where he was greeted with obloquy by the victims of his own persecutions and condemned to play dice for ever with a dice-box lacking a bottom. This entertaining skit was entitled the 'Pumpkinification of Claudius'.

IV. NERO, A.D. 54–68

It was an interesting commentary on the disfavour with which Roman society had regarded Claudius' innovations that the reign of his successor was ushered in by a sort of 'Declaration of Rights'. Seneca prepared and Nero read out in the Senate a speech which promised, amongst other things, that the power of freedmen ministers should be strictly curtailed and all unconstitutional methods of trial abandoned.

The Senate was highly gratified, and for a time all went well. Nero himself was a youth of only seventeen years of age with a strong taste for rollicking horseplay. His old tutor's influence seems to have had but superficial effects; for, truth to tell, Seneca was something of a fraud. He could write elegant poems about the virtues of Stoic self-control and the wise man's contempt for worldly wealth. But he himself amassed an enormous fortune, and his private morals, if half the tales are true, were no better than they should have been. The one noticeable result of his pupil's education was a passionate enthusiasm for the arts. Nero fancied himself as a musician and a singer, and developed an inordinate vanity about his talents. As for affairs of State, he was content to leave them in the hands of Seneca himself and the honest, capable commander of the Guard, Burrus. At the outset these two men were in virtual control of the Empire; and according to a well-known saying of the Emperor Trajan the first five years of Nero's reign compared favourably with any other period of the Principate. Certainly there was a marked vigour in the conduct of both domestic and foreign policy. At home the senatorial treasury was rescued from bankruptcy by an enormous grant from the Emperor's privy purse; and, what was more important, its administration was transferred from senatorial quaestors to prefects of the Emperor's choosing. In the provinces great vigilance was exercised over the misbehaviours of governors; and many trials were held before the Senate at which convictions were secured. The malpractices of *publicani*, too, came in for some attention. Nero himself seems to have proposed, though no doubt on Seneca's initiative, that harbour-dues (which was all that the companies now controlled) should be altogether abolished. This free trade project had much to recommend it, since that sweeping away of restrictions could hardly have failed to stimulate trade; but after discussion in the Senate it was dropped, and all that was done was to make certain fiscal remissions, chiefly to the shipowners responsible for the corn-supply of Rome.

The most notable events of the reign, however, occurred on the Eastern frontier. There the Augustan policy of maintaining a pro-Roman prince on the throne of Armenia was rudely challenged by the new Parthian King Vologeses, who in 53 invaded the country and handed it over to his own brother Tiridates. Swift action was taken. Corbulo, who had won a big reputation by his German campaigns, was sent out as governor of Cappadocia with a couple of legions at his command. He found the troops so much demoralized by years of service in the Levant that not till 57 did he enter Armenia. Then he carried all before him; working from Trapezus, he destroyed Tiridates' northern capital Artaxata in 59 and next year by a daring march into the interior occupied the southern capital Tigranocerta. Finally, having set a pro-Roman Cappadocian named Tigranes on the throne, Corbulo left a body of troops to keep him there and departed. No sooner was his back turned than the foolish prince by his aggressive behaviour gave the Parthians an excuse to dethrone him. All Corbulo's work was therefore undone; and as he had meantime been placed in command of Syria, a certain Caesennius Paetus was given the task of recovering Armenia. So far from succeeding, he actually allowed himself to be surprised and surrounded in his winter quarters at Randeia near the Cappadocian border. Instead of awaiting the arrival of Corbulo's reinforcements, Paetus made an abject surrender and, having given an undertaking to evacuate Armenia, he decamped at high speed, leaving baggage and wounded behind him. At Rome the catastrophe was compared to the disaster at the Caudine Forks, and the blow to the imperial prestige was serious. But in the last resort it led to a compromise— so successful that it settled the frontier problem for two generations to come—whereby Tiridates, the Parthian candidate, resumed the throne of Armenia, but came to Rome to receive his investiture at the hands of the Emperor. Nero thoroughly enjoyed the chance for a pageant, and solemnly closed the Temple of Janus to celebrate the end of hostilities (A.D. 65).

Apart from these operations, the only other serious troubles of the reign were a native rising in Britain in 61,[1] which was accompanied by the massacre of 80,000 traders and settlers,

[1] See page 334.

and a Jewish rising in 66,[1] concerning both of which it will be more convenient to speak in subsequent chapters.

The comparative tranquillity of the provinces was the more surprising, since the direction of affairs was all this time passing out of the grip of the Emperor's two capable ministers. As Nero grew to manhood, the sense of power went to his head and he became recklessly wilful. One of the first victims of his self-assertion was his own mother. Agrippina's calculation had been that, with her son on the throne, she would be mistress of Rome. But she soon found her mistake. When she tried to associate herself with him at court ceremonies Nero ostentatiously snubbed her. In 55, the second year of the reign, Pallas, her freedman ally, was dismissed from his ministry. Her rash talk about Britannicus' claim to the throne brought swift retribution on that unhappy young man. He was invited to dinner and poisoned. But there was worse to come. In A.D. 58 the charms of a young beauty called Poppaea won Nero's heart and he determined to divorce his own wife Octavia, Claudius' daughter. But to this he knew Agrippina would never consent. So Agrippina, he decided, must die. While staying at Baiae near the Bay of Naples he summoned her to him, affected reconciliation, and conducted her to a barge which was to carry her home. In mid-sea the deck of the barge, which had been specially so constructed, collapsed and tipped Agrippina into the water. The indomitable lady kept afloat and was presently rescued by a passing ship. But all in vain—the word went out for her assassination and a party of soldiers found her and stabbed her to death. The Senate obsequiously passed a vote congratulating the Emperor upon *his* escape; but the scandal was terrible, and for six months he dared not enter the capital.

It still remained to get rid of his queen, Octavia; but opposition to his scheme was gradually weakening. First in 62 Burrus died, and the command of the Praetorian Guard was entrusted to Tigellinus,[2] a courtier of low birth and coarse character. Next Seneca, feeling himself incapable of continuing the struggle alone, retired into private life. Meanwhile Poppaea's husband, M. Salvius Otho, had already been got

<hr>

[1] See page 305.   [2] Conjointly with Faenius Rufus.

out of the way by the simple expedient of sending him to
govern Lusitania; and nothing could now prevent her marriage
to the Emperor. Public opinion raged impotently; and Octavia
was first divorced, then banished, and finally executed; and
the Senate, obsequious as ever, loaded the new queen with
compliments.

Under the evil influence of Poppaea and Tigellinus life at
the court lapsed swiftly into an orgy of giddy and vicious
dissipation. All decent folk were deeply shocked; and even
such popularity as Nero enjoyed with the masses by reason of
his lavish expenditure on public entertainments was soon to
be rudely shaken by a terrible catastrophe. In 64 a great
fire raged through the city. Some shops in the neighbourhood
of the Great Racecourse started the conflagration. The
houses of the city were largely built of timber. The streets
were narrow and the flames spread rapidly. For nine days
nothing would check them, and a large portion of the city was
destroyed. The opportunity of reconstruction was on the
whole well used, and fine straight streets replaced the narrow,
winding alleys of the past. Nero reserved for his own use a
vast area at the south end of the Forum and turned it into
a pleasure park full of woods and lakes and gardens and
splendid porticoes which he christened the Golden House.
But the poor had suffered terribly, and they not unnaturally
vented their anger on the man who had so selfishly exploited
the public calamity. Whether or no it be true that Nero
'fiddled while Rome burned', it is certain that men believed
him to have been the originator of the fire; and in his desire
to escape the odium of this rumour he looked round for some
scapegoats on whom to divert the charge. He fastened on
the Christians; and the story of the persecution which ensued
shall be told in the following chapter.

That the mob was genuinely placated by this subterfuge
is certainly improbable; but in any case so long as they were
kept tolerably well fed and amused they were little likely
to cause serious trouble. Nevertheless it must seem strange
in view of Nero's growing unpopularity that the Roman world
should so long have tolerated his odious rule. The truth is
that no alternative readily suggested itself. The legions, who,

as events were soon to prove, could at any time have placed their nominee on the throne, were slow to realize their power. The tradition of three generations had accustomed men's minds to the continuance of the Julio-Claudian dynasty; and, except to a few sentimental theorists, a restoration of the Republic was unthinkable. This last fact will explain why plots against the Emperors from Augustus onwards, though by no means infrequent, were usually ill-supported, and, except in the case of Gaius, invariably unsuccessful. A certain lack of resolution, too, seems to have characterized such attempts as were actually made. By now the best elements of the old aristocracy had been well-nigh destroyed by the continuous persecutions of successive emperors. What remained had either retired into a dreamland of philosophic idealism or been drawn into the corrupt influences of court life. In the year that followed the Great Fire a widespread conspiracy was hatched in which many leading men were implicated. Its purpose was to place a certain noble named Gaius Piso on the throne, and it won the support of many Pretorian officers. But the plans were ill-laid. Some of the conspirators blabbed, and Tigellinus was able to suppress it with ease. Piso himself committed suicide, and many of his associates were put to death. Among the victims, though it is most unlikely that he joined the plot, was Seneca himself. Poppaea, it seems, had never forgiven his opposition to her marriage, and the order went out for him to end his life. The form of death he chose, as was not uncommon at this time, was by opening the veins in his arms. Despite the agony of the slow exhaustion, he dictated his thoughts to a faithful secretary, and these were subsequently published. His wife Paulina was actually following his example when orders to desist came from the Emperor, and despite the loss of blood she was nursed back to life.

Another victim was Seneca's nephew, a young poet named Lucan. He was the author of an epic on the war between Caesar and Pompey, in which his strong Republican sympathies were but little disguised; and whether he was guilty or no, it was characteristic of the coterie to which he belonged to look back with wistful regret to the era of political liberty.

A wiser emperor would have ignored such harmless senti-mentality; but, whereas Augustus had conciliated the intellectuals of his day by tactful patronage, his successors distrusted and estranged them. Even the literary-minded Claudius had banished Seneca and caused the death of a well-known Stoic philosopher named Paetus. Since then the Stoic persuasion had come even more into the limelight. It was natural enough that the licence and immorality of the times should provoke its protest; but there was perhaps a touch of extravagance about the way in which its more strait-laced disciples now began to air their moral superiority. Their pose of puritanical austerity even ran to the wearing of long, tousled beards and the coarsest of homespun cloaks. Like Cato of Utica, who, as the last champion of Republican liberty against Caesarian despotism, was taken as their beau ideal, they lost no opportunity of parading their independence. Yet there was something heroic as well as histrionic about these stalwart diehards; and many noble souls were prepared to uphold their principles even to the point of martyrdom. One Paetus Thrasea, who had married the daughter of the older Paetus, had aroused the wrath of Nero by refusing to identify himself with the Senate's shameless connivance at Agrippina's murder; and in 66, without any proper charge being formulated against him, he was ordered to commit suicide. At the same time his son-in-law Helvidius Priscus was banished; and at least one other member of the Stoic school was put to death.

It is scarcely surprising if Nero felt the sting of these philosophers' criticism, for his outrageous behaviour had begun to pass all bounds. The craze for advertising his musical talents completely got the better of him. In 64 he had insisted on appearing on the public stage, first at Naples and then, to the horror of the aristocracy, at Rome. Finally, in 66, wishing perhaps to escape from the unpopularity he had aroused at home, he undertook a tour round the chief cities of Greece, where he played the lyre and sang at several of the famous public competitions—and of course received the prize. It was no joke, we are told, to be a member of Nero's audience; for soldiers were in attendance and failure to applaud at the right point was sometimes rewarded with a flogging.

Meanwhile the state of affairs at Rome had begun to stir the patriotism or ambition of military commanders in the provinces. In 68 came news that Julius Vindex, governor of Gallia Lugdunensis, was raising a revolt. Vindex' family, it appears, was of Gallic origin, and his real intention seems to have been not so much the overthrow of Nero as establishment of an independent empire in Gaul. This threat aroused the legions of the upper Rhine, and under their general, Verginius Rufus, they came down upon the rebels who, though 100,000 strong, were an undisciplined rabble, and were utterly routed in a pitched battle near Vesontio. Meanwhile, however, the emissaries of Vindex had won the adhesion of Galba, the governor of Hither Spain, and, despite the collapse of the Gallic rising, this man determined to make a bid for the Principate himself. At Rome, Nymphidius Sabinus, Tigellinus' co-prefect, won over the Praetorians to the rebel cause by promising them a donative in Galba's name. At this Nero lost his nerve completely and fled from the city, to take refuge in the house of his freedman Phaon. The Senate, mustering courage, passed a decree for his death. Still irresolute, the wretched man waited till the tramp of horses' hooves warned him of his pursuers' approach. He put a dagger to his throat, but even so lacked the courage to drive it home. A companion assisted him. 'What an artist perishes here!' were almost his last words. He died as he had lived—an egoist and a coward.

CHAPTER XXII
CHRISTIANITY AND ITS RIVALS

I. MYSTERY RELIGIONS

THE story of the reigns, which we have just recounted, presents a gloomy picture; and though the metropolis itself, with its vicious court and wastrel proletariat, can scarcely be regarded as typical, yet there can be little doubt that throughout the Roman world, and more especially in the Eastern half of it, there was a widespread decay of morals and, what often goes therewith, a deep-seated *malaise* bred of spiritual dissatisfaction. The old creeds and ceremonies, however punctiliously observed, were losing their hold on men's hearts. The more intellectual took refuge in Stoicism; but though Stoicism might brace their courage to face danger or trouble, its fatalistic doctrines could give no comfort to those whose souls were burdened with a sense of sin or who desperately craved some assurance of a life beyond the grave. It is no mere accident that during this epoch we can observe a growing enthusiasm for several cults—for the most part of Eastern origin—which claimed to offer to men and women some better satisfaction of their inward needs. These cults—known under the general term of 'Mystery Religions'—were quite dissociated from the official forms of worship. Only a comparatively small number of folk, as a rule, were initiated into their secret rites. Initiation involved a preliminary course of abstinence or other forms of purification; and it was followed by the revelation of some mysterious vision in a darkened shrine. Details of the ritual, which was doubtless well staged by the priests, are often difficult to ascertain, since strict secrecy was enjoined. In Greece mysteries of this kind had been practised for centuries at Eleusis near Athens; and attendance at them had recently become fashionable with certain Romans. But more popular still was the cult of Isis which found its way westwards from Egypt. The legend round which this cult centred told how the goddess Isis came to earth in human form and wandered in quest of her murdered husband Osiris, and how Osiris himself eventually undertook to deliver the souls of the dead from the clutches of ravening demons. The cult had originally come to Italy in the first century B.C., doubtless as a result of the influx of Levantine slaves and traders. The secrecy of its rites and the excitable fervour of its worshippers—particularly women—aroused the suspicion of the authorities, and though, as we know, there was no feeling at Rome that foreign religions were wrong in themselves, there had been a vigorous attempt to suppress it. Nevertheless, in the long run it won its way; and Antony and the other Triumvirs had actually erected a temple in Isis' honour. Another mystery religion (which, as time went on, gained great popularity among the armies) was the cult of the Persian god Mithras, an offshoot of Zoroastrian creed. It first seems to have taken real root in the West during the second half of the first century A.D., and was probably brought thither by legionaries returning from service in the East. To soldiers there was a special appeal in this belief in a young warrior god who, according to legend, had come to earth in human form and there slain a monstrous bull and done other labours in the service of mankind. The worship was carried on in an underground chapel, and the ritual included not merely baptism by water, but a banquet at which the initiates partook of bread, water, and wine. At one time it would seem that Mithraism was a serious rival to Christianity itself; nor is it difficult to discern a more than superficial resemblance between these mystery cults and the faith of the Early Church—the celebration of a secret rite or sacrament by a small select band of worshippers, the assurance of relief from the burden of sin and the hope of a better life hereafter, and, above all, belief in a God who came to earth and there laboured or suffered for mankind.

II. CHRISTIANITY

Christianity, then, like the rival cults of Isis and Mithras, made a very direct appeal to those elements in human nature which the outworn ceremonial of the orthodox State religion was failing to satisfy. Nevertheless, at the outset there was a real risk that the Christian message might never reach the ears of the world. After Jesus' death in A.D. 29 (or thereabouts) His humble Galilean disciples were so far from realizing the universality of its appeal that the Church was in danger of remaining a mere sect of Judaism. It was the genius of Paul of Tarsus that broke down the barriers of prejudice; and in A.D. 49, just twenty years after Jesus' death, a council of leading Christians at Jerusalem decided at his instance to admit Gentile converts to the Church. During the following decade Paul's missionary journeys founded small communities of Christians at Ephesus, Corinth, Philippi, and many other centres in Asia Minor or Greece—centres which, with a shrewd organizing instinct, he seems to have chosen as being situated

on the main arteries of the Empire's traffic and so calculated
to spread the Gospel farther afield. Meanwhile Christianity
had made its way to Rome, and when Paul himself was
brought there for trial before the Emperor in A.D. 59, he was
able to count converts among the Pretorian Guard and even
in 'Caesar's household'. In the capital, as elsewhere, Paul was
pursued by the bitter hostility of those Jewish opponents to
whom his idea of admitting Gentiles to the Church was utterly
abhorrent; and it seems not improbable that it was such
Jewish enemies that in the aftermath of the Great Fire, when
Nero was seeking a scapegoat, directed his attention to this
little-known sect.

Normally, as we have said, Roman officialdom was tolerant
of external religions, provided they in no way conflicted with
the established rules of order and morality. At first, as the
Acts of the Apostles testifies, Christians received fair treatment and even protection at the hands of provincial governors
and officers. But their refusal to take part in pagan sacrifice
gave them a reputation for aloofness. The secrecy of their
meetings aroused suspicion, and rumour began to credit them
with practising unseemly rites. Though it was now nearly
thirty years after their Founder's death, they still clung to the
belief that His Return in glory was momentarily at hand, and
since they expected this event to be accompanied by a violent
and universal cataclysm, some garbled version of their belief
may well have lent colour to the charge that they had set
Rome on fire. Such at any rate is the most probable explanation of the account which Tacitus has given of the Neronian
persecution. 'He inflicted,' so it runs, 'the most exquisite
tortures on this class well hated for their abominable practices
and called Christians by the mob. Christus (who gave them
their name) was put to death in Tiberius' reign by the procurator Pontius Pilate; but the mischievous superstition,
though momentarily checked, broke out again not merely in
Judaea, but in Rome itself, where all things foul and shameful
find a welcome and a home. So arrests were first made of all
such as pleaded guilty; and then, on their evidence, a vast
number were convicted not so much on the charge of incen-
diarism as of hatred for all mankind. They were gibbeted in

various ways for the popular amusement, some wrapped in wild beasts' skins and torn to bits by dogs, some nailed to crosses, or burnt alive to illuminate the night when day expired. Nero opened his gardens for the spectacle and held a show in the Circus Maximus, mingling with the crowd in the dress of a charioteer.' It is probable that St. Peter and St. Paul lost their lives at this time or soon after.

The Neronian persecution was a brief and exceptional episode; but the belief was spreading that Christians were somehow or other setting themselves in opposition to the Empire, and it soon became the fashion, perhaps as early as Domitian's reign, to test their loyalty by demanding an act of homage to the Emperor's statue. Refusal was punished with death.

Hitherto many, if not most, converts to the Faith had been drawn from the lower orders of society—slaves, freedmen, and other downtrodden folk for whom life was miserable and harsh. But in Domitian's reign (A.D. 81–96) we hear of Christians who were members of high society; and a certain relative of the Emperors' own family called Flavius Clemens became a proselyte to the Faith. Nevertheless persecution went on; and in the reign of Trajan (A.D. 98–117) we find a most interesting correspondence between the Emperor and Pliny, who, as governor of Bithynia, was faced with the problem of dealing with Christians. 'Hitherto,' wrote Pliny, 'I have cross-examined confessed Christians under threat of torture and have had the recalcitrant executed. Anonymous letters have come into my hands denouncing a large number of persons. Many of these admit to having been Christians years ago; but say that the sum of their offence was simply that on a fixed day (presumably Sunday) they were wont to foregather before dawn and to pledge themselves by a sacrament not to any improper behaviour (Christians were popularly supposed to eat human flesh—an obvious misconstruction of the Eucharist), but simply to abstain from theft, immorality, and any form of dishonesty. This done, they dispersed and met later for a meal of an ordinary and harmless sort. Even this they had discontinued, so they said, after the edict which I issued in accordance with your instructions against Guilds (the Roman Government was always suspicious of societies formed even for purely social purposes). To ascertain the truth of all this I thought fit to examine under torture two young women called deaconesses, but discovered nothing beyond a morbid fanaticism. So many people are involved that I have decided to consult you. For the mischief has spread from the towns to the countryside; but can quite clearly be checked. For already temples, recently deserted, are once more resuming their normal round of sacrifices, and there is a market for fodder for sacrificial animals which till yesterday was unsaleable.' Trajan's reply is a masterpiece of businesslike brevity. 'You have followed the right course, my dear Pliny, in your examination of alleged Christians. Search must not be made; but, if accused and convicted, they must be punished—with the proviso that any who deny themselves to be Christians and prove the same by venerating our gods, should have the benefit of their recantation, whatever your suspicions of their past. Anonymous letters are not evidence; to treat them as such would be a shocking precedent, unworthy of our age.'

Hadrian, Trajan's successor, made it still more clear that charges against Christians should be proved up to the hilt before action were taken; and such an attitude was on the whole typical of Rome's treatment of them. Persecution was neither systematic nor continuous; but if any disaster, such as a plague or a fire, occurred to rouse popular feeling, the scapegoats were ready to hand; and the mob lost no chance of demanding that the Christians should be thrown to the lions for their amusement.

III. THE EXTINCTION OF THE JEWISH NATION

Partly because it was not without significance in relation to the spread of Christianity and partly because its main events coincided with the transition from Nero's to Vespasian's reign, it will be well to say something here of the great catastrophe which now overtook the nation of the Jews.

Soon after the death of Herod the Great in 4 B.C. Judaea had been converted into a province, governed by a series of procurators of whom Pontius Pilate was one. After a brief

TRAJAN'S COLUMN (DETAIL)

period during which Claudius restored the throne to the native prince Herod Agrippa, it had reverted to procurator's rule; and during the term of Gessius Florus in A.D. 66, riots broke out simultaneously in Caesarea and at Jerusalem, where the out-and-out nationalist party of Zealots succeeded in massacring the Roman garrison. So serious was the rising that Flavius Vespasianus, who had served with great distinction in Britain, was sent out with a special commission to suppress it. He began by reducing the region of Galilee, where the historian Josephus directed the defence of the chief stronghold Jopatata and incidentally, after surrender, became a member of Vespasian's suite. The outlying districts had been systematically mastered and the armies were concentrating for the final attack on Jerusalem when the death of Nero and the subsequent struggle for the throne called Vespasian away from Palestine, and his son Titus was left to conduct the siege of the city. By now it was crowded to overflowing by refugees from the country-side and could easily have been reduced by starvation. But Titus was eager for some exploit which would shed lustre upon the beginning of his father's reign; and he pressed the attack with a ferocity which was only equalled by the desperate resistance of the inhabitants. Their sufferings were so terrible that some, it is said, were driven to cannibalism. They were even quarrelling among themselves; but every inch of the Roman advance was disputed. The position was naturally strong and very skilfully fortified; and it was three months before the Tower of Antonia and the second line of defences were carried. Then followed a desperate struggle for the Temple Area, which was eventually mastered by the use of fire-darts, and in the ensuing conflagration the Temple itself was destroyed. The upper part of the city, known as the Hill of Zion, still held out under the more determined leaders; and, when this too was entered at last, the end came amid hideous scenes of pillage and slaughter. Altogether, in the course of the war, it is reckoned (though this is probably an overestimate) that a million lives were lost. Jerusalem became a heap of ruins on which a Roman legion pitched its camp. The spoils of the Temple were carried off to grace Titus' triumphal procession; and a carved representation of the Seven Golden Candlesticks, which formed part of this treasure, may still be seen on the arch which was erected in his honour at the south end of the Forum. As a nation the Jews ceased to exist.

CHAPTER XXIII

THE YEAR OF THE FOUR EMPERORS

I. GALBA

THE nineteen months which elapsed between the death of Nero in June 68 and the final triumph of Vespasian's cause in December 69 were among the most dramatic and critical of Roman history. The reason for the upheaval is not far to seek. 'The secret was out,' says Tacitus (whose narrative of the period has by sheer literary brilliance enormously enhanced its interests for ourselves). 'Men knew now that Emperors could be made elsewhere than at Rome.' The Julio-Claudian dynasty was finished and done with; for Nero had left no heir, nor, if he had, would it have made any difference. The field was open to other candidates and any one who could command a backing of troops was free to enter. Would-be emperors sprang up like mushrooms—at Rome, Nymphidius Sabinus the Praetorian Prefect; on the Rhine, Fonteius Capito the legate of 'Lower' Germany; in Africa, Clodius Macer the governor of the province, ostensibly standing for a restoration of the Republic. The odds lay, however, with the governor of Spain, Galba, who had been first in the field. He was a fine old aristocrat of seventy-three, popular with the troops and 'by common consent well fitted to rule', so Tacitus declared—with the acid addition, 'until he tried'. Though he had diplomatically proclaimed himself the Senate's obedient servant, there was no doubt he was aiming at the throne. Luck favoured him. Macer and Capito were assassinated by his partisans. The Praetorians, deposing Sabinus, declared for him; and by October he was master of Rome.

Galba was an officer of the old school; and the strictness of his discipline struck an unpleasant contrast to his predecessor's laxity. An empty Treasury, too, compelled him to an almost niggardly economy. He refused to give the Pretorians the donative promised in his name. He tried to compel the recipients of Nero's unscrupulous bounty to disgorge their ill-gotten gains, and thus made countless enemies. He even alienated the mob by refusing to put Nero's hated prefect, Tigellinus, to death. Then on January 1st 69 came the ominous news of serious unrest among the Rhineland legions, and Galba decided that, to strengthen his position, he must adopt a consort. His choice fell on Piso Licinianus, a man of unimpeachable character, but, as ill-luck would have it, unpopular with the Praetorians, who had favoured a rival candidate Marcus Salvius Otho. Otho had been a member of the fast set at Rome, until sent by Nero into what amounted to exile as governor of Lusitania; and he had come back in Galba's train in a rebellious mood, heavily in debt and ready for any desperate fling. His lax reputation attracted those who regretted the change from Nero's gaiety to Galba's straitlaced ways. The Praetorian Guard was already smarting under a sense of grievance, and a couple of privates, acting as Otho's agents among them, prepared a *coup d'état*. On January 16th, while Galba was engaged in offering a sacrifice, Otho stole away from the ceremony to the Praetorian camp. The soldiers rose in his favour, caught and murdered Galba as he ventured into the Forum, and compelled the Senate to proclaim Otho Emperor.

But during this critical fortnight events had been moving no less swiftly on the Rhine. There Galba's elevation had been most unpopular; and, conscious that they had given offence by their suppression of his friend Vindex in Gaul, the legions of the 'Upper' or Southern Province refused to take the oath of allegiance. They now made up their minds to show that, if the Spanish army could create an emperor, they could do the same. In the army of the Lower Province Capito's place had been filled on Galba's order by a certain Aulus Vitellius, a lazy, good-natured nonentity. Though he had only been a few weeks at his post, both armies agreed to support his candidature for the throne. He himself had no special enthusiasm for the adventure, and was left behind to move towards Italy at his leisure, while two legionary commanders,

Caecina and Valens, posted ahead with two columns of roughly 40,000 apiece. By now Otho had of course taken Galba's place on the throne; but his overtures to Vitellius were rejected and he was forced to fend for himself. Had he chosen to take time by the forelock he might well have held the approaches to Italy and then awaited with confidence the arrival of reinforcements from the Danubian provinces, to say nothing of the East, which had declared in his favour. But Otho was no soldier; nor, though there were several able officers in his service, did he care to appoint one of these as *generalissimo* in his stead. The result was that the enemy were left to enter the northern plains unopposed. While Valens made a circuit by way of Gaul and the Cottian Alps (where a diversion made by Otho's fleet against the coast involved them in some delay), Caecina struck directly south through Switzerland and the Great St. Bernard pass, and in March, arriving a month ahead of his colleague, seized Cremona on the north bank of the Po. For Otho it was essential to hold the line of that river. He hastened north, crossed to the northern bank somewhat lower downstream than Caecina, and occupied an advantageous position at Bedriacum, commanding the junction of two important roads whereby reinforcements might reach him from Rome and the Danubian district respectively. A preliminary engagement at Locus Castorum went in his favour, the enemy's plan for an ambush having come to his general's knowledge, which enabled them to turn the tables neatly. Then, in April, Valens' arrival set the balance of numbers against Otho ; and more than ever he would have been wise to await the mustering of his reserves, for time was on his side. But he was in a fit of hot impatience; and, though he was induced to leave the direction of strategy in the hands of Suetonius Paulinus and two other lieutenants, the plan for an immediate decision was pressed on. An advance westwards towards Cremona—the prelude, it would seem, to an encircling movement which should have struck in between the enemy's base and his communications with Gaul—provoked a general engagement. In the complicated terrain of vineyards and orchards no co-ordinated tactics were possible; and after some obstinate fighting between scattered bands of soldiers the issue was determined by the flight of the Othonian commanders. The army capitulated; and Otho himself, who on the advice of his lieutenants had retired before the battle to the south side of the Po, abandoned all thought of continuing the struggle. His reinforcements from Illyria were by now well on their way, but he was sick of bloodshed and he made up his mind to commit suicide— perhaps the most creditable action of an ill-spent life.

The victorious troops signalized their triumph by plundering Italian cities on their march towards Rome; and the Emperor, in whose name these excesses were committed, proved himself no better than the troops he led. Vitellius possessed neither capacity nor ideals; and he used his new-won power simply as a means of rewarding his followers and gratifying his own bestial appetites. Disbanding the Pretorians who had fought for Otho, he filled their places with drafts from his own legions of the Rhine. The morale of the soldiers, fresh as they were from the rigours of camp-life on the frontier, broke down altogether in the luxurious city. Caecina and Velens had everything their own way, and while they lined their pockets with the proceeds of controlling the patronage, the Emperor, indifferent to their misbehaviour, gave himself up to the pleasures of the dinner-table. Vitellius was a drunkard and a gourmet of the most extravagant description, and his brief reign of eleven months is said to have cost the exchequer no less than nine million pounds.

But it was now the turn of the legions of the East to put forward their candidate. They had accepted Galba and they had accepted Otho; but when they heard of the triumph of the Germanic armies jealousy was too much for them. Their choice fell on Vespasian, the general in charge of the Jewish War, and on July 1st he was proclaimed Emperor at Alexandria. It was arranged that he should leave his son Titus to continue the siege of Jerusalem and himself take up his quarters in Egypt, where he could cut off the vital corn-supply of Rome and await in safety the decision of arms. The advance against Italy was entrusted to Mucianus, the Syrian governor who had himself refused an offer of the Principate on the ground that he had no son to succeed him. He was proceeding slowly on his way through Asia Minor when a startling development occurred in the West. The armies of the Danubian provinces, smarting under the recent defeat of their vanguard at Bedriacum, were eager for their revenge against Vitellius, whose wrath they not unnaturally feared; and they had decided to throw in their lot with the 'Flavians', as the followers of Flavius Vespasianus came to be called. But, impatient at Mucianus' slow progress, they determined to strike a blow for themselves. Antonius Primus, the commander of one of the Pannonian legions, took the lead and pushed forward to the invasion of Italy. In a whirlwind campaign he penetrated the passes, swept down through Aquileia at the head of the Adriatic and by the very speed of his advance rushed the line of the River Adige (or Athesis) north of the Po. The Vitellian troops, which should have held it, were doubly handicapped by the treachery of their commander Caecina and the defection of the Ravenna fleet on their flank, and they fell back southwards on Hostilia. Simultaneously by a more westerly route Primus was also racing for the Po. He had got quite near to Cremona; the Vitellians posted there had come out against him, but had been beaten back, and his troops were clamouring to be led to the assault, when suddenly came the dramatic news that the enemy forces he had left retreating on Hostilia had entered the town. By incredible marching they had crossed to the south bank of the Po, and moving along it arrived at Cremona, covering the distance of a hundred miles in four days. But despite their travel-worn condition they were in such a fever of excitement that they insisted on attacking Primus' army that same evening. It was nearly nine o'clock when the battle was joined on the old field of Bedriacum, and all through the night the two armies fought on under the light of the moon. At dawn the Vitellians broke and fled to Cremona. The pursuit followed, and entering the town gave it over to pillage. Primus betook himself to the town bath. On his complaining of the tepid water, the attendant replied, 'It will be hotter presently.' The remark was picked up and handed on among the troops, who interpreted it as a hint. Within a few hours the whole town was in flames.

Vitellius' position was hopeless, but a final tragedy was still to be enacted at Rome. There, as it so chanced, Vespasian's brother, Flavius Sabinus, was city prefect and so commander of the urban cohorts. Acting on his brother's behalf he had arranged for Vitellius' abdication when he was attacked by the Praetorians, driven on to the Capitol, and after a desperate resistance, in the course of which the Temple of Jupiter was set on fire, he was overwhelmed and slain. His avengers, however, were not far away. When Primus' army entered Rome there was a hideous scene of carnage as the wretched Vitellians were hunted through the streets. Fifty thousand are said to have perished, the old Emperor himself among them; and all the while, so Tacitus declares, the civilian population went their ways pursuing business—and pleasure—as usual.

Not the least horrible feature of these civil wars was the utter callousness with which soldiers slaughtered fellow-soldiers or turned equally to looting civilians. There was a strong sense of *esprit de corps* among the legions of the different commands, but none of real patriotism. The fact was that the army was now recruited either from the riff-raff of Italy where the influx of aliens had done much to obliterate the old native stock, or else from provincials who had not yet learnt to regard soldiering except in the light of an adventure. Their sole motive for fighting their commander's battles was the prospect of loot or the other rewards which victory would bring. The Empire, in short, was paying dearly for the fact that the authority which held it together rested on the power of the sword. Happily on this occasion the commander, whose elevation was achieved in so deplorable a manner, was a man of outstanding ability; and Vespasian's arrival at the capital in October 70 was to mark a new era in the history of the Principate.

CHAPTER XXIV

THE FLAVIANS AND A NEW START

I. VESPASIAN, A.D. 69–79

FEW men raised to power by such haphazard methods as Vespasian can have more abundantly justified their elevation. He was not indeed a genius of the calibre of Julius Caesar or Augustus; but if shrewd judgment and conscientious zeal for efficiency can make a man great, then he assuredly deserved that title. The first and most important thing to be noted about him was his origin. Vespasian was not, like all preceding emperors, an aristocrat. He hailed from Reate, a small town in the Sabine hills. His father had been a tax-collector and moneylender; and thus he himself, (though he had a fair education, knew some Greek and, as Emperor, went so far as to patronize the arts) had nevertheless been brought up in a very different environment from the average Roman gentleman and had gained an early experience of business methods such as that gentleman would undoubtedly have despised. In appearance he was of a coarse, thick-set, bull-necked type; but he possessed the old Italian qualities of practical energy and financial integrity. He even appears to have enjoyed a sense of humour. 'I believe I am turning into a god,' he is said to have remarked during his last illness. Power did not turn his head. He stuck to his simple soldierly habits, and instead of using Nero's luxurious palaces, he took up his residence in a modest house on the Esquiline. Hard work was meat and drink to him; and even the members of his secretariat and suite were compelled to rise at cock-crow in imitation of their master—a strange contrast to the ways under Vitellius or Nero!

Now the accession of such a man meant something more to the Empire than a mere change in the personality of its ruler. It meant the beginning of a new social order. Circumstances were ripe for such a change. The old aristocracy of Rome was fast disappearing. Many noble families had died out, and few men of real character had escaped the persecutions of Tiberius, Caligula, and Nero, to say nothing of the final havoc of the Civil Wars. Here, then, lay the importance of Vespasian's freedom from class-prejudice. Of *bourgeois* origin himself, he was prepared to take the *bourgeoisie* into the administration of the Empire. Henceforward the ladder of promotion was open to talent irrespective of class, and the highest offices of State, both at home and abroad, were occupied by men who hitherto would only have been admitted to lower posts of the civil service. The employment of freedmen in really responsible positions would seem to have been discontinued; and under Domitian at any rate knights were admitted side by side with senators to the Emperor's inner Council of State. As for the Senate itself, Vespasian, assuming the censor's office, drafted into it many members of middle-class origin without the usual formality of election to a magistracy. Nor was the 'new aristocracy' confined to Italians only. Already the imperial regime had brought to the fore many soldiers, politicians, and writers of provincial extraction; Seneca, for instance, hailed from Spain and Burrus from Gaul, whither, so far as we can tell, their ancestors had gone but from Italy as settlers and perhaps even married native wives. But, whereas in the past such cases had been exceptional, from Vespasian's time onwards the administrative services were more and more recruited from the civilized population of the Western provinces, till in Trajan and Hadrian the Principate itself was to fall to men whose place of birth was in the province of Spain.

The new blood thus infused into the imperial organism brought an energy of action and freshness of outlook which were sorely needed. In such a man as Agricola—born in southern Gaul and governor of Britain under Vespasian, Titus, and Domitian—Tacitus, his son-in-law and biographer, could not sufficiently praise the high seriousness of purpose and sense of responsibility which inspired his brilliant career; and there is no special reason to suppose Agricola to have been exceptional. At Rome the contrast must have been most marked between the riotous indecency of Nero's or Claudius' court and the sober self-restraint and efficiency of the new regime. To Vespasian and his successors it meant everything that in such reliable subordinates, drawn from so comparatively wide an area of the Empire, they could count on a genuine loyalty and devotion which had too frequently been lacking in the somewhat disgruntled members of the old aristocracy of Rome. For now more than ever the Emperor's will was the centre and focus on which all authority depended. Vespasian never attempted to disguise the fact that he meant to be master. By his use of the censorship he had ensured that the members of the Senate should be his tame nominees.[1] Indeed, the pretence that the House was a real partner in the imperial system was wearing more than a little thin. Its vote was still valuable as a means of registering the Emperor's wishes, and Hadrian a little later was to employ it—without any real pretence of consulting the House's opinion—as the simplest method of promulgating laws. But, as such a development indicates, the actual influence of the Senate was gradually dwindling, and the process continued until in the last resort it became little more than the town council of Rome.

There can be no question, then, that Vespasian ruled in a more literal and autocratic sense than any of his predecessors. Happily his zeal for efficiency was accompanied by an unusual talent for organization—military organization above all; for the new Emperor was first and foremost a soldier. His share in Claudius' invasion of Britain had won him recognition, and the recent campaign in Palestine, over which he was commander-in-chief, had given him experience, and experience, as it so happened, of a somewhat unique sort. For this was the first war for over a century in which a Roman army had been called upon to overcome the prolonged resistance of a civilized foe; and there is reason to believe that many lessons of military science here learned were later applied to the problems of the frontiers elsewhere. There was urgent need, too, after the reigns of Gaius, Claudius, and Nero, for an Emperor who had some first-hand knowledge of the troops, more especially since the recent civil wars had seriously undermined not merely their discipline and morale, but also their allegiance. How far such a state of things had gone was revealed by a

[1] His son Titus shared the office, and Domitian, when Emperor, was censor for life. The constitutional change thus effected in the character of the Principate was of far-reaching importance.

terrible upheaval—half mutiny and half rebellion—which took place upon the Rhine at the outset of Vespasian's reign, but before we describe it in detail it will be well to say something about the geography of the frontier itself.

Since the close of Germanicus' campaigns in A.D. 17 the frontier belt had been divided into two areas, Upper (i.e. Southern) and Lower (i.e. Northern) Germany, in each of which was stationed an army under a separate *legatus*. The legions of the Upper Army were posted at Vindonissa near Basel, Argentoratum (or Strasbourg), and Moguntiacum (or Mainz); the Lower Army had fortified camps at Bonna (Bonne), Novaesium, and Castra Vetera. Being the most northerly of all, Vetera lay nearest to the so-called 'Island' at the Rhine mouth, in which dwelt the Batavi, hitherto loyal subjects of Rome and the recruiting-ground of her finest auxiliary troops. It was among these Batavi that the trouble began. Antonius Primus, during his march on Cremona, had sent messengers appealing to the Rhineland troops to desert Vitellius in favour of Vespasian. Among the Batavi a certain nobleman, Julius Civilis by name and till recently an officer of auxiliary troops, grasped at this pretext of using Vespasian's name to shelter what in reality was to be an insurrection. Eight thousand Batavian auxiliaries from Mainz at once marched up to join him. Volunteers from the Tencteri and other German tribes flocked to his banner, and with a formidable army at his back he was soon leading the attack on Castra Vetera. Now the withdrawal of troops for Vitellius' march on Italy had seriously depleted the garrison of both this and other stations. Added to this, the general left in command of both the Upper and Lower Armies, Hordeonius Flaccus by name, acted with lamentable indecision, if not with actual treachery; and it was only the vigour and dash of Dillius Vocula that availed to bring relief to the half-starving defenders of Vetera, from which after revictualment he once again withdrew.

But now affairs took a fresh and even more serious turn. The news of Vespasian's accession compelled Civilis to abandon his pretence of partisanship and declare himself in open rebellion against Rome. Meanwhile his success had fired the nationalist aspirations of three Gallic nobles—Julius Classicus,

Julius Tutor of the Treveri, and Julius Sabinus of the Lingones. The old idea, started by Vindex, of forming an independent 'Empire of the Gauls', caught hold. The burning of the Capitol at Rome had made a deep impression on the superstitious provincials, among whom the Druid priests were busily prophesying the imminent downfall of the tyrant city; and early in A.D. 70 many of the Gallic tribes were up. Thus attacked upon the west as well as on north and east, the threat of complete encirclement was too much for the nerve of the legions. They turned on Vocula and slew him as they had already slain Flaccus, and then both at Novaesium and Mainz undertook to save their skins by swearing allegiance to the 'Empire of the Gauls'. The garrison at Vetera, now once again under siege and reduced to devouring the very weeds that grew on the walls, held out for a while, then surrendered on promise of safe conduct, and when five miles out of their camp, were massacred almost to a man.

But just when Rome's hold upon north-eastern Gaul and the Rhineland appeared completely lost, dissension began to arise among the ranks of the rebels. Civilis and his Germans had no enthusiasm for an Empire of the Gauls; and even among the Gauls themselves the tribes were already quarrelling over the question of leadership. So when Petilius Cerealis was sent north by Vespasian at the head of three legions, he found more than half his work could be done by diplomacy. By playing on their old fears of Teutonic irruption, he won over the rebel Treveri, and then near their capital Augusta Treverorum (now Trèves) he defeated the German host in a pitched battle. So the insurrection petered out and the terms accorded were merciful. Even the turncoat legions were merely disbanded, and the rebels settled down peacefully. As for Civilis, the account of Tacitus here breaks off short, and what happened to this romantic leader is lost to history. We should like to know.

The lesson of the rising was not lost upon Vespasian. The defection of the Batavian cohorts in response to the call of their countrymen showed how unsafe it was to leave native regiments to serve in the land of their birth. Accordingly there followed a sort of 'general post', and henceforward, so we find, the auxiliaries on the Rhine were drawn from Spain,

Africa, or even farther afield, while auxiliaries recruited from the German tribes were employed in Britain or the Danubian provinces. For additional security the commissions in such regiments were no longer given to native nobles like Civilis, but reserved almost exclusively for Italians. On the other hand, recruitment for the *legions*, as opposed to the auxiliaries, was now spread far more widely through the Empire, Italy being left simply to supply the men for the Praetorian Guard. In the Western provinces Romanization was proceeding apace —Vespasian himself enfranchised even the larger villages of Spain[1]—so that there was a plentiful supply of citizen-soldiers who felt they had some stake in the Empire; and accordingly it was found that legionaries, unlike the less dependable and less civilized auxiliaries, could safely be recruited from the districts in which they were stationed.

To the problem of the frontier Vespasian gave special attention; and indeed for the first time that problem was tackled in a really scientific manner. On the Rhine the danger of invasion had become almost negligible; but in the countries beyond the Danube there were already symptoms of a restless stirring among barbaric peoples who later were to become a perpetual menace to the Empire's very existence; and Vespasian saw the necessity of planting a series of forts along the middle reaches of that river, starting from Vindobona (or Vienna) and continuing eastwards past Carnuntum (already founded by Claudius) to Viminacium, Ratiaria, and Oescus in northern Moesia. Here too, as on the Rhine, a fleet of boats was started to accelerate communication between these legionary stations. Vespasian's real stroke of initiative, however, lay in a scheme for a closer co-ordination between the two great river fronts. Their upper waters, as a glance at the map will show, form an awkward re-entrant angle. Nothing was easier than to annex this angle (for the district—now the Black Forest—was then apparently held by a drifting and sparse population), and diagonally across it to draw a new and shorter frontier. Along this frontier was constructed a series of small forts and watch-towers—an innovation which

[1] He gave them 'Latin' or half-rights, which meant that their magistrates, at any rate, would receive full citizenship automatically.

was ultimately to lead to such great frontier-works as Hadrian's Wall in Britain. Finally under cover of this fortified line ran a military high road, forming a link whereby the co-operation between the Rhine and Danube garrisons was considerably facilitated.

In the East, where no natural barrier was available, similar treatment of the frontier problem was out of the question; but by a redistribution of provincial areas Vespasian did much to strengthen the approaches through Armenia or the upper Euphrates where hitherto about 300 miles of frontier had been undefended by a single Roman soldier. The client kingdoms of Cappadocia and Lesser Armenia were incorporated in the province of Galatia, Commagene in the province of Syria; and the garrisons of these provinces were thus enabled to move their quarters forward to important strategic points such as Satala and Samosata on the Armenian border, Melitene and Zeugma on the Parthian. New legions had to be transferred to the defence of the East. But, on the other hand, it is well to note that this careful planning was aimed at an economical use of man-power; and, though the number of auxiliary troops was somewhat increased, it is highly significant that, whereas Augustus had started the Empire with twenty-eight legions, the number still stood at roughly the same figure, or thirty legions at the most. Yet Rome's commitments were greater and her external foes not less active; so that only by a scientific and economical use of the forces at her disposal could she hope to hold her own.

Reorganization of the army, however, was only one-half of Vespasian's problem. For armies cost money; and if at his accession the military situation was unsatisfactory, the financial situation was scarcely less so. Nero's extravagance had left the Treasury empty. The civil wars had shattered public confidence; and Vespasian himself declared that some forty million pounds were needed to re-establish the Exchequer. So he taxed unmercifully. He increased the tribute due from the provinces, and, what is more, appointed a much larger staff of procurators, to see that it was properly collected. He cancelled the immunity hitherto allowed to Greece. He restored a tax on sales which Galba had remitted. Above all he made a great effort to reorganize and develop the imperial resources in land. An attempt was made to bring all public property under the same administration as his own estates. Cultivators were found for vacant districts by offering them at low rents free of taxation, and such would seem to have been the treatment of the Black Forest annexations which came to be known as the 'Tithe-lands'.

In Vespasian's policy there is in fact plenty to show that the accusations of niggardly meanness, which his critics were fond of bringing, were very wide of the mark. He was a constructive as well as a cautious economist. In all quarters of the Empire evidence of his energetic road-building can still be traced. He could find money, if need be, for public works at Rome. The restoration of the Capitoline Temple was taken in hand, and, where Nero's pleasure park had stood, was now built an enormous amphitheatre, the Colosseum, capable of holding nearly 90,000 persons. Most remarkable of all perhaps, this shrewd old financier had the taste and foresight to found professorships of Greek at Rome and pay the salaries out of the public purse.

Like most Emperors of the epoch, Vespasian was unpopular in certain quarters at the capital; and this unpopularity is reflected in literature where the approval of inarticulate millions goes unrecorded. Certainly he was a hard master; and seeing what the times were, he had no other choice. He was already sixty-one at his accession and could not count on many years in which to restore a State which he found in ruins. Above all, remembering how terrible had been the chaos attendant upon a vacant throne, he was determined, like Augustus, to secure the succession in his own family before he died. He had two sons, Titus and Domitian, and he lost no opportunity of associating the elder with himself in every conceivable capacity. Like Augustus' consorts, Titus received tribunician and proconsular powers. Year after year he was elected to the consulship along with his father. He shared with him the censorship too. He was even made Prefect of the Praetorian Guard; and, if we can trust a hint of Suetonius, acted as Vespasian's Secretary of State. Like all upstart monarchs, this *bourgeois* Emperor was desperately anxious to establish the 'legitimacy' of his family; and it was statecraft, not vanity, which induced him to encourage the imperial cult and to found, like Augustus, a special order of priests—known as the Flaviales, whose special duty it was to superintend the worship of his family *genius*. The sanctity of the blood royal is always a convenient theory for the founder of a hereditary dynasty. But in his heart of hearts it is clear that Vespasian realized the hollowness of the pretence. He could laugh at the poets' effort to provide him with a heroic pedigree; and in truth the real dignity of the man stood in need of no such adventitious aids. When it came to the last, he showed a sense of his position worthy of the finest of aristocrats. 'An Emperor should die standing,' he said, and, struggling to his feet, fell dead.

II. TITUS, A.D. 79–81

Vespasian's dynastic plan succeeded brilliantly. Nobody disputed the succession of his son and consort. Titus, say Tacitus, was the world's darling, and, as his portraits seem to indicate, a somewhat spoilt darling at that. He was handsome; he had great charm of manner. His success in Palestine brought him a high military reputation. He was a great favourite with the troops. It was not unnatural for an Emperor, who had witnessed the unpopularity of his predecessor's economy, to court approval by a lavish use of the resources which that economy had built up; and Titus valued power for the opportunities it brought of airing his own good-nature and winning the plaudits of the mob. 'I have lost a day,' he once exclaimed on discovering that twenty-four hours had passed without his bestowing any gift on a friend. He built a magnificent bath-house for the public use; and when the Colosseum was nearing completion he celebrated the event by providing gladiatorial and other shows which lasted a hundred days. When sated with the shambles, he had the arena filled with water and a mimic sea-fight enacted before the delighted populace. As for governing, he scarcely bothered his head about that; and unscrupulous officials made hay while the sun shone. The only two important incidents of his reign showed him at his best. When another great fire devastated part of the capital, Titus sold some of the Palace furniture in aid of the homeless victims. In 79 occurred the famous eruption of Vesuvius in which Pompeii and Herculaneum were overwhelmed, and the Emperor appointed a committee to organize relief, himself contributing generously towards the purpose. Unfortunately the open-handed extravagance with which he conducted his charities and his amusements alike put a severe strain on the exchequer. Perhaps it was fortunate both for his own reputation and also for the welfare of the State that he died prematurely, after two years' reign, at the age of forty-one. He left no son to succeed him on the throne.

III. DOMITIAN, A.D. 81–96

Titus died where his father had been born, at Reate among the Sabine hills. His brother Domitian, who was with him at the time, got to horse and rode full speed for Rome; there he promised the Praetorians a donative and was proclaimed Emperor. It was his first real taste of power. Apart from formal honours, neither his father nor his brother had entrusted him with any important command, though he had ardently begged for it. So the energy of his nature, lacking an outlet, had become warped, and, as he brooded over his disappointments, his less pleasant traits, which might have been sloughed off in useful action, had grown.

For Domitian's character, as Vespasian doubtless knew, was a curious mixture. On the one hand he inherited much of his father's efficiency and organizing talent. In the course of his reign he spent long stretches of time in the frontier-camps of the Rhine and the Danube, supervising the operations of the troops or engineers. This side of him received scant justice from historians such as Tacitus, whose judgment was gravely biased by the unfortunate interactions of the Emperor's touchiness and the ill-judged pretensions of the intellectual clique at Rome. For Domitian could not bear criticism. He lacked the sense of humour of his father, who refused to take a 'barking dog' too seriously. Determined at all costs to rule, he learnt to domineer, and the result was an autocracy stripped of all the disguises with which Augustus' tact had veiled it, but an autocracy which, unlike the rule of Domitian's great successors, could not command a merited respect. The Senate, which Vespasian had at least made more representative of the Empire, was now treated like dirt. Domitian attended its debates clad in his imperial purple, and violated all etiquette by insisting on voting first. He assumed the censorship for life and therewith the power to keep a permanent check on the personnel of the House. Above all, when asked to guarantee that members should be immune from arbitrary execution without due trial by their peers, he bluntly refused; and his refusal proved once and for all that the pretence of partnership was at an end. The senators were the Emperor's subjects, not his partners now. Meanwhile he surrounded himself with ministers drawn from the equestrian class; and few things were more unpalatable to the remnants of the old aristocracy than the inclusion of such *bourgeois* upstarts in his Council of State, now often used not merely for discussion of policy but for trials of high treason. This Council frequently met in the Emperor's favourite country-seat among the Alban hills outside the capital; and Juvenal the satirist has given us a lifelike and amusing skit on its deliberations. It certainly was a motley gathering. Alongside with Pegasus the City Prefect and the leading lawyer of the day, Fuscus the Praetorian Prefect and other reputable persons, it included Crispinus, a native of Egypt who had come to Italy as a fishmonger, made a fortune, and gained equestrian rank; Veiento, a fat rogue notorious as the Emperor's evil genius; and, most unpopular of all, a blind old sycophant called Catullus Messalinus, whose tell-tale tongue brought many a man to his doom. A midnight summons calls them to the Emperor's presence, where they find themselves confronted with a peculiar problem —a prodigious mullet has been brought to the Palace and the question is how should it be cooked—divided into portions or served whole? Opinions are divided. The blind Messalinus affects admiration of the splendid monster—all the time looking in the wrong direction. Finally the gourmet Montanus clinches the issue by advising the manufacture of a special dish capable of containing the bulk of the fish.

> Henceforth, great Caesar, on the far campaign
> A staff of potters shall attend thy train.

The atmosphere reeks with grovelling adulation more reminiscent of some Sultan's court than of a Roman Emperor's—so far have we travelled since Augustus' day.

But entertaining as is Juvenal's lampoon, it shows only one side of the picture. The best of Domitian was seen upon the frontier, and of his military activities something must now be said. In 83 he superintended in person a campaign against the Chatti, whose recent raids across the Rhine seemed to call for punitive measures. While efforts were made to induce the Cherusci to attack the enemy in the rear, the Roman forces started from Mainz and pushed north-eastward into the thickly wooded district of Mount Taunus. The victories there won were deemed sufficient to entitle the Emperor to a 'triumph', though Tacitus characteristically scoffs at such exaggerated claims and declares that the war captives, who marched in the procession, were hired and dressed in wigs for the occasion. Unhappily literary evidence is too scanty to establish the truth about the campaign; but archaeologists have been busy, and across the angle between the Rhine and Danube, and well in advance of Vespasian's original frontier, their researches have revealed a new fortified line which unquestionably belongs to this reign. It began north of Mainz, encircled the Taunus district, followed the course of the River Main, struck across country to the river Neckar, and thence to the Danube itself. It consisted of a series of forts built of earth with frequent watch-towers between, while in the rear of these were stronger forts of stone to serve as bases. A generation later the Emperor Hadrian, pushing the line slightly farther east, gave it additional strength by erecting a timber palisade. The motives of Domitian's enterprise were probably mixed. As the heir to a strong military tradition, he could scarcely escape the temptation to a forward policy. At this very time Agricola, his representative in Britain, was engaged in a similar advance into Scotland, and the discontinuance of his efforts were most likely due to the diversion of troops from Britain to the Emperor's Rhineland campaign. Besides this, it may well be that the process of Romanization which was proceeding apace in the Tithelands and in adjacent districts on the east bank of the

Rhine,[1] required a more adequate protection than Vespasian's frontier had given them. In any case the new frontier meant a further shortening of the line and thus a corresponding economy of troops; and so secure was it now considered that half a century later the number of the Rhineland legions had been reduced to four.

The truth is that not here, but on the line of the Middle Danube, lay now the real threat to the frontier. Already we can detect the premonitory symptoms of a grave unrest which not long hence was to become the crucial problem of the Empire's security. From far away on the Russian steppes a great movement westwards was beginning, headed by the Sarmatians, a populous tribe of wandering nomads and the forerunners of the great barbarian migrations which three centuries later were to accomplish the overthrow of Rome. At present the effect of this movement was to exercise pressure on the Daci, Quadi, and other tribes which dwelt north of the Danube basin, and which, as the result of such pressure, were now tending to encroach upon the Roman borders. Till recently the scattered tribes of which the Daci were composed had remained disunited and comparatively harmless; but the appearance of an ambitious and capable chief named Decebalus had completely altered the situation. Knowledge of Roman military methods, gleaned apparently from deserters, had enabled this man to organize a well-disciplined army; and in 85 he crossed the Danube and, after defeating and killing its governor Oppius Sabinus, had overrun Moesia. Cornelius Fuscus, being sent to restore the position, first pushed the invaders back across the Danube, then building a bridge of boats, rashly ventured over himself to the invasion of Dacia— only to be driven back, pursued, and overwhelmed in a battle in which he and his whole army appear to have perished (87). No worse disaster had befallen Roman arms since the loss of Varus' legions; but happily Fuscus' successor Julianus proved a better strategist. He inflicted a bloody defeat upon the Dacian forces and was marching on Decebalus' capital, Sarmizegethusa, when the king sued for peace. At the moment

[1] There had been silver-mining in Mount Taunus as early as Claudius' reign.

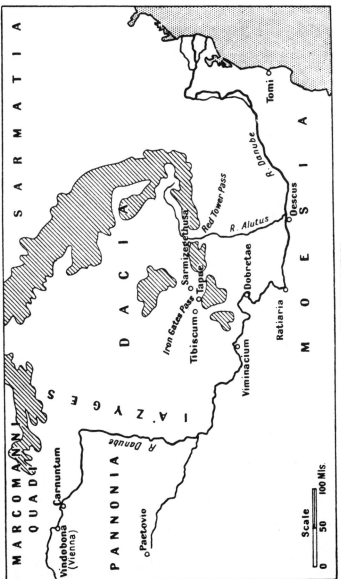

THE DACIAN WARS

an attack was threatening from the Quadi and other neighbouring tribes; and Domitian's hands, too, had recently been
full with a rebellion on the Rhine. He therefore determined on
a compromise. On condition that Decebalus restored his prisoners of war and undertook to accept his crown from Rome
(much in the same way as Tiridates of Armenia had done in
Nero's reign), Domitian agreed to pay him an annual subsidy
of money and allow him the loan of some Roman engineers.
The terms were perhaps more tactful than honourable, and
critics spoke scathingly of 'tribute paid to the barbarian';
but for the time being at least the menace was staved off, and
by the construction of new forts along the Danube frontier
Domitian unquestionably left the situation more secure than
he had found it.

As far as provincial administration was concerned, everything goes to show that the machine worked smoothly and
efficiently under Domitian's rule. The one serious trouble was
the revolt above alluded to when in 88 Antonius Saturninus,
commander of the Upper Rhine Army, made a bid for the
throne. As he succeeded in buying the co-operation of the
Chatti, the position looked critical; and Domitian, who had
recently been on the Danube, hurried to the scene of the
rebellion. Before he could arrive, however, Norbanus, commander of the Lower province, had acted. Assisted by a sudden
thaw which opportunely broke the river ice, and so stopped
the Chatti from crossing, he caught Saturninus' two legions
near Mainz and utterly defeated them. The lesson of the
episode led to one important change. Of recent years the very
security of the frontier had left the Rhineland legates dangerously idle. So, to keep them better occupied, Domitian transferred to them the civil government of their districts which
hitherto had been administered from Gaul; and Saturninus'
place was filled by a man more versed in legal than in military
science.

It seems clear that, in general, Domitian's choice of men for
provincial posts was sensible; and even his critics gave him
credit for keeping a tight hold on them. Nor again in the field
of public works and monuments did his policy lack vigour.
Like his father, he was responsible for the construction of many

new roads both in Italy and elsewhere. Like his father, too, he was prepared to spend money on the adornment of the capital. Indeed, no Emperor since Augustus had built on so lavish a scale; and apart from a new Senate House, a new palace, and several new temples which stood to his credit, the havoc wrought by the fire of Titus' reign gave him a special opportunity. The Capitoline Temple, then under process of reconstruction, had been entirely gutted, and it was now rebuilt with golden roof and splendid porticoes of marble imported from Greece. In the Campus Martius, which had also suffered severely, Domitian erected a Hall of Music and a Circus. For, autocrat though he was, he well realized the importance of keeping the populace amused. Gladiatorial shows, chariot races, and distributions of free food were becoming a regular charge on the imperial exchequer; and when to this lavish outlay upon public works and public entertainments was added the cost of continual frontier wars, it is not surprising that the Treasury, already depleted by Titus' extravagance, was left in a state of complete exhaustion at Domitian's death.

But a desire for popularity was not the only motive for some of these expenditures, which reveal in fact a very different side of this strange Emperor's character. The truth is that he possessed certain traits so unexpected in the son of a strictly practical father that some historians think them to have been derived from the Etruscan blood of his mother Domitilla. In the first place he clearly had something of an artist's temperament. As a young man he had been much addicted to literary pursuits; and the primary purpose of his Hall of Music seems to have been the inauguration of public competitions to which poets, singers, and orators were invited in imitation of the famous festivals of Greece. In building, too, he seems to have been indulging a personal taste for beauty, or at any rate for splendour, as in the gorgeous palace which he erected for himself on the slopes of the Palatine Hill. Yet here again there was another trait to be distinguished in him. For his very generous outlay on religious architecture must probably be traced to a superstitious tendency that revealed itself in various forms. He consulted astrologers. He was an ardent votary of the Egyptian goddess Isis and built her a temple at

Rome. He even made a point of enforcing obsolete rules of morality; and one Vestal Virgin who had broken her vows, he condemned to be buried alive. What seems certain is that he regarded himself in some sense as the defender of the orthodox creeds. For he did his best to check the spread of the Jewish faith among members of upper-class society, and (so far as can be judged) of the Christian faith too. We know at any rate that the charge of 'atheism' was brought against the Emperor's cousin Flavius Clemens and Domitilla his wife; and since archaeological evidence shows the catacombs to have been dug on Domitilla's property, it is a natural guess that Christianity was the real root of their offence. As Clemens' children were heirs presumptive to the throne, his conversion must clearly have presented awkward problems, and this may well have accounted for his execution. Furthermore, the appearance of the Christian faith within the Flavian family must have been an unwelcome challenge to the imperial cult itself, to which Domitian, even more than his father, attributed great importance. Not merely had Vespasian and Titus received their due deification, but also Domitian's own son who had died before he came to the throne, and, what is stranger still, the female members of the family. As for Domitian himself, there can be little doubt that the cult flattered his exaggerated sense of self-importance. Vain he certainly was, and Suetonius relates how he filled the streets of Rome with portrait-statues of himself, till some wag scrawled 'Enough' across one of them. It is therefore not surprising that after some show of demur he assumed the resounding title of 'Dominus et Deus', or, as we might style it, 'Potentate and God'. Such a claim to *present* divinity went far beyond the usual practice whereby the Emperor's 'genius' was worshipped in his lifetime and deification of his person was deferred till death. To ourselves the extravagance of the claim can scarcely fail to suggest some degree of megalomania; but it may help us to understand how little such a man, obsessed by the consciousness of his own omnipotence, could tolerate the somewhat futile criticisms of the intellectuals at Rome.

For once again the Stoic philosophers were lifting up their voice. One, Senecio, composed a panegyric in memory of

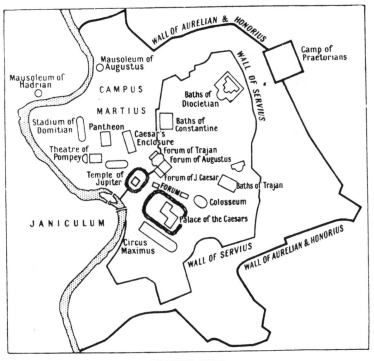

IMPERIAL ROME

Helvidius Priscus, whose book *In Praise of Cato* had brought down Vespasian's wrath upon his head. The gesture of independence, however harmless, was a gratuitous insult, and Senecio paid for it with his life. Helvidius' own son suffered a similar fate for a tendentious play he had written; and the compliant Senate passed a general decree of banishment against all philosophers in Italy. Tacitus, whose whole outlook upon life was embittered by his enforced silence throughout these unhappy years, declared that all freedom of speech was completely extinguished; and, if but one half of his accusations should be true, Domitian must have yielded, in the latter part of his life, to the same impulses of nervous suspicion and bloodthirsty revenge which had marked the climax of Tiberius' reign. It was said that the real motive of the numerous executions was a desire to replenish the exhausted treasury by the confiscation of the victim's wealth. But any tale was good enough wherewith to blacken the memory of the detested tyrant; and the likelihood is that the Emperor's nerves had simply got the better of him. A lonely figure, morose and self-contained, he lent a ready ear to the least hint of the 'informers', taking a sinister pleasure in devising fresh methods of conviction and watching with satisfaction for the guilty blench on his intended victim's cheek. The atmosphere at Rome grew tense with dread. No one could feel himself safe, least of all were he a man of any prominence; and the darkest rumours were credulously believed. Tacitus broadly hints that his father-in-law was poisoned, for no better reason than that during his last illness the Emperor sent so frequently to inquire after his health. Conspiracies there doubtless were among the aristocracy. It was the failure of one such in 88 which led indirectly to Saturninus' revolt on the Rhine. But in the final issue it was among the Emperor's own family that the fatal coup was planned. His wife Domitia, finding evidence among his papers that her own life was in danger, suborned a freedman of her suite named Stephanus to undertake the deed. Concealing a dagger in the folds of a sling which he assumed for the occasion, Stephanus entered the presence, unfolded a pretended disclosure of some new conspiracy, and, as Domitian read it, stabbed him in the groin. He died fighting gamely, and, though the Senate greeted the news with cheers, the soldiers undoubtedly regretted him; but since he left no son, the dynasty which his father had so much hoped to found, died with him. That dynasty had indeed fulfilled its difficult mission; and the motto 'Rome Resurgent' which Vespasian had imprinted on many of his coins, had been abundantly justified—in a more than literal sense—by the strong rule of the Flavian House. Nevertheless, in the coming years, the choice of a new Emperor was to be determined on other principles than hereditary succession by blood.

CHAPTER XXV

THE EMPIRE IN THE FIRST AND SECOND CENTURIES

THE idiosyncrasies of an autocrat may greatly influence for better or for worse the fortunes of millions; and much space in the foregoing chapters has necessarily been devoted to the characters and personal doings of successive Emperors. Yet, taken as a whole, the life of the Empire was curiously little affected by the change from one ruler to another; and there could be no worse error than to suppose that its history consisted solely in what happened on the frontiers or in the court at Rome. The era of the Flavian Dynasty and their immediate successors has rightly been regarded as the Golden Age of the imperial régime, and probably in many ways one of the happiest periods in all human history. It is therefore no inappropriate moment to pass under review the various aspects of the Empire's life which have hitherto been little considered. The provinces shall stand first; and partly because it must possess a special interest for ourselves, partly because it well illustrates the effect of Roman rule upon more backward countries, we will begin with our own island.

I. BRITAIN UNDER ROMAN OCCUPATION

The history of the Roman occupation of Britain falls roughly into three phases. The first phase ended, as we said above, with the thorough subjugation of the south-eastern half of the country, clearly marked by the drawing of a temporary frontier along the line of the Fosse Way. The next phase was distinguished first by an advance into the wilder districts of north and west, and second by a nationalist revolt analogous to those which Varus met in Germany and Julius Caesar in Gaul.

Ostorius Scapula, the governor who was responsible for the construction of the Fosse, was not long content with this frontier, but pushed his military posts to Deva (Chester), Uriconium (Wroxeter), and probably Glevum (Gloucester) in the west, and from these bases he was able to attack the two chief tribes of Wales, the Ordovices of the north and the Silures of the south. In his struggle with the latter he overcame and captured Caractacus or Caradoc, a son of Cunobelinus, and so worthy to be considered the last surviving champion of the national resistance. The conquest of Wales was still very far from complete. But a lull followed; and then in A.D. 60 Suetonius Paulinus determined to strike a blow at the island of Mona or Anglesey—the stronghold of the rebellious Druid priesthood. Proceeding presumably from Deva and accompanied by a fleet of barges built on the Dee, he reached the straits, his men dashed through the shallows, and overcoming the resistance of the astonished natives, slaughtered the Druids on their own altar-stones. Meanwhile, however, behind the governor's back trouble was brewing in East Anglia. There the Iceni were bitterly resenting their treatment at the hands of the conquerors. Apart from the tribute they were forced to pay, they had several special grievances. Agents of Seneca, who had lent them large sums of money at high interest, were calling in the loan. At the outset, moreover, they had been accepted as allies, but, when their old chieftain Prasugates died and bequeathed his whole kingdom to Rome, they had found themselves treated as slaves. Lands had been taken from them, most probably to make provision for fresh veteran settlers; and imperial officials had brutally maltreated Boadicea, Prasugates' widow, and insulted his daughters. Seizing the opportunity of Paulinus' absence the tribesmen rose *en masse*, and sweeping down on the unfortified town of Camulodunum they slaughtered its inhabitants, men, women, and

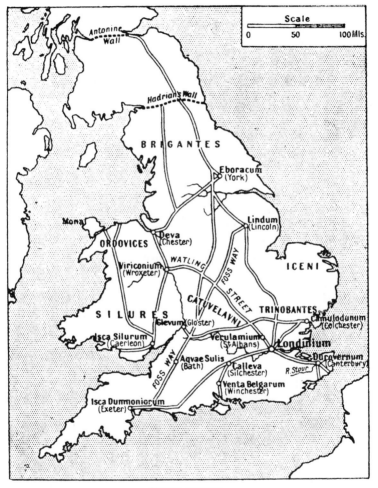

ROMAN BRITAIN

children, with hideous barbarity. The Ninth Legion under Petilius Cerialis, marching down from Lindum (Lincoln), was cut up by the rebels; and Paulinus, returning hot-foot from Anglesey, had not the forces to hold Londinium, which suffered from the same fate as Camulodunum (Colchester.) Charred remains of its buildings are still sometimes laid bare; and the total number of victims (Verulamium, or St. Albans, also was sacked) is said to have run to 80,000 'Roman citizens and allies'—a remarkable indication of the scale on which commercial exploitation had been pressed. Eventually, as he fell back north-westwards along Watling Street, Paulinus succeeded in forcing a pitched battle in which his disciplined troops wellnigh annihilated the British hordes. Boudicca committed suicide and the rebellion was suppressed in so thorough-going a fashion that it was more than a century before East Anglia recovered from the appalling devastation it endured.

We now enter the third phase of the conquest, in which a permanent delimitation of the provincial frontier was to be achieved. Under Cerialis and Frontinus, two first-class generals, whose appointment to Britain may well have been due to Vespasian's special interest in the island, a marked advance was made. Cerialis pushed his northward legionary station to Eboracum (now York). Frontinus overcame the Silures and established a new base at Isca Silurum or Caerleon-on-Usk. But the outstanding governor of the Flavian period was Agricola, the father-in-law of Tacitus. He completed his predecessors' work in Wales by reducing Ordovices and Mona; and this done, he turned his attention to the north. By establishing a series of block-houses or forts he effectually pacified the warlike tribe of the Brigantes in Yorkshire; and then secured his communications for a systematic invasion of Caledonia or Scotland. In A.D. 80 he reached the line of Forth and Clyde; and at this stage of his advance a fresh line of forts was built next year, thus isolating the Lowland country from the Highlands, which were to be his next objective. In 83 and 84, with a strong fleet in attendance, he pushed up past Stirling and Perth, and at an unknown position called the Graupian Mount, he won a resounding victory over the wild tribes of the north. The thorough reduction of Caledonia now seemed scarcely beyond his power, but Domitian, who, as we have seen, needed reinforcements on the Danube, decided to recall him. There can be little doubt that Agricola's project of incorporating Scotland, had it been realized, would have enormously diminished the size of garrison required for holding the province.[1] But it was not to be. The line of the Clyde and Forth isthmus, which he had established, remained the boundary of Roman rule until the Emperor Hadrian's time. What caused Hadrian to pay a visit to Britain we do not know for certain; but some disaster is indicated by the fact that the Ninth Legion, until then stationed at York, disappeared from the Army list. Feeling presumably that the existing frontier was too far north for safety, the Emperor decided on the systematic fortification of the Tyne and Solway isthmus instead.[2] This fortification, which we know as the 'Roman Wall', is still largely in existence. It consisted of a stone rampart, seven and a half feet thick and stretching seventy-three miles in length from sea to sea. At intervals along it were seventeen forts, affording quarters for the garrison troops; at every mile were small forts, now known as the 'mile castles' with a couple of watch towers between each. The purpose of this elaborate work was not so much to form a defensive shelter behind which the garrison might fight, but rather to enable them to watch for raiding-parties and rally swiftly to any threatened point. The garrison itself consisted of about 15,000 auxiliary troops, drawn from all over the Empire; and one would have supposed such arrangements quite sufficient to prevent any successful raiding of the border. Apparently it was not so; for under Hadrian's successor, Antoninus Pius, the governor Lollius Urbicus pushed forward once again to the line of Clyde and Forth and there built another defensive work, this time of turf and clay, furnishing it with forts so close together that there were upwards of a score to its thirty-six miles of length. Even so, the new policy proved

---

[1] On the other hand, the conquest of Scotland would have been economically useless. The real resources of the island lay in the south and west.

[2] A vallum or mound and ditch which runs south of the wall had apparently been constructed as a temporary measure in the years immediately preceding Hadrian's visit.

a failure; and about 180 the defence of the north broke down so seriously that the raiders actually overwhelmed the legions and killed the governor. Eventually Septimius Severus abandoned the Antonine frontier and reverted to Hadrian's wall, which he thoroughly rehabilitated. Meanwhile by punitive expeditions he succeeded in breaking the spirit of the Highland tribes, and so gave Britain peace for a century to come, and until a new menace arose from raiders from over the sea.

South of the wall the whole of what we now call Northern England remained in a wild, semi-civilized state; for its inhabitants were of a far more savage type than the folk of the south-eastern districts, who even before the coming of the Romans had enjoyed some degree of culture. The fact is that nearly all the towns and nine-tenths of the 'villas' which have been discovered lay south of a line drawn between the Rivers Humber and Severn; and of this district by far the most populous part lay south of the Thames. Here very soon had sprung up many townships planned on the Roman pattern. Of these Londinium—a purely Roman foundation—was by far the largest. It covered half a square mile in area, and was provided with a good water-supply and an efficient drainage-system. Bath, with its magnificent bathing-halls, which are still in a great measure extant, was another town that owed its rise to the Roman occupation and the needs of gouty officials. But more interesting in many ways are the converted British towns of which Calleva or Silchester is an excellent example. This formidable stronghold, the capital of the Atrebates of North Hampshire, had originally been encircled by a high earthwork of polygonal plan. The process of its reconstruction must have begun under the Flavian Emperors—a period when, according to Tacitus, Agricola did much to accelerate the Romanization of the province, starting schools for the sons of nobles, encouraging the erection of temples, baths, and forums, and even popularizing the adoption of the 'toga' in the place of the native breeches. At Silchester the enclosed area of the town, though still kept to its polygonal shape, was greatly contracted; for there was no longer any necessity for keeping herds inside the city bounds. As was usual in Roman town-planning, the streets were laid out in a rectangular pattern.

HADRIAN

TIMGAD — THE FORUM

In the centre stood a market-place lined with stately colonnades and dominated by a town hall the size of a small cathedral. A cluster of temples, a public bath, an hotel, and even an amphitheatre outside the walls, were also gradually erected, and finally, perhaps some time in the second century, a substantial wall of stone and flint was built on the new polygonal rampart, not so much for defence (which at this period can scarcely have been necessary), but because such a circumvallation was considered appropriate for any self-respecting city. For, though it contained no more than three- or four-score houses, Calleva clearly served not merely as a market, but also as an administrative centre for the surrounding districts. Its inhabitants were not Romans, but well-to-do Britons, habituated to Roman methods of life. The same is true of the numerous 'villas' or country-houses which are so freely scattered through the south and midlands. These villas were normally planned, not, as in Mediterranean countries, round a central court, but abutting on a long corridor or veranda in which the sun's warmth could be conveniently enjoyed despite the colder climate. Usually too the living-rooms were heated by hot air admitted to a hollow space under the floor through flues from a neighbouring furnace. A 'Turkish bath' and a cold plunge would be available in a special wing of the house; and the fine tessellated pavements, many of which may still be seen, show how readily the Romanized Britons accepted the luxurious fashions of their conquerors.

In articles of domestic use, however, such as pottery and metal-work, there was a closer adherence to the old native tradition of craftsmanship. At first large quantities of so-called 'Samian' ware were imported from Italian or still more from Gallic factories. But in the second century the Britons began to manufacture a similar ware for themselves,[1] in which the embossed patterns of animals and other objects were much more lively and spontaneous than in the stereotyped output of Continental mass-production. In the same way the exquisite skill of the old British metal-workers was not wholly forgotten; and side by side with imported brooches and

[1] The chief centre of manufacture being Caistor in Northamptonshire, this type of native pottery is known as Caistor ware.

mirrors we find similar objects far more delicately modelled by the native craftsmen, though in partial imitation of the Roman designs.

In religion equally there was a tendency to fall into line with the ways of the imperial race. Local gods and goddesses were assimilated with their supposed Roman counterparts; so that we hear of 'Mars' Cocidius the patron deity of Northumberland and the 'Nymph' Brigantia among the Yorkshire dales. At the same time foreign cults must clearly have taken root in the island. Among the garrison-troops of the Wall, Mithraism was very popular, and its altars have been found. Eventually too when Christianity became the religion of the Empire, it must have found its way across the Channel; and though evidences of its dissemination are rare, a small apsidal chapel at Silchester can scarcely have been other than a sanctuary of the Church. How far the Latin language was adopted by the natives is difficult to say. It was certainly used in all official documents, in the law courts, and among the more educated classes; but there is also sufficient evidence to show that ordinary workmen knew a smattering at least, for on tiles and bricks have been found such scrawlings as *satis* ('enough') and *puellam* ('the girl'), and even the entertaining inscription '*Austalis dibus XIII vagatur sibi cotidim*', which means 'Augustalis has been off on his own every day for a fortnight.'

II. SELF-GOVERNMENT IN THE PROVINCES

The principal features which we have observed in the Romanization of Britain, were even more strongly marked among the other Western provinces. The colloquial use of Latin, for example, became so firmly established both in Spain and Gaul that it has remained the basis of their native tongues ever since. Again the country-houses of the Romanized Gallic landlords were of a far more sumptuous and elaborate character than the modest villas of Britain. Above all, the towns not merely of Gaul and Spain, but also of Africa and the Balkan provinces, were of an almost incredible magnificence, with fine broad streets, covered markets, theatres and amphitheatres, public baths and hotels, and, outside the walls, cemeteries full of exquisitely carved tombs. In Provence, for instance, Oranges and Nîmes and Arles are rich in the remains of such lordly monuments. Near Nîmes, too, may be seen the soaring arches of a Roman aqueduct, now called the Pont du Gard; and an even larger one exists at Segovia in Spain. Dalmatia can show, amongst other things, a triumphal arch at Pola; and most imposing of all perhaps are the ruins of great cities, such as Timgad, lying amid the sands of the African desert. All these bear witness to a civilization not imposed by force, but embraced for its obvious attractions and developed with a dignity that stands in striking contrast to the sordid process of industrialization which is the dubious boon bestowed by modern Europe on the more backward lands of other continents.

The parallel between Roman and modern methods, however, is in one respect very significant; for then, as now, it was a distinctively *urban* culture which formed the natural vehicle for the extension of civilizing influences. Among the Italians, as among the Greeks before them, town-life was considered not merely as a means to greater comfort and more varied entertainment, but also as the proper basis for efficient government. So among the Western provinces towns grew up as centres of administration as well as of marketing and trade; and one of the most interesting features of the imperial system was the skill with which the institutions of local self-government were adapted to the needs of both the ruling and the subject race. For it is clear that a provincial governor, even with a staff somewhat increased since Republican days, could do little more than supervise the administrative work of local bodies; and with their shrewd political instinct the Romans were always content to allow a slow and natural evolution from the more primitive methods of self-government to the more advanced and sophisticated. Thus among backward peoples, as in Gaul or Britain, where the existing political unit was the tribe, the tribe was utilized, its council of nobles being made responsible for the maintainance of order, the administration of justice, and the collection of the prescribed quota of tribute. What had originally been the tribal stronghold now became the natural meeting-place for such councils; and in course of time, as at Silchester, this centre would grow into a thoroughly Romanized town. When such a town was considered ripe for further privilege, it became more and more the custom to confer upon it a charter of urban self-government after the Roman pattern. There is no space here to describe in detail the various grades of status, varying from the 'Latin' cities, in which the magistrates alone received the full Roman franchise, to the *municipia*, in which all the inhabitants received it, and the *coloniae*, which often enjoyed, in addition, immunity from taxation. By the individual inhabitants of such towns the possession of Roman citizenship[1] was very highly prized; for, besides securing them certain legal advantages very useful in commercial and other transactions, it gratified their pride to feel themselves, as it were, members of the ruling race; and what is more, the responsibilities of public service, which the charter of self-government imposed, were accepted in a patriotic spirit thoroughly worthy of the best Roman traditions. The constitution conferred by the charter was usually modelled on the political institutions of the capital itself. It included two mayors or *duoviri*; two aediles, half surveyors and half police superintendents; and a council or senate of *decuriones* recruited from ex-magistrates and numbering usually about a hundred. In the hands of this town council lay the control of all local business, such as the maintenance of order, finance, the control of religious cults and festivals, and the upkeep of public works. At the annual elections, if we may judge from the 'posters' found painted on the street walls at Pompeii, the competition for magistracies was keen; and though the posts carried no salary, so strong was the local pride in their townships that the successful candidates paid out of their private purse for the provision of very expensive gala spectacles as well as for the erection of schools, bathing-halls, and other buildings of public utility.

In the Western provinces it will thus be seen that a very considerable latitude of self-government was allowed to the

[1] The progressive increase of the number of citizens is noteworthy. The census lists of 69 B.C. showed just under one million; in 28 B.C., as the result of Julius Caesar's work, over four millions, under Augustus' more cautious administration about 900,000 were added; under Claudius again nearly one million.

urbanized areas (for along with such towns was of course included a considerable tract of the surrounding country). The interference of the governor, and, parallel with him, of the imperial procurator or financial supervisor, was limited not so much by law as by a wise tradition; and since the Emperor's ear was usually open to the complaints of the provincials, unjustifiable intervention or serious malpractices were rare.

In the Eastern half of the Empire a somewhat different state of affairs prevailed. Here, in the thoroughly Hellenized countries, where towns were numerous, and the practice of self-government was well understood, the Romans, as we have seen, left the local institutions as they found them already operating. The problem was therefore not so much how to stimulate self-government as how to regulate it along sound and healthy lines. For the provincials of Hellenized countries, once deprived of all real political independence, seem to have grown irresponsible, especially in financial affairs. In some cases intervention was a necessary remedy. One interesting example occurred in Trajan's reign. The extravagance of the Bithynian towns had reduced them to a state of bankruptcy, and, though the province was properly under senatorial management, the Emperor preferred to send out a special commissioner of his own. This was Pliny the Younger, nephew of the man who lost his life during the eruption of Vesuvius; and we are fortunate in possessing not merely many of Pliny's reports and queries, but also the answers which Trajan sent back. The minute details, with which this correspondence is often concerned, are striking proof of the very close surveillance kept by the imperial secretariat over provincial affairs. 'Is the jail to be guarded by soldiers or public slaves?' Pliny asks. 'Follow the usual course,' comes the answer. 'Two runaway slaves have been found among the recruits; should they be executed?' 'It depends on the circumstances of their enlistment.' 'There has been a bad fire at Nicomedia; shall I start a guild of firemen?' 'Not if the guild is likely to turn into a political society; the folk must put out the fires for themselves.' But most important are the letters which deal with financial problems. 'May the folk of Prusa restore a dilapidated bath-house at the borough's expense?'

'Only if they can afford it.' 'A half-finished gymnasium at Nicomedia has been burnt down; should it be rebuilt?' 'Greeks must have gymnasia; but they must not be extravagant.' 'Nicomedia has already spent a small fortune on building two aqueducts, both of which have been abandoned; shall I start them on a third?' 'Yes; but find out who has been responsible for this waste.' The necessity of exercising some discipline over these extravagant municipalities is perhaps self-evident. Bithynia was not the only senatorial province to whom a special commissioner had to be sent; nor was Pliny, it seems, the last commissioner to be sent to Bithynia. But this fact alone seems to show that such measures could be no permanent remedy for a state of things which could only be cured by a spontaneous effort of the municipalities themselves.

There is another and even more serious criticism to be passed on the imperial régime. It is that no attempt was made to give the provincials any real share in the formulation of higher policy; the responsibilities of even the self-governing communities ended at their district boundaries. In Gaul, it is true, representatives of the various tribal units assembled from time to time at Lugdunum (or Lyons), but the sole purpose of their meetings was to unite in an act of loyal homage at the shrine of the Emperor's cult. Somewhat similar assemblies of 'Asiarchs' and 'Armeniarchs' in Asia Minor were convened for nothing more important than the control of public festivals or the passing of a vote in praise or criticism of the provincial governor. But all this was in no genuine sense a devolution of authority;[1] and the truth is that a system of government in which all the threads of administration were gathered into the hands of a single omnipotent autocrat at Rome and in which every official from the lowest to the highest was directly or indirectly taking his orders from the self-same source, could never breed a healthy and spontaneous vigour of political life. Self-reliance and self-control could never be developed even by the most efficient paternalism; and it is not surprising that in the long run stagnation set in, and first indifference, then

[1] In fairness to Rome it must be admitted that any form of self-government which would have involved a provincial control of the armed forces would have been out of the question in an Empire so constituted as was hers.

distaste began to replace the enthusiasm with which municipal affairs had at one time been conducted.

III. ECONOMIC DEVELOPMENTS

What on the other hand the Empire proved itself supremely capable of doing, was to secure a high level—we may safely say an unprecedented level—of material prosperity for the great mass of its inhabitants.

One of the greatest boons which the Romans conferred upon the world they ruled was an extraordinary freedom of communication both by land and sea. The great arterial roads which radiated out from Rome and Italy into every quarter of the Western provinces were so solidly constructed that right down through the Middle Ages they remained in use, and not till quite modern times have they been bettered. An efficient post-chaise system under official control made it possible to travel at an average of fifty miles daily, and, in a case of emergency, much faster. It is reckoned that a journey from London to Rome at the beginning of the nineteenth century and before the invention of railways, took at least as long as in the days of Domitian or Trajan. By sea the rate of progress was slower. The service between Puteoli and Alexandria may have taken as much as fifty days; even so it was dependent on fine weather, and no winter sailing was undertaken, unless absolutely necessary. The seas were now well policed. Merchant ships ranged freely round Spain and Gaul and even penetrated the Baltic. There was a regular traffic with India too, and as early as Augustus' reign a fleet of 120 vessels left annually from one Red Sea port alone. We even hear (from Chinese sources) of a visit paid by Marcus Aurelius' envoys to China. Within the Empire itself commerce passed freely from province to province; for the custom dues levied at provincial frontiers were trifling. The existence of the standard imperial coinage was an immense aid to business transactions and the prevalence of a uniform language, too, Greek in the East and Latin in the West, was scarcely less so. There was thus little to discourage a man from leaving his home-country and settling wherever trade or industry might open out better prospects. Rome became a completely cosmopolitan city.

Puteoli was so full of Levantine skippers and agents that it wore every appearance of an oriental port. Jews, with their peculiar talent for commercial operations, swarmed everywhere. Even Britain, which Horace regarded as the 'other end of nowhere', had become a happy hunting-ground for profiteers. There is a remarkable tombstone found in the north of England, commemorating a native of Palmyra, a town on the edge of the Syrian desert, who came to Britain, married a British wife, and died in the country.

The extraordinary facilities for rapid and unrestricted transit within the Empire had two important results. The first was what we should call a boom in every sort of productive activity. No time was lost in exploiting the natural wealth of the Western provinces. Lead, silver, and even gold were mined in the mountains of Wales. Still more prolific was the output of the Spanish peninsula. Tablets have been found containing regulations laid down by Hadrian for the management of some copper-mines in Portugal. In them every detail is carefully prescribed—the amount of ore due to the imperial treasury, rules for shopkeepers, hours for the opening of the public bath, and even the conditions under which the local barber and the local schoolmaster should ply their trade. As here, so in many other districts, the exploitation of natural resources was sedulously fostered by the central government. The Flavians and their successors well realized the importance of increasing the Empire's wealth. It is often difficult for us to remember by how narrow a margin the ancient world, notwithstanding every appearance of prosperity, succeeded in keeping its population properly fed. In 91 a year of bad harvests so scared Domitian that he forbade the extension of viticulture in Italy and ordered the suppression of half the provincial vineyards simply in order to increase the acreage under corn. In the absence, too, of scientific manuring and crop-rotation the soil was apt to become exhausted. Sicily, once the granary of Rome, was no longer able to fulfil its function. Egypt, fertilized as it was by the Nile floods, contributed steadily to the needs of the swollen metropolis; but even this was not enough, and in the African provinces, the greater part of which was now taken up with what we should call crown-estates, tremendous efforts were made, by irrigation and other means, to increase their productivity. Lands which had never been cultivated before and which have relapsed into sterility since were then brought under the plough; and flourishing communities sprang up, the architectural remains of which may still be seen incongruously emerging in the midst of desert sands.

But the wide dissemination of commercial and industrial effort had another and a less satisfactory result. The technical methods of manufacture which at the beginning of the imperial era had been successfully exploited by Italian enterprise, were transmitted, in the natural course of things, to the Western provinces; and soon the Western provinces began to manufacture for themselves. The case of pottery is a good example. We have already seen how a native industry grew up in Britain; and a good deal earlier the same thing had happened in Gaul. There the 'Samian' ware, hitherto made chiefly at Arezzo in North Italy, began to be copied first in the southern districts of the Auvergne, and later northwards along the Rhineland. Enormous numbers of furnaces and storehouses have been discovered, from which the output of vigorous mass-production flowed out into every quarter of the world. Even at Pompeii, which, as we know, was destroyed in 79, there has been discovered a box containing more Gallic than Italian vessels. The deduction is obvious. The factories of the home-country were being 'cut out' by the provincial; and it is highly significant that about this time, presumably owing to a decline of the Campanian export-trade, Puteoli began to dwindle in importance; while Ostia, recently improved by the Emperor Claudius, attracted more and more merchant ships. Theirs, however, must have been a 'one-way' traffic; for Rome still had nothing to export.

With the loss of its industrial markets it became all the more important for Italy to develop its agriculture; and in this there was indeed a partial revival. The owners of large estates were beginning to realize that the labour of slaves, whose heart was not in their job, was apt to be unskilful and therefore unremunerative. So they tended to lease out their farms to freeborn tenants. This in itself was a healthier development;

and in the neighbourhood of the capital the culture of vegetables and other delicacies seems to have flourished. In the
northern districts, however, as in the vicinity of Comum, where
the younger Pliny had considerable estates, it was another
story; and his correspondence shows that his tenants were
usually in arrears with their rent, while many went bankrupt.
There is much evidence to show that even the imperial government were gravely concerned about the decay of rural life.
One interesting remedy, originally devised by the benevolence
of a private citizen in Julio-Claudian times, was applied on a
larger scale by Domitian's successor Nerva. Loans were made
to landowners on the security of their estates and the interest
on these loans, at the rate of 5 per cent, was made over to the
local municipality to form a fund out of which poor children
might be maintained by free allowances, and possibly assisted
with a lump sum on coming of age. It was thus hoped to 'kill
two birds with one stone'—encourage landownership and
breed a healthy rural population. Though continued by
Nerva's successors, this beneficent scheme can have had little
real effect; and while the population of the Empire was
steadily rising, that of Italy remained stationary or even
shrank. Trajan found it necessary to compel all provincials
who attained senatorial rank to buy estates in Italy; and
more significant still, he actually forbade emigration from
the home-country, so great was the temptation for men
to seek an easier livelihood abroad.

But, if the economic initiative was thus passing away from
Italy[1] to the provinces, she was also losing something that
mattered far more—the energy of her native manhood, which
during three centuries past had conquered, organized, and
administered the Mediterranean world. For the provinces
were henceforth to furnish not merely a larger and larger
number of leading officials, but even, in many cases, the
Emperors themselves. Not indeed the Eastern provinces, for
apart from a wholesale migration of Hellenized artists, teachers,
doctors, and mathematicians to Rome and the West, the

[1] It is noteworthy that Italian business-men who formerly, as
members of the ruling caste, had used their privileged position to
exploit the provinces, had by now more or less disappeared from the
eastern parts of the Empire.

Levantine countries scarcely contributed much of value except literature. Their inhabitants remained the unstable, feckless folk they had long since been. At any crisis of the Empire it was useless to look to them for support. Except for the less civilized districts such as Galatia, they did not even furnish their fair share of recruits to the forces. Morally, socially, and intellectually, in short, they belonged to a different world. It was therefore from among the Western provinces, and most of all from the Gauls, that the Empire was in the future to renew its strength. While learning much from Roman methods and culture, they had kept their robust energy untainted by the vices of civilization which had done so much to weaken Italy. Even their abortive attempts at secession betokened a certain independence of character; and from their ranks were drawn not merely a large proportion of the new aristocracy of the imperial service, but also an unfailing supply of admirable soldiers who were long to prove the backbone of the imperial troops. It is no exaggeration to say that had it not been for Julius Caesar's conquest of this virile people, the barbarian overthrow of the Roman Empire would have taken place at least a century earlier than it did.

IV. THE ARMY

It would be a serious omission if in this review of the Empire nothing was said concerning the life of its soldiers, not merely because it was upon them that its very security depended, but also because in their far-flung outposts on the frontier lines they did much to familiarize its outlying districts with Roman manners and ideas.

In theory at least the Roman army was still, as it had always been, a conscript army—that is, every citizen was liable for service; and at times of special crisis levies were still occasionally held. As a rule, however, especially in the Western provinces, there was a more than adequate supply of volunteers. Military service was in fact, a life career. The terms of enlistment which under Augustus had been for twenty years, was raised to twenty-five under the Flavians. Apart from material rewards, of which more shall be said later, the prospect of promotion was fair. A pretty firm line was drawn, it is true, between what we should call commissioned and non-commissioned officers. To the first belonged the military tribunes or staff-officers, young aristocrats, as a rule, serving their apprenticeship in the imperial service and entrusted with little more than the management of the commissariat and various 'orderly-room' duties. Apart from what they could pick up in the twelve months of their appointment, there was little or no systematic military instruction; and their next experience of soldiering would come when they attained the rank of *legatus* or commanding officer of a legion. Here again it is clear that many who filled such a post regarded it as a step towards obtaining a provincial governorship or even political office, and were not of necessity primarily interested in military science. The result was that the maintenance of a legion's tradition and even, to a large extent, its operations whether in camp or in the field, devolved on the centurions—the staunchest and most reliable body of non-commissioned officers that any army has ever possessed. For these men the prospects were excellent. Sometimes they were promoted to commissioned rank in auxiliary regiments or even in the Praetorian Guard. On discharge they were rewarded by equestrian status and sometimes by civil posts, not excluding the governorship of a smaller province. Their pay was high, about £180 a year for the ordinary centurions, while the senior centurions, who corresponded to staff-officers, received as much as £360 or even £720; and it is not surprising that they often stayed on with the colours well after their term of twenty-five years was expired. There were sixty centurions to each legion, which was between five and six thousand strong. They were not, as a rule, very popular; for their discipline was very severe. The death-penalty was enforced for desertion or cowardice; and for lesser offences brutal floggings were frequent. '*Cedo alteram*', or 'Give us another', was the nickname of one muscular sergeant who was fond of the stick. In battle the senior centurions seem each to have commanded a cohort of roughly 600 men. During peace-time efficiency was maintained by regular arms-drill, open order exercises, practice in swimming, and other athletic sports; and ten-mile route-marches were held three times a month. The soldiers were frequently employed in the construction of roads, canals, or fortifications. Camp-making played an important part in the routine; for, though a legion always fought in the open, it never spent a night except under the shelter of a palisaded mound. So every private carried a trenching-tool as a part of his equipment which otherwise consisted of helmet, cuirass, cylindrical shield, throwing-spear or *pilum*, short sword, boots, trousers, and military cloak. Pay was at the rate of ten asses a day or eight pounds a year. Domitian increased it by roughly a third, and even a junior centurion got ten times as much. Out of this pay certain sums were apparently stopped for boots, bedding, and food (which incidentally consisted of soup, bread, vegetables, and cheap wine). On the evidence of papyri it would seem that a man could live on five-sevenths of his pay. Savings-banks existed in every legion, and though as a rule payments into it were voluntary, on the occasion of a 'donative' or bonus distribution half of it was compulsorily diverted to the recipient's account. Besides this, booty taken on campaign, went to swell the normal remuneration.[1]

Under the Republic the settlement of discharged soldiers had always been a difficult problem. Augustus therefore started a fund, known as the 'Military Chest', which was fed by the proceeds of an inheritance duty and a tax on auction sales; and from it a man received on discharge a lump sum of £25 or alternatively was settled on the land, perhaps in some colony such as Camulodunum. Many ex-soldiers chose of their own accord to settle down in the country where they had served their term of service. For it was not the practice to move legions about from province to province. As time went on, too, and the progressive enfranchisement of the provincials created an ample supply of eligible recruits, it became more and

[1] Parker (the *Roman Legions*) quotes the following amusing letter written by a young soldier: 'Dear Mother, I hope this finds you well. On receipt of this please send me £2. I've not a farthing left, as I bought a donkey cart and am quite cleared out. Do send me a riding-coat, some oil and my monthly allowance. When last I was home, you promised not to leave me quite broke, and now you treat me like a dog. Father came to see me the other day and gave me nothing. Every one laughs at me and says, "His father's a soldier, his father gave him nothing". Valerius' mother sent him a pair of pants, some oil, a box of food and £2. Do send me some money and don't leave me like this. My love to all at home. Your loving son.'

more the tendency to enlist a legion locally. Though strictly speaking a legionary was not allowed to marry, irregular unions with native wives were winked at; and behind the frontier stations (as for instance Hadrian's Wall) there grew up regular towns, containing shops, taverns, temples, and places of amusement. Here soldiers' sons were bred up and, when of age, were free to be legitimized and receive citizen-rank, provided they too joined the colours. The result was that in the later days of the Empire soldiering became almost a hereditary profession, sons following in their father's calling as did their own sons after them. From Hadrian's time onwards even the old class-distinction between legionaries and auxiliaries began to fade away. For as the imperial officials became more cosmopolitan, racial prejudices were forgotten; and with citizens entering auxiliary regiments and provincials entering the legions, the Roman army became a homogeneous whole.

V. LIFE AT ROME

It is a sorry contrast when from this picture of provincial energy and legionary staunchness we turn to contemplate the vicious, pampered, vulgarized population of the metropolis itself. Outwardly indeed imperial Rome was in all probability the most magnificent city in the history of the world. Neither of the great capitals of the Levant, Alexandria or Antioch, could compare with it in architectural monuments. It contained temples without number, theatres, libraries, museums, courts of law, triumphal arches, and enormous baths in which there were facilities for every form of luxury and exercise. Open squares or forums, lined with colonnades, opened one upon another; and yet a fresh one was added by Trajan in commemoration of his Dacian Wars. The comfort of the inhabitants had been carefully studied. The streets were well paved. The drainage-system was efficient, and water was conveyed into the city from a distance by huge aqueducts the remains of whose towering arches may still here and there be seen bestriding the plain outside the walls. The houses of the rich were sumptuous to a degree; but for the poorer class conditions were very different. They lived huddled together in great rabbit-warrens called 'Islands', vast tenements many stories high and filling the entire space between surrounding streets.

The inhabitants of the city were drawn from every nation under heaven. A large proportion hailed from the East, whence many had originally been brought as slaves and subsequently won their freedom. 'The rivers of Asia,' declared Juvenal in disgust, 'have flowed into the Tiber.' The 'hungry Greekling', too, he complains, is everywhere in evidence—a versatile Jack-of-all-trades, picking up all the best jobs from 'schoolmastering and rhetoric to tight-rope dancing, fortune-telling, or medicine'. For this swarming population the government were careful to make due provision of sustenance and amusement—*panem et circenses*, as the oft-quoted saying ran. The round of entertainments was endless. It was the recognized business of the annual magistrates to furnish expensive spectacles, and the emperors, as we have seen, often supplemented these on a still more lavish scale. Among the most popular was chariot-racing. Four capitalist companies arranged for the teams, the drivers of which wore coloured favours of white, red, blue, and green. The excitement of this extremely dangerous sport was further enlivened by reckless betting. Another favourite entertainment was the wild beast shows, performed in the arena of the Colosseum. It is said that quite early in imperial times Mediterranean countries had been completely denuded of the requisite species, so that panthers, bears, and lions had to be fetched from farther afield. In the Colosseum too were held gladiatorial contests which threw so ugly a sidelight on the Roman character. Some gladiators were condemned criminals; others made it a profession. The commonest form of fighting was a duel between a man equipped only with net and dagger and another man fully armed. Thousands attended these bloody scenes with morbid enthusiasm, dictating death or mercy for the defeated duellist by the gesture of turning their thumbs either *up* or *down*.

The maintenance of the idle populace was a serious charge on the exchequer. Over two hundred thousand were still in receipt of free corn. Many of the poorer class, too, still attached themselves as clients to some wealthy patron, waiting on him

at sunrise, attending him as he strutted through the streets—
to be duly rewarded by a regular morning dole of money or
food. The atmosphere of toadyism and snobbery, which so
often existed at the court, was unpleasantly reflected in other
walks of society. The successful man found himself burdened
by a host of hangers-on who managed, by flattery or a reputation for wit, to 'cadge' an invitation to dinner. One particularly obnoxious feature of the times was the blatancy of the
attentions paid to rich persons of whom a legacy might be
expected. To send presents of fish or some such delicacy
was a common method by which *captatores*, as they were called,
laid siege to the favours of ladies or gentlemen who happened
to have no children. Childless marriages were still, as in
Augustus' day, unwholesomely common—so much so that
Domitian sought to revive some of the laws whereby Augustus
had tried to combat the tendency. Among the aristocracy
at any rate ennui—or selfishness—seems to have sapped the
natural desire to raise a family, though not, on the other hand,
the desire to grow rich. Fabulous fortunes were often piled
up by men who started at the bottom of the social scale; and
another favourite butt of the satirist's ridicule was the vulgarity of the parvenu millionaire. Petronius, a writer of Nero's
day, has left us a ludicrous sketch of a banquet given by one
such man, Trimalchio by name. Trimalchio, we are given to
understand, came originally as a slave from Syria, bought his
freedom, inherited a large bequest from his master, invested
it in ships, and made a fortune, then to give himself the airs
of a gentleman, purchased some landed property and built a
magnificent 'villa'. We then hear how this half-educated host,
himself dressed 'up to the nines', his arms loaded with bangles
and his fingers with rings, endeavoured to impress his snigger-
ing guests with the lavishness of the entertainment. Slaves
on their arrival pare their nails and pour iced water over their
hands. An entrée is served on a bronze stand shaped like a
donkey with panniers loaded with olives. Troupes of ballet-
dancers remove the dishes. Negroes bring skins of wine for
the guests to wash their hands in. The climax of the feast is
the entry of an enormous plate containing a hare, and stuffed
capons, surrounded by fanciful imitations of the twelve signs

of the Zodiac, a pair of kidneys for the 'Twins', a bull's eye for the 'Archer', a lobster for 'Capricorn', and so on. Still more ridiculous is the wild boar from whose side, when cut open, there issues a flight of live thrushes. Meanwhile an acrobat performs with ladder and hoops of fire, and finally a contrivance descends from the ceiling bearing bottles of scent for each guest.

There were many in Rome, however, who loathed and despised such flaunting vulgarity, and to whom life at the capital, for all its brilliance and gaiety, was extremely distasteful. Juvenal in a famous satire has depicted the feelings of a man who had determined to make his escape from the intolerable conditions; and his description, if allowances are made for altered circumstances, has a curiously modern ring: the bawling, jostling crowds, the sedan-bearers elbowing their way through the throng, the fires that broke out in the highly inflammable houses, the tiles that crashed down from the roofs overhead, the tipsy revellers reeling home at night, the footpads lurking at street-corners, the wagons lumbering along with their load of marble and spilling it with fatal effect upon some luckless wight. Even those who had enjoyed a successful career and made their mark in Roman society often longed to escape from the bustle and noise to the peace of their countryside villas. This was certainly true of the Younger Pliny, whose letters give us an admirable picture of the best type of second-century gentlemen. A native of Comum in Cisalpine Gaul, where incidentally he inherited large estates, he passed through the usual offices of a public career—first as a subaltern with the troops, then quaestor, tribune, praetor, prefect of the Treasury, consul, and finally, as we have seen, as special commissioner in Bithynia. He also practised assiduously as a barrister; but his heart was really in writing, and he often laments the necessities of public duties which kept him from his beloved country-house and the literary pursuits which he could there pursue at leisure. His industry was extraordinary, and even in the hunting-field he carried a note-book to jot down any passing idea. Wealth gave him every comfort, and the description of his country-house near Ostia, with its sun parlours and plunge-baths, shady walks and flower-gardens, makes it clear that he was no ascetic. But how sober and enlightened were his tastes is proved by a letter written about his friend Spurinna, an old man of seventy-seven, which is an excellent illustration of how a gentleman of this period spent his day. At seven he calls for his boots and takes a three-mile walk, talking the while to his friends on serious subjects. Then some reading out loud by a secretary. Then a seven-mile drive in a carriage, after which he retires to his room for some writing (he composes in Greek and Latin indifferently and is the author of some scholarly verses). At bath-time (two o'clock in winter, an hour earlier in summer) he strips naked, walks about in the sun, plays a hard game of ball, and after his bath reads light literature till dinner-time. This meal, simple but elegant, is served on plain old silver; entertainers diversify by the repast; and the evening's conviviality is carried on 'far into the summer night'.

The zest for reading and writing which this picture discloses was characteristic of a wide circle of contemporary society. Rome was full of third-rate littérateurs who, as Pliny tells us, gave public recitations of their works at social gatherings; and though he plumes himself on his own conscientious attendance at such tedious performances, he makes it quite clear that the majority of the audiences were supremely bored. The truth is, as we shall see in the following section, that, though after the Golden Age of Augustus there were still a few writers of outstanding merit, the literature of the Empire was in its decadence. Men were tending to write more because they wished to be writers than because they had something to say.

VI. EDUCATION AND LITERATURE

The literature of any age must inevitably be influenced to a considerable degree by the character of contemporary education; and before we pass on to describe the authors of imperial epoch it will be well to say something about its schools and studies. Never before in the history of the world had instruction of a sort been so widely or so easily available. The Hellenized East was of course well provided with schools already; though it is important to note (since the cultural division between the two halves of the Empire was hereby greatly intensified) that no Latin was taught in the Eastern half. What is really surprising, is that throughout Gaul, Spain, Africa, and even Britain there seem to have been schools in all the towns; even the little Portuguese mining village above mentioned could boast one. Such schools were normally controlled and financed by the town council; but individuals of a generous turn of mind often helped to endow them; and Pliny, for instance, contributed to the foundation of a local academy at Comum because he found its boys were compelled to go and reside at Milan some distance off. So, though the poorest folk were probably illiterate, the children of the middle and upper class were able to attend these so-called 'Grammar' schools. When the rudiments of reading, writing, and arithmetic had been mastered, together with some slight training in music, the course of instruction concentrated mainly on literary appreciation and criticism. The chief classical authors to be studied were Aesop's Fables, Livy, Cicero, Virgil, Demosthenes, and Homer, of which considerable quantities would be learned by heart and recited. Such training prepared the way for the more advanced course of study to which at the age of fifteen or thereabouts the abler and richer pupils would pass on in the schools of Rhetoric. Here they would begin to practise original composition, writing 'themes' or essays on a variety of subjects, carefully graded for their difficulty. First would come simple historical questions as, 'Why did Hannibal not march upon Rome after the battle of Cannae?' Then, slightly more advanced, came the delineation of typical characters, especially those to be avoided, such as the 'spendthrift' or 'debauchee'. Finally the course worked up to problems of behaviour: 'Is the murder of a tyrant morally permissible?' In these themes the method of composition was reduced almost to a formula. Arguments, illustrations and quotations were drawn mainly from text-books; and there was in fact little scope for original thought. For the chief purpose of these Rhetoric schools whose tradition was rooted in the old days of Republican freedom, was to fit men for political or forensic careers, in which public speaking was all-important. Method and manner were therefore more considered than matter; and great pains were taken to practise style and delivery. Parents and friends were frequently invited to hear the pupils declaim. Even at the Universities (as, for instance, at Alexandria, Athens, or Rome) the study of philosophy, mathematics, medicine, and law was sadly hidebound; and that eager zest for truth and discovery which had been the inspiration of Greek culture at its prime was lost in the lifeless monotony of stereotyped instruction. It can scarcely be denied that Roman education was capable of producing first-rate officials, but it did not produce great originators fit to solve the manifold problems, on the solution of which the Empire's life depended; nor did it give rise to profound ideas or sincere appreciation of beauty.

From what has been said it will seem only natural that the chief characteristic of post-Augustan literature was emphasis on style. Even among poets rhetorical tricks of antithesis and epigram produced a sense of artificiality. Manilius[1] the greatest poet of Stoicism, could rise to heights of noble eloquence, but he lacks the passionate inspiration of Lucretius. That brilliant historical epic, the *Pharsalia*, written by Seneca's young nephew Lucan, contains much fine writing and many notable sayings,[2] but its over-elaborate style smells too much of the midnight oil, tending more to the sententious than to the poetical. The same is more or less true of Seneca himself. Some of his poems possess considerable delicacy and pathos, but even in these there is an excess of artifice,[3] while his scholarly tragedies were so far removed from real life that they never would have done upon the stage. Sincerity, as we have seen, was not his strong point; but he was an indefatigable writer, and in his philosophical essays and treatises he pronounced many noble sentiments which were not without their influence on succeeding generations. His prose style was marked by a striving after brevity which distinguished the authors of the Imperial Epoch from those of the Late Republic. The resounding periods of Cicero would have been inappropriate in an age when there was no longer need to play on the

---

[1] Manilius began his career under Augustus.
[2] e.g. the famous line, *Victrix causa deis placuit, sed victa Catoni*.
[3] e.g. The strange pun, *Flentes Eurydicen Juridici sedent*.

emotions of the Senate or the mob. Both writers and speakers preferred to be practical and to the point; and terseness of style was reduced to a fine art. Meanwhile the repression of independent thought, begun under the Julio-Claudian Emperors and continued by the Flavians, drove many men of talent to concentrate on the less dangerous fields of research and criticism. Thus the Elder Pliny wrote thirty-seven books on Natural History; Vitruvius (whose work may possibly have begun under Augustus' reign) was an expert upon Architecture; Quintilian wrote a handbook for would-be Orators. After the accession of Nerva, the wider licence allowed to men of letters provoked a new outburst of activity. Tacitus, free at last to utter his pent-up thoughts, began to publish the productions of his pungent pen. An unsparing critic of Rome's decadence, he began with a treatise upon Germany, in which he slyly sought to point the contrast between barbarian virility and civilized corruption. His laudatory biography of his father-in-law Agricola was similarly intended as a counterblast to cynics. Finally in his 'Histories' he compiled a matchless narrative of the Civil Wars of 69, and in his 'Annals' a full-length record of the reigns of Tiberius, Caligula, Claudius, and Nero. Though far from accurate as an historian, he conveys in his short, tense sentences an incomparable picture of those terrible times. In style he was an unrivalled master of epigram, and in half a dozen words he managed to convey more meaning than any writer before or since.

For direct criticism of contemporary life we must turn to the poets. Juvenal, the most brilliant of Latin satirists, wrote with bitter sarcasm about the state of things at Rome; and his writings, as we have seen, provide interesting sidelights upon the habits of the rich. Martial, who had managed by flattery to keep on the right side of Domitian, was responsible for what was almost a new *genre* of verse—the epigram; not, as among the Greeks, merely an epitaph or inscription intended to be carved upon stone, but a brief poem often no more than a couple of lines long, which nevertheless gave admirable scope to Martial's amazing gift for concentrated irony:

> On seven husbands' tomb-stones Chloe scored
> 'My handiwork'—Well, that's the very word!

But the real impetus of Latin literature was almost spent; and for its final spurt we must look far ahead to the fourth-century poet Ausonius, the author of a charming descriptive piece on the River Moselle. The fact is that from the Flavians onwards there had been a strong revival of Greek literature— a serious challenge to the native Italian tongue. The revival began with Plutarch, the author of the famous 'Lives', a series of biographical sketches comparing the great men of Greece and of Rome in carefully chosen pairs. Epictetus, a philosopher exiled by Domitian, wrote on ethics under the patronage of Trajan. A little later under the Antonines Pausanias, the well-known globe-trotter, compiled a guide to the best-known sites in Greece, while Lucian wrote charmingly fanciful dialogues or tales—such as the *Ascent to the Moon*, and finally in the third century Plotinus the philosopher helped to resuscitate the doctrines of Plato and found the school of neo-Platonism.

As will have been seen, however, the great bulk of second and third-century literature was rather critical than creative. Something had crushed out the spontaneous fount of inspiration, so promising in the early days of Lucretius, Catullus, and Cicero. Yet self-criticism is not unwholesome; and it can at least be said of these Silver Age authors that they were acutely aware of the national shortcomings. It will not perhaps be inappropriate to close this chapter with a famous passage from Tacitus—placed actually in the mouth of a certain Scottish chieftain, but beyond doubt the most scathing indictment of commercialism masquerading under the guise of Imperialism that has ever yet been penned:

'Vain hope,' he says, 'to evade the Romans' clutches by obsequious submission. The whole world is to them a prey. They have ransacked the continents, and now they must search the seas. If their foe be rich, they are ravenous for gold, if he be poor, for glory; and neither East nor West can sate an appetite, unique in this, that plenty or dearth is alike to them a lure. Empire is the name they give to a policy of plunder, bloodshed and rapine; and when they have created a wilderness, they call it "Peace".'

CHAPTER XXVI

NERVA, TRAJAN, AND HADRIAN

I. THE REIGN OF NERVA, A.D. 96–98

EVEN before Domitian's assassination, Nerva had been picked upon by those privy to the plot as his most suitable successor. He was to all intents and purposes the Senate's choice; and thus the doctrines of the Stoic opposition, so bitterly at odds with his predecessor's tyranny, came at last to fruition. A ruler, they held, should regard himself as servant rather than as master of the State; and an Emperor should be chosen on no other grounds than that he appeared the best man for the post.[1] Nerva—already past sixty at the time of his accession—was essentially a gentleman, by birth a member of the old nobility, by character courteous, conscientious and self-effacing, but scarcely a strong personality. 'It is go-as-you-please now,' said some one, recalling the repression of the previous reign. Yet Nerva was not without courage; and after recalling those exiled on the evidence of informers, he refused to surrender the informers themselves to the vengeance which was hotly demanded. As the Senate's nominee he could hardly do other than treat it with consideration; and to the oft-repeated demand that no member of the House should be arbitrarily executed, he replied with a formal guarantee—and kept it. He often consulted it; and in appointing a committee for the rehabilitation of the public finance—left by Domitian in a parlous condition—he invited the Senate to select its members. Free speech was once more possible; and Tacitus declared with enthusiasm that Liberty and the Principate, once diametrically opposed, had at last been brought into harmony. Yet the liberty of which he boasted was no better than a sham; and behind the flattering attentions whereby the new Emperor gave a false air of reality to the futile deliberations of the House, his own monopoly of power remained quite unimpaired. He and his successors

---

[1] Another point in Nerva's favour was that he had no son, so that on his death the field would be left free for a fresh choice of the best ruler.

were as thoroughgoing autocrats as ever Domitian had been, and the truth is that the aristocracy, at last inwardly convinced that the Principate was inevitable, were prepared to offer their co-operation as a graceful return for being let down so lightly.

The one awkward clash which the new Emperor encountered was with the Praetorian Guard. Domitian had been their favourite—for had he not considerably increased their pay?— and in loyalty to his memory they demanded the death of his assassins. There was an ugly scene; and though at the risk of his own life Nerva gallantly confronted them, they insisted in taking the law into their own hands. The mild old man was after all no soldier; and this episode appears to have so preyed upon his mind that he determined to appoint a consort forthwith. In October of 97 he wrote a letter to Marcus Ulpius Trajanus, commander of the legions of the upper Rhine, and without waiting for an answer he went through the ceremony of formal adoption at Rome. In January of the following year he died; and Trajan's succession to the throne was accepted as a matter of course.

II. THE REIGN OF TRAJAN, A.D. 98-117

Nerva's choice of a successor was the best act of his reign; for not only did it confirm the principle that merit alone should be the basis of such a choice, but it brought to the head of affairs a man of most outstanding capacity. Trajan was born near Seville in the south of Spain, but was of Roman ancestry and the son of a father who had governed in two provinces. At forty-four he was a strikingly handsome figure, wearing on his face a look of firm decision; yet his unaffected charm of manner made him popular with all classes. He moved about freely among the crowd at Rome. He dined and hunted with his friends as an equal among equals. Once, on receiving a hint that one of his favourite officers was plotting against his life, he went straight to the man's house, took dinner with him unattended, and actually let himself be shaved by the alleged conspirator's barber. He had, in short, a happy knack of winning people's confidence by simply showing that he trusted them. As an administrator he was indefatigable, supervising every detail of his various departments and, as his letters to Pliny show, possessing a singular gift for going straight to the heart of a problem. But it was as a soldier that he had risen to power—he commanded a legion in Spain before his Rhineland appointment—and it was as a soldier that he was destined to spend much of his reign in a series of stern wars against Rome's external foes. With the troops he was a tremendous favourite; for he was always ready to share with them the rigours of camp-life or the hazards of a campaign; and the story is told how once he cut up his own tunic to make bandages for the wounded.

On his assumption of the Principate military concerns were his first preoccupation and, instead of hurrying to the capital, he paid a visit to the upper Danube where there had recently been trouble. He spent the winter of 98 in reorganizing the army and improving the defences of the Pannonian frontier; and undertook negotiations with the German tribes across the border with a view to securing their promise of neutrality in the event of war with Decebalus. There can be little doubt that the project of a Dacian campaign was already moving in the Emperor's mind.

In the spring of 99, however, he returned to Rome. The mob turned out to cheer him as though he had been a conqueror returning from the wars. His courteous affability won the hearts of the aristocracy, and the harmonious relations with the Senate which Nerva had established were confirmed by the deference the new Emperor paid them. He was always at pains to keep them well informed of his movements and activities. He even allowed them the privilege of ratifying his measures. Nevertheless, he kept the initiative entirely in his own grasp, and his strong handling of affairs was of itself sufficient to have silenced criticism.

At the end of two years Trajan set out for the Danube once again. Some sort of forward policy was clearly his intention; but how far he had been forced to it by positive aggression is difficult to determine. It must suffice to say that year by year the Danubian provinces were becoming much more civilized and the threat of invasion thus correspondingly more to be dreaded. Year by year, too, the power of the Dacians, which Domitian's peace had left quite free to develop, had been steadily growing under the strong rule of Decebalus. So, if a struggle was imminent (as it almost certainly was), it must have seemed sound strategy for Rome to get her blow in first. Now, for an invader of Dacia the natural objective was its capital Sarmizegethusa. But since Sarmizegethusa was protected on the south by the almost inaccessible chain of the Transylvanian Alps, approach to it was limited to two somewhat circuitous routes. One started from Viminacium, and leading up through a pass known as the Iron Gates, came in upon Sarmizegethusa from the west. The other started much farther down the Danube, followed up the course of the River Alt or Alutus, then turned left-handed through the Red Tower Pass and so came in on Sarmizegethusa from the east.

In 101, the first year of the campaign, it was by the western route that Trajan chose to deliver his attack. For many details of what followed, it should be said, in passing, the literary evidence is scanty and untrustworthy. Indeed, for the reconstruction of the whole campaign we have mainly to depend upon the interpretation—often much disputed— of the scenes depicted on Trajan's Column at Rome. As a source of information about Roman military methods it is full of interest; and it conveys the impression of a highly scientific organization. In this wonderful series of bas-reliefs, containing, it is said, no less than 2,500 figures, we can see the engineers at work, building bridges, making bricks, and mani- pulating their *ballistae* or catapults, the army surgeons attend- ing to the needs of the wounded, the legionaries at an assault adopting the famous 'tortoise' formation with shields inter- locked above their heads as a shelter against enemy missiles. On this occasion, to judge by such pictorial evidence Trajan must have begun his campaign by building a couple of boat- bridges in the neighbourhood of Viminacium. Crossing the river by these, he then marched up in the direction of the Iron Gates Pass without apparently meeting any opposition till he arrived in the neighbourhood of Tibiscum. Here stood one of the many strong positions which Decebalus had fortified according to methods learnt from Roman engineers. A great battle was fought near by at Tapae; but, though apparently it went in the Romans' favour, Tibiscum was not stormed, and abandoning his project of penetrating the Iron Gates Pass, Trajan returned to winter in the Danube camps. The off-season, however, was by no means wasted; for near Dobretae, some eighty miles downstream from Viminacium, a great permanent bridge of brick and stone—no mean feat of engineering—was begun across the Danube; and at this point in the following spring Trajan once more crossed over into the enemy's country. But instead of resuming his strategy of the previous year he struck across country to the River Alutus, followed up its course, and, penetrating the Red Tower Pass, debouched from the mountains into the heart of Dacia. One, at least, of Decebalus' fortresses was taken by storm, and his troops being again beaten in battle, the threat to his capital was soon so serious that the King sued for peace. The terms which were imposed upon him involved the dismantling of his fortresses, the quartering of a Roman garrison in his capital, and possibly the cession of the western part of his Kingdom. Trajan, for his part, returned home to celebrate a triumph at Rome; and it seems clear that at this point he regarded the Dacian problem as solved. The country was to be treated as a Roman protectorate and used as a buffer-State against the restless tribes beyond.

In reality, however, the problem was not solved; and Decebalus was far from being beaten. Three years he waited, secretly reorganizing his army and repairing his dismantled fortresses. Then in 105 he struck. Under pretence of a parley he kidnapped Longinus, the commander of the garrison. Negotiations with Rome were begun; and Longinus, rather than embarrass the home-government by concern for his safety, took poison. The negotiations broke down; and then in a twinkling the Dacians were once more on the warpath. The garrison of Sarmizegethusa having fallen into their hands, they swept down south across the Danube, to attack the Roman troops in the frontier camps of Moesia. Trajan's work was all undone; but he lost not a moment. He took ship across the Adriatic and by a long march up-country arrived in time to relieve his hard-pressed garrisons. Winter set in; but with the spring of 106 two columns, advancing one by the western and one by the eastern route, converged on Sarmizegethusa. This time it was war to the knife. There was no parleying. Sarmizegethusa was laid under siege and set on fire. Decebalus fled, and when the pursuit came up fell on his sword. Many of his followers took poison rather than surrender. Meanwhile the whole population of the country-side was driven out into the mountains eastward. A new policy had, in fact, been decided upon. Annexation now seemed the only alternative to an unending series of tiresome frontier wars. So Dacia became a province. Sarmizegethusa was made a 'colony' and renamed Ulpia Trajana. Colonists were imported in vast numbers to repopulate the country. On the evidence of inscriptions the majority seem to have been drawn from the Eastern provinces. Many towns were founded. Gold mines were sunk; and considerable wealth must have flowed into the Imperial Treasury from this now prosperous province. But the new frontier, unhappily, was more than ever exposed to the attack of barbarian hordes which were pressing down out of the north. There was indeed a respite; and the occupation of Dacia lasted a century and a half before its evacuation became necessary. During this time, however, so thorough had been the process of its Romanization that the inhabitants of what to-day is called Roumania speak a language largely derived from the Latin tongue.

After his return to Italy, Trajan spent seven years at the centre of affairs attending to the duties of government. To call him a great statesman would be an exaggeration, for he initiated no reform of major importance; but he pursued the ideal of efficiency with all the zeal of a somewhat 'official' mind. He knew how much was expected of him; and he seems to have felt (as doubtless his subordinates felt too) that they were living in an age of high standards. 'A precedent wholly unworthy of our times,' he replied to Pliny's doubt whether anonymous denunciations of Christians should be accepted as evidence. In the interests of efficiency the tendency towards bureaucratic management was pressed still further; and where-ever there were serious indications that things were not being kept up to the mark, particularly in the sphere of finance, special commissioners like Pliny were sent, to supervise the affairs of self-governing communities. Such interference was not confined to the Eastern provinces only. Even in Italian townships, which, as a rule, were left much to themselves, Trajan had once or twice to put in a commissioner. The welfare of the home-country was, in fact, one of his primary concerns. Its economic life, as we have seen, was in danger of breaking down; and in addition to the measures which he took to revive agriculture and which have been described in the preceding chapter[1] he also did much to improve communications, constructing new roads (notably a shortening of the route from Beneventum to Brundisium) and further developing the harbours at Ostia and Ancona. In the capital itself he was perhaps more concerned to cut a popular figure than to tackle the real problems which beset it. After his Dacian victories he distributed the sum of over twenty pounds per head among the citizens; and, as we have seen, he celebrated his successes by the construction of a new forum, the magnificence of which must have eclipsed all the monuments of his predecessors. It was approached from the Forum of Augustus through an arch, which was surmounted by a gilded figure of Trajan riding in a chariot drawn by gilded steeds. Beyond this lay a colonnaded square, at one end of which was a vast Hall of Justice, and, flanking it on either side, two libraries, while in the centre between the libraries rose the majestic column 130 feet high and decorated by a spiral series of bas-reliefs to which allusion has previously been made.

Fine architecture is a taste of which no one need be ashamed. But it is difficult to resist the suspicion that Trajan had been a little spoilt by power. In his Eastern campaigns, which were presently to follow, there is a hint of something very like megalomania and a zest for military achievement not altogether justified by the necessities of the situation. Anecdotes told about emperors are by no means always trustworthy; but there may be a real truth underlying the tale that when Trajan, after his triumphal progress through Mesopotamia, reached the head of the Persian Gulf, he looked wistfully towards India and said with a sigh, 'If only I were Alexander!'

[1] See page 346.

That Trajan's Eastern policy was dictated by mere motives of vainglory would, however, be an absurd supposition. It is clear in the first place that quite early in his reign the question of some readjustment of the Eastern frontier had engaged his attention. On the eastern and southern flank of the province of Syria lay a desolate region bordering on the great Arabian Desert and inhabited by nomadic tribes. Their organization was naturally of the loosest character; but their sheiks acknowledged the rule of a common chief or king and the passage of important caravan-routes, north-eastwards through Palmyra to Mesopotamia and south-westwards through the Sinaitic Desert to Egypt, had led to the formation of a few commercial settlements. Of recent years the ruling chief had been friendly towards Rome; and when in 106 the throne fell vacant the Syrian governor, Palma, was ordered to annex the whole of this border country. Its northern district round Damascus was attached to Palma's province and the southern district formed into a separate province entitled Arabia Petraea. Under Roman control the commercial prosperity of the region increased by leaps and bounds; and several flourishing towns sprang up of which the architectural remains may still be seen. The caravan-routes were secured against the interference of brigands; and what may perhaps have been the original purpose of the annexation, considerable revenue seems to have flowed into the exchequer from the tolls levied upon passing merchandise.

Great as was the wealth of the Empire, it is always to be remembered that the upkeep of its army and civil service was a heavy burden on the public funds, and the Dacian Wars were especially costly; so it is not unlikely that when Trajan embarked upon a policy of more extensive conquests in the East, financial considerations were present in his mind. But that this was not his only motive is certain. For, as in Central Europe, so equally in the Middle East the peoples bordering on the Roman frontier were beginning to experience a slow but steady pressure from the uneasy westward movement of barbaric hordes, the Sarmatians, the Alani, and, in their rear, the Huns. Armenia was certainly exposed to occasional raids from the north-east; and though at this date the Romans can scarcely have realized the magnitude of the menace, it may have occurred to Trajan that here, as in Dacia, a forward policy would be the wisest strategy.

However that may be, he picked in 113 a quite needless quarrel over the question of the Armenian throne with the Parthian King Chosroes (the successor of Pacorus). It is true that without waiting to obtain the Romans' sanction (as by Nero's settlement of 64 he was strictly bound to do) Chosroes had appointed his nephew Exedares to the vacant throne. But without attempting negotiations Trajan declared war at once. He ignored Chosroes' apology. He ignored the substitution of another nephew, Parthamisires, in Exedares' place; and late in 113 he took ship to Antioch. In the following spring he invaded Armenia. At Elegeia he gave an interview to the grovelling Parthamisires. But despite his protestations of submission the wretched prince was deposed, and Armenia made into a province.

But this was only a beginning. In the absence of any natural barrier which might form a defensible frontier, the simplest way of securing Armenia against Parthian aggression was to conquer Parthia too.[1] Such a conquest presented no great difficulties. Under the influence of Hellenism the once virile Parthians had ceased to be formidable. Their unwieldy realm had been further weakened by frequent disaffection among its outlying principalities; and at this very moment Chosroes was engaged in suppressing a revolt of an Arab chief, Manisares. It was under such circumstances that Trajan decided to pursue his victorious advance. In 114 he marched across northern Mesopotamia to Nisibis in the neighbourhood of the Tigris, receiving on his way the ready submission of one at least of Chosroes' vassals. After returning for the winter to Antioch, he rejoined his army at Nisibis in the spring of 115. Boats which had been constructed in this wooded district were transported to the Tigris, and, with the support of these as commissariat carriers, the whole force proceeded downstream towards Ctesiphon, the Parthian capital. The ease of their advance was very different from the painful

[1] It is further said that the Parthian King had been in league with Decebalus—an additional reason for mistrusting him.

progress among the Dacian mountains; and apart from some trouble with the principality of Abiadene in the north, which required a special diversion, all opposition seems to have melted away before the appearance of the Roman host. Ctesiphon soon fell. Chosroes fled; and in 116, after following the Tigris to the head of the Persian Gulf, Trajan turned his steps towards the Euphrates valley, where he occupied Babylon.

But his success had been, as it proved, too swift to be permanent. For suddenly at this point came terrible tidings from the north. An insurrection had broken out on the upper Tigris. Nisibis and other important posts on the lines of communication had been overwhelmed. The news of the catastrophe spread like wildfire through the whole Levant. The Emperor, it was believed, was cut off and probably doomed; and the Jews, smarting under the humiliation of their national extinction, instigated a general rising in Cyprus, Cyrene, and Egypt, where thousands of their race had long since taken up their abode. With true Semitic fury they turned on the civilian population. In Cyprus alone they slaughtered a quarter of a million[1]; in Cyrene not far short of that number. In Egypt the Roman governor was forced to take refuge in his citadel. Trajan acted with promptitude. One of his generals named Turbo was sent at once to Egypt. In Cyprus the Romans regained the upper hand and slaughtered the Jews in their turn. In Mesopotamia, Lusius Quietus, a Moorish lieutenant highly trusted by Trajan, got the situation once more under control. The Emperor was thus free to proceed to a final settlement of the Parthian Kingdom. The northern half of it he had already annexed and organized in two provinces Mesopotamia and Assyria, but deeming it wiser to leave the southern half as a protectorate under native control, he placed a relative of Chosroes, named Parthamaspates, on the throne at Ctesiphon. It was impossible for him, however, to stay longer in the East or to complete the settlement which he had thus imposed. Bad news was arriving from Europe. The Sarmatians were threatening the Danubian front. There was trouble in Britain and in Africa. So Trajan was forced to hurry homewards; but on his journey through

[1] Allowance must probably be made for some exaggeration.

POMPEII —THE AMPHITHEATRE

CONSTANTINOPLE—INTERIOR OF SANTA SOPHIA

Cilicia he was seized by a stroke and within a few days he was dead. It was an ironical comment on the incompleteness of his Eastern conquests, that no sooner was his back turned than Chosroes re-entered Ctesiphon; and among the first acts of his successor Hadrian was an order for the evacuation of all the newly acquired provinces, Armenia included.

There has been endless dispute about the wisdom or un-wisdom of Trajan's attempt to solve the thorny problem of the Eastern frontier, and seeing what was the burden his cam-paigns had laid on an exhausted treasury, and what additional responsibilities the extended front imposed upon a military organization already strained to its uttermost, the issue of the controversy must remain in doubt. But in one respect at any rate it is impossible to acquit him of a certain lack of states-manship; for if one thing more than another was demanded by the ideal of efficient government, it was continuity of foreign policy. Yet so far from having communicated his plans to a successor and thus ensured that, if he himself died, they would be carried through, the extraordinary thing is that he had not even appointed a successor at all. It was only on the selfsame day that Trajan died, that his cousin Hadrian, then governor of Syria, received a letter by which he was adopted as the dead man's son and heir. Whether Trajan himself was responsible for the choice is actually uncertain. For the tale was put about and by many credited that the real author of the letter was the Emperor's wife, Plotina. Scandalmongers added that she had long been in love with Hadrian.

III. THE REIGN OF HADRIAN, A.D. 117-137

Whatever may be the truth about the circumstances of his adoption, Hadrian certainly employed the most consummate tact in securing his succession to the throne. He wrote to the Senate apologizing for his failure to obtain their formal sanc-tion. He gave the now customary guarantee that no member of the body should be put to death without due trial by his peers; and, while he himself went off to deal with the troubles on the Danube, he sent to the capital a certain Attianus, once his guardian in the days of his childhood, now his trusted confidant. It was not long, however, before serious events brought him quickly back to Italy. The Senate had somehow got wind of a conspiracy among four of Trajan's most prominent generals—Nigrinus, Celsus, Palma, and Lusius Quietus. Of the latter two, Palma had been the conqueror of Arabia Petraea, and Lusius, as we have seen, played an important part in the Parthian campaigns. Disgusted to find themselves deprived of a job by their old master's death and to see all his conquests in Armenia and Mesopotamia abandoned by the new Emperor's policy, they had apparently determined to get rid of him. The Senate took no risks and, acting probably under Attianus' advice, had the four conspirators executed out of hand. It was an unfortunate prelude to Hadrian's reign; and on reaching Rome he took particular pains to remove all impression of tyrannical behaviour by making a handsome distribution of money to the mob. At the same time it is by no means certain that he was not privy to the removal of this dangerously militarist group.

The statecraft of Hadrian, as this episode seems to indicate, was extraordinarily subtle, and in some ways typical of a character which more perhaps than any of the preceding Emperors appears almost to defy analysis. In him the practical qualities of the Roman were combined with the intellectual versatility of the Greek. He was a hard worker, and a highly efficient organizer. He was a competent general, and never flinched from sharing the rigours of camp-life with the troops. He fulfilled all the duties of his arduous office with extreme conscientiousness. Yet he found leisure at the same time to indulge a rare taste for art, literature, and scientific inquiry which a Greek education had given him. He wrote poetry. He painted and sang. During his provincial tours he lost no opportunity of visiting any notable monument. Once he made the ascent of a mountain to witness the sunrise. He was indeed a strange mixture. His whimsical temperament made his actions somewhat incalculable. Mean and generous by turns, he appears to have made no firm friend, and Roman society, while outwardly deferential, sneered at him under its breath as the 'Greekling'. Nevertheless he held a complete mastery over the affairs of the Empire both in large and in detail; and under his rule it reached perhaps the height of its strength and enjoyed a period of tranquillity almost without precedent.

Peace was certainly the keynote of Hadrian's foreign policy. In the East we have seen that he preferred a withdrawal to the traditional frontier rather than accept the risks of more extensive commitments; and when in 123 trouble was once again threatened from Parthia he set out at once in person. He held an interview with Chosroes, promised to restore his daughter and his golden throne which had been carried off to Rome by Trajan; and by such tactful concessions managed to smooth matters down. Hadrian's diplomacy, however, was by no means a veil for any weakness of military policy. His experience of service in the Dacian Wars, during which he had commanded a legion, had given him an excellent introduction to the military science of the day, and he used his knowledge to strengthen the defences of more than one frontier. The most notable instance was, of course, the construction of the famous wall in northern Britain. But somewhat similar fortifications, as we have seen above, were now probably erected between the Danube and the Rhine. He paid visits of inspection to all the European frontiers, and to Africa as well. Here he held a review of the troops, and his comments on their efficiency have actually been preserved. He praised their javelin-practice and the nimbleness of their jumping, and added that, 'if there had been fault to find, as, for instance, for overshooting the targets, he would certainly have found it; but all their work had been pat by the drill-book'. Everything goes to show that he clearly realized the temptations of peace-time soldiering. Leave was closely restricted, extravagance in the officers' messes was carefully checked, and the standard of discipline rigorously maintained.

Hadrian's success in maintaining external peace was doubtless due in a considerable measure to the hammer-blows which Trajan had dealt, especially on the Danube. But Rome's enemies would scarcely have remained quiescent if these had been followed by a slack or incompetent régime. The one internal disturbance of any real importance was a fresh Jewish rising (132–134)—this time confined to the remnant still residing in Palestine. It was the outcome of Hadrian's provocative decision to stamp out the last vestige of their national life by founding a colony on the site of Jerusalem. Under a fanatical priest called Bar-cokbar, who gave himself out to be the Messiah, the rebels regained possession of their old sacred capital. Their ejection was no difficult matter, but it took three years of bitter guerrilla warfare before the Romans succeeded in killing Bar-cokbar and suppressing his followers. When the end came, all Jews were banished from the country, which henceforward they were only permitted to visit once in each year.

Hadrian's determination to Romanize Palestine was no mere act of thoughtless tyranny. It was part of a process whereby it was sought to weld the various races of the Empire into a more homogeneous whole. Already the wide diffusion of the franchise had begun to obliterate the old jealousies and distinctions; and about this time, as we have seen, citizens were coming to enlist in auxiliary regiments hitherto reserved for non-citizens only. If this process of amalgamation was to be still further developed no more suitable agent could possibly have been found than the cosmopolitan Emperor who now sat on the throne. In studying the interests and welfare of his multifarious subjects, Hadrian displayed a unique width of outlook; and whereas his predecessors' motive in leaving the metropolis had usually been to deal with some frontier emergency, he himself made it a regular part of his routine to tour the provinces of East and West alike. Out of the twenty-one years of his reign thirteen at least were spent outside Italy. There is no space here to describe his travels in detail. Suffice it to say that between 121 and 125 he visited Gaul, traversed the Rhineland frontier, spent a considerable time in Britain, and then, after a winter in Spain, hurried East to deal with Chosroes of Parthia. Doubling back through Asia Minor to Greece, he passed six months at Athens studying art and philosophy, touring round to places of historic interest, and, amongst other acts of munificence, adorning the city by rebuilding the Temple of Olympian Zeus, left unfinished by Pisistratus the Tyrant seven centuries before. His insatiable curiosity even led him to seek initiation in the Eleusinian

Mysteries before returning to Rome after an absence of nearly
six years. In 126 he made a tour of inspection through North
Africa; and between 128 and 132 he was again in the East,
at one time staying at Athens, at another making his head-
quarters in Egypt, where the ancient monuments made a
special appeal to his romantic imagination. Even the oasis-
city of Palmyra and the shores of the Black Sea as far as the
Crimea were visited. But, though no quarter of the Empire
was neglected, it is clear that the Eastern provinces came in
for special attention. Nor was this simply the result of
Hadrian's individual tastes; for his repeated journeys to the
East were the symptom, rather than the cause, of an important
change which was coming over the Empire. Culturally, as
some one has said, its centre of gravity was shifting; and from
this time onwards ideas and superstitions, Oriental in origin
rather than Greek, began to exercise a spell over the mind of
European civilization. So the wheel was to come full circle
and the old Augustan policy of upholding the supremacy of
the West against the menace of dictation from the East was
in the ultimate issue to be signally reversed.

Though in the course of his travels Hadrian seized every
opportunity of indulging his many-sided tastes, their real
motive was unquestionably the thorough overhauling of the
whole administrative machinery of the Empire; and the result
of his efforts was that the imperial bureaucracy, which had
grown up bit by bit and largely at haphazard, was now
reduced to a more scientific system. In the central secretariat,
for instance, where in the past freedmen and equestrians had
often worked side by side, Hadrian made a clean sweep of
the freedmen element and employed equestrians only. Then
again the old requirement that some service with the legions
should be an essential preliminary to a public career was
now greatly modified. For Hadrian realized that efficiency
demands some degree of specialization, and in appointing
equestrians to provincial or financial posts he was often
willing to waive the military qualification. Not that equestrians ceased to hold high positions in the army. The Prefect
of the Praetorians continued to be drawn from their ranks;
and some offence was even caused by the promotion of an

equestrian, Marcius Turbo, to be commander-in-chief over all the Danubian provinces. Broadly speaking, however, Hadrian was responsible for a far-reaching reform, whereby the executive was divided into two parallel branches—on the one hand the army, on the other the civil service. The latter, which was recruited exclusively from the equestrian middle class, was organized on a regular system of graduated promotion—from the financial agents or procurators at the bottom to the ministers of the central secretariat at the top. A progressive scale of salaries was laid down, ranging from 60,000 sesterces to 300,000 yearly. It is even probable that titles such as 'His Excellency' and 'His Eminence',[1] which a little later were certainly in use, also dated from this reign.

All this systematization had of course very obvious advantages; but a less healthy, though perhaps inevitable, development was a corresponding increase in the number of these civil servants. The abolition of the 'publican' companies, for instance, must have involved the appointment of a whole host of new agents; and side by side with the regular staff of imperial 'collectors' there was created a new type of officials called *advocati fisci*, whose duty it was to recover overdue debts for the Treasury and, if needful, take proceedings at law. Last, but not least, the informal Council of State, which previous Emperors had made a habit of calling into consultation, was now entrusted with executive powers during Hadrian's lengthy absences, and was for the first time recognized as an official institution. Salaries were paid to its members. One of its chief functions was to tender advice upon knotty questions of law, and it contained many men selected for a specialized knowledge of jurisprudence.

The prominence given to jurists was, in fact, typical of the age; for as the life of the Empire developed there was an increasing demand for legal decisions on all sorts of questions, fiscal, financial, commercial, and the rest. This not merely meant a multiplication of law courts and judges and lawyers; it also emphasized the importance of continuity and uniformity in the administration of justice. Now, justice of its very nature

[1] *Vir egregius* and *Vir eminentissimus*—corresponding to the title reserved for senators, *Vir clarissimus*.

implies that the individual's rights and liabilities should be recognized as fixed and invariable—in other words, that the individual should know precisely where he stands under whatever circumstances. A deep-seated instinct for justice had indeed been a marked characteristic of the Roman State ever since its earliest days. Moreover, as its territory and commerce increased, its magistrates had gained a wide experience of the legal institutions of other Mediterranean peoples. Underlying principles, too, had been studied; and the Stoic conception of a universal law (or *jus gentium*), common to all the nations of the world, found a very practical application in an Empire the inhabitants of which were more and more coming to enjoy the rights of a common citizenship. Nevertheless, the Roman legal system, having grown up by slow evolution, was in a very complicated, not to say a muddled, condition. There were of course many statutory laws, set down, so to speak, in black and white, about which there was no real uncertainty. Many of these dated from the Republic, having been passed by the popular Assemblies. To these may be added the decrees or rulings of successive emperors, and the Senate's motions or *consulta* which, with an Emperor's approval, carried virtually the authority of law. But no law, however carefully drafted, could be expected to meet every contingency. New points were bound to arise over questions of inheritance, the transference of property, business transactions, and so forth; and under such circumstances it was for a magistrate, sitting in judgment, to interpret the law and pronounce on its application to a particular case. Such pronouncements, furthermore, came to be regarded as precedents for future decisions upon any similar case; and in the praetors courts so much regard was paid to these precedents that every praetor on entering office usually issued an 'edict' embodying the interpretations which his predecessors had placed upon the statutory laws. But an individual praetor would also add to this *edictum perpetuum* certain interpretations of his own; and thus the growing mass of judicial formulae remained in some degree fluid and ill co-ordinated. It was for this reason that on Hadrian's initiative a certain Salvius Julianus, a native of Africa, was entrusted with the task of codifying the 'edicts'.

The code, which was completed in 129, was henceforward regarded as permanent, unalterable except by the will of the Emperor, completely binding on all magistrates, and universal in its application. Universal, that is to say, in its application to citizens throughout the Empire; for not merely was appeal to the Emperor's jurisdiction extremely frequent and easy, but provincial governors themselves would necessarily base their decisions on the Julian code, a copy of which must almost certainly have been kept in each provincial capital. Among the unfranchised provincials, on the other hand, disputes continued to be settled in the native courts according to native law. Of these, unfortunately, we know but little; and we can scarcely gauge to what extent they were influenced by Roman legal principles. In Egypt, of which we possess some information, the influence was certainly slight, but in the highly Romanized Western provinces, such as Spain and Gaul, it seems probable that the legal methods employed in the municipalities, would in some measure be carried outwards to the country-side.

It is a significant fact that even in Italy Hadrian found it expedient to regulate the local administration of justice by appointing special assize judges, whose business it was to supervise the courts of the self-governing communities. This step was not popular, for it implied that the home-country, the primacy of which Augustus and many of his successors had striven to maintain, was now reduced to a status little better than that of an ordinary province. The Empire, in short, was now to be regarded as a homogeneous whole; and the man who ruled it was henceforth scarcely less in theory, than in fact, its absolute sovereign. The Senate, though still treated with deference, had simply ceased to count. With the growing influence of the equestrian order its prestige was rapidly declining. Its debates, which could not conceivably run counter to the Emperor's wishes, were a mere matter of formality; and it remained an obsolete figurehead of a régime which had passed away.

The one boon which Hadrian may be said to have conferred on the Italian people was a further beautification of their capital. He was a great builder and, as we have seen, his munificence extended to many provincial centres, not merely, for instance, his favourite town of Athens, but also Corinth, which received a public bath, Ephesus a temple, and Smyrna a gymnasium. At Rome he was responsible for many monuments, notably a Temple of Venus and Rome in the Forum, which he is said to have designed with his own hand. He also restored the Pantheon, which seems to have been almost totally destroyed by a fire in Domitian's reign. But it was perhaps characteristic of the extreme pomp and circumstance with which even this hard-working and conscientious Emperor was invested at Rome that two of his most striking architectural achievements were designed to minister to his own dignity and comfort. One was a huge mausoleum, the circular shell of which may still be seen on the north bank of the Tiber and which is now called the Castle of St. Angelo. The other was an extensive country-house or palace near Tivoli, where its ruins, standing among beautiful olive groves, are to-day the most famous memorial of their author's name. This palace covered acres of ground, and included not merely a vast series of halls, corridors, and bath-houses, but also many replicas of famous buildings which Hadrian had noted and admired in Greece.

For the artist-Emperor who had conceived and planned this astonishing building there was not much remaining of life in which to enjoy its amenities. Three years after his return from the East in 132, he fell victim to a fatal and lingering disease. He suffered much, and it was a happy release when in 138 he died. If ever man did, he had served his generation well; but, like many of his contemporaries, he seems to have been burdened by a sense of the futility of life. Few things in literature are more pathetic than the wistful, whimsical little poem of farewell which, shortly before he died, he addressed to his departing soul:

> Frail little, fond little waif of a soul,
> Comrade and guest of this body of clay,
> Whither away now, O whither away—
> Naked and stark and so woefully wan,
> Yesterday's whimsies all over and done.
> Poor little droll!

CHAPTER XXVII

THE ANTONINES

I. ANTONINUS PIUS, A.D. 138–151

HADRIAN, unlike Trajan, had looked ahead over the problem of the succession. He had no children of his own; and, as soon as the first symptoms of his fatal malady declared themselves, he had selected for adoption a certain Lucius Commodus Verus, who therewith took the new name of Aelius Verus. It would not seem to have been a wise choice; for Aelius, though he had literary tastes, was of an easygoing, self-indulgent nature; but, fortunately perhaps, he died of consumption in January 138. Hadrian's days were obviously numbered, and he lost no time in making a new arrangement. This time he adopted a middle-aged senator, Titus Aurelius Antoninus, making the additional stipulation that Antoninus in his turn should adopt two sons of Hadrian's own choosing. One was Aelius' son, Lucius Verus; the other was Antoninus' nephew Marcus, one day to be better known as the Emperor Marcus Aurelius. These arrangements appear to have given umbrage in certain circles; and the execution of Servianus, Hadrian's brother-in-law, and Servianus' grandson, Fuscus, seems to point to some sort of conspiracy. Nevertheless, on Hadrian's death his choice of Antoninus as successor was duly endorsed.

Under Trajan and Hadrian the Roman Empire attained, as we have said, the pinnacle of its strength; and, though thanks to their labours the period of the Antonines (as their immediate successors were called) began in an atmosphere of prosperous security, it marked in reality a turning-point from which set in, slowly but surely, the long and painful decline that eventually was to end in utter ruin. For this change the personality of the two Emperors Antoninus Pius and Marcus Aurelius were, directly at least, in no wise to blame. Antoninus was an exemplary character—an amiable soul, generous to his friends, simple in his habits, a lover of outdoor sports, and a sociable host. Every one liked him; and the Senate, with whom he maintained the most cordial relations, bestowed on him the name of Pius, in token, perhaps, of his kindly attentions to his adoptive father. Though by no means a strong or forceful individuality, he was not without his parts, having long since won a considerable reputation as a jurist. But, as might be expected of so gentle a nature, his policy was chiefly marked by a dislike of interfering. He even withdrew the assize judges recently imposed on Italy. He seems to have felt that, thanks to his predecessors' energetic measures, the machinery of the Empire was working well enough, so that he had better leave well alone; and he discontinued the practice of touring round the provinces—a practice which incidentally threw a heavy burden of entertainment on the provincial towns. As for the frontiers, though he did not visit them in person, his subordinates were responsible for some slight readjustments. In Britain, as we have seen, the defences were pushed forward to a point well north of Hadrian's Wall; and a similar advance of about ten or twenty miles may be traced in the angle between the Rhine and Danube fronts, where a new palisaded line was established. The comparative tranquillity of the reign was, however, somewhat deceptive. Detailed historical evidence is unfortunately meagre; but there is sufficient to show that the barbarian pressure had been no more than temporarily checked by the strong policy of Trajan. We hear of trouble on the Dacian front. The Alani from the Caucasus made raids into Armenia, and the new Parthian King Vologeses was apparently desirous of avenging the recent humiliation of his country. Antoninus, as his manner was, dispatched a diplomatic letter to the bellicose monarch; but there are hints that even so he regarded war as inevitable. Nor can there be much doubt that Vologeses was not the only enemy of Rome who interpreted the new passivity of her policy as evidence of weakness. It is true that against such external aggression her frontiers were now amply furnished with a highly scientific system of continuous fortifications; and it is impossible to accuse Antoninus or his successor of unpreparedness. The ultimate failure to stem the tide of barbarian invasion was due to causes which lay deep in the condition of the Empire itself; and if any criticism can be passed upon them it was that they lacked the imagination or the power to revitalize the failing initiative which alone could have arrested the process of decay. Already in the first half of the second century A.D. the symptoms of this decay were observable; and the reasons for it must apparently be sought in a lack of vigorous leadership in the economic sphere. Just when brains were badly needed in dealing with the vital problems of production, we find not advance towards better technical methods, but a relapse into more primitive. Thus in agriculture, for example, the large landowners tended more and more to lease their lands to small tenants, with the result that the science of farming began to decline. Again, the working of the State mines, which in the past had been entrusted to large-scale contractors, was now left to petty exploiters and a loss of efficiency was inevitable. There can be little doubt that the authorities were conscious of the shrinkage of production. Not least among the reasons which led to the annexation of Dacia were the valuable mines it contained; and the extension of the cultivated area, especially in Africa, was dictated by the same reason. Nevertheless, the full significance of the decline can scarcely have been appreciated. Human beings can rarely discern in their own epoch the latent forces which are destined to produce catastrophe in the next; and when Antoninus died every one regarded his reign in the light of a Golden Age. It is interesting and somewhat ironic to recall the fulsome eulogy which was passed upon his rule by a certain Aelius Aristides:

'The whole world commonwealth is governed by one good ruler, and every member thereof may have recourse to one common centre whence all may receive their rights. Everywhere your rule is equal. Every order is obeyed upon the instant. You have but to decree a thing and it is done. Yours is a universal Empire, distinguished herein that your subjects are all free men. The whole world keeps holiday; the age-long curse of the sword has been laid aside; and mankind turns to happiness. Strife is stilled, leaving only the rivalry of cities, each eager to be the fairest and most beautiful. Every city is full of gymnasia, fountains, porticoes, temples, workshops, and schools. The whole earth is adorned as it were a garden.'

II. MARCUS AURELIUS

The Greek philosopher Plato once declared that the ideal system of government would only be attained when a philosopher became king; and now on the accession of Marcus Aurelius Plato's improbable dream came true. From his earliest years Aurelius had been of a serious turn of mind. It was his earnestness of character which had attracted the attention of Hadrian; and it was by Hadrian's wish that he became the adopted son of Antoninus Pius, who not merely gave him his daughter in marriage, but in 146 appointed him as his consort. A great friendship sprang up between the two men; and the Emperor's gentle nature was one of the main influences in Marcus' life. Early training under the orator Fronto had soon given way to more serious studies; and the Stoic philosophy had gained a firm hold upon his mind. Though the Stoics' insistence on self-discipline doubtless helped to develop his high sense of duty, it was not so much their doctrine of austere self-sufficiency which appealed to him; it was rather their humane outlook on life, bred of a deeply rooted belief in the rights of all God's creatures, and their emphasis on the virtues of self-abnegation, patience, forgiveness, and philanthropy. In his private *Meditations*, composed during the intervals of campaigning on the Danube, but never actually intended for publication, we have an extraordinary revelation of the heights to which a pagan soul could rise. 'Do not feel despondency,' he writes, 'if thou dost not invariably succeed in acting from right principles'; or again, 'To what use am I putting my soul? Fail not to ask thyself this question and cross-examine thyself.' 'Thou canst live on earth as thou purposest to live when departed.' 'The best way thou canst avenge thyself is not to do likewise.' 'Love the men amongst whom thy lot is cast—but wholeheartedly.' 'Train thyself to pay careful attention to what is said by another, and so far as is possible enter into his soul.' 'Let any do or say what he will, I must for my part be good.'

The *Meditations* had not of course been written when in 161 at the age of thirty-nine Aurelius came to the throne; but, as an index of his character, such sayings tell their own tale.

Intensely self-critical almost to the verge of morbidity, he was also weak in health; and we can well understand how tremendous must have appeared to him the burden of the responsibility which he was called upon to shoulder. When we add to this the fact that he had received no military training, it is not difficult to guess the reason why he took the unprecedented step of appointing a consort at the very outset of his reign. At the time of Marcus' adoption by Antoninus Pius, Lucius Verus, it will be remembered, had been adopted too. He had grown up a somewhat self-indulgent, slap-dash fellow; and it is clear that by Antoninus at least he was not considered fit for the throne. But, if the disappointment rankled, there was abundant compensation when Marcus immediately made him his consort upon equal terms, intending him presumably to undertake the military duties of the Principate, while he himself dealt with the civil.

The policy of Marcus was based, as we should expect, partly on a philanthropic conception of his imperial obligations, partly on a profound study of law, which was with him a lifelong interest. Though responsible for no sweeping changes, he showed his sympathy for the poor and the down-trodden by several beneficent measures. He did much to encourage the emancipation of slaves. He made a regulation that during acrobatic entertainments a net should be stretched under the performers; and when his wife Faustina died he celebrated her memory by founding a charitable institution for 5,000 poor children. In the control of finance his instinctive generosity made him a somewhat short-sighted economist. Bankrupt municipalities which appealed for a remission of taxes were always sure of receiving liberal concessions. Funds were readily advanced to districts stricken by earthquake or famine. The result was that the Treasury was often in straits, more especially under the heavy demands of long wars on the frontier; and on one occasion Marcus even sold the crown jewels. At length, with a falling revenue, he found it so difficult to make two ends meet that he depreciated the currency—a disastrous precedent for less scrupulous successors. The fact is, as we have hinted, that the Empire was beginning to experience an inescapable dilemma, which continued to perplex its rulers for two centuries to come—on the one hand, the failure of its internal resources, and, on the other, an increasing demand made on those failing resources for the defence of its sorely pressed frontiers.

It was a cruel fortune which called a man of Marcus' character to spend himself in fighting back the most serious menace that Rome had encountered for many a long day. Trouble came first in the East. In the year after the Emperor's accession the Parthian King Vologeses invaded Armenia (now no longer of course subject to the Roman rule), cut up the garrison of Cappadocia under its general Severianus, and even put to flight the legions of the Syrian province. Aurelius acted promptly. He gave his consort Lucius Verus the supreme command of the expedition with Avidius Cassius and other able generals on his staff. The local troops were reinforced by large drafts from other frontiers; and with such numbers at their command the lieutenants of Lucius carried all before them. In 163 Artaxata was captured by Statius Priscus and burnt to the ground—presently to be rebuilt on the model of a Roman city; and a thoroughly Romanized princeling called Sohaemus was installed on the throne of Armenia. In the following year Mesopotamia was entered; and in 165 Ctesiphon the Parthian capital, fell once more into Roman hands. The war was even carried, far beyond the point reached by Trajan, into Media Atropatene. But Vologeses had by now been taught a sufficient lesson. So the legions were withdrawn and only a small district in north-west Mesopotamia was retained on the farther side of the Euphrates, where Carrhae, Singara, and perhaps Edessa were made Roman colonies. Avidius Cassius, who had been chiefly responsible for the Parthian campaign, was appointed governor of Syria with wide powers of control over all the Eastern provinces—a commission which, as we shall see, he tragically misused. Meanwhile Lucius Verus, who had spent most of his time enjoying himself at Antioch, had returned to Rome, and there in token of his victories he assumed the resounding title of 'Armeniacus Parthicus Maximus Medicus'.

The expedition had, for the time being at least, achieved its intended purpose; but it had a disastrous sequel. For, when the detachments which had been drafted out from the European legions came home again, they brought with them the infection of a terrible pestilence. Some think it was small-pox, others the bubonic plague. But however that may be, Italy and the West now suffered with the East. In Rome men and women died like flies. In the country-side whole districts were depopulated. Famine only served to intensify the horror of the time; and the government were hard put to it to relieve the stricken people. The appalling character of the calamity is obvious, and its consequences hard to overestimate. The Empire, when it emerged from the ordeal, seems to have suf-fered a loss of energy from which perhaps it never recovered; yet never had energy been more urgently needed than now.

For the barbarian hordes of Central Europe were renewing their attack. While within the Empire the birth-rate was de-clining, these virile tribes bred rapidly, and behind them the inexorable pressure of yet more adventurous warriors—Sarma-tians from Russia and perhaps even Slavs from farther east—were beginning already to bear upon their rear. Langobardi or Lombards from the neighbourhood of the Elbe Valley, had appeared on the Danube and asked for permission to settle in Pannonia. Their request was refused; and the restless move-ments of these homeless folk set Central Europe in a sudden turmoil. The Marcomanni, the Quadi, and other neighbouring tribes united for a determined assault upon the Roman border. They swept into Dacia, but failed to take Sarmizegethusa; they broke across the Danube, where the Roman garrisons, weakened by the recent withdrawal of troops for the East, were powerless to check them. They overran Raetia, Noricum, and Pannonia, and even stood upon the threshold of Italy itself. Aquileia was besieged, and Opitergium on the road to Verona was sacked.

It was nearly three centuries since a barbarian enemy had set foot on Italian soil; and we can well understand how the peaceful inhabitants, by now quite unaccustomed to arms, must have quaked in their shoes. The Emperor, however, rose magnificently to the occasion. He called for recruits, and even slaves were enlisted. He recalled the remaining detachments from the East; and, taking Lucius Verus with him, assumed

personal command of the campaign. After some initial reverses, in which a Praetorian Prefect was killed, the Romans
were successful in driving back the invaders and compelling
them to restore the booty and the 60,000 prisoners they had
captured. In the following year (167) all the Danubian provinces were cleared of the enemy. But this did not satisfy
Aurelius. The successful resistance of Dacia to the enemy
seemed fully to have justified Trajan's extension of the frontier north of the Danube; and it was now decided to imitate
him in assuming the offensive. The Emperor took up his head-
quarters at Carnuntum, a more or less central point on the middle
reaches of the river. It was a well-chosen base for the coming
operations. For the enemy's pressure was felt from two
directions—from the north-west came the Germanic tribes the
Quadi and Marcomanni, from the north-east, the Iazyges and
their kindred tribes the Sarmatians. Thus from Carnuntum
it was possible to divide these two hostile groups and strike
left or right at discretion. On the other hand, since the
Romans' man-power was never quite sufficient to drive their
offensive home in both fronts simultaneously, their successes
in one direction were apt to be cancelled by fresh trouble in
the other. Thus when, after suppressing the Quadi, Aurelius
struck north-east against the Sarmatian group, the Marcomanni and the Quadi broke over the Danube once more, and
he had to hurry back. The brunt of the fresh invasion fell this
time upon Raetia; but under the leadership of Pertinax, the
future Emperor, its troops succeeded in throwing back the
intruders, and carrying the war far north into their native
territory of Bohemia. It was now possible to attack the Sarmatians once again, and happily with more success. Here,
too, the Romans' offensive seems to have been pushed home
with great audacity, and it penetrated, some say, as far as the
Carpathian Mountains. So complete indeed was the triumph
upon either front that Aurelius appears to have planned the
annexation of two great northern areas. Between the Danube
and Dacia the country of the Iazyges was to be made into a
province called Sarmatia, and to the north-west of this again
was to be formed another province under the name of Marcomannia. As the result of such a policy a continuous frontier

would have been formed from the mouth of the Danube to the upper waters of the Elbe. Thus a great wedge was to be thrust across the lands of Central Europe, dividing the Germanic from the Sarmatian peoples; and it is not improbable that in the sequel the idea conceived by Augustus nearly two centuries before might at last have been carried through, and the whole of Germany enclosed by a frontier ultimately reaching as far as the North Sea.

But, whatever project was shaping itself in the brain of Aurelius, there now occurred an interruption fatal to its execution. For in another quarter of the Empire a thing happened which he might well have foreseen. When he gave Avidius Cassius the command over the East, there were not wanting those who warned him of the man's untrustworthy character. 'He is a good soldier,' the Emperor had replied, 'and the State requires his services.' Avidius used his position to make himself personally popular, and when in. 175 there came a false rumour of Aurelius' death he proclaimed himself Emperor. The governor of Egypt supported him; and, though the rumour was soon contradicted, it was too late to draw back. Aurelius left the Danube and hurried through Italy for the East. His haste, however, proved needless; for while he was on his way Avidius was murdered by the officers of his own staff. In the course of his return journey Aurelius took the opportunity to visit some of the Eastern provinces, and stayed some while in Athens; but by the time he was back in Rome he learnt that the Marcomanni had been stirred to fresh activity by his absence from the front. So in 178 he once more took up the weary task and travelled north to the Danube. His campaign was successful and the territory of the invaders was again overrun. The situation began to look brighter; and the relentless pressure of the barbarian hordes had been to some extent lightened by the adoption of a policy, not indeed originated by Aurelius, but by him carried much farther than by any of his predecessors.

Since the reign of Augustus barbarian border-tribes had occasionally been admitted across the Roman frontier and allowed to settle upon vacant lands. Hitherto such transplantation had been on a comparatively small scale; but Aurelius' policy was much more drastic. Owing to pestilence, famine, the bloody losses of the war, and, perhaps most of all, the disinclination of its civilized inhabitants to undertake military service, the Empire's resources of man-power were sadly exhausted; and already Aurelius had been compelled to enlist detachments from the tribes which he had conquered. An extension of this policy had manifest attractions; but to secure the dubious loyalty of such auxiliaries it was plainly better to settle them under the civilizing influences of Roman provinces. Room for such settlement was not difficult to find. The havoc of the war had left many areas desolate. The food-resources of the Empire, too, had been seriously declining. Famine had been frequent of late, and rather than allow precious land to go untilled there was much to be said for letting barbarians till it. So in Dacia, Moesia, Pannonia, and (though this proved a failure) in north-east Italy itself, large numbers of Marcomanni, Quadi, and other tribes were planted on the soil. Any who had sided with Rome and came of their own free will were given some latitude of choice and treated on equal terms with the provincials among whom they settled. Others, who were compelled to migrate under the enforced terms of their submission, received more stringent treatment. They were tied to the soil like serfs, and laid under obligation to military service in case of a fresh invasion. Thus was begun the policy of relying on barbarians to keep barbarians out, a precedent, as it proved, which later Emperors followed and which merely served in the long run to facilitate the task of the invaders.[1]

For all this it would be unfair to blame Marcus overmuch, since no better alternative was readily to hand. But a more serious error of judgment must certainly be laid to his charge; and it concerned his choice of a successor. The hard blows which fortune had dealt him afford indeed some explanation of his action. His consort, Lucius Verus, was dead, worn out by the earlier campaigns of the Marcomannic War (169). The

---

[1] The policy was not, in point of fact, a new one. Under Augustus, numbers of the Ubii and other German tribes had been transferred into Gaul; under Claudius Suebi into Pannonia; under Nero immense numbers of barbarians from the northern to the southern side of the Danube.

treachery of Avidius Cassius cannot have failed to shake even his loyal faith in his subordinates. The death of his wife Faustina, too, must have left him a very lonely and disheartened man; and under such circumstances it was perhaps only natural that he should have abandoned Trajan's and Hadrian's policy of choosing the man best fitted for the post, and reverted to the theory of a hereditary succession. On his return from the East he had appointed his own son Commodus, then but fifteen years of age, to be his consort in the Principate. He took the boy with him to his final campaign on the Danube front; and when in 180 he died at Vindobona (now Vienna), utterly worn out by his long exertions, Commodus duly came to the throne. His first act was to disregard his father's wishes and the advice of his staff-officers, and to negotiate a peace with the enemy. No sooner was this decision taken than he hurried back to Rome. It may be that it was the wisest course for a new Emperor—and still more for a young Emperor—to be at the centre of affairs during the dangerous transitional period of his accession; but, if this were so, it was one of the very few wise acts of Commodus' lamentable reign.

III. COMMODUS

Commodus was ill served by the historians, who liked to paint his character black as a foil to his father's virtues; yet, with all allowances made, he seems to have been a worthless sort of fellow. Emperor at nineteen, he thought more of his favourite pleasures, horse-racing and the arena, than of the serious task ahead of him. He relied on a short-sighted policy of pampering the Praetorians—a policy which after his death produced most troublesome consequences. He promoted his low-born favourites to important offices of State; and one by one he got rid of his father's trusty advisers. Finally one of these, Pompeianus, who had married Commodus' sister, attempted to assassinate him, but badly bungled the job; and with that all the devilry of the Emperor's savage temper was let loose. He executed senators right and left. A fresh conspiracy followed, and again heads fell. The realization of his power seems to have driven the man half crazy, and he threw all sense of decorum to the winds. They say that he used to get himself up in the fancy-dress of Hercules and belabour his courtiers with a club His crude tastes were indulged to the uttermost. He took to driving his own team in the races, and, if tales be true, actually appeared in the lists at the arena. At length the members of his household could stand it no longer, and a new conspiracy was hatched. His mistress Marcia gave him poison; and, when this failed to work, a gladiator was called in to finish him off.

So ended the 'Golden Age' of the Antonines; and the reign of the philosopher's son proved the prelude to an era beside which even the horrors of the earlier civil wars appear mild by comparison.

CHAPTER XXVIII

THE DYNASTY OF THE SEVERI

WHEN we pass from the Antonines to the age of the Severi and their successors it is to enter an atmosphere in which all that was noble and dignified in the Roman character seems completely to have vanished. Chaos is followed by tyranny and tyranny by chaos; and murderous scrambles for power alternate with the reigns now of a Sultanic potentate, now of a religious fanatic, and now of a sergeant-major promoted from the ranks. It is not easy to attribute this rapid plunge downhill to any single direct cause. The ordeal of the plague (as such experiences often will) must have left men sour and embittered and ready for desperate courses. The administration of the Empire, we must remember too, was rapidly changing hands. The respectable class of senatorial 'gentlemen', though still held socially in high repute, were losing their monopoly of leadership whether in the army or in the provinces. The traditional standards of patriotism and public service were being degraded by the unscrupulous and selfish vulgarity of the equestrian middle class, recruited as this was not merely from men of every profession, but also from men of all races—African Moors, unstable Levantines, and rough Illyrian peasants. More than all, however, we can begin to appreciate the disastrous consequences of the distinction which Hadrian had drawn between the military and the civil branches of the imperial service. Now that an official career no longer included a training for both branches, the army tended, even more than before, to become an exclusive professional caste, and its commanders, losing touch with the ideals of sound government, pursued their own selfish interests by the power of the sword. The State was henceforward more and more at the mercy of the army and of men who sought to climb into power by the gratification of its exorbitant demands.

I. SEPTIMIUS SEVERUS

On Commodus' death there were several leading generals who had their eye upon the throne. But the conspirators, being on the spot, chose Pertinax, Aurelius' able lieutenant, and the Praetorians accepted their choice. Pertinax, however, was not a man to humour the troops. The Praetorians were utterly spoilt by Commodus' indulgence; and they were disgusted when they found their request for a donative refused and strict discipline imposed on them once more. At the end of three months they murdered the unpopular Emperor; and, offering the throne to whoever would pay highest, gave it to a senator named Didius Julianus.

In Pannonia, meanwhile, the legions, growing restive at the Praetorians' effrontery, put forward their governor Lucius Septimius Severus, marched down on Rome, and installed him in Julianus' place. His first act was to disband the Praetorians and replace them with drafts from his own Illyrian troops. The accession of Septimius Severus, like the accession of Vespasian, marked a new chapter in imperial history. For the man was an African—not in the sense that Trajan and Hadrian had been Spaniards, for at least they were descended from Roman settlers in the province—but an African by blood whose native tongue was Punic and who even lacked the education and culture of most Roman citizens. His wife was a Syrian lady, hailing from Emesa, north of Damascus, though in place of her true name Martha she assumed the title of Julia Domna.

But, whatever his origin, the rude strength of Septimius' character soon made itself apparent. Other rivals were already in the field, and he dealt his blows swiftly. In the East, Pescennius Niger, who had the backing of the Euphrates troops, was soon overwhelmed. His adherents were ruthlessly punished, and the town of Byzantium, which had held out in his cause, was razed to the ground. Albinus, the governor of Britain, had meanwhile raised an army in Gaul, and a fresh campaign thus became necessary. It ended in a great battle near Lyons; and Septimius celebrated his victory by handing over this ancient and highly civilized city to the fury of his troops. The act was typical. The African Emperor had no sense of decency or mercy in his composition, and in asserting his authority he cared little how much blood might flow. On the other hand, there was method in his ferocity. He realized well enough that the Roman nobility, who had been the bitter opponents of Commodus, were likely to prove the most serious obstacle to his own rule, and he was determined to teach them a terrible lesson. Though he had previously given the usual promise to put no senators to death, he now executed more than a score of them on suspicion of complicity in Albinus' revolt. The confiscation of his many victims' property augmented the 'crown lands' to such a degree that a complete reorganization of imperial finance was undertaken; and the whole revenues both of the *fiscus* and of the crown lands were concentrated in a common treasury which Septimius henceforward treated entirely as his own. The *aerarium*, which the Senate controlled, thus came to be little more than the 'municipal chest', and the Senate itself the town council, of Rome. It lost its valued powers of appointing provincial governors. Its personnel was flooded with the Emperor's favourites, no longer sober, cultured nobles of the western provinces, but African half-breeds, Syrian degenerates, and half-civilized peasants from the Illyrian hills.

The one merit of Septimius Severus' policy was that it at least united the Empire at a moment when unity was essential but he achieved this result only by the rough and ready method of ruthlessly stamping out every form of opposition. He governed, in short, like some despot of the Orient; and, despite his ridiculous attempts to disguise his usurpation—he called Aurelius his 'father' and rechristened his own son

Antoninus—the plain fact was that he had come to power by the sword and by the sword alone he held it. He kept a Parthian legion stationed on the Alban Mount within easy hail of the capital. He increased the pay and the privileges of the soldiers, making promotion rapid and removing the ban upon legitimate marriages. 'Enrich the troops' was the last piece of advice he gave to his heirs.

But if the growing dissociation between the military and civil executive gave an added prestige and importance to the former, the process of specialization was not without its influence upon the latter too. Little as Severus can have cared for the traditions of Roman jurisprudence, he at least realized that under a despotic monarchy the control of legal procedure required a further measure of centralization. Henceforward, accordingly, we find that one at least of the two Praetorian Prefects was invested with new powers of administering justice. As a judge of final appeal, this official handled cases brought up from both Italy and the provinces; and his decisions naturally did much to develop the civil code already formulated by Julianus. It stands to the credit of Severus that he entrusted this responsible function to a highly trained lawyer, Papinianus, while under Alexander Severus, his great-nephew, a scarcely less eminent juristic authority named Ulpian served in the same capacity. The work of these men went far to infuse a more human and liberal spirit into the administration of the law. Even the rights of slaves were recognized; and the interests of lower-class provincials were studied with greater sympathy[1] and understanding by men who themselves hailed from the provinces—for Papinian was a native of Syria and Ulpian of Tyre.

The condition of the frontiers during Severus' reign was comparatively peaceful. In 197 a Parthian attack on Nisibis, which was now in Roman hands, required an expedition for its recovery; and the campaign led to a demonstration of force into the heart of Parthia, where Babylon and Ctesiphon were once again entered. It seems, indeed, to have become a more

---

[1] It is not improbable that Septimius, himself a provincial, appreciated the importance of favouring the poorer classes of the Empire, since it was from those very classes that the army was recruited.

or less accepted principle that peace in the East was best to be maintained by thus, from time to time, 'showing the flag'; and since the Empire's military man-power was insufficient to concentrate a striking force in more than one quarter at a time, it was more convenient to do so in the East when the European frontiers were quiet. In 209, however, Severus' presence was required in Britain, and he is said to have pushed far north into Caledonia. Whatever may have been his plans for a complete conquest of the island, he never lived to complete them; for in 211 he died at Eboracum (now York).

II. CARACALLA

'Stick together; enrich the troops; nothing else matters,' was the parting advice said to have been given by Severus to his two sons and joint-heirs Caracalla and Geta. The initial precept was wasted upon them; they hated one another bitterly, and, after an attempt at compromise on the basis of partitioning the Empire, Caracalla had Geta murdered in his mother's arms. He followed up this brutal act, we are told, by massacring 20,000 persons on suspicion of having favoured his brother. It was a characteristic prelude to the reign of a boor and a bully. Caracalla had all his father's vices without his ability. He pampered the soldiers according to instructions and again raised their pay. Then, lacking the ready money, since the silver-mines were becoming exhausted, he proceeded yet further to depreciate the currency by an admixture of cheap alloy. He fleeced the richer classes of the Empire without mercy; and it was probably a desire to draw more taxpayers into his net that led to the one important measure of his reign. In 212 he extended the rights of citizenship to all the freeborn inhabitants of the provinces. There were certain taxes—notably an inheritance duty—to which citizens alone were liable. But apart from the gain which this reform must have brought to the Exchequer, some such unification of political status was long overdue. The existing varieties of privilege and liability had been a tiresome complication not merely to the machinery of fiscal collection but of military recruitment too. Nor can it be doubted that it was a shrewd stroke on Caracalla's part to gratify the savage swashbucklers, on whose swords his power depended, by thus placing them on an equality with his more civilized subjects. For to this half-breed Emperor, son of a Punic father and a Syrian mother, the old traditions of Rome's culture meant nothing whatever. He hated men of education, having little himself; and if anything flattered his pride it was the idea that, as a military despot, he could bend all men to his will. Like Alexander of old, whom he greatly admired, and whose exploits, queerly enough, he pretended to emulate, he determined to conquer the East. Great preparations were made for a fresh invasion of Parthia; and when the inhabitants of Alexandria made fun of him, he had all their young men called out on parade and massacred in cold blood. But retribution was at hand. In 217 a Moor named Macrinus, his own Praetorian Prefect, encompassed his murder and was appointed Emperor in his stead.

III. THE SEVERI FROM SYRIA

The sequel of Macrinus' rise to power was perhaps the most fantastic tale in all the annals of Rome. Severus' wife Julia Domna had a sister Julia Maesa, a dangerous and ambitious woman; and Macrinus with some foresight had her hounded out of Italy. She went home to Emesa and there began to plot. Having only daughters of her own, she set to work in the interest of their two sons, Elagabalus and Alexander Severus. Being very rich, she was able to corrupt some troops then stationed near Emesa; and when Macrinus came back from an unsuccessful expedition into Parthia her followers attacked him, and, with Maesa herself leading at the head of the charge, succeeded in defeating him. So Elagabalus became Emperor and a more ludicrous figure to be seated on the throne it is scarcely possible to imagine. He was the high-priest of a debased Syrian cult of the Sun God, fanatical, unbalanced, and completely Oriental in his ways and ideas. There can be little doubt, however, that this curious creature took himself very seriously. His intention was to impose his Syrian cult upon the Empire as a whole. He actually imported to Rome the sacred black-stone which was the object of his superstitious veneration; and, as though to symbolize the union of the new religion with the old, he went through the form of marriage with a Vestal Virgin. He kept a luxurious court after the style of some Eastern monarch and conferred the highest offices on favourites of his own, among whom were a charioteer, an acrobat, and a barber. Roman society was not unnaturally outraged; and the scandal was ended, as so many times before, by the Praetorian Guard, who murdered him and put up his cousin, Alexander Severus, in his place.

Alexander Severus being only thirteen, some delegation of authority was essential; and, seeing what had been the history of the past few years, there was clearly no trust to be placed in the army-commanders. So, under the influence of Alexander's strong-minded mother Mamaea, a committee of sixteen senators was set up to hold the reins of government during his minority. The most important post of all, the Prefecture of the Guard, was entrusted to Ulpian, the famous lawyer, and, maybe as the result of his authority, we can at length discern some rational attempt to arrest the fatal progress towards bankruptcy. The depredations of the demoralized soldiery, the outbreak of piracy and brigandage, and, perhaps worst of all, the depreciation of the currency had produced an almost complete breakdown in the economic life of the Empire; and, as a consequence of all this, the collection of taxes had become increasingly difficult. Two main remedies were applied which, though often used in the past, now began to assume an ever-increasing importance. First, the town-councillors of each municipality were made personally responsible for producing the sum required—if necessary out of their own pockets. Second, under the prevailing shortage of ready money, recourse was frequently had to exacting labour or commodities instead of actual cash. Thus, to supply the needs of the army, craftsmen's guilds were compelled to furnish gratis their respective articles of manufacture. The tenants on the crown estates were laid under obligation to make over part of their produce to the State; and the labour of transporting food to the capital was requisitioned in a similar manner.

To add to the difficulties of the imperial government the situation on the frontiers became once more precarious. In the East, among the mountains of Persia, the Sassanid princes, hitherto vassals of Parthia, had recently thrown off her yoke;

and in 227 Ardashir, their ruling monarch, embarked on a career of conquest which brought him to the confines of Asia Minor itself. In 231 Alexander Severus went out to meet the invaders. One of his armies was completely destroyed; and, though Ardashir failed to follow up his victory, the disaster so frightened the Emperor that he shrank from pushing home the campaign. Nor in any case was it wise for him to linger in the East. The withdrawal of troops from the Danube foi this Asiatic campaign had exposed the European frontier to a fresh barbarian attack; and in 234 Alexander's presence was required on the Rhine. Instead of taking the offensive, how- ever, he proposed to buy off the invaders with gold; and so infuriated were the soldiers at this humiliation that in March 235 they murdered both him and his mother. So the dynasty of the Severi ended in ignominy, and the policy of their founder had brought its appropriate penalty. For the army to which Septimius had given so exaggerated an importance had begun to get out of hand as soon as ever the control of his strong personality was removed. Greedy for plunder or rewards, and resentful of discipline, the soldiers had proved too much for the weaker members of Severus' line, and in the pursuance of their selfish ends they were now ready, even at the worst crisis of its history, to plunge the unhappy Empire into still further chaos.

CHAPTER XXIX

THE ANARCHY

ALEXANDER SEVERUS' death was followed by fifty years of anarchy, during which rulers rose and fell in such bewildering succession that it would be tedious and unprofitable to recount their story in detail. No less than twenty-three emperors were, for a brief period at least, officially recognized. Nearly all were nominees of this or that body of troops; and after a reign sometimes of a few months, seldom more than a few years, nearly all came to a violent end. Only one of the whole number died in his bed.

First Maximinus, a Thracian and the commander of the

Illyrian troops, was acclaimed by the murderers of Alexander Severus; but this grim barbarian was bitterly detested by the noble class. In pursuance of his schemes for a further campaign into Germany, he laid his hands on any source of revenue he could find, not excluding temple treasures. Even a worm will turn, and the outraged Senate seized desperately at the chance of conferring the throne on two pretenders in Africa. These men, Gordianus father and son, were promptly murdered by their garrison troops; and a second pair of senatorial nominees were set up, but as promptly slain by the Praetorian Guard. Maximinus himself having meanwhile met the same fate at the hands of his legions, there remained Gordianus' grandson, a boy of fourteen. When, however, this courageous lad went out East to deal with the Persians he in his turn was made away with by one of his generals—the son of an Arab sheik, known as Philippus Arabs. Five years later he too fell victim to the revolt of an Illyrian pretender named Decius (249).

All this while the state of things had rapidly been going from bad to worse. Even in the East the Persians were sufficiently dangerous, but in Europe a far more serious situation had arisen. The old tribes of Germany—the tribes against which Augustus and his successors had fought, and which since then had settled down to comparative tranquillity—had suddenly been swamped and perhaps almost obliterated by the irruption of wild hordes from the north. Franks descending from their home on the Baltic had pushed through to the northern reaches of the Rhine. Farther south the Alamanni were bursting across the river. Meanwhile on the Danube Goths from the Vistula were an even more terrible menace. To these wandering and predatory peoples the lure of the rich lands which lay behind the Empire's frontier and the prospect of still richer booty to be won in its peaceful cities proved an irresistible stimulus. Though some tribes even banded together for a concerted strategy, their onslaught as a rule was fitful and haphazard; but so inadequate were the numbers of the Roman defence that the frontier crumbled now here, now there, like some wall of sand before the incoming tide.

In the reign of Decius the Ostrogoths, or Eastern Goths, broke across the lower Danube, overrunning Thrace and even

Macedonia. The havoc they wrought was indescribable; and at Philippopolis, it is said, 100,000 of its inhabitants were put to the sword. Decius himself went north to do battle with the invaders, and lost his life in the attempt. They were bought off by his successor Trebonianus, who agreed to pay them an annual subsidy. But the respite thus won could not last and in 253, when Valerianus and his son Gallienus became its joint rulers, the whole fabric of the Empire seemed on the point of collapse. Leaving Gallienus to deal with the West, Valerian himself hurried off to save, if possible, the frontier of the East —only to fall prisoner into the hands of Shapur, the new Persian dynast (258). The Asiatic provinces seemed as good as lost; and both Syria and Cilicia had already been overrun when a remarkable rally was made by the oasis city of Palmyra on the edge of the Syrian desert. Odenethes, its commander, gathering together what was left of the Roman troops in this region, inflicted a severe defeat upon the Persians and proceeded to establish a semi-independent hegemony in the East.

Thus, while a new vigour was thus infused into the defence of its frontiers by the gallantry of a free-lance commander, the Empire itself appeared to be splitting into fragments; and in the meantime a similar development had occurred in the West. For there too the position seemed equally desperate. Valerianus' son, Gallienus, had been simultaneously distracted by attacks from every quarter. The Goths had overwhelmed Dacia, which was now lost for ever to Rome. Another party of them had seized the Black Sea shipping, sailed into the Aegean, laid siege to Athens, sacked Ephesus, and invaded Asia Minor. On the Rhine front the defences of the Neckar region broke down before the Alamanni, who struck down by the Rhône valley, and, thence penetrating into Italy itself, were only beaten back by a great victory won by Gallienus in the neighbourhood of Milan (258). At the same time the Franks were pouring over the frontier in the farther north, and, sweeping across Gaul, even crossed the Pyrenees. Here again, as in the East, it was the initiative of a local commander which alone availed to save the Western provinces from utter ruin. For proclaiming himself Emperor, Latinius Postumus, the commander of the Rhine garrison, proceeded to establish

an independent 'Empire of the Gauls'. Its capital was at
Trèves; and its constitution was planned upon the Roman
model with senate and consuls of its own. This was not, as
in earlier days, an attempt to reassert the nationalist aspirations
of the Gallic people, for any sense of racial antagonism to Rome
was long since dead. But it was felt that, whereas emperors,
rushing hither and thither to stem the barbarian onset, had
failed to protect Gaul, a more localized authority might possibly succeed; and indeed the independent action of Latinius
Postumus went far to justify the hope. The Franks and the
Alamanni were driven back across the Rhine; and the defences
of the river (no longer including the district of the Neckar) were
to some extent restored. To counter this new threat to the
Empire's unity the distracted Gallienus turned home from the
Danube, seeking to reassert his lost authority, but he was killed
outside Milan, while attacking another pretender—struck in
all probability by an arrow aimed from behind by one of his
own men (263).

Hitherto the long sequence of 'barrack Emperors' had
produced scarcely a man at all capable of coping with the
double problem of a demoralized, mutinous army and a frontier rapidly crumbling. But in Claudius, the stout-hearted son
of an Illyrian farmer, such a man was at last forthcoming. It
was none too soon. Huge bands of Goths, numbering it is
said, 300,000 warriors, were roaming about in Macedonia and
elsewhere, and dealing devastation far and wide. On Claudius'
approach they left Thessalonica, which they had been besieging, and retreated towards the Danube. He caught them
near Nish and won a decisive victory. Vast numbers of the
enemy were slain and many prisoners, who were eventually
rounded up, were placed as serfs on the land. Claudius assumed the title of Gothicus in honour of his triumph; and had
he lived to follow it up, he might have succeeded in reasserting
the unity of the Empire. In 270, however, he fell a victim
to a renewed outbreak of the plague; and he handed on the task
to an even more competent successor, Aurelianus.

This man too was of Illyrian stock. Having risen from a
private in the ranks, he was a martinet for discipline, and, as a
ruler. unswerving in the severity of his justice. When he came

to the throne, the German tribes were once again upon the war-
path; and once again the Alamanni swept down through the
Alpine passes upon the valley of the Po. Italy seemed doomed;
but, though defeated in a great battle, Aurelian gathered a
fresh army of recruits and, returning to the attack, drove back
the invaders on the historic field of the Metaurus, then, pursuing them to the River Ticinus, destroyed them utterly. It
was a telling indication of the extreme peril in which even the
capital had stood, that he proceeded to fortify its undefended
suburbs by building a great brick wall, the remains of which
may still be seen. The territory of the Empire being now
cleared of foreign foes, Aurelian turned to the no less important
task of arresting the process of its internal disintegration.
Odonethes of Palmyra was now dead; but the official recognition which at first the Roman Government had accorded to
his successful self-assertion had been ill requited. Under his
widow Zenobia, Palmyra, so far from losing its mastery of the
East, was beginning deliberately to cut adrift from all imperial
control. Zenobia's son Wahballah, now ensconced as governor
of Egypt, assumed the title of Augustus and issued his own
coinage as an independent ruler. Such pretensions were a
challenge which Aurelian could not overlook. Palmyra was
besieged and Zenobia taken prisoner. Egypt moreover was
already reduced, and Aurelian was at last free to turn westwards and deal with the independent Empire of the Gauls. Pos
tumus, its founder, was now dead; and Tetricus, his successor
after the defeat of his army near Chalons, came readily to
terms. Thus not merely the Gallic province, but also Britain
which had thrown in her lot with the rebels, was brought
once more under the Empire's rule.

But the author of this remarkable recovery was not long permitted to enjoy his triumph. The severity of his rule had
brought him many enemies; and one of his private secretaries,
who was threatened with punishment, determined in self-
protection to encompass Aurelian's dispatch. By forging a
death-warrant against some leading officers, he persuaded
them to murder his master; and the throne passed once more
into less capable hands (275). Claudius Tacitus was murdered
after the briefest of reigns. Probus, another Illyrian, did well

for a while, but he too was murdered. Other short-lived successors followed till in 284 the Praetorian Guard gave the throne to a man who was to prove himself the greatest statesman of the Empire's decline—the famous Diocletian. The period of anarchy was ended; and under the forceful rule of this extraordinary man a complete reorganization of the administrative system was to offer a hope, though it proved but a passing hope, of the Empire's survival.

CHAPTER XXX

DIOCLETIAN

THE agony of the years through which the Roman Empire had been passing can scarcely be exaggerated. The security of the Age of the Antonines had been replaced by chaos. No man knew from day to day how long his life would be safe or his livelihood forthcoming. Plague had raged for years at a time. Famine was frequent. The inroads of the barbarians no longer stopped short at the frontier districts. Ancient cities, the very birthplace of civilization, had been sacked. Predatory hordes roamed at will through peaceful provinces; and the defenceless inhabitants, softened by centuries of luxury and comfort, could do nothing better than strengthen the fortifications of their towns, leaving the countryside a prey to the invaders. Crops were destroyed, farms looted and burnt, and large areas went out of cultivation altogether. Men's hearts were utterly failing them; and, worst of all, the whole intricate system of industry and commerce was breaking down. The depreciation of the currency alone was a source of infinite confusion. Successive emperors, lacking money to pay their troops and officials, had resorted to 'inflation'. Eventually they had come to coining thin disks of copper, and, washing them over with silver, issued them as *denarii*. The disastrous consequences were twofold. Men who possessed genuine silver coins refused to part with them on equal terms with the new and worthless money; and hoarding increased the shortage of the much-needed precious metal.

In the second place, as always happens under similar circumstances, the producers of goods, realizing the diminished value of the *denarius*, put up their prices; so that more and more coins were required to meet their growing demands and there was nothing for it but for the government once again to increase their issue with an even lower quality of metal-content. The result was that the *denarius*, which had been worth roughly eightpence halfpenny in the time of Augustus, dropped in the third century A.D. to the value of a farthing. With the failure of production, prices soared to intolerable levels, until the same quantity of corn which in earlier days would have fetched seven or eight drachmae was sold in Egypt for a hundred and twenty thousand. In such a state of affairs commerce became impossible. Instead of passing freely from one quarter of the Empire to another, goods locally produced were locally sold; and in the absence of a stable currency, the value of which could be counted on as permanent, men preferred to make their transactions by the awkward method of barter. Industry too was equally hard hit. Mass-production for export was no longer possible; and we consequently find a reversion to local types of pottery and other wares, markedly inferior in workmanship.

Worst of all, however, was the condition of agriculture. First there was the damage done by the barbarian invaders. Not merely had the farmsteads and stock been destroyed, but their stricken owners lacked the wherewithal to make a fresh beginning. For there were no banks to lend on credit, as in modern times. In the second place, the urbanization of the provinces had produced an unfortunate effect. For the high standard of living enjoyed by the inhabitants of the towns made an excessive demand on the produce of the land. Some think that the soil was becoming exhausted; and though this is doubtful there were certainly recurrent shortages of corn. On the farming class, too, fell by far the heaviest burden of an exorbitant taxation. The requisitions in kind which the central government made were inevitably levied on the primary producers; and in raising their local taxes the townships tended more and more to rely upon the landowners, and the landowners not unnaturally passed the burden on to their tenants. Many of these tenant-farmers, having fallen into arrears of payment, were reduced to a state of dependence little better than serfdom.

Nor must we forget that the civil servants of the Empire, in whose hands lay the responsibility of seeing justice done in such matters, were by now most unfit for their duties. Administrative posts had been increasingly filled by semi-civilized soldiers, first promoted for military distinction, then claiming their reward in some well-paid administrative post. To such a pitch had come the unfortunate departure from the Empire's earlier tradition. Once the higher positions in both army and civil service had been the monopoly of the more highly educated and politically experienced classes. Now ruffians from the Balkans, Moors from Africa, and wild mountaineers from Asia Minor claimed and received appointments for which they were totally unsuited. Emperors themselves, as we have seen, were only too frequently drawn from these more backward regions; and the miracle is that, when at last a man with some real claim to statesmanship appeared, he too was of low origin— lower indeed, so far as we can tell, than any who had previously attained the throne.

Though born in Illyria, Diocletian was apparently not a native of the province, but the son of an ex-slave from the East. Certainly when he rose to be Emperor he showed a taste for pomp and ceremony which was truly Oriental. He wore a diadem and robes of purple silk. He held his receptions seated upon a throne. Even the members of his court were compelled to stand in his presence. In short, he was more completely the despot than any man before him. There can be no doubt that this extraordinary display was deliberately intended to enhance the dignity of his imperial office. For, if ever a man knew what he was doing, it was Diocletian. There was indeed no great originality in his methods of government. Most of his policies were merely a continuation of developments which had already taken place under preceding emperors; but, being gifted with an extraordinarily clear head, he reduced to system what had previously been mere haphazard practice, and carried to their logical conclusion tendencies which had long been observable in the slow evolution of the imperial organism.

One such tendency was towards a decentralization of authority. During the early Empire, as we have seen, the effort of rulers had been to concentrate the mechanism of administration more and more in their own hands; no sooner, however, was the process complete than it was realized that the mechanism was too unwieldy and its problems too intricate for a single man to control them efficiently. Even Marcus Aurelius had begun his reign by appointing a consort. Valerian and Gallienus had divided the Empire between them; and now in 286, the third year of his reign, Diocletian proceeded to do the same. He appointed Maximian, a native of Pannonia and a capable general, to be his colleague or fellow-Augustus, and leaving this man to deal with the western half of the Empire, himself took up his quarters at Nicomedia in Asia Minor, from which he ruled the eastern half. In the interests of efficiency even this partitionment proved inadequate, and seven years later Constantius and Galerius were appointed as subordinate partners under the title of Caesars. Henceforward the Empire was divided into four areas. Maximian kept Italy, Africa, and Spain, leaving Gaul and Britain to the control of Constantius; and Diocletian kept the Eastern provinces, leaving the Danubian and Balkan districts to the control of Galerius. It was further arranged that at the end of twenty years of rule the two Augusti should resign and the two Caesars take their place, thus paving the way for a continuous succession without risk of civil war.

It must not be supposed, however, that by such a delegation of authority Diocletian intended in any real sense to abdicate his sovereignty. He remained the Empire's master, and his was the brain that conceived the elaborate series of reforms which followed. His first concern, as always in these days, was with the army; and if one thing was clear it was that a force, which in the days of Augustus had been adequate for the defence of the frontier, was no longer adequate; and yet in the course of over three centuries its numbers had but little increased. Diocletian certainly doubled them—one authority says quadrupled them—but this in itself was not enough. The barbarian attacks, as we have said, were spasmodic, but when their fury fell on some particular part of the frontier the local garrison alone were unable to hold it. The need for some more mobile striking-force which could be rushed at a moment's notice to the threatened point had already been recognized by Gallienus, who had organized a special corps that had its head-quarters in Italy and included for greater mobility a large proportion of cavalry. This corps Diocletian developed into a special branch of the service, giving it special privileges and placing its detachments under the direct control of himself and his consorts. Its recruits were almost exclusively drawn from the wilder parts of the Empire, and many barbarian mercenaries were also incorporated. Its fighting quality therefore was vastly superior to the garrison troops of the frontier, which henceforward became a completely immobile force. Such troops were given lands to till in the proximity of their station and were forbidden to quit them. So all along the frontier grew up a continuous line of military settlements, in which families were raised and lived, and in which sons were compelled to follow in their father's calling. The garrison troops, in short, became a hereditary caste, and lacking the stimulus of experience or ambition the standard of their efficiency sank very low.

In his reorganization of the army Diocletian recognized and (as his habit was) stereotyped the divorce which had already begun to take place between the civil and military branches of the higher executive. Henceforth it became the rule for the armed forces in a province to be commanded by a soldier pure and simple under the title of '*Dux*'. Side by side with such military commanders was a vast staff of civilian officials, so graded as to correspond with the elaborate new re-grouping of the administrative districts. In each of the four main areas assigned to the two Augusti and the two Caesars, there was to be a high-commissioner, or *prefect*, responsible of course (as were the army commanders too) to his imperial master. Each of these areas was again divided into *dioceses*, over which was set a sub-commissioner or *vicarius*, and each diocese in its turn was sub-divided into provinces, controlled by governors, termed proconsuls, presidents or correctors. Taken all together, there were over a hundred such provinces; and, as may easily be seen, the whole method of reorganization involved an enormous multiplication of officials. In the first place, where formerly a single provincial governor had combined the functions of military commander and civil administrator, two men were now required. Added to this was the fact that Diocletian was unable or unwilling to trust his subordinates; and an enormous secret service of imperial agents was set up to spy upon the ordinary officials and report on what they saw. In short, the growth of the bureaucracy was such that one authority declares, no doubt with exaggeration, that half the population of the Empire were now the salaried servants of the Crown. In other words, at a time when every man's labour was required to keep the economic life of society in action, enormous numbers of men were occupied in superintending what the others did.

The strain of financing these overswollen state services was naturally tremendous; and the collection of revenue was perhaps the most difficult problem which Diocletian had to face. He began by reforming the currency; and for a time at least succeeded in putting it once more on a sound basis. But the bulk of the taxes had still to be paid in kind or by compulsory labour. Farmers had to furnish their quota of corn; clothiers and armourers were compelled to supply their goods at less than the market price. But here an unforeseen difficulty arose. Men who found it impossible to meet their dues took to absconding from their farms or abandoning their trades, and the only remedy was to compel them to continue at their tasks. Tenants were forbidden to quit the estates to which they were attached. It was even made obligatory on artisans to remain in the craft-guilds to which they belonged and so become tied to their existing occupation. Eventually, too, sons were forced to carry on their father's trade; so that, what was scarcely better than a veiled form of State slavery or serfdom, became hereditary. Even the local government of towns came to a standstill, for the citizens very naturally sought to evade the burdens of public office, which involved, amongst other things, the responsibility for finding the quota of taxes. So it became necessary too to force the members of the middle class to undertake these municipal duties, and they were forbidden to quit their native township.

On the top of all came further financial problems. Despite Diocletian's reform of the currency, prices still soared, and to meet the difficulty the Emperor proceeded in 301 to issue his famous edict whereby he sought to fix a maximum price for ordinary commodities. There was a maximum for wheat and rye and a maximum for butter, cheese, beef, and bacon, a maximum also for boots and articles of clothing; and, as a natural result, it further became necessary to fix a maximum wage for various sorts of labour. Every effort was made to enforce the decree. The penalty ordained for disobedience was death. But such a hard and fast system proved impossible to maintain. It was not indeed unusual in the ancient world to take similar measures against profiteering at a special crisis. But the present state of things was no passing emergency. It was a permanent and deep-rooted disorder of the economic life of the world, and the only consequence of Diocletian's decree was to discourage production. Finding it impossible to grow food or manufacture goods at a profit, men simply abandoned the struggle and swelled the ranks of the unemployed.

Such, then, was the tragic climax to which Rome's thousand years of history had brought her. Her political and social institutions had been built up by a slow accumulation of reforms and adjustments improvised to meet the needs of the moment, seldom logically thought out, but based on a profound instinct for continuity of tradition. Even under the Empire this evolutionary development had been for a while continued; but the inherent character of the imperial régime and of the many problems which it was called upon to face, had step by step impelled its rulers towards a new conception of government, till at length the old elastic process of organic growth had been replaced by a stereotyped, cast-iron system that was a complete negation of all that Rome had stood for. Constitutionalism had given way to despotism. The old passion for freedom had been swallowed up in a condition of society scarcely distinguishable from State slavery. The civilization which Rome had given to the world had by its very nature destroyed all chance of its survival. The best that can be said for Diocletian's system was that many of its features were continued under the rule of his successors, and that for nearly a century the threat of extinction by the barbarian invaders was successfully staved off.

For this respite Diocletian's military reorganization must have been to a large extent responsible. But in the first instance, as seems probable, the reorganization itself was due to a serious *débâcle* in the East. For in 297 Galerius, being summoned by Diocletian to meet a new threat from the Persians, suffered severe defeat; and though he swiftly retrieved it by a subsequent victory, the incident may have opened the Emperor's eyes to the need for a permanent striking-force. In Europe the barbarians' activities both on the Rhine and the Danube were held well in check; and the only important trouble was the revolt of a certain Carausius, commander of the flotilla then stationed at Boulogne against raids of German pirates. In 287 he established in Britain an independent Empire which lasted till 297, when his successor Alexander was at length overthrown. Apart from this temporary defection the unity of the Empire was successfully maintained. In 305, in accordance with his own arrangement, Diocletian duly resigned; and though troubles which immediately followed compelled him to come out of his retirement and intervene to put things right, he promptly returned to the luxurious palace which he had built at Spalato on the Dalmatian coast. From his comfortable seclusion no further appeals could drag him. 'If you could see my cabbages,' he is said to have written, 'you would not wish me to abandon this happy life.' Nine years later he died peacefully in his bed.

CHAPTER XXXI

THE EMPIRE IN DECLINE

I. THE CAUSES OF DECAY

THE reforms of Diocletian, though for the time being at least they regalvanized it into fresh life, could not disguise the fact that the Empire was slowly dying; and it is time to ask ourselves the question—what was it dying of? The diagnosis is not easy; and many varied causes have been suggested by historians; but it goes without saying that no one cause was of itself responsible. In the first place, it is obvious that no civilization will survive unless the standard of life, necessary to its continuance, can be permanently maintained. At the present day the provision of adequate supplies presents no difficulty, and it is rather the problem of distributing them that puzzles our statesmen. In the Roman world it was different. The slow but steady growth of large urban populations, the multiplication of unproductive services such as the administrative bureaucracy, and the necessity of keeping the armed forces clothed and fed—all these combined to place an intolerable strain on the producers of primary commodities.[1] From the second century onwards successive rulers had recognized the need for increasing the Empire's supply of food, metals, and other raw materials. The method they had adopted was the very natural one of bringing more land under cultivation and sinking fresh mines. But this alone was not sufficient; for soil becomes exhausted and mines are soon worked out, unless scientific devices are discovered for their further exploitation; and the trouble was that in the Roman Empire not merely was the skill of both farmers and miners declining, but the progress of applied science had come to a standstill. Few, if any, new tools appear to have been invented; and, though manuring was carefully studied, no adequate rotation of crops was employed. Worst of all, the use of labour by masters, who were intent on quick profits, was sadly unintelligent.

Nothing, indeed, is more significant than the fact that the brilliant promise of scientific research which began in the period of the Hellenistic Empires had dwindled and decayed under the influence of Rome. It is true that the pundits of Alexandria continued their studies under the imperial rule; and in the field of medicine at any rate there was considerable advance. Galen, who flourished in the second century A.D., was accounted one of the greatest medical authorities in antiquity. Greek physicians were widely employed in the

[1] Added to all this was the fact that with the decline of wealth the demand for commodities also declined. Men cannot grow corn or make goods when nobody will buy them.

west; doctors were provided for the poor and surgeons for the army; and Rome itself became the centre of a school of medicine. Nevertheless, the Romans themselves produced no great physicians. They were by nature too practical to bother their heads about experimental inquiry for its own sake, and it is notable that even in Alexandria dissection of the human body ceased altogether by the middle of the second century A.D. Astronomy too was studied mainly for the purposes of navigation and the calendar; and the most characteristic achievement of imperial times was the perfection of architectural construction and of drainage systems. The absence of originality and enterprise in other directions was the more deplorable since during the first century B.C. the Greeks had seemed to be upon the verge of great discoveries. Heron of Alexandria had even got so far as experimenting with the principle of steam-power; and it is not impossible that if research had been pushed farther in this or other fields, inventions might have resulted which would have altered the whole future of Mediterranean civilization.

It is difficult to resist the conclusion that the loss of political liberty had somehow stifled the spirit of individual initiative. It is a striking fact, as we have seen, that after the second century A.D. literature and art had suffered complete decay. The same phenomenon occurred in the sphere of local self-government. Finding that they were in no real sense the masters of their own destiny, men lost the sense of individual responsibility. The better of them, too, were naturally tempted away into the imperial civil service; and thus a condition of affairs arose which inevitably discouraged real enterprise. Under a bureaucratic government subordinates came to rely on the guidance of their chief; and few were likely to undertake the responsibility of independent action, the credit for which, if it succeeded, would go to their imperial master, the blame, if it should fail, be visited upon themselves. Only too often emperors were jealously suspicious of real merit, and the civil servant who gained most approval was apt to be the one who asked no questions and obeyed.

So the spirit of originality and independence was slowly but surely crushed out; and men, deprived of a real ideal to live for, began to lose heart when times became dangerous and critical. Parents even ceased to care about raising a family, and the decline of the birth-rate among the more cultured class became a constant perplexity to the authorities. The practice of infanticide was one of the darkest features of life in the ancient world; but the fact is that men and women were weary and sick at heart, and their minds centred more and more on getting through life with a maximum of pleasure and a minimum of pain. 'Let us eat, drink, and be merry, for to-morrow we die.' The morale of the well-to-do was sapped by luxury; and among the proletariat of the towns the popularity of gladiatorial shows and other hideous spectacles was a symptom of callous degeneracy. Meanwhile, for the poor tiller of the soil innumerable misfortunes bred utter despair. No wonder that Diocletian found it difficult to bring back vital energy to a society so moribund.

II. MORAL AND RELIGIOUS TENDENCIES

But there was another side to the picture. For it would be absurd to deny that in the moral sphere Greco-Roman civilization had brought gain as well as loss. Education had taught men to use their reason; and the Stoic philosophy in particular, though by the nature of things it could only reach the more intellectual minds, had wrought many beneficent results. 'All men are members of one brotherhood', Seneca had said, and the great lawyers of the third century had applied the principle in their juristic practice. Throughout the imperial era, in fact, we can discern the growth of a humaner outlook. The treatment of slaves, for example, steadily improved. Under the Republic the slave possessed no rights, being completely at the mercy of his master; and in the reign of Augustus so fine a gentleman as Horace could callously rate the crucifixion of a slave—for gobbling up the dinner scraps—as less heinous an offence than to backbite an acquaintance. But in the better households relations between master and slave were cordial; and a century later the Younger Pliny tells how on festal occasions he used to retire into an out-of-the-way corner of his house so as not to be a spoil-sport to his servants' merrymaking. Manumission too became increasingly common. Slaves were allowed to save up pocket-money and so purchase their freedom, and step by step legislation was enacted to protect their rights. Hadrian prohibited masters from torturing them; and Antoninus transferred maltreated slaves from the offending owner to another. Finally we find the great lawyer Ulpian insisting that by nature all men are equal, and that when disputes arose about rights of ownership the alleged slave should be given the benefit of a doubt.

The humanitarian tendency of the later Roman Empire had been frequently illustrated by the charitable benefactions made in the interest of poor children. The status of women, too, had shown a marked advance, and in the ordinary affairs of life the ladies of the upper class came to play a more open and more active part; so that we hear of women who became barristers and doctors. Even animals came in for an increasing share of attention, and amongst other poems written about pets there were two by the Emperor Hadrian, commemorating a favourite horse and a favourite hound.

So far had four centuries of Greco-Roman civilization and its attendant philosophies served to humanize men's relations with their fellow creatures. But individuals have, before all else, to face their own difficulties in life; and as these difficulties grew and world-wide misery prevailed, their hearts began to fail them. The stern doctrine of the Stoic, defiant of adversity, was too coldly rational to appeal to more than a few. The orthodox religion of the State could no longer stir enthusiasm. The natives of the Western provinces still maintained the worship of their local gods, considering them potent to ensure good harvests or avert a plague. But in such crude magic-mongering there was nothing to satisfy the cravings of the human soul; and under the miserable circumstances of their precarious life on earth men and women ardently desired some assurance of a better life hereafter. Some found it in the worship of the Jewish Jehovah; for thousands of Jews had settled in Italy and there were several synagogues in Rome. Others found it, or thought they found it, in the mystery religions of the East, which, since the time when we first spoke of them, had gained an increasing hold upon the West. But besides these, all manner of superstitious practices had been brought from the Levant by slaves or traders. The cult of the great Earth Mother from Asia Minor had long since taken root in Rome. The worship of Baal had been imported from Heliopolis, now Baalbeck in Syria. Even Emperor worship had been contaminated by ritual borrowed from the worship of the Sun and introduced by Aurelian after his campaigns in the East.

During the third century A.D., in short, religion was becoming a dominant factor in men's lives. Superstition was rampant. The reign of reason was over. For men, feeling that it had failed them, relinquished the belief (first learnt from the Greeks) that hard thinking would solve all problems whether human or divine. So abandoning the effort to *understand* the mysteries of existence, they turned to seek comfort and hope in the blind working of their own inner emotions. Ecstasy was the principal feature in the oriental cults—ecstasy in which the worshipper was uplifted by a sense of communion with the deity. But in spite of much talk of ritual purification and release from the burden of sin, there is little to show that the devotees of such religions came to lead better lives; and it was a short step from such shallow emotionalism to a condition of fatalistic despair. 'What will be, will be,' was coming more and more to be the prevailing attitude towards life. But out of the darkness of pagan despair there was to dawn a new hope—the hope of the Christian Faith.

To a superficial observer there might have seemed to be little reason to distinguish Christianity from the other numerous cults; and the striking resemblances between them have already been noted. The differences, however, were fundamental. In the first place the central figure of the other religions, such as Isis or Mithras, for example, were legendary heroes; whereas the foundation of the Christian creed was laid on the known character of an historical man. Then, again, it is obvious that among the early Christians, uplifted as they were by an ecstasy of devotion, which often led them to speak with unintelligible tongues, there was at first a danger lest they should have remained content with a faith precariously based on mere emotional inspiration; for, when emotions fade, as they are bound to do, little or nothing is left behind. But such a danger was averted by the genius of St. Paul. With an intellectual honesty, as profound as it was penetrating, he strove to understand what he felt, and to define the relation between God and Jesus in terms which became the basis of the Church's theological doctrine. At the same time, too, and in part under the influence of St. Paul's missionary zeal, the organization of the local Christian communities had developed rapidly. At the head of each was an overseer or *episcopus*, from which term our own word 'bishop' is derived. He was assisted by a council of elders or *presbyters*, and by an inferior order of servitors or *deacons*.

As time went on and as the new sect spread from one city to another its stirring and hopeful message caught the imagination of innumerable converts, who were weary to death of the unsatisfying make-believe of paganism. But it made many enemies too. The uncompromising stand which Christians made against the gross immorality of the times was a challenge which provoked an inevitable reaction. Nor were Christians, like the followers of Isis or of Mithras, prepared to acquiesce in the orthodox religion of the State. Their refusal to do homage to the pagan gods, and, in particular, to the statues of the Emperor, brought them into defiant opposition towards the government authorities, and from time to time fierce persecution was the result. Even Marcus Aurelius seems to have permitted stern measures, perhaps due to the difficulty of forcing Christians into the army. Under Decius and Valerian, too, there were many martyrs for the Faith, and Aurelian in his effort to impose Sun-worship on the Empire, issued a severe edict, the execution of which, however, was anticipated by his death. But a more tolerant spirit was growing among the officials of the Empire, and it was not until the reign of Diocletian that the persecution reached its height. Christians were then disfranchised, turned out of all official posts, their property was confiscated and their gatherings proscribed. The savagery of this attempt to suppress it was a true index of the enormous growth of the sect. Diocletian, in fact, had realized that against his despotism was pitted a force which, if not once and for all suppressed, would end by capturing the Empire.

The success of the Church was the more remarkable since its ranks were anything but united. Bitter controversies had long been dividing its members into rival groups. The first generation of Christians had lived their lives in the daily expectation of the immediate return of their Master. But, as the impulse of their enthusiasm began to wane, it was inevitable that more and more their thoughts should turn to thinking out what their religion meant. The theological ideas, formulated by St. Paul in the course of his extemporized letters, and further developed by the writer of the Fourth Gospel, were now endlessly discussed. Controversy centred round the exact significance of the Incarnation—in what sense was Jesus both human and divine? In such discussions the conception and terminology of Greek philosophy—the only existing vehicle of accurate reasoning—played a highly important part. In particular, Christian theologians were much influenced by a school of thought known as the Gnostics, who believed that the key to personal salvation lay in the intellectual contemplation of the nature of the Deity and of His relationship with human kind. That, God having made man in His own image, there was necessarily a link between the human and divine, was not difficult to argue; but to define the personality of Christ was a more perplexing problem. In the second century a certain Marcion declared that Jesus was in no true sense man at all, but God masquerading, as it were, in human form. A little later Clement of Alexandria, starting from a different basis, sought to identify Him with the Spirit of Divine Wisdom or Reason which permeated the Universe, and so to show that there was nothing illogical in the idea that God should take human form. So the controversy ran on until at the beginning of the fourth century, and almost simultaneously with Diocletian's abdication of the throne, it blazed up with yet greater violence in Alexandria once more. This time the champion of the new conception was the famous Arius. Jesus, he declared, if something more than man, was also something less than God; and the Church was rent in twain by this tremendous challenge to the Apostolic Faith.

Denunciations and counter-denunciations were flung this way and that; and nothing is more significant of the change which had come over the world than the vehement intensity with which these theological problems were debated. It seemed as though all the ardours and emotions of the human mind, long paralysed by the slow stagnation of the imperial régime, had burst suddenly into new life. A society which had long since ceased to care much about anything had at last found something about which it cared very much. The world stood upon the threshold of a new epoch. As the culture of ancient civilization—political and social, literary and artistic—sank into irretrievable decay, it was to become the seed-bed of a new order of things; and when we pass from the reign of Diocletian to the reign of Constantine the Great we enter a new phase of human development in which the supremacy of the religious motive in the actual practice of men's lives was universally acknowledged and in which the foundations of medieval Christendom were destined to be laid.

CHAPTER XXXII

EPILOGUE

ON May 1st 305 Diocletian, according to the plan which he had himself laid down, abdicated his sovereignty and Maximian his fellow-Augustus did the same. Constantius in the West and Galerius in the East then automatically assumed the vacant roles. Their places as lesser partners or Caesars were by rights to have been filled by Maximian's son Maxentius and Constantius' son Constantine; but here a hitch occurred. For Galerius promoted in their stead two creatures of his own; and, to make doubly sure, detained the young Constantine at his court at Nicomedia in north-west Asia Minor. One night, however, Constantine succeeded in slipping away, crossed into Europe, and rode for dear life to join his father in Britain. A hue and cry went after him; but at each stage, as he passed, he destroyed the horses of the imperial post and so the pursuit was foiled. A year later, in 306, when Constantius died at York, the troops saluted this adventurous young man as his successor and Augustus of the West.

The title thus conferred was not to go unchallenged, and for several years, though maintaining his hold upon Britain and Gaul, Constantine's position remained in jeopardy. For the whole Empire was in turmoil. Maxentius assumed the throne in Italy, and his old father Maximian reappeared to assist him. Severus, a nominee of Galerius, being sent to contest this usurpation, was defeated, captured, and killed. Licinius, arriving on a similar mission, proved more successful; and Diocletian himself emerged from his retirement to give him official recognition as Augustus of the West. Meanwhile, though chafing under the interruption of his larger ambitions, Constantine held on to his provinces and bode his time.

In 311 Galerius' death brought him the opportunity at last; Licinius, though still officially the Augustus of the West, was severely pressed. On one side he was threatened with attack by Maximinus Daia, Galerius' co-ruler in Asia. In Italy Maxentius was openly defying him; and he was glad to leave the task of crushing this old rival to the hands of Constantine. Accordingly in 312 Constantine marched down on Rome. At the Mulvian Bridge across the Tiber he met and overthrew the enormous army which was marshalled for the city's defence. The river was in flood, the bridge collapsed, and thousands of fugitives, Maxentius among them, were lost in the swollen stream. In the following year Daia also was defeated by Licinius; and the two victorious rulers, after a brief inconclusive struggle, agreed to divide the Empire between them (314). But the truce could not last. Constantine had no faith in Diocletian's system of partitionment and was determined, if possible, to reunite the Empire once more under his own single rule. For nine years he nursed his resources and maintained a precarious peace. Then in 323, with an enormous host over 100,000 strong, he struck his blow. Licinius was first beaten at Adrianople, then driven out of Byzantium, and finally went down in a great battle fought near Chrysopolis, the modern Scutari. Constantine was thereby left in sole occupation of the imperial throne.

The importance of Constantine's victory lay in something far more than the restoration of the Empire's political unity. His mother Helena, if tales are true, had been a Christian; and in the early days of his Gallic rule he himself must clearly have pondered on the meaning and appeal of the persecuted faith. As he was about to march on Italy to the overthrow of Maxentius he is said to have seen in the sky the vision of a cross athwart the sun and above it the legend *In hoc vince* or 'Herein conquer'. Whatever the truth of the story, it is certain that he took the Christian monogram ☧ as the badge he wore on his helmet, and after the victory at the Mulvian Bridge inscribed it also on his soldiers' shields. It was not till eleven years later that he formally undertook to receive Christian instruction as a catechumen and only shortly before his death was he actually baptized. Nevertheless, from the moment when after the battle of the Mulvian Bridge he attained the supremacy of the West, he must have made up his mind that the long-drawn conflict between the Empire and the Church must end, and could only end, in the triumph of the latter; and in the following year he issued at Milan his historic Edict proclaiming toleration of the Christian Faith. His championship of the cause assisted him greatly in his struggle with Licinius, and upon it was set the seal of his final victory in 323. From that moment it was certain that the Empire must be one not politically alone but in religion too. Nothing could be more significant of the momentous change than the fact that two years later Constantine himself was called upon to mediate in a great internal controversy which was rending the Church in twain. The Alexandrian preacher Arius, as we have seen above, was at this time expounding his doctrine that Jesus was not in a full sense God. To decide this crucial question, a great Church Council—the first ever to be held—was summoned at Nicaea on the southern shore of the Sea of Marmora. Three hundred bishops were present. The vast majority of these rallied strongly to the vigorous lead given by another Alexandrian called Athanasius, then a mere deacon of the Church. In accordance with his view a creed was formulated[1] denouncing as heretical whoever might maintain that

[1] Not the creed nowadays known as the Nicene Creed.

'there was a time when Christ was not'. Thus was established the orthodox doctrine of Jesus' Divinity. But, despite this decision, Arianism persisted, and even Constantine himself received his baptism at the hands of an Arian bishop. By an unlucky accident, too, the heresy gained a strong hold upon the barbarian invaders who settled in the European half of the Empire and thus served to intensify the widening rift between the West and the East.

Even more, however, was this fatal cleavage hastened by the policy of the very man whose main ambition was to check it. For, as every one knows, the reign of Constantine was marked by the great decision to transfer the imperial capital from Italy to the shores of the Bosphorus. Rome had long since ceased to count for very much as a political centre. Diocletian did not even trouble to set foot within the city till the year of his retirement; and from a strategic point of view it is not difficult to see the advantages of a capital more centrally placed between the European and the Asiatic fronts. In 326, accordingly, on the site of the old Byzantium were traced the foundations of the new city, Constantinople. For four years thousands of slaves and craftsmen were employed on the great work. Streets were laid out, leading to a fine oval market-place or Forum. Circuses, baths, churches, and theatres rose on the beautiful shores overlooking the waters of the Golden Horn; and when in 330 the town was solemnly dedicated, Roman aristocrats and other important persons from all over the Empire were compelled to leave their homes and settle down in the new quarters so magnificently prepared for them. Yet, for all the splendour of its execution, the grandiose conception was an irretrievable mistake. For the new capital, while it became the home and stronghold of what remained of Hellenic culture, was too much exposed to Asiatic influences to escape their dangerous lure. Brilliant as was the civilization which for a thousand years and more was destined to survive in proud isolation upon the shores of the Bosphorus, it owed at least as much to the Orient as to Europe. In other words, with the transference of the Empire's capital east-wards, the centre of the Empire's gravity shifted eastwards too; and whatever hope there still might have been of saving the Western provinces from their impending doom was now lost beyond recall.

For the unity of control, which Constantine himself had so laboriously re-established, did not survive his death in 337. His three sons redivided the Empire; and at the very moment when its frontiers were once again beginning to crumble both in East and West, its strength was sapped by a fresh series of disputes, murders, and usurpations. Another quarter of a century passed in the confused turmoil of internal and external wars; and then in 361, on the death of Constantius, the last survivor of Constantine's three sons, the sole charge of the Empire passed for a brief period into the hands of their cousin Julian. This remarkable man had already won considerable success in the defence of Gaul against the Alamannic and Frankish invaders; but, though called upon to spend most of his days in campaigning, he was a philosopher at heart, sensitive, earnest, and humane. As a result of his studies, he had abandoned the Christian faith, and on attaining supreme power he made it his object to restore an enlightened paganism as the official creed of the State. He revived old cults, removed Christians from posts in the army, and by an organized campaign of propaganda and preaching endeavoured to re-convert the mass of his subjects. Some of his subordinates were less squeamish than their chief, and adopted more violent methods. But whether by sweet reasonableness or by active persecution the tide of Christianity was not to be turned; and when after a reign of two years Julian fell in battle against the Persians beyond the Tigris the religious issue no longer stood in doubt. Some twenty years later Theodosius (379–395) completely turned the tables. Himself a baptized Christian, and profoundly influenced by Ambrosius the Bishop of Milan, he abolished the old State cults, demolished the pagan statues, and converted the temples into Churches of the Faith. It was highly significant that towards the end of his reign he himself fell under the bishop's ban for atrocities committed by his troops, and was only readmitted to the Christian communion after doing public penance in the cathedral at Milan. Henceforward, in short, the Church was not merely, as Constantine had intended, the prop and ally of the imperial monarchy: it had become the sovereign power in the State; and thus were laid the foundations of a new form of society in which the authority of kings and princes was held to be derived not merely from God, but from God's representative on earth.

The medieval conception of the Papal Church was indeed the most important legacy of the Empire, on the institutions of which its ecclesiastical machinery was to a large degree modelled. But at the very moment of giving birth to this great religious conception, the Empire itself, as a political unit, fell finally into the throes of dissolution. During the aftermath of Constantine's reign, the Persian Empire in Mesopotamia had seemed the most dangerous enemy; but in reality far worse trouble was brewing on the Danubian front. There on the north bank of the river in the abandoned province of Dacia, as well as farther east along the Black Sea littoral, vast numbers of Goths had settled down to peaceful and civilized habits; and many, as we have hinted, had even been converted to Christianity by Arian missionaries. But now, suddenly as a tempest, out of the heart of Russia there burst the destructive hordes of a new and more barbarous folk. Foiled in their long attempt to conquer China, the Huns had travelled westwards through the Asiatic wastes, a hideous, dwarfish people with dark yellow skins and narrow, beady eyes, great riders, living on horseback, irresistible in the charge of their swarming squadrons, tireless in slaughter, and utterly without remorse. In 375 they had crossed the River Volga on rafts and swept down towards the south. Fleeing in terror, the unhappy Goths crowded in hundreds of thousands to the Danube bank, supplicating permission to cross. Vast numbers were ferried over, but at last the Romans would take no more. But though the refugees were starving, fresh bands soon forced an entrance and spread confusion and destruction through the Balkan provinces. In 378 they found their way to the gates of Adria-nople, and there was fought a great battle in which the Emperor Valens fell and the flower of the Roman army was utterly destroyed. After pressing forward within view of Constantinople itself, the Goths turned away again. Theodosius, who in the following year succeeded to the throne, persuaded them to settle in Dalmatia. But the respite was brief. In 395, when Theodosius died, the Empire was entrusted to his two feeble sons, the Eastern half to Arcadius, and the Western to Honorius, assisted by the Vandal general Stilicho. Within a few weeks the Goths were up once more. Alaric, their leader, who had grown weary of serving under the Roman flag, led a great band southward to plunder and ravage Greece. In 400 he marched on Italy itself. Panic reigned, and the Emperor Honorius fled. But on Easter Day 402, when the Goths were celebrating the festival, his general, Stilicho, took them by surprise and by a great victory won in the neighbourhood of Turin succeeded in driving them back. But the defence of the frontier was now breaking down hopelessly. In 406 Vandals and Suevi, harassed by the Huns, pressed through the Alpine passes. Once again through Stilicho's efforts Italy was saved. But Gaul was left at the invaders' mercy. The legions deserted Britain; and the Western provinces were lost beyond recovery. Meanwhile Honorius, who had taken up his quarters in the safe seclusion of the Ravenna marshes, remained selfishly indifferent to his subjects' fate. In 408, as the result of some mean intrigue, he put Stilicho to death; and Alaric, learning of the removal of his chief antagonist, marched down on Rome itself. The inhabitants bought him off with gold. In 409 he again appeared outside the walls, and then again retired. Finally in 410 the tragedy came. The city was entered, and despite Alaric's instructions a hideous massacre ensued. Houses and churches were ransacked and then the barbarians drifted away to seek plunder in other towns.

It would serve no purpose to continue further the story of the Empire's dismemberment. Though emperors continued to reign in Italy,[1] no permanent rally occurred; and while behind the strong walls of Constantinople the Emperors of the East maintained a precarious safety by paying tribute to the Huns, Gaul and Spain were gradually repeopled by the invading hordes who crossed the Rhine. When at last the

---

[1] The last of these was Romulus, nicknamed the 'Little Augustus', whose abdication in 476 was followed by the barbarian rule of Odovacer, a mercenary leader from the North.

Hunnish inroad under Attila was beaten back at the battle of Châlons in 451, it was more to the prowess of the Visigoth settlers than to the Roman troops, which fought beside them, that western Europe owed its escape from this last and most terrible menace.

So ended the history of the Roman Empire in a welter of human misery most terrible to contemplate. Few fates can have been more tragic than the plunge of this highly civilized society into a condition of semi-barbarism. Where prosperous cities had stood were smouldering ruins. Men and women, bred in the security of comfortable homes, were driven out to die in the waste country-side. Desperate peasants rose and murdered their masters and then perished themselves from starvation. Cultivated fields reverted to moorland and forest. The Dark Age had set in.

Yet it must not for a moment be supposed that all Rome's work was lost. The barbarian invaders, settling down side by side with the remnant of the Romanized inhabitants, were ready to learn from these. The provincialized Latin speech, for instance, developed under Frankish domination into the earliest form of French. Latin too was utilized for a primitive codification of unwritten Germanic law. Many Roman customs, such as the personal tenure of land, were in part at least adopted; and Roman methods of building—to which the great architectural developments of the Byzantine or Eastern Empire gave a new and brilliant trend—inspired the erection of great Christian basilicas and churches in Italy and the West. It was indeed in the religious sphere that the influence of Rome was most permanent and profound. We have already noted how the Papacy itself was based on a conception deriving in the last resort from the secular institutions of the imperial monarchy. The unity of Christendom under its single head became the ideal of the medieval Church just as the unity of the civilized world had been achieved under the Emperor's rule. Even the organization of ecclesiastical machinery was modelled on the lines of the old civil administration. Bishops had been posted at the chief city in each province and ruled it as their 'diocese'. The discipline which they enforced on their subordinates owed much to the old

Roman conceptions of official authority; and the 'Canon' law administered in the Church courts was closely related to the principles of Rome's jurisprudence. The language of liturgy and theology alike was of course exclusively Latin. Above all, whatever intellectual activity survived through the Dark Age was nurtured in the Church; and monastic establishments, when these arose, were the chief repositories of classical manuscripts as well as the homes of scholars and the educators of the young.

As time advanced the tradition of Roman culture, thus jealously preserved, became increasingly the object of study. As the Western World emerged from the chaos of the Dark Age and a more or less stable society was rebuilt upon the basis of national or feudal States, the chief need which confronted their rulers was to find methods of enforcing law and order; and nothing was more natural than that they should have looked back to the only example of settled government of which written record was available. From the twelfth century onward, therefore, much attention was devoted to the study of Roman law. The importance of this revival can scarcely be exaggerated. Indeed, the most valuable legacy which the Roman people bestowed upon posterity was beyond a doubt their legal system. To the building up of that system various factors had contributed—first and foremost, of course, the instinct for just dealing which seems to have been from the earliest times a part of the national character. At the same time it should be remembered that the tendency of Roman lawyers was to concentrate upon cases which actually arose, or might arise, *in practice* rather than upon the search for abstract principles of justice; and in co-ordinating and simplifying the resultant mass of contradictory or redundant formulae, much was due, as we have seen, to the influence of Greek philosophic thought. In the Byzantine Empire this process reached its culmination in the great work of codification accomplished under the Emperor Justinian in the sixth century A.D. In Justinian's *Digest*, as it was called, we find a clear enunciation of such fundamental principles as that 'No man shall be a judge in his own case', 'No appeal for mercy shall be made while the case is being tried'; and even that 'it befits the Monarch to declare himself bound by the laws'. At the same time the conception of 'the Monarch's right both to make and to interpret the laws' was very deeply rooted in the mind of the late Empire; and during medieval times this conception was to play a highly important part in establishing and justifying the absolute power of kings. Thus side by side with the authoritative claim of the Church a similar and scarcely less authoritative claim was eventually made by the secular rulers. Under such circumstances it was not surprising that an almost blind obedience to authority became the prevailing attitude in an age, which, in the absence of other ideals and knowing no other example of a well-ordered society, inevitably drew its political and intellectual inspiration from the example of Rome. It was not until at the Renaissance the rediscovery of Greek ideals reawoke in men's minds the spirit of fearless inquiry, that they ventured once more to think freely for themselves. The results are with us still.

Thus in the fabric of Western civilization both past and present there are inextricably interwoven the twin threads of our classical inheritance. But, when all is said, it was the Roman faculty for organizing life far more than the Hellenic subtlety of thought and taste which has served to transform for ever the destinies of Europe. For, if to Greece we owe in a large measure our artistic and literary forms, our methods of reasoning, and, in the last resort, our science, the influence of Rome's political and legal codes—to say nothing of her language, her engineering, and her architecture—may be traced on every hand. So our debt to the *aesthetic and theoretic* genius of the one ancient people is balanced or rather supplemented by our even greater debt to the *practical* genius of the other. Without either Greece or Rome our whole outlook on the world would be something very different from what it is; and according to the bias of personal temperament or of the age in which we live, we incline to draw our inspiration from the one or the other in varying degrees. Where men seek to solve the problems of existence by an intellectual effort to understand more fully the mysteries of their own selves or of the world around them, there, consciously or unconsciously they are following in the wake of the Greek pioneers of thought, and such an effort will tend inevitably to produce the old result—a reasoned distrust of traditional beliefs and conventions, an opposition of the individual judgment to the dictates of authority, and a reaching forth to fresh and often disturbing experiments for the enlightening or improving of the world. Where, on the other hand, they prefer the more secure but less adventurous guidance of some well-established system of discipline and habit, where the moulding of character is held of more importance than the unfettered exercise of intellectual powers, where, above all, the independence of the individual is kept in strict subordination to the claims of community or State or Church, there—sometimes to our advantage, and sometimes to our bane—breathes the Spirit of Ancient Rome.

CHRONOLOGICAL TABLES

I. IMMIGRATIONS

c. 2000. Italian tribes cross Alps and settle round Northern Lakes.
c. 1500. Italians push southwards into Umbria, Latium, etc.
c. 900. Etruscans settle in Etruria and Western Umbria.
From 800 onwards, Greeks found colonies in Sicily and S. Italy.

II. ROME UNDER THE KINGS

*753. Foundation of Rome by Romulus from Alba Longa.
*715–673. Numa Popilius (Sabine), traditional founder of religious institutions.
*673–642. Tullus Hostilius (Latin) destroys Alba Longa.
*642–617. Ancus Martius (Latin) bridges Tiber and founds Ostia.
*616–579. Tarquinius Priscus (Etruscan) makes war on Latins.
*578–535. Servius Tullius (Etruscan ?) builds wall : Constitution by ' classes '.
*535–510. Tarquinius Superbus (Etruscan) completes Temple on Capitol.
510. Expulsion of Tarquin, who summons aid of fellow-Etruscans.
496. Defeat of Lars Porsenna at Lake Regillus.
(* These dates are purely traditional.)

III. THE EARLY REPUBLIC

External	*Internal*
494.	Secession of plebs to Sacred Mount : creation of tribunes
493. Roman alliance with Latin League.	
c. 480. Volscian War (Coriolanus)	
477. War against Veii : battle of *Cremera*.	
474. Etruscans defeated at *Cumae*.	
c. 460. War against Aequi (Cincinnatus)	

External	*Internal*
451.	Decemviri begin tabulation of Laws.
450.	Decemviri (Appius Claudius) deposed.
449.	Valerio-Horatian Laws : rights to plebeians.
445.	*Lex Canuleia :* permitting inter-marriage of Orders.
431. Aequi defeated at *Mt. Algidus.*	
396. Capture of *Veii* by Camillus.	
390. Rome sacked by Gauls.	
376.	Licinian proposals : violent strife results.
367.	Licinian proposals become law : one consul plebeian, etc.
360–50. Gallic Invasions.	
287.	*Lex Hortensia* gives plebescita authority of law.

IV. CONQUEST OF ITALY

A. First Samnite War (343–41) : Rome intervenes in Campania to aid *Capua.*

B. Latin War (340) : Latins and Campanians defeated at *Veseris* : end of League.

C. Second Samnite War (327–04) : Rome intervenes at *Naples* : defeated at *Caudine Forks* (321) : founds *Luceria* and is defeated at *Lautulae* (315) : Via Appia begun (312) : Samnites joined by Marsi (308) : peace (304).

D. Third Samnite War (299–290) : Romans capture *Bovianum* (298) : defeat Samnites and Gauls at *Sentinum* (296) : found colony at *Venusia* (291).

E. War with Pyrrhus (282–75) : Pyrrhus defeats Romans at *Heraclea* (280) : and at *Ausculum* (279) : crosses to Sicily (278) : returns and is defeated at *Beneventum* (275) : *Tarentum* surrenders (272).

F. Extension of citizenship : civitas given to Latium : to Sabines (268) : half-franchise, to Campania and S. Etruria : Greek cities of South become free allies : rest of Italy, Socii.

G. Foundation of colonies : *Ardea* (442) : *Setia* (382) : *Sutrium, Nepete* (383) . Antium (338) : Anxur (329) : *Fregellae* (328) : *Luceria* (314) : *Saticula* (313) : *Interamna* (312) : *Sora* (303) : *Alba* (303) : *Carsioli* (302) : *Narnia* (299) : Sinuessa (296) : *Venusia* (291) : *Hatria* (289) : Sena (283) : *Ariminum* (268) : *Paestum* (273) : *Beneventum* (268) : *Cremona, Placentia* (218) : *Bononia* (189) : Parma, Mutina (183) : *Aquileia* (184).

(*N.B.*—Latin Colonies in italics.)

V. FIRST PUNIC WAR (264-41)

A. *Romans gain hold on Sicily :* seize *Messana* and defeat Hiero and Carthaginians (264) : joined by Hiero (263) : defeat Hanno at *Agrigentum* (262).

B. *Romans gain control at sea :* defeat Carthaginians off *Mylae* (260) : off *Ecnomus* (256) : send Regulus to Africa (256) : where he is defeated (255) : capture *Panormus* (254).

C. *Romans' failure at sea :* fleets wrecked (255 and 253) : defeat off *Drepana* (249) : siege of *Lilybaeum* foiled by tactics of Hamilcar Barca (247).

D. *Romans' final effort :* new fleet built : Catulus wins victory off *Aegates Islands* (241) : Carthaginians compelled to evacuate Sicily and pay large indemnity.

VI. BETWEEN THE WARS

239.   Annexation of *Sardinia* (made province with *Corsica,* **227**).

232.   C. Flamininus parcels out *Ager Gallicus.*

229.   Illyrian Queen Teuta's pirate lieutenant Demetrius defeated.

228.   *Corcyra* and strip of coast brought under Roman protectorate.

226-22. *Gallic invasions :* Romans defeat Gauls at *Telamon* (225) : capture *Mediolanum* (222) : carry *Via Flaminia* to *Ariminum* (220).

237-219.   *Carthaginian conquest of Spain :* Hamilcar overruns south-west (237-29) : Hasdrubal founds *New Carthage :* under pressure from Rome and Massilia, undertakes not to cross Ebro (226) : Hannibal attacks *Saguntum* (219).

VII. SECOND PUNIC WAR

	Spain, Africa, etc.	Italy.	Sicily and Macedon.
218.	Hannibal leaves New Carthage (May).	Battles of *Ticinus* and *Trebia* (Dec.).	Sempronius' army returns from Sicily.
217.	Naval repulse of Carthaginians at Ebro.	Battle of *Trasimene*: Hannibal enters Apulia: Fabius, as Dictator, avoids open battle.	
216.		Battle of *Cannae*: *Capua*, etc. join Hannibal.	Philip of Macedon invades Illyria.
215.	Carthaginian attack on Sardinia: Hasdrubal repulsed at Ebro.	Hannibal attempts to win port at *Naples*.	Philip's alliance with Hannibal.
214.	Hasdrubal recalled to Africa: Romans capture *Saguntum*.		*Syracuse* besieged by Marcellus. Carthaginians aid *Syracuse*.
213.		Hannibal captures *Tarentum*.	Marcellus captures *Syracuse*.
212.		Romans blockade *Capua*.	
211.	Scipios defeated on *Baetis*.	Hannibal's dash on Rome: *Capua* reduced.	Rest of Sicily reduced.
210.	P. Scipio arrives in Spain.		
209.	Scipio takes *New Carthage*.		
208.	Scipio defeats Hasdrubal at *Baecula*.	But Hasdrubal escapes towards Italy.	
207.	Scipio defeats Carthaginians at *Ilipa*.	Hasdrubal defeated at *Metaurus*.	
206.	Scipio captures *Gades*.	Hannibal at bay in *Bruttium*.	
205.		Scipio (consul) prepares invasion of Africa.	Rome makes peace with Philip.
204.	Scipio lands in Africa: besieges *Utica*.		
203.	Scipio defeats Syphax and Gisco.	Mago driven from *Liguria*: Hannibal recalled.	
202.	Battle of *Zama*.		

VIII. EXTENSION OF EMPIRE

A. *Conquest of Cisalpine Gaul, etc.*
    (i) Defeat of *Insubres* (196) : defeat of *Boii* (191) : colony at *Aquileia* (181).
    (ii) Conquest of *Liguria* (180).

B. *Spain.* Divided into Hither and Further Province (197) : insurrection quelled by Cato (195).

C. *Second Macedonian War* (200–196).
    Philip defeated at *Cynoscephalae* (197) : Flamininus proclaims freedom of Hellas (196).

D. *War with Antiochus of Syria* (192–190).
    Antiochus invades Greece (192) : defeated at *Thermopylae* (191) : retires to Asia Minor and is defeated at *Magnesia* (190) : Volso attacks *Galatians* (189).

E. *Third Macedonian War, etc.* (172–167).
    (i) Perseus (successor to Philip in 179) defeated at *Pydna* by Aemilius Paullus (168).
    (ii) Macedon split into four (167) : 1,000 Achaeans deported to Rome (167).
    (iii) Revolt of Andriscus quelled by Metellus (148) : Macedon becomes a province (146).
    (iv) *Corinth* sacked by Mummius : Greece under Macedonian governor (146).

F. *Third Punic War* (149–146)
  153. (i) Commission of Cato to settle between Carthage and Massinissa (153).
  149. (ii) Death of Cato : Romans attack *Carthage*.
  147. (iii) Scipio Aemilianus (consul) sent out to *Carthage*.
  146. (iv) Capture and destruction of Carthage. Africa becomes province.

G. *Spanish Wars*
  179. Governorship of T. Sempronius Gracchus.
  171. Latin colony at *Carteia* : natives protest against extortion.
  154. Revolt of Lusitanians.

150. Treachery of Galba prolongs revolt.	153. Revolt of Celtiberians partially quelled.
148. Rising of Viriathus.	
140. Treaty repudiated by Caepio : murder of Viriathus.	143. Revolt encouraged by Viriathus's success.
	141. Siege of *Numantia* begun.
138. D. Junius Brutus quells revolt.	
	137. Mancinus forced to surrender.
	133. Scipio Aemilianus takes Numantia.

H. *Asia Minor.* Attalus III of Pergamum bequeaths kingdom (133) : made Province (128).
I. *Transalpine Gaul.* Campaign against Allobroges and Arverni (125) : formation of Gallia Narbonensis (122) : colonization of *Narbo* (118).

IX.   PERIOD OF THE GRACCHI

A. *Tiberius Gracchus.* Tribune : land reforms : seeks re-election and is murdered (133).
B. *Interval.* Scipio champions Italians, death (129) : expulsion of allies from Rome (126) : F. Flaccus proposes Italian enfranchisement (125) : revolt of *Fregellae* (125).
C. *Caius Gracchus.* Returns from Sardinia (124) : tribune (123) : second tribunate and visit to Carthage (122) : death (121).
D. *Senatorial Reaction.* Land Commission dissolved (118) : squatter-tenants allowed free possession (111) : equestrian juries not upset.

X.   RISE OF MARIUS

A. *Jugurthine War*
    (i) Senate adjudicates between Adherbal and Jugurtha : Jugurtha seizes *Cirta* (112) : Bestia sent out but makes peace (111).
    (ii) Albinus's surrender (110) : Metellus makes headway and attacks *Zama Regia* (109).
    (iii) Marius elected consul for 107 : secures Eastern Numidia (107) : advance against *Mauretania* (106) : capture of Jugurtha by Sulla (105).
B. *Cimbrian War*
    (i) Previous disasters : Carbo defeated by Cimbri at *Noreia* (113) : Silanus defeated in Transalpine Gaul (109) : Cassius Longinus defeated by Tigurini near *Tolosa* (107) : Caepio and Manlius annihilated at *Arausio* (105), but Cimbri make for Spain.
    (ii) Marius on return from Africa reorganizes Roman army (104–102).
    (iii) Marius defeats Teutones and Ambrones at *Aquae Sextiae* (102) : but Cimbri and Tigurini invading Italy from north-east drive back Catulus on *R. Athesis.*
    (iv) Marius defeats Cimbri at *Vercellae* on Raudine Plain (101).
C. *Internal affairs and Marius's fall*
    (i) Piracy in East induces M. Antonius to annex Cilician coast (103).
    (ii) Revolt of Sicilian slaves (sequel to revolt of 134–31) led by Tryphon (104) : finally suppressed by Aquilius (100).

100 (iii) Marius, consul for sixth time, outshone by Saturninus and Glaucia, who, desiring re-election, seize Capitol and are killed (100).

98 **(iv)** Marius leaves Rome.

XI.   RISE OF SULLA

A. *Social War*

    (i) Expulsion **of** Italians from Rome (95).

91. (ii) Italian hopes roused by Drusus's programme : revolt follows his death.

90. (iii) Samnites penetrate *Campania* : Marsi overwhelm Rutilius : Marius takes command : siege of *Asculum* : Lex Julia placates waverers.

89. **(iv)** Sulla's successes in Campania : Lex Plauta Papiria gives franchise to individual Italians : rebels capitulate except at *Nola*, etc.

B. *Sulpicius and Marius*

88. (i) Sulla blockades *Nola* : is given command against Mithridates.

    (ii) Sulpicius. championing enfranchised Italians, offers command to Marius.

    (iii) Sulla marches on Rome : flight of Marius.

87. (iv) After strengthening Senate Sulla sails for East.

C. *Mithridatic War and Marian Reaction*

Mithridates of Pontus annexes Paphlagonia (105) : seizes Cappadocia (96) : ousted (92) : invades Bithynia and Roman province (88) : sends Archelaus to Greece, where Athens under Aristion rises against Rome (87).

Eastern Front	*Italy*
87. Sulla lands in Greece and reduces	Cinna and Marii seize Rome : massacres.
86. Athens : defeats Archelaus at *Chaeronea.*	Marius dies : Cinna in control of Rome.
85. Defeats Archelaus at *Orchomenos* : Fimbria drives Mithridates into Pergamum.	
84. Sulla imposes terms on Mithridates : overcomes Fimbria : returns to Greece.	Democrats prepare to resist Sulla. Cinna murdered by troops.

D. *Sulla's Return*

83. Sulla wins South Italy : democrats retire into the north.

82. Democrats held in north by Pompey and Crassus : younger Marius besieged at *Praeneste* : Samnites' dash on Rome : battle of *Colline Gate* (Nov.).

81–80. Sulla dictator. Reactionary Constitution : retires (79) : dies (78).

XII. RISE OF POMPEY

A. *Risings of Lepidus, Sertorius and Spartacus*

    (i) Lepidus's *coup* defeated by Catulus : Pompey gets Spanish command (77).

    (ii) Sertorius tries to secure Spain for Marians (83) : driven to North Africa : leads Lusitanian rising : reinforced by Lepidus's lieutenant Perpenna (77).

    (iii) Pompey reaches Spain (76) : Sertorius murdered (71) : Pompey returns home (71).

    (iv) Slaves rise under Spartacus (73) : overcome by Crassus (71) : remnant cut up by Pompey (71).

    (v) Consulship of Crassus and Pompey (70) : Sullan constitution annulled : Trial of Verres (70).

B. *Pirates and Mithridatic War*

Mithridates	Pirates
75. Claims Bithynia which Nicomedes bequeaths to Rome : supported by Tigranes of Armenia.	Expedition of Servilius Isauricus.
74. Lucullus and Cotta proceed against him.	
73-2. Mithridates driven from kingdom: flees to Tigranes	
69. Lucullus takes *Tigranocerta.*	Expedition of Metellus.
68. Lucullus abandons march on *Arxtaxata.*	
67. Senate orders supersession of Lucullus.	Lex Gabinia gives Pompey command : pirates suppressed.

C. *Pompey and Cicero.* Appointed under Lex Manilia (66).

Pompey	Italy
66. Mithridates flees to Crimea : dies (63).	Riots in Rome : Catiline plots with Piso.
65. Tigranes submits : Pompey in *Caucasus.*	Plot fails : Catiline's trial for extortion.
64. Gabinius in Syria : Pompey at *Jerusalem.*	Rullus's Land Bill : Rabirius's trial.
63. Settlement of East.	Cicero defeats Catilinarian conspiracy.
62. Pompey returns to Italy and disbands army (Dec.)	Manlius and Catiline killed (Jan.) : Clodius's profanation of Bona Dea (Dec.).

D. *Julius Caesar*

    Born (102) : escapes Sullan massacres (82) : serves in East (81) : returns to Rome (78) : studies in Rhodes (75) : elected Pontifex, returns to Rome (74) : quaestor in Further Spain (68) : aedile (65) : Pontifex Maximus (64) : praetor (62) : pro-praetor in Further Spain (61).

XIII. RISE OF CAESAR

A. *Caesar's Consulship* (59)

60. (i) Equites dispute contract for Asia : *concordia ordinum* breaks down : FIRST TRIUMVIRATE, Pompey, Crassus and Caesar : Caesar elected consul for 59.

59. (ii) Caesar consul : ignores Bibulus : confirms Pompey's acts and settles veterans.

58. (iii) Clodius procures Cicero's exile : Cato sent to Cyprus : Caesar goes to Gaul.

B. *Period of Caesar's Gallic Wars* (58–49)

Gaul	*Italy, etc*
58. Caesar rounds up *Helvetii* : drives *Suebi* (Ariovistus) beyond Rhine.	Clodius in control.
57. Subdues *Belgae* : sells *Aduatuci* as slaves : Crassus invades *Veneti*.	Cicero recalled (autumn) : Pompey food-controller : Ptolemy in Rome.
56. Brutus subdues *Veneti* : Crassus overruns *Aquitania* : conquest complete.	Clodius aedile : disunion of Pompey and Crassus : conference at *Lucca*.
55. Caesar defeats *Usipetes* : pursues across Rhine : reconnoitres *Britain*.	Pompey and Crassus consuls : Cicero retires : Gabinius restores Ptolemy.
54. Second invasion of Britain : *Cassivellaunus* overcome. Indutiomarus of *Treveri* heads revolt : *Eburones* under Ambiorix ambush Sabinus and Cotta.	Pompey gets Spanish command for five years but stays in Rome : Crassus invades North Mesopotamia winters in Syria : death of Julia.
53. Caesar crosses Rhine : hunts Ambiorix.	Crassus's disaster at *Carrhae*.
52. Vercingetorix of *Arverni* leads revolt : Caesar besieges *Avaricum* and *Alesia*.	Milo kills Clodius at *Bovillae* : Pompey sole consul : law of provinces.
51. Caesar captures *Uxellodunum*: completes settlement of Gaul.	Cicero in Cilicia : Marcellus works against Caesar.
50. Caesar cedes two legions to Pompey.	Curio negotiates at Rome : retires (Dec.).
49. Caesar crosses *Rubicon* (Jan. 11) : reduces Domitius at *Corfinium* (March) : reaches Rome (April).	Ultimate decree, Jan. 7 : Antony and Cassius flee to Caesar : Pompey sails East.

XIV. CIVIL WARS

Italy, Spain, Africa	*Sicily, Greece and East*
49. Caesar defeats Afranius at *Ilerda* : *Massilia* surrenders : Valerius secures Sardinia : Curio secures Sicily but is killed by Varus in Africa.	Pompey organizes army in Macedonia : Dolabella defeated by Pompeian fleet.
48. C. Rufus promulgates debt laws.	Caesar lands in Epirus (Jan.) : blockades Pompey at *Dyrrhachium* : battle of *Pharsalia* (Aug.) : Pompey killed in Egypt : Caesar in Alexandria.
47. Dolabella suppressed by Antony : Spain restive under Q. Cassius : Caesar quells legions (Sept.) : reaches Africa (Dec.).	Caesar gets upper hand at Alexandria : defeats Pharnaces at *Zela* : Pompeian fleet, defeated by Vatinius, retires to Africa.
46. Defeats Pompeians at *Thapsus* (April) : returns to Rome (July) : goes to Spain.	
45. Defeats Pompey at *Munda* (March) : Sext. Pompeius escapes : Caesar returns to Rome (Sept.).	
44. Preparations against Parthia: death (March 15) : Octavian arrives (April) : Antony besieges D. Brutus at *Mutina* (Nov.) : Cicero's ' Philippics '.	Brutus occupies Macedon : Cassius goes to Syria.
43. Antony defeated by Octavian and consuls : joins Lepidus in Gaul : Octavian consul : Triumvirate, Antony, Lepidus, Octavian : Proscription : death of Cicero.	Dolabella kills Trebonius : is defeated by Cassius : Brutus joins Cassius in Asia : coerce *Rhodes*, etc.
42. Sextus Pompeius in Sicily.	Brutus and Cassius defeated at *Philippi*.
41. Octavian settles veterans : L. Antonius besieged in *Perusia*.	Antony settles East : joins Cleopatra in Egypt.
40. Fall of *Perusia* : Compact of *Brundisium*.	Parthians overrun Syria.

Italy, Spain, Africa	*Sicily, Greece and East*
39. Bargain with S. Pompeius.	Ventidius defeats Parthians.
38. Octavian attacks Pompeius: is defeated.	Ventidius defeats Parthians at *Pacorus.*
36. Pompeius crushed : Lepidus's revolt.	Antony invades Parthia.
34. Octavian subdues *Dalmatia.*	Antony with Cleopatra.
32. War declared on Cleopatra.	Antony winters in Greece.
31.	Battle of *Actium* (Sept.).
30. Mutiny of Veterans in Italy.	Octavian in Egypt . death of Antony.

XV.   CONSTITUTIONAL

Magistrates	*Senate and Assemblies*
509. 2 consuls : quaestors : pontifex.	*Servian Constitution* adopted : comitia centuriata supreme : curiata ceremonial.
494. 2 tribuni plebis : soon raised to 10.	Comitia tributa elects tribunes.
449.	*Valerio-Horatian Law* : sanctions plebescita (i.e. resolutions of comitia tributa).
444. Military tribunes instead of consuls—as often during next 80 years.	
443. Censorship created for enrolment, etc.	
367. *Licinian Law* : one consul plebeian : creation of praetor for justice : 2 aediles.	
350. Plebeian first censor : praetor (337) : priest (300).	
327. *Pro*-consular power for Campanian War.	
311. Duo-viri navales instituted.	
287.	*Lex Horiensia* : Plebescites have force of law : power of popular Assembly grows.
242. Praetor peregrinus instituted.	
241.	Centuriata reorganized more democratically.
227. 2 additional praetors for Sicily and Sardinia	Punic War weakens power of Assembly and Senate becomes supreme.

Magistrates	*Senate and Assemblies*
180. *Lex Vilia* regulates cursus honorum.	
153. *Lex Aelia* gives religious ban on assembly.	
139.	Secret ballot in Comitia.
133, 123. Gracchi assert power of tribunate.	Senate's ultimate decree exercised.
88.	Sulla adds 300 equites to Senate.
81. Tribunate degraded by Sulla : who adds 2 praetors, thus providing 10 pro-magistrates.	Sulla gives Senate complete control of legislation and administration.
70. Tribunician power completely restored.	Assembly's power recovered.
67-6. Tribunes used by Pompey to gain command through popular vote.	

XVI. JUDICIAL

(i) *Lex Valeria de provocatione.* Appeal to Assembly (509).

(ii) XII Tables adopted by *Valerio-Horatian Law* (449).

(iii) Creation of praetor (367) : praetor peregrinus (242).

(iv) *Quaestio de Repetundis* created by *Lex Calpurnia* (149) : courts *de vi* and *de majestate* added subsequently.

(v) Juries transferred to equites (123) : restored to senators by Sulla, who adds courts *de peculata, inter sicarios, de falsis* (82).

(vi) Juries shared between senators, equites, tribuni aerarii (70).

(vii) Caesar reorganizes procedure (59) : abolishes tribuni aerarii (46).

I. AUGUSTUS (31 B.C.–A.D. 14)

A. CONSTITUTIONAL, etc.
    (i) *First scheme:* Augustus receives annual consulship (31–23) and proconsular powers for ten years (27).
        Second scheme: Tribunician powers and permanent proconsular powers (23).
    (ii) *Encroachments on senatorial sphere:* Curators of food-supply (22); prefect of food-supply (A.D. 6); curators of roads (20); prefect of watch (A.D. 6); prefect of city during Augustus' absences.
    (iii) *Finance:* Besides personal *patrimonium*, Augustus organizes *fiscus* for military expenditure, and gives assistance to senatorial *aerarium*.
    (iv) Laws for promotion of marriage, etc.: *Lex Julia* (18): *Lex Poppaea* (A.D. 9).

B. FOREIGN POLICY, etc.
  27–24. Augustus in Western provinces.
  22–19. Augustus in Greece and Asia Minor: settlement with Parthia and Armenia (20).
     17. Secular games.
     17. Sugambri cross Rhine and defeat Lollius: Tiberius given command and with Drusus' aid annexes *Raetia* (15): Silius annexes *Noricum* (15): Tiberius transferred to Danube and annexes Pannonia (12): Moesia becomes a province (11).
  12–9. Drusus' German campaigns (see Table XII): dies (9).
   9–6. Tiberius given German command: retires to Rhodes (6).
    4 A.D. Tiberius resumes German command.
  6–9 A.D. Diverted by Pannonian revolt: 9 A.D., Defeat of Varus.

C. PLANS FOR SUCCESSION:
    (i) 25. Julia marries *Marcellus* (dies 23).
    (ii) 21. Julia marries *Agrippa* (granted proconsular power, etc. 18: dies, 12.)
    (iii) 11. Julia marries *Tiberius* (trib. powers 6: retires 6): Julia disgraced, 2.
    (iv) After death of *L. Caesar* (A.D. 2) and *C. Caesar* (A.D. 4), Tiberius restored to favour: equal powers with Augustus (13 A.D.).

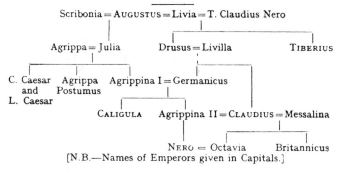

Scribonia = AUGUSTUS = Livia = T. Claudius Nero

Agrippa = Julia   Drusus = Livilla   TIBERIUS

C. Caesar Agrippa Agrippina I = Germanicus
and Postumus
L. Caesar

CALIGULA   Agrippina II = CLAUDIUS = Messalina

NERO = Octavia   Britannicus

[N.B.—Names of Emperors given in Capitals.]

II.   THE JULIO-CLAUDIAN EMPERORS

A.   TIBERIUS (A.D. 14–37).
   14. Mutiny of Rhineland and Pannonian legions.
   15. Germanicus' campaign in Germany (see Table XII).
   16. Germanicus' mission in East (see Table XIV).
   19. Germanicus quarrels with Piso: dies A.D. 19.
   23. Death of Tiberius' son Drusus.
   27. Tiberius retires to Capri: Sejanus (prefect of Praetorians since A.D. 17): supreme at Rome.
   29. Death of Livia: Agrippina and her children imprisoned.
   31. Fall of Sejanus.
B.   CALIGULA (37–41).
   40. Caligula's mock campaign on Rhine: embassy of Jews.
C.   CLAUDIUS (41–54).
   (i) *Policy of centralization:*
      (*a*) Growing importance of freedmen: secretaries of finance, correspondence, petitions, etc.
      (*b*) Concentration of imperial *fiscus* at Rome: imperial procurators receive judicial powers.
      (*c*) Trials *intra cubiculum.*
   (ii) *Extension of franchise:*
      (*a*) By individual grants.
      (*b*) Grants to communities, e.g. Anauni.
      (*c*) Charters of self-government to *municipia*, e.g. Verulamium or *coloniae*, e.g. Camulodunum and Cologne. [N.B.—Gauls promoted to Senate.]
   (iii) *Foreign policy:*
      43. Invasion of Britain (see Table XV).
      47. Corbulo's campaigns, e.g. Frisii and Chauci.
      42. Mauretania becomes province: Lycia (43): Thrace and Moesia (?) (46).
   (iv) *Court intrigues:*
      48. Claudius' wife Messalina marries Silius: forced to suicide.
      49. Claudius marries Agrippina, who marries her son Nero to Claudius' daughter Octavia (53): in his interest murders Claudius (54).
D.   NERO (54–68).
   (i) *External events:*
      (*a*) Under control of Seneca and Burrus (prefect of Praetorians) provincial administration carefully supervised.
      (*b*) *Parthian War* (see Table XIV): Corbulo's campaign in Armenia (57–60): surrender of Paetus at *Randeia* (62): compromise over Armenia (65).
      (*c*) *Rebellions* in Britain under *Boadicea* (61): in Palestine (66).
   (ii) *Internal events:*
      (*a*) 55, Pallas dismissed: Britannicus poisoned.
      (*b*) 61, Agrippina killed: 62, death of Burrus: Tigellinus, Prefect of Praetorians: Seneca retires.
      (*c*) Nero marries Poppaea.
   (iii) *Nero's unpopularity:*
      (*a*) Great Fire (64): persecution of Christians.
      (*b*) Piso's conspiracy (65): death of Seneca, etc.

(c) Nero leaves Rome for Greece (66).
(d) Revolt of Vindex in Gaul suppressed by Rhine legions under Verginius Rufus.
(e) Galba, governor of Hither Spain, makes bid for throne: wins over Praetorian Guard and its prefect, Nymphidius Sabinus: death of Nero (68).

III. THE CIVIL WAR

I. (a) 68, Oct., GALBA enters Rome: his discipline and economy estranges Praetorians.
   (b) 69, Jan., Galba adopts Piso, but is murdered by Praetorians, who proclaim OTHO.
II. (a) 69, Jan., Legions of upper and lower Rhine proclaim VITELLIUS.
   (b) (Apr.), *Caecina*, arriving through Switzerland, occupies Cremona: beaten yb Otho at Locus Castorum.
   (c) Reinforced by *Valens*, arriving via Gaul: defeats Othonians near Bedriacum: Otho commits suicide.
   (d) (Apr.), Vitellius enters Rome: disbands Praetorians.
III. (a) 69, July, VESPASIAN proclaimed at Alexandria with support of Syrian legions.
   (b) While *Mucianus* prepares to lead them against Italy, Danubian legions under *Antonius Primus* march down in Vespasian's cause: force Vitellians back from R. Adige: defeat them near Bedriacum: sack Cremona (Oct.).
   (c) At Rome *Flavius Sabinus*, Vespasian's brother, besieged and killed by Vitellians.
   (d) Primus' army plunders Rome: kills Vitellius and his followers (Dec.).
   (e) 70, Oct., Vespasian arrives in Rome.

IV. THE FLAVIANS

I. VESPASIAN (69–79).
   69. A. *Revolt of Civilis:*
       (i) *Civilis* raises revolt among Batavi (nominally for Vespasian): joined by Batavian auxiliaries and Tencteri and other German tribes: besieges *Vetera*, which is temporarily relieved by *Vocula*.
   70.   (ii) On Vespasian's accession revolt widens: joined by Gauls under Julius Classicus, etc.: and by legions at Novaesium, etc.: garrison of Vetera massacred.
       (iii) Batavi show no enthusiasm for 'Empire of Gauls': *Cerialis*, sent by Vespasian, wins over Treveri: defeats Germans near Trèves: revolt peters out.
       (iv) Auxiliaries henceforth stationed away from home-country.
     B. *Vespasian's policy:*
       (i) Vespasian economizes troops by scientific fortification of Danube: annexation of angle between Rhine and Danube (73), and advance-posts on eastern frontier (see Tables XIII and XIV).
       (ii) To replenish empty Treasury increases taxation of provinces, enlarges staff of collectors.

   (iii) Attempts to bring State lands under imperial control
     encourages cultivation of Black Forest district, etc.
   (iv) Develops high roads throughout Empire: builds
     Colosseum and restores Capitoline Temple at Rome.
   (v) Attempts to found new dynasty.
     (a) Promoting Titus to consulship, censorship and
      prefecture of Praetorians.
     (b) Developing Emperor worship: new order of
      priests, *Flaviales*.

II. TITUS (79–81).
  79. Eruption of Vesuvius.

III. DOMITIAN (81–96).
  A. *Frontier campaigns, etc.:*
   (i) 83–84. Expedition *v.* Chatti.
   (ii) 85–89. War *v.* Dacians (see Table XIII).
   (iii) 88–9. Saturninus' rebellion on Rhine, assisted by Chatti.
   (iv) 92. Marcomanni, etc., invade Pannonia.
  B. *Domestic policy:*
   (i) Employs equestrian ministers: increased power of Coun-
    cil of State.
   (ii) Architectural activity: Capitoline Temple completed:
    Hall of Music and general encouragement of arts.
   (iii) Persecution of Jews, Christians.
   (iv) Development of Emperor worship: deification of female
    members of family: Domitian assumes title of 'Dominus
    et Deus'.
   (v) Persecution of Stoics: Senecio, Helvidius Priscus, etc.
   (vi) Conspiracies in connexion with Saturninus' revolt, etc.
    lead to assassination by Stephanus.

  V. NERVA (96–98) chosen by Senate.

  TRAJAN (98–117) adopted by Nerva

  98. (i) Trajan, before returning to Rome, organizes defences
    of Pannonia.
   (ii) *Dacian Wars.*
    (a) First campaign (101–3): Decebalus accepts Roman
     garrison and demolishes forts.
    (b) Dacians invade Roman provinces (105): second
     campaign (106), Sarmizegethusa taken: Dacia
     becomes province.
106–113. (iii) *Seven years spent in Italy:*
    (a) Home-agriculture encouraged: emigration for-
     bidden: senators forced to buy Italian estates.
    (b) New roads built.
    (c) Harbours at Ostia and Ancona improved.
   (iv) *Eastern campaigns:*
    (a) Arabia Petraea annexed (106).
    (b) 113. Trajan picks quarrel with Chosroes of Parthia
     over Armenia: makes Armenia a province.
114–15.   (c) Campaigns in Mesopotamia: northern Mesopotamia
     and Assyria made provinces: revolt of N. Meso-
     potamia crushed by Quietus: revolts of Jews in

Cyprus and Egypt: Lower Mesopotamia placed under Parthamaspates: on Trajan's departure Chosroes re-enters Ctesiphon (117).

(d) Unrest in Britain and on Danube demands Trajan's return: dies in Cilicia (117): Hadrian appointed successor.

HADRIAN (117–37)

A. *Hadrian's tours:*

117. Hadrian on Danube: Trajan's eastern annexations abandoned: at Rome conspiracy of Trajan's four generals suppressed by Senate and Attianus.

121–5. Hadrian in Western provinces (wall built in Britain) and in East, where interview with Chosroes of Parthia leads to compromise.

126. Hadrian in Africa.

128–32. Hadrian in East: Colony at Jerusalem leads to revolt of Bar-cokbar (132).

B. *Hadrian's policy:*

(a) Army and civil service made distinct: salaries and titles for equestrian civil servants: increased staff of collectors and new *advocati fisci.*

(b) Council of State made official.

(c) Codification of Edict by Salvius Julianus (129).

(d) Much building at provincial towns, e.g. Athens: Hadrian's villa at Tivoli and Mausoleum at Rome.

(e) Succession prearranged. First plan: Aelius Verus adopted (136): died 138. Second plan: Antoninus adopted and made to adopt Lucius Verus and Marcus Aurelius.

ANTONINUS PIUS (138–61)

Frontiers:

(i) Wall farther north in Britain: advance of frontier between Rhine and Danube.

(ii) Trouble on Dacian front: Alani from Caucasus invade Armenia.

(iii) Vologeses of Parthia threatens war.

VI. MARCUS AURELIUS (161–80)

A. *Eastern frontier:*

(i) 161. Vologeses of Parthia invades Armenia and cuts up Severianus' army in Cappadocia.

(ii) *Lucius Verus* (already made consort) sent East with *Avidius Cassius.*

(iii) 163. Artaxata taken by Statius Priscus and rebuilt: *Sohaemus* installed as King of Armenia.

(iv) 164. Invasion of N. Mesopotamia.

165. Capture of Ctesiphon and invasion of Media, followed by withdrawal from all but N. Mesopotamia: Avidius left to control Eastern provinces.

(v) 166. Plague brought back by legions to the West.

B. *European frontiers:*
    (i) Langobardi refused settlement in Pannonia: Marcomanni and Quadi overrun Danube provinces and enter N. Italy (166).
    (ii) Aurelius drives back invaders across Alps (166): clears Danube provinces (167).
    (iii) Aurelius at Carnuntum:
        (*a*) Crushes Quadi and attacks Iazyges (168).
        (*b*) Raetia overrun by Quadi and Marcomanni: repelled by Pertinax: Bohemia invaded: death of L. Verus (169).
        (*c*) Successful invasion of Sarmatian country (170).
        (*d*) New provinces of Marcomannia and Sarmatia planned.
C. 175. Revolt of Avidius Cassius causes Aurelius to go East.
    176. Appoints his son Commodus as consort.
    178. Aurelius resumes campaign on Danube: barbarians settled within Empire: dies at Vindobona (180).

COMMODUS (180–93)
VII.   SEPTIMIUS SEVERUS (193–211)

A. *Struggle for throne:*
    193. (i) On Commodus' death *Pertinax* succeeds, but murdered by Praetorians, who promote *Didius Julianus.*
        (ii) Pannonian legions install *Septimius Severus* in his place.
        (iii) Septimius suppresses Pescenninus Niger in East and overwhelms *Albinus*, governor of Britain, near Lyons.
B. *Policy:*
    (i) Senate, etc., subordinated to *personal* rule of Severus and his non-Italian favourites.
    (ii) Military despotism: Legion on Alban Mts.: higher pay, etc., for troops.
    (iii) Centralization of jurisprudence: one of Praetorian prefects (*Papianus*) made Judge of Appeal.
C. *Frontiers:*
    (i) 197. Parthian attack on Nisibis necessitates expedition.
    (ii) 209. Severus' expedition into N. Britain: dies at York (211).

CARACALLA (211–17)

Murders brother *Geta*: pampers soldiery: depreciates currency: overtaxes rich.
212. Extends citizenship to all freeborn provincials.
217. While organizing expedition against Parthia, murdered by Praetorian prefect *Macrinus.*
218. *Julia Maesa* (Severus' sister-in-law) collects troops at *Emesa*: defeats Macrinus and raises her son Elagabalus to throne.

ELAGABALUS (218–22)

A fanatic who tries to impose Syrian cult on Empire: murdered by Praetorians.

ALEXANDER SEVERUS (222–35)

Elagabalus' cousin, aged thirteen: government by committee of senators: *Ulpian* (lawyer and prefect of Praetorians) introduces financial reforms, etc.

227. *Ardashir* (one of Sarsanids princes of Persia now emerging behind Parthia) defeats Alexander.
234. Barbarians bought off on Rhine.
235. Alexander murdered by troops.

VIII. THE ANARCHY (*Emperors in Capitals*)

A. *Conflict of Pretenders:*

    235. MAXIMINUS, Thracian, alienates Senate, who support GORDIANUS I and II in Africa (till troops murder them), then PUPIENUS and BALBINUS at Rome.

    238. MAXIMINUS murdered. GORDIANUS III rules till murdered in 244 by PHILIP ARABS, who is overthrown in turn by DECIUS, an Illyrian (249).

B. *Barbarian invasions and threatened disruption of Empire:*

    (i) Franks and Alamanni appear on Rhine: Ostrogoths overrun Balkan provinces: sack Philippopolis: Decius killed in battle (251).

    (ii) TREBONIANUS succeeded by VALERIAN and his son GALLIENUS (253).

        (a) In *East*. Valerian captured by *Shapur* of Persia (258): *Odonethes* of *Palmyra* rallies Eastern provinces.

        (b) In *West*. Gallienus fails to check Goths who plunder Aegean, but beats back Alamanni near Milan (258). Against Franks, etc., Postumus forms independent Empire of Gauls: Gallienus killed (268).

C. *The Recovery:*

    CLAUDIUS (268) defeats Goths near Nish: settles many on land: dies of plague (270).

    AURELIAN (270–5):

        (i) Defeats Alamanni at Metaurus and Ticinus: refortifies Rome.

        (ii) Reduces Odonethes' widow Zenobia at *Palmyra*.

        (iii) Recovers Western provinces by defeating *Tetricus*, Postumus' successor in Gaul: Aurelian murdered by officers (275).

    CLAUDIUS TACITUS murdered (275–6).

    PROBUS murdered (276–282).

    CARUS and his sons CARINUS and NUMERIANUS (282–4).

    Accession of DIOCLETIAN (284).

IX. DIOCLETIAN (284–305)

286. Diocletian rules East from Nicomedia: appoints *Maximian* as fellow-Augustus to rule West.

287–97. *Carausius* creates independent Empire in Britain, lost by his successor Alexander.

    293. Redistribution of Empire: Diocletian rules Eastern provinces: Maximian Italy, Africa, Spain: *Galerius* Balkan provinces: *Constantius* Gaul and Britain: these fourfold areas subdivided into *dioceses* under vicarii, which are again divided into *provinces* (100 in all) under proconsuls, etc.

    297. Galerius defeated by Parthians, but restores position: army reforms and increase of striking force originated by Gallienus.

    301. Edict fixing prices, etc.

X.   CONSTANTINE

(i) 305. Maximian replaced by *Constantius*: Diocletian by *Galerius*, who, instead of prospective Caesars *Maxentius* and *Constantine*, appoints nominees of his own.

(ii) 305. Constantine escapes from Nicomedia to his father Constantius in Britain: on father's death is proclaimed Augustus of West by troops (306).

(iii) Maxentius and Maximian assume control of Italy: *Licinius*, sent by Galerius, ousts Maxentius and is made Augustus of West.

(iv) 311. On Galerius' death, Licinius attacks Daia, leaving Constantine to suppress Maxentius at *Mulvian Bridge* (312).

(v) 314. Constantine divides Empire with Licinius: defeats him at Chrysopolis (323): becomes sole Emperor.

(vi) 313. Proclaims toleration of Christianity: presides at Council of Nicaea (325).

(vii) 330. Constantine dedicates Constantinople: dies (337).

XI.   THE FINAL DECLINE

337–61. Rule of Constantine's sons—*Constantine II, Constans,* and *Constantius*.

361–63. *Julian* the Apostate restores paganism: killed in fighting Persians (363).

375. Under pressure from Huns, Goths cross Danube: *Valens* killed in defending Adrianople (378).

379–395. *Theodosius* establishes Christianity as official creed.

395. Theodosius' sons: *Arcadius* takes Eastern Empire: *Honorius*, assisted by *Stilicho*, Western.

400. Goths under Alaric invade Italy: repulsed by Stilicho at Turin.

406. Vandals and Suevi repulsed from Italy: Gaul and Spain overrun by barbarians.

409. Alaric bought off from Rome: returns 409: sacks Rome 410.

451. Huns beaten back at Châlons by Roman troops and Visigoth settlers.

476. *Romulus Augustulus* succeeded by *Odovacer*.

XII.   THE GERMAN FRONTIER

I. 16 B.C. Sugambri destroy legion under Lollius: Tiberius' appointment.

II. 12 B.C. Drusus takes over command and plans conquest of Germany:

    (a) Advances by sea to *R. Ems*: attacking Frisii, Bructeri and Chauci *en route*.

    (b) After building Rhine forts (Castra Vetera, Bonna, Moguntiacum, etc.), advances by R. Lippe

11 B.C.   against Cherusci to *R. Weser*: advance base at Aliso.

10 B.C.   (c) Reduction of Chatti.

9 B.C.   (d) Advance to *R. Elbe*: death of Drusus: Tiberius succeeds, but retires 6 B.C.

III. 4 A.D. Tiberius resumes command: plans reduction of Marcomanni (Bohemia).

6–9 A.D. Tiberius occupied with Pannonian revolt: *Varus* destroyed by Arminius and Cherusci at Teutoberg Forest (9): withdrawal to Rhine.

IV. 14 A.D. Mutiny of Rhine legions quelled by Germanicus.

14 A.D. Germanicus invades Germany:
   (a) March up R. Lippe.
   (b) 15. By sea to R. Ems: reaches Teutoberg: damaged by storm on return.
   (c) 16. By sea to R. Ems: penetrates to R. Weser: defeats Arminius at Idistaviso.

17 A.D. After Germanicus' recall frontier-belt divided into Upper and Lower Germany.

V. 47. Corbulo's campaigns against Frisii and Chauci.

VI. 73. Vespasian annexes and fortifies Black Forest district, connecting Rhine and Danube fronts.

VII. 83–4. Domitian's expedition against Chatti: annexation of Mt. Taunus district; more advanced line fortified between Rhine and Danube.

VIII. Comparative tranquillity until *c.* 250: new tribes (Franks, Alamanni, etc.) begin to threaten the frontier.

XIII.   THE DANUBE FRONTIER

I. *Under Augustus:*
   (a) Frontier advanced to Danube by formation of provinces Raetia and Novicum, 15 B.C.: Pannonia, 12 B.C. (Moesia and Thrace added *c.* 46 A.D.).
   (b) 6–9 A.D. Pannonian revolt crushed by Tiberius.
   (c) On Augustus' death mutiny of Pannonian legions quelled by Tiberius' son Drusus.

II. *Under Domitian:*
   (a) Daci, organized by Decebalus, defeat Sabinus and overrun Moesia (85).
   (b) Fuscus, after invading Dacia, is overwhelmed (87).
   (c) Julianus restores the position: Domitian makes peace (89).

III. *Trajan's Campaigns:*
   (a) Owing to growth of Decebalus' power, Trajan decides on invasion.
   (b) First campaign: 101, Advancing towards Iron Gates Pass, joins battle near Tapae, but retires: 102, Entering Dacia by Red Tower Pass from east, compels Decebalus to terms: Roman garrison in Sarmizegethusa.
   (c) Second campaign: 105, Decebalus having recovered Sarmizegethusa and crossed Danube, Trajan (106) closes on Sarmizegethusa from east and west: Decebalus killed.
   (d) Result: Dacia annexed: Sarmizegethusa renamed Ulpia Trajana.

IV. *Marcus Aurelius' Campaigns.* Owing to unrest in Central Europe—166–80. Expeditions against:
   (a) Quadi and Marcomanni, north-west.
   (b) Iazyges and Sarmatians north-east: plan to annex new provinces of Marcomannia and Sarmatia, but abandoned by Commodus after Marcus' death.

V.   *c.* 250. New wave of invasion begun by Goths from R. Vistula.
     c. 273. Dacia abandoned by Aurelian.

XIV: EASTERN FRONTIER

I. *Under Augustus:*
     (a) 20 B.C. Phraates of Parthia ejects Tiridates, but comes to terms with Augustus.
     (b) 20 B.C. Pro-Roman Tigranes placed on Armenian throne:
     (c) A.D. 2, Parthians recognize another Roman nominee, but feuds between claimants continue, till Germanicus (A.D. 16) again installs pro-Roman prince in Armenia and cultivates *entente* with Artabanus of Parthia.

II. *Under Nero:*
     (a) 53, Vologeses of Parthia invades Armenia and installs Tiridates.
     (b) 57, Corbulo sent East; captures Artaxata (59) and Tigranocerta (60): installs Tigranes, who is soon driven out again by Parthians.
     (c) 62, Paetus' surrender at Randeia: leads to compromise whereby Parthian candidate to Armenian throne receives investiture at Rome (65).

III. *Under Vespasian*: Annexation of Commagene and Lesser Armenia, accompanied by advance of frontier posts to Satala, Samosata, etc.

IV. *Campaign of Trajan:*
     (a) Chosroes of Parthia places Exedares on Armenian throne, Trajan invades Armenia and makes it a province (113).
     (b) Trajan invades northern Mesopotamia. winters army at Nisibis (114).
     (c) Moves down R. Tigris: occupies Ctesiphon (115).
     (d) Visits head of Persian Gulf and thence to Babylon (116).
     (e) Revolts in northern Mesopotamia and Cyprus crushed.
     (f) Northern Mesopotamia and Assyria made provinces, but abandoned by Hadrian (117), who later makes *entente* with Chosroes (123).

V. *Under M. Aurelius:*
     (a) Vologeses of Parthia invades Armenia.
     (b) 163, L. Varus and Avidius Cassius sent out: Statius Priscus captures Artaxata and installs Sohaemus.
     (c) 165, Ctesiphon captured; Media invaded.
     (d) Withdrawal from all except northern Mesopotamia: though occasional demonstrations against Parthia required, e.g. by Septimius Severus (197).

VI. *Rise of the Sassanids of Persia:*
     227. Asia Minor threatened.
     231. Alexander Severus defeated by Ardashir.
     241. Gordianus III's campaign against Persians.
     258. Valerian captured by Shapur: Asia Minor and Syria overrun: Odonethes of Palmyra rallies Eastern forces against Persia.
     273. Independence of Palmyra ended by Aurelian.

XV. BRITAIN

I.   (a) After Caesar's abortive invasion (54) touch with Rome continued through traders.
    (b) Cunobelinus (A.D. 5–40), King of Trinobantes (Essex), holds hegemony of S.E.
    (c) On his death succession is disputed: his son flees to Rome: Caligula plans invasion.

II. *Claudius' Invasion:*
    (a) 43. Under *Aulus Plautius* Romans cross Thames: capture Camulodunum: E. Anglia, Midlands, and southern districts (Vespasian) reduced.
    (b) *Ostorius Scapula* (47–52):
        (i) Defines western frontier by Fosse Way from Lincoln to Exeter: high roads radiating from Londinium.
        (ii) Advanced posts at Deva, Uriconium, Glevum: attack on Ordovices (N. Wales) and Silures (S. Wales): Caractacus' last stand.

III. *Under Nero:*
    (a) *Suetonius Paulinus* (58–61) strikes at Mona, Druid stronghold.
    (b) 61. During his absence Iceni under Boadicea sack Camulodunum, Londinium and Verulamium: defeat Cerealis: overcome by Suetonius on Watling Street.

IV. *Cerealis* (71–4) advances frontier to Eboracum: *Frontinus* (74–7) overcomes Silures and founds base at Isca Silurum.

V. *Agricola* (78–84):
    (a) Subdues Ordovices and Mona (78): Brigantes of Yorkshire (79).
    (b) Invades Caledonia: fortifies Clyde-Forth isthmus (80).
    (c) Invades Highlands: battle at Mons Graupius (83).
    (d) Recalled by Domitian—(owing to Rhine campaigns?)—(84).

VI. *Hadrian* visits Britain *c.* 122 (owing to disaster to 9th legion?): withdraws frontier to Tyne-Solway isthmus: building of the Wall.

VII. *Under Antonius Pius, Lollius Urbicus* (143) re-establishes Clyde-Forth frontier.

VIII. 180. Frontier overrun and legions defeated: Albinus (governor) makes bid for throne: defeated by Septimius Severus (196): Septimius' campaigns into highlands, rebuilds Hadrian's Wall: dies at York (211).

IX. 287. German sea-raids begin: 287–97, independent Empire in Britain under *Carausius* and Alexander: legions withdrawn (407).

LITERATURE

POETRY	PROSE

A. *Primitive:*
  Livius Andronicus (fl. 250 B.C.) — translated Odyssey into Saturnians, etc.
  Ennius (239–169) — introduces hexameter in Annals.
  Plautus (254–184) and *Terence* (185–89)—Adapt Comedies of Menander.
  Afranius (fl. 120)—Attempts purely Roman comedy.
  Lucilius (180–102) — Writes satires.
	Cato (234–149)—Origines and other treatises.

B. *End of the Republic:*
  Lucretius (97–53) — Writes philosophic De Rerum Natura.
  Catullus (87–53) — Love-poems, etc.
	Varro (116–27) — Antiquities, grammar, etc.
	Cicero (106–43)—Speeches, letters, philosophy.
	Caesar—Commentaries and Civil War.
	Sallust (86–35)—Jugurthine War, Catilinarian conspiracy.

C. *Augustan Period:*
  Virgil (70–19) — Eclogues, Georgics, Aeneid.
  Horace (65–8) — Odes, Satires, Carmen Saeculare, etc.
  Tibullus (65–19).
  Propertius (50–18?)—Love-poetry, etc.
  Ovid (43 B.C.–A.D. 17)—Metamorphoses, etc.
	Livy (59–17)—History of Rome.
	Vitruvius (fl. 15 A.D.)—Architecture.

D. *Post-Augustan:*
  Manilius (fl. A.D. 20)—Astronomica, philosophic.
  Seneca (4 B.C.–A.D. 65)—Tragedies, etc.
  Lucan (39–65)—Pharsalia.
  Martial (40–104)—Epigrams.
  Juvenal (fl. 100)—Satires.
  Ausonius (310–395).
	Seneca (4 B.C.–A.D. 65)—Philosophy, etc.
	Petronius (23–79)—Trimalchio's Feast.
	Pliny the Elder (23–79)—Natural History, etc.
	Quintilian (35–95)—On style, etc.
	Tacitus (c. 55–117)—Agricola, Annals, Histories.
	Younger Pliny (61–113)—Letters, etc.

INDEX